Collins

CSEC® CHEMISTRY

Author: Naresh Birju
Reviewer: Michelle Toussaint

Collins

William Collins' dream of knowledge for all began with the publication of his first book in 1819. A self-educated mill worker, he not only enriched millions of lives, but also founded a flourishing publishing house. Today, staying true to this spirit, Collins books are packed with inspiration, innovation and practical expertise. They place you at the centre of a world of possibility and give you exactly what you need to explore it.

Collins. Freedom to teach.

Published by Collins
An imprint of HarperCollins*Publishers*
The News Building, 1 London Bridge Street
London, SE1 9GF

HarperCollins*Publishers*
Macken House, 39/40 Mayor Street Upper,
Dublin 1, D01 C9W8, Ireland

Browse the complete Collins Caribbean catalogue at
www.collins.co.uk/caribbeanschools

© HarperCollins*Publishers* Limited 2022

10 9 8 7 6 5 4 3

ISBN 978-0-00-843199-0

Collins CSEC® Chemistry is an independent publication and has not been authorised, sponsored or otherwise approved by **CXC®**.

CSEC® is a registered trademark of the **Caribbean Examinations Council (CXC®)**.

All rights reserved. No part of this publication may be reproduced, stored in a retrieval system, or transmitted in any form by any means, electronic, mechanical, photocopying, recording or otherwise, without the prior written permission of the Publisher or a licence permitting restricted copying in the United Kingdom issued by the Copyright Licensing Agency Ltd., Barnard's Inn, 86 Fetter Lane, London, EC4A 1EN.

Without limiting the exclusive rights of any author, contributor or the publisher of this publication, any unauthorised use of this publication to train generative artificial intelligence (AI) technologies is expressly prohibited. HarperCollins also exercise their rights under Article 4(3) of the Digital Single Market Directive 2019/790 and expressly reserve this publication from the text and data mining exception.

British Library Cataloguing in Publication Data.

A catalogue record for this publication is available from the British Library.

The publishers gratefully acknowledge the permission granted to reproduce the copyright material in this book. Every effort has been made to trace copyright holders and to obtain their permission for the use of copyright material. The publishers will gladly receive any information enabling them to rectify any error or omission at the first opportunity.

Author: Naresh Birju
Reviewer: Michelle Toussaint
Assistant reviewers: Amanda Eaves, Tim Jackson
Publisher: Dr Elaine Higgleton
Development editor: Tom Hardy
Project leader: Peter Dennis
Illustrator: Ann Paganuzzi
Copy editor: Jan Schubert
Proofreader: Mitch Fitton
Typesetter: Siliconchips Services Ltd
Cover designers: Kevin Robbins and Gordon MacGilp
Photos: P45, Figure 3.5, Jaroslaw Moravcik/Shutterstock; P142, Figure 9.6, TURTLE ROCK SCIENCE / SCIENCE PHOTO LIBRARY; P174, Figure 10.1, Anne Tindale; P346, Figure 23.5, The Sherwin-Williams Company
Printed and Bound in the UK by Ashford Colour Ltd

MIX
Paper | Supporting responsible forestry
FSC™ C007454

This book contains FSC™ certified paper and other controlled sources to ensure responsible forest management.

For more information visit: www.harpercollins.co.uk/green

Contents

Answers

Online at www.collins.co.uk/caribbean

Getting the best from the book

Welcome to CSEC® Chemistry.

This textbook has been written as a comprehensive course designed to help you achieve maximum success in your CXC® CSEC® Chemistry examination. Facts are presented in an easy-to-understand way, using simple and clear language. A variety of formats are used, including diagrams, graphs, photos and tables, to make the facts easy to understand and learn.

Key terms are highlighted in bold type, and important definitions which you must learn, are written in italics and highlighted in colour. These definitions are appropriately positioned within the text itself.

All the information needed to fully cover the syllabus is given within the text, and only the required information is given.

A variety of methods are used to make the facts easy to understand and learn.

Useful techniques on tackling certain types of questions are outlined to provide you with the confidence required to always produce the correct answer. Worked examples are provided that demonstrate how to answer the spectrum of questions on any topic which may confront you in the examination.

The CSEC® Chemistry syllabus is divided into three sections, outlined below.

Each section has been colour-coded and Sections A to C have been divided into chapters presenting their constituent topics.

The book has been divided as follows.

- Chapters 1–13   Section A: Principles of Chemistry
- Chapters 14–17   Section B: Organic Chemistry
- Chapters 18–24   Section C: Inorganic Chemistry

Practice exercises are provided at the end of each chapter to help you test your knowledge and comprehension, and to improve your ability to use your knowledge by developing your thinking, investigative and analytical skills. The exercises are presented in three distinct levels of difficulty as outlined below, and are colour-coded for clarity.

- **Recalling facts:** These exercises are designed to help you assess your knowledge and understanding of the facts, concepts and principles covered in the chapter. You should be able to find the answers to these questions within the chapter and answering them should help you to learn this information.

- **Applying facts:** These exercises are designed to test how you use the facts, concepts and principles covered in the chapter to answer questions about unfamiliar or novel situations. They should help you to develop your ability to apply knowledge and develop critical thinking skills.

- **Analysing data:** These exercises are designed to develop your investigative and analytical skills. You are given data or information to analyse, usually in the form of tables or graphs. You may be asked to read information directly from the table or graph, use data from a table to draw a graph, use data from a graph to construct a table, determine the slope of a graph or perform other calculations using information extracted from a table or graph. You may also be asked to identify patterns or trends, to make predictions and to draw conclusions.

Key features of the book

Learning objectives inform you of what you are expected to learn ►

Key terms in bold for emphasis ►

Learning objectives

- State the four main ideas of the **particulate theory of matter**.
- Describe and explain the evidence that supports the **particulate theory of matter**.
- Explain the everyday effects of **diffusion** and **osmosis**.
- Describe the main properties of the **three states of matter**.
- Explain the **changes between the three states of matter** in terms of **energy changes** involved and the **arrangement of particles**.
- Interpret information gained from **cooling** and **heating curves**.

Real-life situations display applications in chemistry ►

Disposal of solid waste containing plastics

Plastics are organic compounds composed of non-metallic elements. They are made mainly from hydrocarbons obtained from natural gas, crude oil and coal. Most plastics are **non-biodegradable**, so they remain in the environment for a very long time. Because of this, getting rid of solid waste containing plastics is a major problem:

- **Toxic gases** are produced when plastics burn. Disposal of plastics in incinerators can cause air pollution and health problems.
- **Toxic chemicals** are continually released from some plastics. These chemicals can contaminate soil and groundwater when plastics are disposed of in landfills.
- About 25% of all solid waste going to **landfills** is composed of plastics. More and more land is being used up to dispose of these plastics.
- Plastics often end up in **lakes, rivers** and **oceans** when not disposed of correctly and can harm aquatic organisms (see page 281).

Full-colour photos enhance maximum interest ►

The more plastic items that are **recycled**, the more the problem of their disposal will be solved.

Figure 21.13 *Solid waste containing plastics*

Annotated diagrams provide relation between form and function ►

- Water is filtered through layers of sand, gravel and charcoal at reservoirs to remove insoluble particles.
- Home aquaria use fibres in their filters to trap particulate matter.

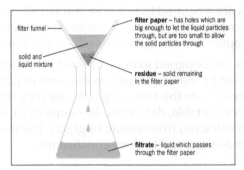

filter funnel

filter paper – has holes which are big enough to let the liquid particles through, but are too small to allow the solid particles through

solid and liquid mixture

residue – solid remaining in the filter paper

Key terms in bold for emphasis ►

filtrate – liquid which passes through the filter paper

Experiments important for School Based Assessments (SBA) are fully described ▶

Experiment 9.1

Aim: to prepare zinc sulfate (soluble salt) crystals by reacting zinc (metal) and sulfuric acid (acid).

1 Add zinc with stirring to 50 cm³ hot dilute sulfuric acid.

2 Keep adding zinc until effervescence (bubbling) stops and the metal is present in excess.

3 Dip a piece of blue litmus paper into the solution; it should remain blue.

4 Filter to remove the excess zinc metal, collect the filtrate.

5 Evaporate the water or evaporate some water and leave to crystallise.

6 Filter the zinc sulfate crystals and dry them between sheets of filter paper.

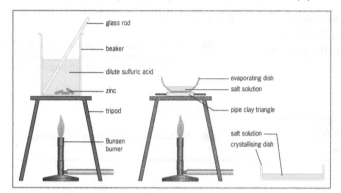

Full-colour diagrams enhance maximum interest ▶

Figure 9.8 *Preparation of zinc sulfate*

Techniques on tackling specific types of questions give students confidence in their approach ▶

When **writing formulae** of ionic compounds, the **sum** of the **positive charges** and the **sum** of the **negative charges** must be **equal**. This is because the **total number** of electrons lost by one type of atom or group of atoms must be the **same** as the total number gained by the other type of atom or group of atoms. Formulae of ionic compounds are **empirical formulae** as they represent the **ratio of ions** present. They are also known as **formula units**.

A spectrum of worked examples greatly strengthen the concepts being taught ▶

Example 6

The chemical formula of boron sulfide is B_2S_3:

- Number of atoms of each element from the formula: $B = 2$

  $S = 3$

- Charge on each ion: $B^{3+} = +3$

  $S^{2-} = -2$

- Sum of the charges: $B = 2 \times +3 = +6$

  $S = 3 \times -2 = -6$

This shows the **sum** of the positive charges and the **sum** of the negative charges are equal.

Important notes give reasons for the approach to the question ▶

Recalling facts questions help you to assess your knowledge and understanding of facts, concepts and principles ▶

Recalling facts

 1 What are the products of complete combustion of an alkane?

a carbon dioxide only

b carbon monoxide and water

c carbon dioxide and water

d carbon dioxide, carbon monoxide and water

Applying facts questions test your use of the facts, concepts and principles ▶

Applying facts

 10 Alkanes are saturated and alkenes are unsaturated. Discuss this statement in terms of the types of bonds or functional groups these compounds possess and their chemical reactivity. Describe a test to distinguish between unsaturated and saturated compounds.

Analysing data questions improve your SBA performance ▶

Analysing data

 13 Are alkanes soluble in water? Explain your answer.

The format of the CSEC® Chemistry examination

The examination consists of two papers and your performance is evaluated using the following three profiles:

- Knowledge and comprehension
- Use of knowledge
- Experimental skills

Paper 01 (1¼ hours)

Paper 01 consists of 60 multiple choice questions. Each question is worth 1 mark. Four choices of answer are provided for each question of which one is correct.

- Make sure you read each question thoroughly; some questions may ask which answer is incorrect.
- If you don't know the answer, try to work it out by eliminating the incorrect answers. Never leave a question unanswered.

Paper 02 (2½ hours)

Paper 02 is divided into Sections A and B, and consists of six compulsory questions, each divided into several parts. Take time to read the entire paper before beginning to answer any of the questions.

- Section A consists of three compulsory structured questions whose parts require short answers, usually a word, a sentence or a short paragraph. The answers are to be written in spaces provided on the paper. These spaces indicate the length of answer required and answers should be restricted to them.

Question 1 is a data-analysis question which is worth 25 marks. The first part usually asks you to take readings from a measuring instrument, such as a set of thermometers, and record these readings in a table. You may then be asked to draw a graph using the information in the table and may be asked questions about the graph or be asked to perform certain calculations. The second part will possibly test your knowledge of tests to identify cations, anions and gases, and there may be a third part which tests your planning and designing skills.

Question 2 and 3 are each worth 15 marks. They usually begin with some kind of stimulus material, such as a diagram or a table, which you will be asked questions about.

- Section B consists of three compulsory extended-response questions, each worth 15 marks. These questions require a greater element of essay writing in their answers than those in Section A.

The marks allocated for the different parts of each question are clearly given. A total of 100 marks is available for Paper 02 and the time allowed is 150 minutes. You should allow about 35 minutes for the data-analysis question worth 25 marks and allow about 20 minutes for each of the other questions. This will allow you time to read the paper fully before you begin and time to check over your answers when you have finished.

Successful revision

The following should provide a guide for successful revision.

- Begin your revision early. You should start your revision at least two months before the examination and should plan a revision timetable to cover this period. Plan to revise in the evenings when you don't have much homework, at weekends, during the Easter vacation and during study leave.
- When you have a full day available for revision, consider the day as three sessions of about three to four hours each, morning, afternoon and evening. Study during two of these sessions only, do something non-academic and relaxing during the third.
- Read through the topic you plan to learn to make sure you understand it before starting to learn it; understanding is a lot safer than thoughtless learning.
- Try to understand and learn one topic in each revision session, more if topics are short and fewer if topics are long.
- Revise every topic in the syllabus. Do not pick and choose topics since all questions on your exam paper are compulsory.
- Learn the topics in order. When you have learnt all topics once, go back to the first topic and begin again. Try to cover each topic several times.
- Revise in a quiet location without any form of distraction.
- Sit up to revise, preferably at a table. Do not sit in a comfy chair or lie on a bed where you can easily fall asleep.
- Obtain copies of past CSEC® Chemistry examination papers and use them to practise answering exam-style questions, starting with the most recent papers. These can be purchased online from the CXC Store.
- You can use a variety of different methods to learn your work. Choose which ones work best for you.

Read the topic several times, then close the book and try to write down the main points. Do not try to memorise your work word for word since work learnt by heart is not usually understood and most questions test understanding, not just the ability to repeat facts.

Summarise the main points of each topic on flash cards and use these to help you study.

Draw simple diagrams with annotations, flow charts and spider diagrams to summarise topics in visual ways which are easy to learn.

Practise drawing and labelling simple line diagrams of apparatus you have encountered. You may be asked to reproduce these, e.g. the apparatus used for fractional distillation.

Practise writing equations. Do not try to learn equations by heart; instead, understand and learn how to write and balance them. For example, if you learn that a carbonate reacts with an acid to form a salt, carbon dioxide and water, you can write the equation for any carbonate reacting with any acid.

Use memory aids such as:

- acronyms, e.g. OIL RIG for oxidation and reduction in terms of electrons; oxidation is loss, reduction is gain.
- **Hi he lives behind brechin castle near our friends never Nancy made all silk purchases for she could always keep cash**: a mnemonic for the first twenty elements: hydrogen, helium, lithium, beryllium, boron, carbon, nitrogen, oxygen, fluorine, neon, sodium, magnesium, aluminium, silicon, phosphorus, sulfur, chlorine, argon, potassium, calcium. Also **Red cat: Red**uction at **cat**hode; and **An ox: An**ode for **ox**idation.
- Cats have paws, hence Cations are pawsitive. Or Ca+ion: The letter t in cation looks like a + (plus) sign.

Test yourself using the questions throughout this book and others from past CSEC® examination papers.

Successful examination technique

- Read the instructions at the start of each paper very carefully and do precisely what they require.
- Read through the entire paper before you begin to answer any of the questions.
- Read each question at least twice before beginning your answer to ensure you understand what it asks.
- Underline the important words in each question to help you answer precisely what the question is asking.
- Re-read the question when you are part way through your answer to check that you are answering what it asks.
- Give precise and factual answers. You will not get marks for information which is 'padded out' or irrelevant. The number of marks awarded for each answer indicates how long and detailed it should be.
- Use correct scientific terminology throughout your answers.
- Balance all chemical equations and ensure that you give the correct state symbols, especially in ionic equations.
- Show all working and give clear statements when answering questions that require calculations.
- Give every numerical answer the appropriate unit using the proper abbreviation/symbol e.g. cm^3, g, °C.
- If a question asks you to give a specific number of points, use bullets to make each separate point clear.
- If you are asked to give similarities and differences, you must make it clear which points you are proposing as similarities and which points as differences. The same applies if you are asked to give advantages and disadvantages.
- Watch the time as you work. Know the time available for each question and stick to it.
- Check over your answers when you have completed all the questions, especially those requiring calculations.
- Remain in the examination room until the end of the examination and recheck your answers again if you have time to ensure you have done your very best. Never leave the examination room early.

Some key terms used on examination papers

Account for: provide reasons for the information given.

Calculate: give a numerical solution which includes all relevant working.

Compare: give similarities and differences.

Construct: draw a graph or table using data provided or obtained.

Contrast: give differences.

Deduce: use data provided or obtained to arrive at a conclusion.

Define: state concisely the meaning of a word or term.

Describe: provide a detailed account that includes all relevant information.

Determine: find a solution using the information provided, usually by performing a calculation.

Discuss: provide a balanced argument that considers points both for and against.

Distinguish between or among: give differences.

Evaluate: determine the significance or worth of the point in question.

Explain: give a clear, detailed account that makes given information easy to understand and provides reasons for the information.

Illustrate: make the answer clearer by including examples or diagrams.

Justify: provide adequate grounds for your reasoning.

Outline: write an account that includes the main points only.

Predict: use information provided to arrive at a likely conclusion or suggest a possible outcome.

Relate: show connections between different sets of information or data.

State or list: give brief, precise facts without detail.

Suggest: put forward an idea.

Tabulate: construct a table to show information or data that has been given or obtained.

Drawing tables and graphs

Tables

Tables can be used to record numerical data, observations and inferences. When drawing a table:

- Neatly enclose the table and draw vertical and horizontal lines to separate columns and rows.
- When drawing numerical tables, give the correct column headings which state the physical quantities measured and give the correct units using proper abbreviations/symbols, e.g. cm^3, g, °C.
- Give the appropriate number of decimal places when recording numerical data.
- When drawing non-numerical tables, give the correct column headings and all observations.
- Give the table an appropriate title which must include reference to the responding variable and the manipulated variable.

Graphs

Graphs are used to display numerical data. When drawing a graph:

- Plot the manipulated variable on the x-axis and the responding variable on the y-axis.
- Choose appropriate scales that are easy to work with and use as much of the graph paper as possible.
- Enter numbers along the axes and label each axis, including relevant units, e.g. cm^3, g, °C.
- Use a small dot surrounded by a small circle to plot each point.
- Plot each point accurately.
- Draw a smooth curve or straight line of best fit which need not necessarily pass through all the points.
- Give the graph an appropriate title which must include reference to the responding variable and the manipulated variable.

School-Based Assessment (SBA)

School-Based Assessment (SBA) is an integral part of your CSEC® examination. It assesses you in the Experimental Skills and Analysis and Interpretation involved in laboratory and field work, and is worth 20% of your final examination mark.

- The assessments are carried out in your school by your teacher during Terms 1 to 5 of your two-year programme.

- The assessments are carried out during normal practical classes and not under examination conditions. You have every opportunity to gain a high score in each assessment if you make a consistent effort throughout your two-year programme.

- Assessments will be made of the following four skills:
  - Manipulation and Measurement
  - Observation, Recording and Reporting
  - Planning and Designing
  - Analysis and Interpretation

As part of your SBA, you will also carry out an Investigative Project which takes the form of a proposal to be done in the first year and then the implementation during the second year of your two-year programme. This project assesses your Planning and Designing, and Analysis and Interpretation skills. If you are studying two or three of the single science subjects, Biology, Chemistry and Physics, you may elect to carry out ONE investigation only from any one of these subjects.

You will be required to keep a practical workbook in which you record all of your practical work and this may then be moderated externally by CXC®.

Answers

Free online answers to questions can be accessed at www.collins.co.uk/caribbean

Section A
Principles of chemistry

In this section

- The states of matter
- Pure substances, mixtures and separations
- Atomic structure
- The periodic table and periodicity
- Structure and bonding
- Chemical equations
- Types of chemical reaction
- The mole concept
- Acids, bases and salts
- Oxidation–reduction reactions
- Electrochemistry
- Rates of reaction
- Energetics

1 The states of matter

Learning objectives

- State the four main ideas of the **particulate theory of matter**.
- Describe and explain the evidence that supports the **particulate theory of matter**.
- Explain the everyday effects of **diffusion** and **osmosis**.
- Describe the main properties of the **three states of matter**.
- Explain the **changes between the three states of matter** in terms of **energy changes** involved and the **arrangement of particles**.
- Interpret information gained from **cooling** and **heating curves**.

Chemistry is often referred to as the central or connecting science because of its role in connecting the physical sciences with the life and applied sciences, medicine and engineering. Chemistry is involved in everything we do. Hearing, seeing, tasting and touching all involve a complex sequence of chemical reactions. In everyday life, chemistry is being done when we cook, wash our clothes using detergents, take medicine when we have a cold, and make juice to drink.

Chemistry is the study of matter and the changes that happen when matter is subjected to different conditions. This field of study seeks to understand the composition, structure, properties and reactions of **matter**.

Matter is anything that has volume and mass.

The word "matter" encompasses all the substances and materials that make up the Universe. This includes buildings (our school), the chair you are sitting on, the air we breathe, sand, soil, plants, human beings and other animals. All matter is made up of **particles** and can exist as solids, liquids and gases. These three forms are called the three different **states** of matter.

The particulate theory of matter

The theory that all substances are made up of very small particles and are in constant motion begins to explain the structure and physical properties of the three different states of matter. There are four main ideas behind the **particulate theory of matter**:

- All matter is composed of **particles**.
- The particles are in **constant motion** and temperature affects their speed of motion.
- The particles have **empty spaces** between them.
- The particles have **forces of attraction** between them.

Evidence to support the particulate theory of matter

Even using the most powerful and sophisticated microscopes, the particles that make up matter cannot be seen. We therefore have to rely on indirect evidence to prove that particles exist. The processes of **diffusion**, **osmosis** and **Brownian motion** provide **evidence** to support the theory that all matter is made of **particles**.

Diffusion

Diffusion is the net movement of particles from a region of higher concentration to a region of lower concentration, until the particles are evenly distributed.

Particles in gases and liquids are capable of diffusing.

Diffusion in gases

Some perfume is sprayed at the back of the classroom through the ventilation blocks. Would the students at the front of the class smell it?

The aroma of cooking curry chicken can be detected throughout the house, even in your bedroom upstairs. Similarly, the sweet fragrance associated with a jasmine flower can be detected from a distance. Why do you think these scenarios are possible? These 'fragrances' are made of minute particles that spread out from a source and are picked up by our senses. This is because the particles that make up the fragrance are bombarded by the particles in the air, causing them to spread out through the air, with some ending up in your nostrils. These scenarios are examples of diffusion.

All gases diffuse to fill the space available.

Example 1

When a small amount of reddish-brown bromine is placed at the bottom of a tall glass jar, the reddish-brown colour of the bromine spreads to fill the jar as it mixes with the air particles in the jar (Figure 1.1).

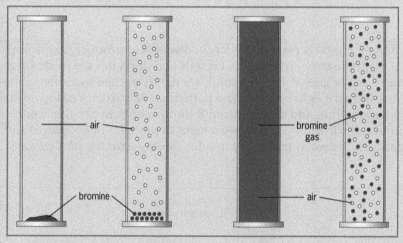

Figure 1.1 *Bromine diffusing*

Example 2

When pieces of cotton wool soaked in concentrated ammonia solution and in concentrated hydrochloric acid are placed simultaneously at opposite ends of a dry glass tube, a white ring of ammonium chloride forms inside the tube. Ammonia solution gives off ammonia gas and hydrochloric acid gives off hydrogen chloride gas. The particles of the gases **diffuse** through the air inside the tube, collide and react to form ammonium chloride:

$$\text{ammonia} + \text{hydrogen chloride} \longrightarrow \text{ammonium chloride}$$
$$\text{NH}_3(g) \ + \ \text{HCl}(g) \longrightarrow \text{NH}_4\text{Cl}(s)$$

Ammonia particles diffuse **faster** than hydrogen chloride particles, so the particles collide and react closer to the source of the hydrogen chloride particles (Figure 1.2). This is because the ammonia particles have a lower relative molecular mass (see page 105) and are therefore lighter than the hydrogen chloride particles and move faster.

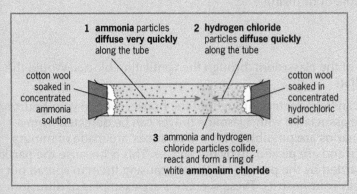

1 ammonia particles **diffuse very quickly** along the tube

2 hydrogen chloride particles **diffuse quickly** along the tube

cotton wool soaked in concentrated ammonia solution

cotton wool soaked in concentrated hydrochloric acid

3 ammonia and hydrogen chloride particles collide, react and form a ring of white **ammonium chloride**

Figure 1.2 *Ammonia and hydrochloric acid diffuse at different rates*

Diffusion in liquids

Diffusion also occurs in liquids but at a slower pace than in gases because the particles of a liquid move much more slowly.

When a blue copper(II) sulfate crystal is placed in water, it **dissolves** to produce a uniformly blue solution (Figure 1.3). Both the copper(II) sulfate crystals and the water are made up of small particles. The particles of the crystal, being a solid, are tightly packed together, while water, which is a liquid, has tiny spaces in between the particles. The particles of the crystals in the water separate from each other and **diffuse** through the spaces between the water particles until they are uniformly distributed. This movement of particles of copper(II) sulfate into the tiny spaces in between the water particles provides evidence for the particulate nature of matter.

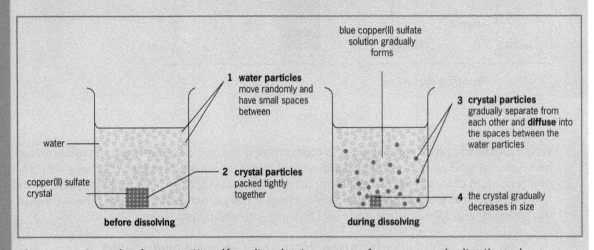

blue copper(II) sulfate solution gradually forms

1 water particles move randomly and have small spaces between

3 crystal particles gradually separate from each other and **diffuse** into the spaces between the water particles

water

copper(II) sulfate crystal

2 crystal particles packed tightly together

4 the crystal gradually decreases in size

before dissolving

during dissolving

Figure 1.3 *Crystals of copper(II) sulfate dissolve in water to form an evenly distributed blue solution*

The following two points can be deduced from the three examples and provide the evidence for the particulate nature of matter.

1 i   for the colour to spread throughout the jar in example 1

   ii for the ammonia and the hydrogen chloride to move towards each other and react to form white rings of ammonium chloride salt, and

   iii for the blue colour of the copper(II) sulfate to spread throughout the water,

   the particles must be able to move.

2 For movement to occur in all three examples, there must be spaces between:

   i   the air particles and the bromine particles

   ii the air, hydrogen chloride and ammonia particles

   iii the water particles in the copper(II) sulfate mixture,

   allowing these particles to move to cause the observed changes.

Other examples of diffusion in gases and liquids include:

- the smell that emanates from the garbage truck when the garbage is collected at the curb next to your home
- the purple colour of potassium manganate(VII) crystal spreading throughout water in a beaker when a few crystals are placed at the bottom of the beaker
- the green colour of nickel(II) sulfate being evenly distributed when a few crystals are placed at the bottom of a beaker of water
- the brown colour of tea, which becomes evenly distributed in the water when a teabag is placed in a cup of boiling water
- when a bottle of fizzy drink is left open, its carbon dioxide diffuses and the soft drink becomes flat
- oxygen and carbon dioxide diffuse back and forth from blood to the body cells
- in plant leaves, oxygen from the leaf cells diffuses out to the air.

Osmosis

Osmosis is a special case of diffusion and is evidence that particles exist and move.

*Osmosis is the movement of **water particles** through a differentially permeable membrane from a solution containing a lot of water particles, for example a dilute solution (or water), to a solution containing fewer water particles, for example a concentrated solution.*

Osmosis can therefore be seen as a special case of diffusion in which water particles move from an area of high concentration of water particles to an area of low concentration of water particles through a differentially permeable membrane.

Example 4

When a dilute sodium chloride solution is separated from a concentrated sodium chloride solution by a **differentially permeable membrane**, water particles move through the membrane from the dilute solution (higher concentration of water particles) into the concentrated solution (lower concentration of water particles), but the sodium chloride particles cannot move in the other direction (Figure 1.4). The **volume** of the concentrated solution **increases** and the **volume** of the dilute solution **decreases**. It must be noted that the sodium chloride particles cannot pass through the pores of the membrane because they are too big and so cannot move to the inside or outside of the membrane.

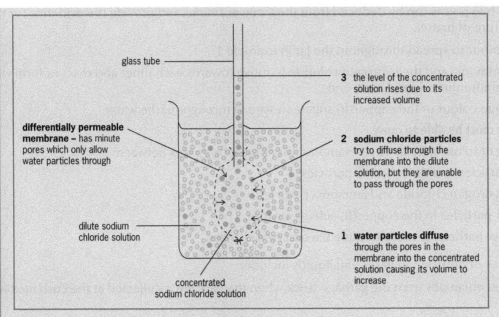

Figure 1.4 *Explaining the phenomenon of osmosis*

Example 5

The membranes of **living cells** are differentially permeable and the cytoplasm inside the cells contains about 80% water.

- When a strip of living tissue (such as a piece of carrot) is placed in **water**, water particles move into the cells through the cell membrane by the process of osmosis. In other words, the water moves from an area of high concentration of water particles (the water surrounding the carrot strip) to an area of low concentration of water particles (inside the cells). This increases the volume of water present in the cells resulting in each cell becoming slightly larger. The strip of carrot therefore increases in length and becomes rigid (or 'turgid').

- When a carrot strip is placed in a **concentrated sodium chloride (salt) solution**, water particles move out of the cells by the process of osmosis. In this case, water moves from an area of high concentration of water particles (inside the cells) to an area of low concentration of water particles (the concentrated solution of sodium chloride surrounding the carrot strip). Each cell loses water particles and slightly shrinks, resulting in the strip becoming shorter and flaccid. Flaccid means a shrinkage or contraction of the contents of the cells, making the carrot strip softer.

- Plants absorb most of the water they need through their root hairs by the process of osmosis. The root hairs behave like a differentially permeable barrier, allowing water particles to move from a high concentration of water particles in the soil to a low concentration of water particles in the roots. As a result, the root cells become more turgid (swollen from the uptake of water, making the plant rigid).

- Another example of osmosis is when salt is sprinkled on a raw vegetable salad. There is no liquid in the salad dish when the vegetables are placed in it, but after the salt is included, liquid is visible in the bottom of the dish. The same can be seen when salt is added to sliced fruits when making 'chow'. Another example is placing raisins in water – they swell up over time.

Uses of osmosis

To control garden pests

Slugs and **snails** are garden pests (Figure 1.5) whose skin is differentially permeable and always moist. When **salt** (sodium chloride) is sprinkled on the moist skin of slugs and snails, the skin acts as a differentially permeable membrane, the salt particles dissolves in the moisture forming a concentrated solution. Water inside their bodies then moves out by **osmosis** to equalize the salt concentration between the inside and outside of the slugs and snails' skin. The slugs and snails die from dehydration.

Figure 1.5 *Snails and slugs are garden pests*

To preserve food

Salt and **sugar** are used to preserve foods such as meat, fish, fruits and vegetables (Figures 1.6, 1.7 and 1.8). They both work in the same way:

- They draw water out of the **cells** of the food by osmosis. This prevents the food from decaying because there is no water available in the cells for the chemical reactions which cause the decay to take place.

- They draw water out of **microorganisms** (bacteria and fungi) by osmosis. This prevents the food from decaying because it inhibits the growth of the microorganisms that cause the decay.

Figure 1.6 *Salted meat*

Figure 1.7 *Jams and jellies are fruits preserved with sugar*

Figure 1.8 *Pickled cucumber preserved with salt*

Brownian motion

Brownian motion is defined as the haphazard motion of microscopic solid particles suspended in a liquid or gaseous medium. The movement of the solid particles results from them being constantly bombarded by the particles in the medium in which it is suspended.

The phenomenon known as Brownian motion was noticed by a botanist, Robert Brown, in 1827, as he observed pollen grains suspended in water under a microscope. He noticed that the pollen grains were moving erratically. This erratic movement of the pollen grains can be explained by the water particles bumping into the solid pollen grains. As the water particles are so small, they were not visible under the microscope.

Erratic movement of dust particles can also be observed in a glass container when it is brightly illuminated. The dust particles are continuously bombarded by the air particles, causing them to move in a haphazard manner.

These examples effectively demonstrate the movement of particles and provide evidence that matter is made up of particles. The ways that matter interacts with each other in space provide evidence to support the theory that matter is made up of particles.

When 50 mls of water is added to 50 mls of isopropyl alcohol, the final volume of the mixture of the two solutions is observed to be less than 100mls. Why would this be? Something must happen between the water and the alcohol when they are mixed to reduce the resulting volume. A reduction of volume implies that the same amount of stuff (50 mls + 50 mls) now fits into a smaller space. To do this, there must be some space within the water and the alcohol that is used up when the two are mixed. Also, the water particles and isopropyl alcohol particles form bonds when they are mixed together, which hold the particles closer together.

Types of particles that make up matter

There are **three** different types of particles that make up matter:

- **Atoms**

  Atoms are the smallest units of a **chemical element** which have all the characteristics of the element. For example, magnesium is made up of magnesium atoms, Mg (see page 19).

- **Molecules**

  Molecules are groups of two or more atoms **bonded** together and which can exist on their own. Molecules may be made up of atoms of the same kind. For example, oxygen molecules, O_2, are made up of oxygen atoms. Molecules may also be made up of atoms of different kinds. For example, water molecules, H_2O, are made up of two hydrogen atoms, H, and one oxygen atom, O.

- **Ions**

  Ions are **electrically charged** particles. Ions may be formed from a single atom, for example, the lithium ion, Li^+. They may also be formed from groups of two or more atoms bonded together, for example, the carbonate ion, CO_3^{2-} (see page 74). These are called **polyatomic ions.**

The three states of matter

The **particulate theory of matter** helps to explain the physical properties of matter and the differences between the three states of matter that are most commonly experienced on Earth. Conditions such as temperature and pressure affect the arrangement of the particles, the types of forces between the particles, and the types of motion that the particles can undergo.

Solids have a regular arrangement of closely packed particles. These particles are strongly attracted to each other with little movement between them. Solids therefore have a fixed shape and volume and are difficult to compress.

Liquids have an irregular arrangement of their particles with small spaces between them allowing the particles to be pushed closer together. Although liquids have a definite volume, they have no fixed shape and will therefore take the shape of whatever contains them and can be compressed slightly. The particles of a liquid can slide over each other and for this reason, liquids flow.

The particles of gases move freely and have small forces of attraction with large spaces between them. For these reasons, gases have no fixed shape or volume but occupy the full space of any container and are easily compressible.

Table 1.1 shows some physical properties of solids, liquids and gases which are explained by applying the knowledge gleaned from the particulate theory of matter.

Table 1.1 *Comparing the three states of matter*

Property	Solid	Liquid	Gas
Shape	Fixed. Many are crystalline in nature.	Takes the shape of the part of the container it is in. The surface is always horizontal.	Takes the shape of the entire container it is in.
Volume	Fixed.	Fixed.	Variable – it expands to fill the container it is in.
Density	Usually high.	Usually lower than solids.	Low.
Compressibility	Difficult to compress.	Can be compressed very slightly by applying pressure.	Very easy to compress.
Arrangement of particles	Packed closely together, usually in a regular way:	Have small spaces between and are randomly arranged:	Have large spaces between and are randomly arranged:
Forces of attraction between the particles	Strong.	Weaker than those between the particles in a solid.	Very weak.
Energy possessed by the particles	Possess very small amounts of kinetic energy.	Possess more kinetic energy that the particles in a solid.	Possess large amounts of kinetic energy.
Movement of the particles	Vibrate in their fixed position.	Move slowly past each other.	Move around freely and rapidly.

Changing state

Matter can exist in any of the three states depending on its **temperature**. It can change from one state to another by heating or cooling (see Figure 1.9), as this causes a change in the **kinetic energy** and arrangement of the particles.

- When a solid is **heated**, it usually changes state to a liquid and then to a gas. This occurs because the particles **gain** kinetic energy, move increasingly faster and further apart, and the forces of attraction between them become increasingly weaker.

- When a gas is **cooled**, it usually changes state to a liquid and then to a solid. This occurs because the particles **lose** kinetic energy, move more and more slowly and closer together, and the forces of attraction between them become increasingly stronger.

Everyday examples of substances that can exist in all three states of matter are water and a burning candle. When water is placed in a freezer, heat energy is removed and solid ice is formed. If water is boiled, heat energy is supplied and gaseous water vapour is formed. When a candle burns, the solid wax with which the candle is made is turned into a liquid by the heat energy supplied by the flame. This liquid wax is then absorbed by the wick and carried towards the base of the flame where it is converted into a vapour which fuels the flame.

The processes of change include melting, freezing, boiling, condensation, evaporation and sublimation (see Figure 1.9). These are discussed in more detail below.

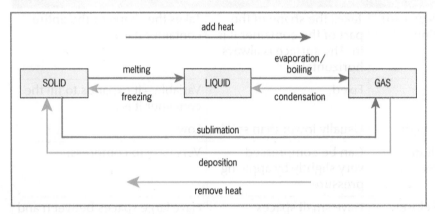

Figure 1.9 *Changing states of matter*

Melting

Energy is gained by the particles in a solid when it is heated. The increased energy causes the particles to vibrate more vigorously. As the temperature increases, the particles vibrate more violently, which results in the forces of attraction holding them in their fixed positions being overcome. The particles can then move more freely, resulting in the solid's structure being broken down, forming a liquid. This is called **melting**. The temperature remains constant during melting because the heat energy being supplied is being used to weaken and eventually overcome the forces of attraction between the solid particles. When the substance becomes a liquid, there are still substantial forces of attraction between the particles, which is why it liquifies. This constant temperature is called the **melting point** of the substance. A pure substance has a fixed melting point. In other words, a pure substance always melts at the same temperature. Examples are: pure gold, which melts at 1064 °C; pure silver, which melts at 961.8 °C; and pure lead, which melts at 327.5 °C.

Freezing

When a liquid cools, heat energy is given out to the surroundings. This causes the particles to move slowly, colliding and increasing the forces of attraction between the particles. The particles eventually take up the fixed and orderly arrangement that exists in a solid. In other words, the liquid changes into a solid. As the solid begins to form, the temperature stays constant until all the liquid solidifies. The temperature at which the liquid turns into a solid is called the **freezing point**.

Boiling

When a liquid is heated, the particles in the liquid gain energy and move faster. As the temperature is increased, the particles' movement increases, eventually gaining enough energy to break the forces of attraction that attach them together. The particles can exist far apart from each other and can move freely, therefore forming a gas within the liquid and at the surface of the liquid. This process is known as **boiling**. The temperature when this transition occurs is constant, and the energy supplied is being used to break the forces of attraction between the particles. None of the energy supplied is used to increase the temperature of the liquid any further and for this reason, the temperature remains constant during boiling. The temperature at which a gas is formed is called the **boiling point**.

Evaporation

When liquids are heated, the particles gain more energy, which allows them to move faster and overcome the forces of attraction holding them together. They can therefore break free and leave the surface of the liquid to form a gas. This process is called **evaporation**. The particles that escape by this process carry a substantial amount of heat energy with them, resulting in cooling of the liquid.

Evaporation and **boiling** are different in the following ways:

- Evaporation can take place spontaneously at all temperatures, whereas boiling occurs at a specific temperature. Usually, the temperature that evaporation occurs at is just below the boiling temperature.
- Evaporation takes place at the surface of the liquid only, whereas boiling takes place throughout the liquid.

Condensation

When energy is removed by cooling a gas, the particles of the gas lose kinetic energy and travel more slowly and move closer together. The force of attraction becomes greater, and the gas is converted into a liquid. This process is known as **condensation**.

Sublimation

Substances that **sublimate** (or **sublime**) change directly from a solid to a gas without going through the liquid phase (Figure 1.10). The reverse process in which a gas changes directly to a solid is called **deposition**. Sublimation occurs in substances where the forces of attraction between the particles of the solid are weak. Only a small quantity of energy is required to overcome these forces of attraction, converting the solids into the gaseous phase and vice versa. Examples of substances that sublime are ammonium chloride, carbon dioxide ('dry ice'), iodine and naphthalene (moth balls).

Heating and cooling curves

Heating and cooling curves can be used to investigate the changes between the different states of matter. Examples of a heating and a cooling curve

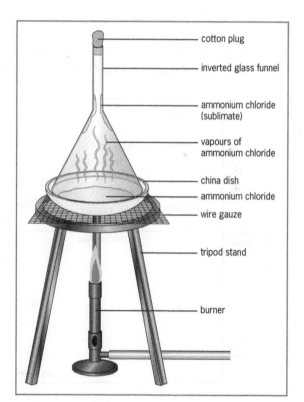

are shown in Figure 1.11 and Figure 1.12. As can be seen, they have the same shape except the heating curve goes in the opposite direction to the cooling curve. The different processes mentioned above, which bring about the changes in the states of matter, are also shown on the cooling and heating curves. Also shown on the curves are the different states that are associated with each distinct region of the graphs.

Figure 1.10 *Ammonium chloride sublimes on heating*

- A **heating curve** is drawn when the temperature of a solid is measured at intervals as it is **heated** and changes state to a liquid and then to a gas. The temperature is then plotted against time.
- A **cooling curve** is drawn when the temperature of a gas is measured at intervals as it is **cooled** and changes state to a liquid and then to a solid. The temperature is then plotted against time.

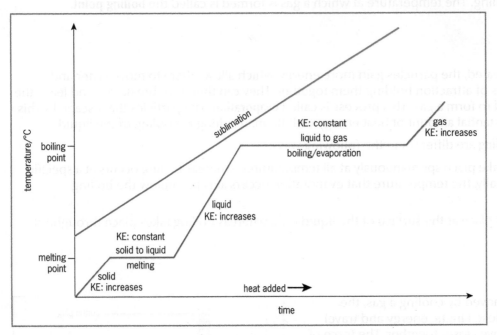

Figure 1.11 *A heating curve (KE = kinetic energy)*

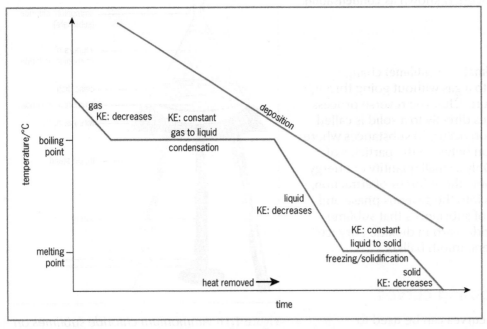

Figure 1.12 *A cooling curve (KE = kinetic energy)*

Figures 1.11 and 1.12 also highlight the definitions of the various temperature points.

*The **melting point** is the constant temperature at which a solid changes state into a liquid.*

*The **boiling point** is the constant temperature at which a liquid changes state into a gas.*

*The **freezing point** is the constant temperature at which a liquid changes state into a solid.*

The energy needed to change the state of a substance is called **latent heat**. Specific latent heat is the amount of energy needed to change the state of 1 kilogram (kg) of material without changing its temperature.

Recalling facts

1. Which of the following observations does NOT give evidence that support the phenomenon that matter is made up of particles?
   a A strip of pawpaw shrinks slightly in concentrated sodium chloride solution.
   b A strip of pawpaw increases in length in concentrated sodium chloride solution.
   c When 50 mls of water and 50 mls of isopropyl alcohol are mixed, the volume occupied is less than 100 mls.
   d Dust particles are seen moving haphazardly in air under a microscope.

2. Which of the following substances does NOT sublime?
   a solid carbon dioxide
   b naphthalene
   c sodium chloride
   d iodine

3. Which of the following takes place at the surface of a liquid only?
   a boiling
   b evaporation
   c solidification
   d freezing

4. Name the constant temperature at which a solid changes state into a liquid.
   a boiling point
   b melting point
   c freezing point
   d condensation point

5. The particles of a liquid:
   a vibrate in their fixed positions
   b move around freely and rapidly
   c move slowly past each other
   d are easily compressed

6 Name the change in state that occurs when heat energy is increased in a solid.

a melting

b evaporation

c freezing

d condensation

7 Two characteristics of _____ are that the particles are packed closely together in a regular way and cannot be compressed easily.

a liquids

b solids

c gases

d solids and liquids

8 A _____ takes the shape of the entire container it is in.

a liquid

b solid

c gas

d none of the above

Questions 9 and 10 refer to the table, which shows the melting and boiling points of four substances

Substance	Melting point/°C	Boiling point/°C
A	1064	2700
B	−218.8	−183
C	327.5	1749
D	−38.83	356.7

9 Which of the substance(s) is/are solids at room temperature?

a D   b B   c A and C   d B and C

10 Which of the substance(s) is/are gases at room temperature?

a A   b B   c A and D   d B and C

11 Define the following terms:

a osmosis

b diffusion

c melting point

d boiling point

12 Define the terms boiling and evaporation. State the differences and similarities between evaporation and boiling.

13 Name the three different types of particles that make up matter.

Applying facts

14 Choose the word from those provided below which best describes the process occurring in each of the following statements. You can use the words once, more than once, or not at all.

| diffusion | sublimation | condensation | osmosis | evaporation |
| freezing | condensation | melting | freezing | |

a You remove the cover from a boiling pot of water and there are droplets of water on the cover.

b You notice the volume of ethanol has decreased from a beaker of ethanol left sitting on the desk in the laboratory for a few hours on a warm day.

c A spoon was dipped in a coloured substance and placed in a pot of water. After a few hours you noticed that the colour of the water was the colour of the substance the spoon was dipped in.

d You just had a hot shower and went to look at your face in the mirror in the bathroom, but the mirror was steamed up and you had to wipe it to see your face.

e Ice forms around the edges of your non-frost freezer.

f The smell of a rotting potato gradually disappears from the kitchen after it is thrown out.

g You are looking at a documentary on jewellery making and see that solid gold is placed in a crucible and heated and then this liquid is placed in a mould and a solid ring is obtained.

h Ammonium chloride is heated in a test-tube and white fumes are seen rising; at the mouth of the test-tube a white salt deposit is noticed.

i A liquid is seen in a salad bowl after salt is added to the dry sliced vegetables.

15 In terms of shape, volume, arrangement of particles, movement of particles and forces of attraction between the particles, describe the differences between the following states:

a gas and a liquid

b solid and a gas

16 Diffusion and osmosis are evidence that support the particulate theory of matter.

a List the main ideas of this theory.

b Using an example of either diffusion or osmosis, explain how the named phenomenon supports the particulate theory of matter.

Analysing data

17 A few crystals of nickel(II) sulfate were placed at the bottom of a beaker and after a few hours it was observed that the water turned to the green colour of the nickel(II) sulfate.

a Name the phenomenon that has occurred, giving a definition.

b Explain, using the particulate theory of matter, the observation made in the experiment.

c Using solid circles to represent the nickel(II) sulfate particles and hollow circles to represent the water particles, draw diagrams to show what happens at:

  i the start of the experiment

  ii the end of the experiment

18 In an experiment, temperature readings were recorded while molten stearic acid was gradually cooled.

a Use the data in the table to plot a graph of temperature against time. Remember to correctly label the axes of the graph and to give the graph a suitable title.

Time/min	1	2	3	4	5	6	7	8	9	10	11	12	13	14	15
Temperature/°C	95	80	79	70	64	61	55	55	55	55	55	50	48	47	44

b Describe the general shape of the line of the graph.

c Explain the shape of the graph between minute 1 and minute 5, between minute 6 and minute 10, and between minute 11 and minute 15. At each stage, give the state in which the stearic acid exists and name the process and temperature range in which they occur.

d Draw suitable diagrams to show what happens in terms of the particles in the named process mentioned in part c.

e State the solidification temperature of the stearic acid. Justify your answer.

2 Pure substances, mixtures and separations

Learning objectives

- Understand the difference between **pure substances** and **mixtures**.
- Define and give examples of **elements**, **compounds** and **mixtures**.
- List the differences between **mixtures** and **compounds**.
- Explain the difference between a **homogeneous** and a **heterogeneous mixture**, giving their properties.
- Define the term **solubility**.
- Obtain **solubility data** and perform calculations using a **solubility curve**.
- Describe **methods of separation** and **purification** for the components of **solid–solid, solid–liquid, liquid–liquid** (**miscible** and **immiscible**) **mixtures**.
- Describe and explain the processes involved in the **extraction of sucrose from sugarcane**.

As seen in the previous unit, matter makes up everything around us. Matter can be classified into **pure substances** and **mixtures**. These can be further classified as shown in Figure 2.1.

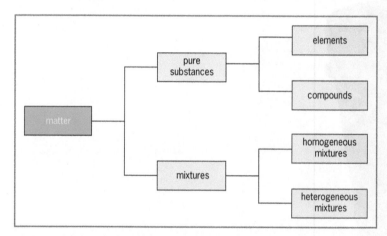

Figure 2.1 *Classification of matter*

All the objects that we see in the world around us are made of **matter**. Matter makes up the air we breathe, the ground we walk on, the food we eat and the animals and plants that live around us. Even our own human bodies are made of matter! Chemists study the structures, physical properties and chemical properties of material substances. We see mixtures all the time in our everyday lives. A soup, for example, is a mixture of different foods such as meat and vegetables; sea water is a mixture of water, salt and other substances; and air is a mixture of gases such as carbon dioxide, oxygen and nitrogen.

Pure substances

*A **pure substance** is composed of a single type of material only.*

Any pure substance possesses certain general **characteristics**:

- Its **composition** is fixed and constant. For example, in carbon dioxide, the ratio of carbon to oxygen is always the same. The chemical formula for carbon dioxide is always CO_2.

- The boiling and freezing points are fixed and constant. At atmospheric pressure, pure ethanol has a boiling point of 78.37 °C and melting/freezing point of −114 °C; the boiling point of acetone is 56.2 °C and its freezing/melting point −94.8 °C.

- It has distinct and predictable chemical properties. Magnesium reacts very slowly with cold water and vigorously with dilute hydrochloric acid. Sodium reacts with chlorine to form sodium chloride. Potassium reacts vigorously with water to produce potassium hydroxide and hydrogen gas.

- The component parts cannot be separated by any physical process. Sodium chloride, (NaCl), can be broken down into sodium and chlorine by electrolysis, which is not a physical method of separation.

To find out if a substance is **pure**, its melting point or boiling point can be measured. If any impurities are present, they will usually **lower** its melting point and **raise** its boiling point.

Have you ever wondered why, when churning ice cream in a hand-turned ice cream freezer, salt is added to the ice (Figure 2.2)? Pure ice melts/freezes at 0 °C and the ice cream mixture freezes at a lower temperature than water (0 °C). Therefore, a colder temperature is required for the ice cream to freeze. Mixing salt (an impurity in this case) with the ice lowers the melting/freezing point of ice (to values between −5 and −25 °C depending upon the mass of salt added), which allows the ice cream mixture to freeze before the ice totally melts.

Figure 2.2 *Hand-cranked freezer*

The boiling point of water (100 °C) is elevated when salt is added to water. When salt is added to water the specific heat capacity is lowered (see page 224) and the boiling point is elevated.

Elements

Elements are the simplest form of matter.

*An **element** is a pure substance that cannot be broken down into simpler substances by using any ordinary physical or chemical process.*

An **atom** is the smallest particle in any element. Each element is composed of atoms of **one kind** only. Most elements are made up of **individual atoms**. For example, gold (Au) is made up of individual gold atoms, chromium (Cr) is made up of chromium atoms only. A few elements are made up of **molecules**.

Section A: Principles of chemistry

For example, chlorine (Cl_2) is made up of chlorine molecules, each molecule being composed of two chlorine atoms.

There are 118 known elements. They can be classified as **metals** or **non-metals**.

Table 2.1 *The physical properties of metals and non-metals compared*

Physical property	Metals	Non-metals
Melting and boiling points	Usually high	Usually low
State at room temperature	Solid (except mercury)	Can be solid, liquid or gas
Appearance of the solid	Shiny	Dull
Bendability of the solid	Malleable (can be hammered into different shapes) and ductile (can be drawn out into wires)	Brittle
Density	Usually high	Usually low
Electrical and thermal conductivity	Good	Poor (except graphite, a form of carbon)

Each element can be represented by an **atomic symbol**. The atomic symbol represents **one atom** of the element.

Table 2.2 *Common metals and their atomic symbols*

Element	Atomic symbol	Element	Atomic symbol
Aluminium	Al	Lithium	Li
Barium	Ba	Magnesium	Mg
Beryllium	Be	Manganese	Mn
Calcium	Ca	Mercury	Hg
Chromium	Cr	Nickel	Ni
Cobalt	Co	Potassium	K
Copper	Cu	Silver	Ag
Gold	Au	Sodium	Na
Iron	Fe	Tin	Sn
Lead	Pb	Zinc	Zn

Table 2.3 *Common non-metals and their atomic symbols*

Element	Atomic symbol	Element	Atomic symbol
Argon	Ar	Iodine	I
Boron	B	Krypton	Kr
Bromine	Br	Neon	Ne
Carbon	C	Nitrogen	N
Chlorine	Cl	Oxygen	O
Fluorine	F	Phosphorus	P
Helium	He	Silicon	Si
Hydrogen	H	Sulfur	S

Note When an atomic symbol consists of two letters, the first letter is always a capital.

Compounds

*A **compound** is a pure substance formed from two or more different types of elements that are chemically bonded together in fixed proportions and in a way that changes their properties.*

Example 1

magnesium + chlorine $\longrightarrow$ magnesium chloride
(element)   (element)   (compound)

The proportions, by mass, of magnesium and chlorine in any pure sample of magnesium chloride are always the same and the elements cannot be separated by physical means because they are **chemically bonded** together. The properties of magnesium chloride are different from those of both magnesium and chlorine.

Compounds can be represented by **chemical formulae**. For example, the chemical formula for magnesium chloride is $MgCl_2$ and for glucose it is $C_6H_{12}O_6$.

As can be seen in its chemical formula, the compound magnesium chloride, $MgCl_2$, is made up of two elements – magnesium and chlorine.

Glucose, $C_6H_{12}O_6$, is made up of three elements – carbon (C), hydrogen (H) and oxygen (O).

The general characteristics of compounds are:

- The chemical and physical properties are different from those of the individual elements.
- There is a fixed ratio of the elements present.
- Energy is given off or taken in when forming a compound. Hence the elements that make up the compound cannot be separated by physical means.

Mixtures

*A **mixture** consists of two or more substances (elements and/or compounds) which are physically combined together in variable proportions. Each component retains its own individual properties and is not chemically bonded to any other component of the mixture.*

Any mixture possesses certain general **characteristics**:

- Its **composition** can vary.
- Its physical and chemical **properties** are variable because its component parts keep their specific properties. Therefore, its physical properties are an average of those of the particular substances. Mixtures melt and boil over a range of temperatures. The chemical properties are the result of the substances in the mixture.
- Its **component parts** can be separated by physical means. Examples of physical methods include evaporation, filtration, distillation and chromatography (see pages 25–31). This is because little or no energy is released or absorbed when a mixture is formed.

Examples of mixtures:

- Sea water is a mixture of solids dissolved in water.
- Alloys are mixtures of elements. For example, sterling silver is a mixture of copper and silver; brass is a mixture of copper and zinc.
- Some gases, such as air, are a mixture of elements and compounds.
- Solutions, such as carbonated drinks, are a mixture of several compounds: water, sugar, extracts, colourings and carbon dioxide.

Mixtures can be classified as homogeneous and heterogeneous mixtures.

Homogeneous mixtures

A **homogeneous mixture** is a **uniform** mixture. It has the same composition and properties throughout the mixture. It is not possible to distinguish the component parts from each other. All **solutions** are homogeneous mixtures. Examples of homogeneous mixtures include sugar dissolved in water; bronze: a mixture of tin and copper; bitumen; and air.

Heterogeneous mixtures

A **heterogeneous mixture** is a **non-uniform** mixture. It is possible to distinguish the component parts from each other, though not always with the naked eye. Heterogeneous mixtures include **suspensions** and **colloids**. Examples of heterogeneous mixtures include sand, oil and water; chicken noodle soup; sand and gravel; orange juice with pulp; and blood.

Solutions, suspensions and colloids

Solutions

*A **solution** is a homogeneous mixture of two or more substances. One substance is usually a liquid.*

When a substance dissolves in a liquid, the resulting mixture is a solution.

$$\text{solute + solvent} \longrightarrow \text{solution}$$

For example:

$$\text{sugar + water} \longrightarrow \text{sugar solution}$$

The **solvent** is the substance that does the **dissolving**. In the example above, water is the solvent. It is present in the solution at a higher concentration than the solute.

The **solute** is the substance that **dissolves**. In the example above, the solute is sugar and is present at a lower concentration than the water.

A solution may contain more than one solute. Solutions in which the solvent is water are known as **aqueous solutions**. Solutions can contain more than one solute; for example, lemonade (sugar and flavourings) and air (many gases). Solutions can be made up of solvents and solutes in the same or different phases, as seen in Table 2.4.

*A **saturated solution** is a solution in which the solvent cannot dissolve any more solute at a particular temperature. The resulting solution will have sediment which is undissolved solute that cannot dissolve.*

Table 2.4 *Different types of solutions*

State of solute	State of solvent	Example	Components
Solid	Liquid	Sea water	Sodium chloride dissolved in water
Liquid	Liquid	White vinegar	Ethanoic acid dissolved in water
Gas	Liquid	Soda water	Carbon dioxide dissolved in water
Solid	Solid	Bronze (a metal alloy)	Tin dissolved in copper
Gas	Gas	Air	Oxygen, carbon dioxide, noble gases and water vapour dissolved in nitrogen

Suspensions

*A **suspension** is a heterogeneous mixture in which minute, visible particles of one substance are dispersed in another substance, which is usually a liquid.*

The particles of a suspension are larger than those of a solution and as such gravity can pull them down from the medium that they are distributed in, allowing them to settle at the bottom of the container.

Example 2

- **Flour** in **water** and **paints (dyes suspended in turpentine oils)**. These are suspensions of solid particles in a liquid.
- A puddle of water on asphalt has an oily feel to it; this is **oil on water**. This is a suspension of liquid droplets in a liquid.
- **Soot** in the **air** or **powdered aerosol sprays for athlete's foot**. These are suspensions of solid particles in a gas.

Colloids

*A **colloid** is a heterogeneous mixture in which minute particles of one substance are dispersed in another substance, which is usually a liquid. The dispersed particles are larger than those of a solution, but smaller than those of a suspension.*

Colloids are **intermediate** between a solution and a suspension. The particles are not as large as those in a suspension. They do not settle upon standing but remain spread uniformly throughout the medium. The medium can be a solid, liquid or gas. Table 2.5 gives examples of different types of colloids.

Table 2.5 *Different types of colloids*

Type of colloid	Composition	Examples
Gel	Solid particles dispersed in a liquid	Gelatine, jelly, paint, blood, butter, cheese
Liquid emulsion	Liquid droplets dispersed in a liquid	Mayonnaise, milk, hand cream
Foam	Gas bubbles dispersed in a liquid	Whipped cream, shaving cream
Solid aerosol	Solid particles dispersed in a gas	Smoke, dust in air, smog
Liquid aerosol	Liquid droplets dispersed in a gas	Fog, aerosol sprays, clouds, mist

Figure 2.3 compares the particle sizes and Table 2.6 compares the characteristics/properties (size of particles, visibility, sedimentation, appearance and passage of light) of the different types of mixtures.

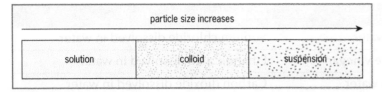

Figure 2.3 *Comparing the particle sizes in a solution, a colloid and a suspension*

Table 2.6 *Comparing the properties of solutions, colloids and suspensions*

Property	Solution	Colloid	Suspension
Size of dispersed particles	Extremely small Less than or equal to 1 nm	Larger than those in a solution but smaller than those in a suspension 1 to 1000 nm	Larger than those in a colloid Greater than or equal to 1000 nm
Visibility of dispersed particles	Not visible, even with a microscope	Not visible, even with a microscope	Visible to the naked eye
Sedimentation	Components do not separate if left undisturbed	Dispersed particles do not settle if left undisturbed	Dispersed particles settle if left undisturbed
Passage of light	Light usually passes through	Most will scatter light	Light does not pass through
Appearance	Usually transparent due to light passing through	Translucent due to the scattering of light, or may be opaque	Opaque due to light not being able to pass through

Solubility

Solubility is the mass of solute that will saturate 100 g of solvent at a specified temperature.

The solubility of a solute in a solvent is influenced by temperature (it increases the movement of the particles resulting in more mixing), the nature/structure of the solvent and solute, and pressure. In general, the solubility of a **solid** solute in water **increases** as the temperature increases.

Solubility is also influenced by increasing the surface area of the solute so that there is more contact with the solvent. Stirring the mixture brings more solvent in contact with the solute. The faster the mixture is stirred the more solute will dissolve.

Solubility curves

A **solubility curve** is drawn by plotting solubility against temperature, as shown in Figure 2.4. The solubility of a given substance at a given temperature can be determined from its solubility. A solubility curve can be used to determine:

* the quantity of solute deposited when a solution is cooled
* the solubilities of different solutes at a particular temperature
* which solute from a solution containing two or more solutes will crystallise first

Solubility curves can also be used to compare the solubility of various compounds at the same temperature.

The solubility curve line represents a solution with a fully dissolved mass of solute in 100 g of water; in other words, a saturated solution (Figure 2.4). Any value above the line indicates a supersaturated solution and any value below the line indicates an unsaturated solution.

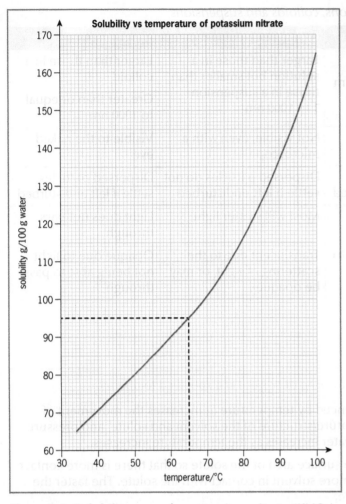

Figure 2.4 *Solubility curve for potassium nitrate (KNO₃)* in water

Solubility curves are useful to obtain different pieces of **information**, as shown in the following questions.

Sample questions

1 What is the **solubility** of potassium nitrate at 65 °C?

The solubility of KNO_3 at 65 °C = **95 g per 100 g water**

2 A potassium nitrate solution containing 100 g water is saturated at 65 °C. What mass of potassium nitrate must be added to **re-saturate** this solution if it is heated to 80 °C?

At 65 °C, **95 g** of KNO_3 saturates 100 g of water

At 80 °C, **117 g** of KNO_3 saturates 100 g of water

∴ the mass of KNO_3 to be added to re-saturate a solution containing 100 g of water

= 117 − 95 g

= **22 g**

3 A potassium nitrate solution which contains 101 g of water is saturated at 70 °C. What mass of potassium nitrate would **crystallise out** of this solution if it is cooled to 63 °C?

At 70 °C, **101 g** of KNO_3 saturates 100 g of water

At 63 °C, **93 g** of KNO_3 saturates 100 g of water

∴ the mass of KNO_3 crystallising out of a saturated solution containing 100 g of water

= 101 − 93 g

= **8 g**

and mass of KNO_3 crystallising out of a saturated solution containing 300 g of water

$= \dfrac{8}{100} \times 300$ g

= **24 g**

4 At what **temperature** would 267 g of potassium nitrate saturate 300 g water?

267 g of KNO_3 saturates 300 g of water

∴ $\dfrac{267}{300} \times 100$ g of KNO_3 saturates 100 g of water

= **89 g of KNO_3**

Temperature at which 89 g of KNO_3 saturates 100 g water = **59.5 °C**

Separating the components of mixtures

Mixtures can be separated into their component parts as pure substances because they are formed by physical changes only. To carry out the separation, physical methods, which do not entail any chemical reactions, are used. The methods used are simple and include filtration, evaporation, crystallisation, sublimation, the use of a separating funnel, simple and fractional distillation and paper chromatography. The **technique** used to separate the components of a mixture depends on the **physical properties** of its components.

Filtration

Filtration is used to separate a **suspended** or **settled solid** and a **liquid** when the solid does not dissolve in the liquid, for example, powdered chalk and water. The components are separated due to their different **particle sizes.**

Figure 2.5 shows suitable apparatus for carrying out the technique of filtration. The chalk and water mixture is poured into the funnel, which is lined with a filter paper. The filter paper has tiny holes in it which allow only the particles of water to pass through. The solid chalk particles are too large to pass though the holes and are trapped on the filter paper. The filter paper acts as a selective barrier. The solid (chalk particles) collected on the filter paper is known as the **residue**, while the liquid (water) which passes through the filter paper is known as the **filtrate**.

Filtration is not only used by chemists in the laboratory but has applications in our everyday lives. The following are some applications:

- Tea is infused into a cup of hot water by either using a tea bag (paper filter) or a metal tea ball (metal filter). The solid tea remains on the filter paper or metal filter and the liquid tea is the filtrate.
- Air conditioners and many vacuum cleaners use High Efficiency Particulate Air filters (HEPA filters) to trap dust from the air.
- Tap water is filtered through charcoal in a water filter pitcher.

- Water is filtered through layers of sand, gravel and charcoal at reservoirs to remove insoluble particles.
- Home aquaria use fibres in their filters to trap particulate matter.

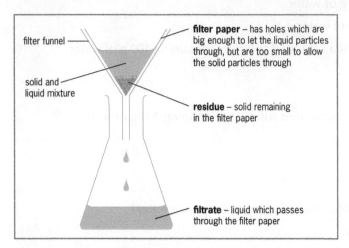

filter funnel

filter paper – has holes which are big enough to let the liquid particles through, but are too small to allow the solid particles through

solid and liquid mixture

residue – solid remaining in the filter paper

filtrate – liquid which passes through the filter paper

Figure 2.5 *Separating components of a mixture by filtration*

Evaporation

Evaporation is used to separate and retain the **solid solute** from the liquid solvent in a **solution**. It is used if the solute does not decompose on heating or if a solid without water that is chemically bonded into a crystal lattice structure (water of crystallisation, see page 142) is required, for example, to obtain potassium chloride from potassium chloride solution. The components are separated due to their different **boiling points**. Figure 2.6 shows suitable apparatus that can be used during this method of separation. The boiling point of the solvent (here water) must be lower than that of the solute (here potassium chloride) so that it is converted to a gas and leaves the solute behind. The potassium chloride is collected in the evaporation dish and the water as water vapour escapes into the atmosphere. Sugar, copper(II) sulfate and sodium carbonate crystals cannot be separated by this technique.

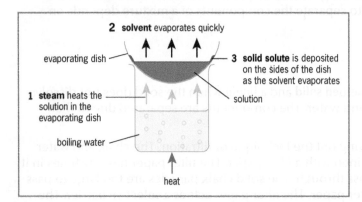

evaporating dish

2 solvent evaporates quickly

3 solid solute is deposited on the sides of the dish as the solvent evaporates

1 steam heats the solution in the evaporating dish

solution

boiling water

heat

Figure 2.6 *Separating components of a mixture by evaporation*

Crystallisation

Crystallisation is used to separate and retain the **solid solute** from the liquid solvent in a **solution**. It is used if the solute decomposes on heating or if a solid containing water of crystallisation is required, for example to obtain hydrated sodium sulfate from sodium sulfate solution. The components are separated due to their different **volatilities**. **Volatility** refers to how easily a substance vaporises or turns into a gas. The solvent must be more volatile than the solute so that it evaporates and leaves the solute behind. Figure 2.7 explains how the components are separated in a mixture by crystallisation.

The sodium sulfate solution must be heated in an evaporating dish until it becomes saturated. This hot saturated solution is then allowed to cool. As the solution cools, pure crystals of sodium sulfate are formed and settle to the bottom of the container and the impurities remain in the solution. The slower the cooling process, the larger the crystals formed.

An explanation of the formation of crystals while the solution is cooled is that most solutes are less soluble as temperature decreases. When the hot saturated solution is cooled, less solute is dissolved in the solution. Therefore, this extra solute, that cannot be dissolved, forms crystals.

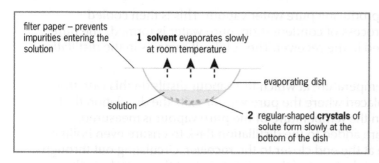

filter paper – prevents impurities entering the solution

1 **solvent** evaporates slowly at room temperature

evaporating dish

solution

2 regular-shaped **crystals** of solute form slowly at the bottom of the dish

Figure 2.7 *Separating components of a mixture by crystallisation*

Sublimation

When a solid that sublimes needs to be separated from a mixture of solids, the process of **sublimation** is used (see Figures 2.8 and 2.9). Recall that some substances undergo sublimation. That is, a solid substance can be converted into its gaseous phase directly upon heating or the gas changes back into a solid when cooled.

A mixture of iodine and sand can be separated by the process of sublimation. Iodine undergoes sublimation whereas sand does not. When the iodine–sand mixture is gently heated, purple iodine vapours are seen to rise and crystals of iodine are formed on the cooler bottom of the evaporating dish. The sand is not affected by the heat and stays in the beaker.

Solid carbon dioxide, anhydrous iron(III) chloride, anhydrous aluminium chloride and ammonium chloride are all examples of substances that sublime.

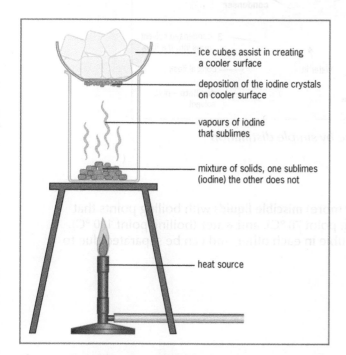

ice cubes assist in creating a cooler surface

deposition of the iodine crystals on cooler surface

vapours of iodine that sublimes

mixture of solids, one sublimes (iodine) the other does not

heat source

Figure 2.8 *Sublimation of iodine from sand and iodine*

Figure 2.9 *Sublimation of dry ice*

Simple distillation

Simple distillation is used to separate and retain the **liquid solvent** from the solid solute in a **solution**, for example, to obtain distilled water from tap water or sea water. The solute can also be obtained by **evaporation** or **crystallisation** of the concentrated solution that remains after distillation if no impurities are present. The components are separated due to their different **boiling points**. The boiling point of the solvent must be lower than that of the solute.

An example of a simple distillation is the distillation of salt water to obtain pure water (Figure 2.10).

Salt water is heated in a distillation flask producing pure water vapour. This is then cooled down in a condenser and, through the process of condensation, pure water is formed. The pure water is called the **distillate** and is collected in the receiver. The solid salt remains in the distillation flask and is called the **residue**.

A thermometer is used to measure the temperature at which the vapour distils (in this case the water). The bulb of the thermometer is placed where the pure vapour exits the distillation flask and enters the condenser. In this position the temperature of the pure vapour is measured. Anti-bumping granules or boiling chips are added to the distillation flask to ensure even boiling. The coolant enters the condenser sleeve at the end closer to the receiver, circulating out through the end at the top. This ensures that the coolest part of the condenser is at the end where the vapour escapes.

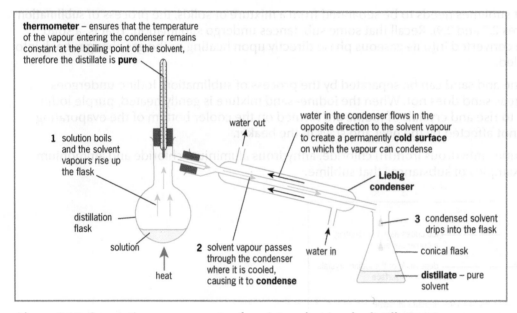

Figure 2.10 *Separating components of a mixture by simple distillation*

Fractional distillation

Fractional distillation is used to separate two (or more) **miscible liquids** with boiling points that are close together, for example, ethanol (boiling point 78 °C), and water (boiling point 100 °C). Miscible liquids mix completely, so they are soluble in each other, and can be separated due to their different **boiling points**.

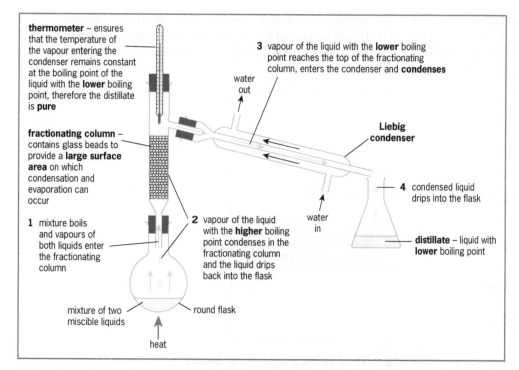

Figure 2.11 *Separating components of a mixture by fractional distillation*

As the mixture boils, vapours of both liquids rise up the fractionating column where they condense and evaporate continually, and the vapour mixture becomes progressively richer in the **more volatile** component (the one with the lower boiling point). The vapour reaching the top of the column and entering the condenser is composed almost entirely of the more volatile component and the temperature remains constant at the boiling point of this component.

As can be seen in Figure 2.11, the apparatus is like that used in simple distillation except for the fractionating column. This column is usually packed with some sort of unreactive material, such as glass beads. This increases the surface area for condensation of the vapours to occur. When a mixture of ethanol and water, for example, is placed in the distillation flask and heated, the ethanol, having the lower boiling point, 78 °C, is converted into the vapour state first. The ethanol vapour reaches the top of the column first and exits into the condenser. The ethanol vapour is cooled in the condenser and condenses into liquid ethanol. The liquid ethanol is collected in the receiver. The vapours of the water, having a higher boiling point, 100 °C, condense in the fractionating column and return to the flask. When most of the ethanol has boiled off, only then does the temperature at the top of the column increase to 100 °C, signalling that the water vapour is entering the condenser. The water vapour is now cooled in the condenser and pure water is collected in another receiving vessel. It should be noted that complete separation of the ethanol and water is not possible. The ethanol distillate will have some trace amounts of water which could be removed by adding a drying agent.

Fractional distillation has wide applications in the alcohol industry, refining crude oil (see pages 254–255) and separating the components of liquid air.

Separating funnel

A **separating funnel** is used to separate two (or more) **immiscible liquids**, for example, diesel and water. Immiscible liquids do not mix and are separated due to their **different densities**.

When a mixture of diesel and water is placed in a separating funnel and left undisturbed, the lighter or less dense diesel collects at the top and the water, being heavier or denser, collects at the bottom. In other words, two distinct layers can be seen (see Figure 2.12). The tap is then opened, and the water is allowed to drain into a beaker. The top layer of diesel remains in the separating funnel and can be collected in another beaker. It should be noted that complete separation of both these components is never achieved. Other examples of mixtures being separated by this method are cooking oil and water; and kerosene and water.

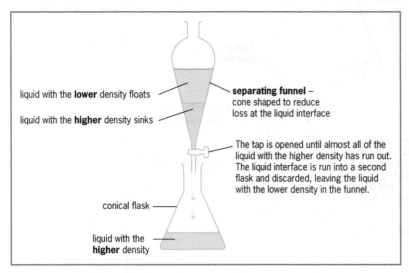

Figure 2.12 *Separating components of a mixture using a separating funnel*

Paper chromatography

Paper chromatography is another method that can be used to identify a substance, to separate mixtures of soluble substances, or to purify a substance by separating it from its impurities. These are often coloured substances, such as food colourings, inks, dyes or plant pigments.

The principle involved depends upon the relative solubilities of the substances in the mixture:

- how **soluble** each substance is in the solvent used
- how strongly each one is **attracted** to the paper used; in other words how strongly each substance adsorbs (sticks/adheres) to the paper.

Chromatography also relies on two different 'phases':

- The **mobile phase** is the solvent that moves through the paper, carrying different substances with it.
- The **stationary phase** is when the solvent and substances are contained on the paper and do not move through it.

Figure 2.13 shows the apparatus used to carry out this method of separation.

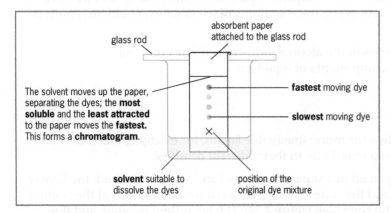

Figure 2.13 *Separating components of a mixture by paper chromatography*

To separate substances by paper chromatography

- Using a capillary tube, place a spot of the mixture about 2 cm from the bottom of a strip of filter or chromatography paper (this is known as the **line of origin**).
- Allow the spot to dry and then spot the paper again in the same place. Repeat this so that the paper has been spotted (and allowed to dry) three times.
- Draw a line of origin on the filter/chromatography paper with a pencil (do not use pen as the ink will dissolve).
- Suspend the paper in a chromatography tank (or beaker) containing a suitable solvent. Ensure that the lower edge of the paper is below the surface of the solvent and that the line of origin does not touch the solvent. If the origin does touch the solvent it will dissolve in the solvent and not separate on the chromatography paper.
- Cover the chromatography tank with either a lid or foil paper. This ensures that the atmosphere in the tank is saturated with solvent vapour. Doing this prevents the solvent from evaporating as it ascends the paper.
- Observe that as the solvent travels up the paper, it carries and begins to separate the dyes. This happens because the substances have different solubilities in the solvent and are **adsorbed** to different degrees by the paper. The dyes that are more soluble travel faster and move further up the paper than the less soluble dyes. Note that identical dyes travel up the same distance on the paper. Dyes that are not soluble do not move but stay on the line of origin.
- Remove the chromatography paper just before the solvent reaches the top of the paper (**the solvent front**). Allow the paper to dry. This paper, with different spots (each one representing a different component in the mixture) is called the **chromatogram**.
- Obtain the **R$_f$ value** from the chromatogram for a particular spot by measuring and relating the distance travelled to the position of the solvent front.

The R$_f$ value is the ratio of the distance travelled by the solute to the distance travelled by the solvent.

Paper chromatography can be used to analyse colourless substances. The colourless substances can be sprayed with **a locating agent** to make them visible.

A locating agent reacts with the substances to form coloured products, or products that glow under ultraviolet light.

Ninhydrin is a chemical that, when sprayed on colourless amino acids, produces a purple stain. Another example is iodine vapour which reacts with fats and oils, turning them brown.

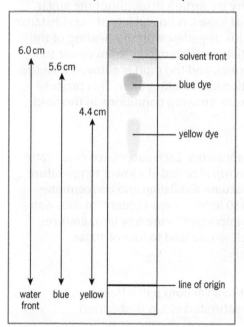

An example of the R$_f$ value calculation

In Figure 2.14:

The R$_f$ value for the yellow dye is given by $= \dfrac{4.4}{6.0}$

$= 0.73$

The R$_f$ value for the blue dye is given by $= \dfrac{5.6}{6.0}$

$= 0.93$

Figure 2.14 *An example of a chromatogram*

Chromatography can be used in the laboratory to assist in crime detection, and to identify pollutants in air and substances such as dyes, pigments and amino acids. In industry it can be used to separate pure substances for making medical drugs, food flavourings and colourings.

The extraction of sucrose from sugar cane

The production of sugar from sugar cane was once a very important financial contributor to all the Caribbean islands. The industrial process of sucrose production from sugar cane utilises many of the **separation methods** discussed above. The extraction process is summarised in Figure 2.15.

Cane sugar processing includes the following steps: sugar cane is crushed, the juice is heated and filtered, then sent to a series of crystallisation steps to create raw sugar, followed by centrifugation to remove any remaining juice or syrup.

Harvesting

The sugar cane stalks are cut in the fields and transported to the factory, where they are washed. Washing takes place on belts that are sprayed with water. After washing, the stalks are conveyed on belts into the factory. The stalks are then **cut** into smaller pieces using rotating knives in a shredder. This process uncovers the inner material of the sugar cane, allowing for more efficient extraction of sugar cane juice.

Crushing

The shredded cane stalks are then **crushed** using roller mills to extract the juice. Water is squirted onto the crushed stalks to dissolve the sucrose present. The crushed stalks then pass through further roller mills to extract the juice by compressing the sugar cane fibres, separating the juice from the **bagasse** (pulp). The initial cane juice which is **acidic** and cloudy is collected in large vats. This juice contains impurities. The sugar concentration of the juice is determined (about 8 to 20% sugar). The bagasse produced is burnt in the boiler furnace, supplying heat to the boilers in the factory. The juice is heated, and then pumped to the clarifier. The heat helps to **denature** naturally occurring **enzymes** in the juice, which would breakdown the sucrose.

Clarification

Slaked lime or calcium hydroxide is added to **neutralise** the acidic cane juice. The impurities are **precipitated** out. The lime also prevents the sucrose from breaking down into glucose and fructose. Preventing decomposition of sucrose is very important throughout the sugar manufacturing process because this would lead to financial losses. A flocculant aide (a substance that promotes clumping) is also added to the juice and this, together with the heating of the juice, causes the impurities to form larger insoluble particles, which makes them easier to settle out. The **clarification** process usually takes a few hours, and the mud is allowed to settle. The clarified juice is then removed by a process of **filtration** in a rotating filter. This process produces factory mud which is used as fertiliser to enhance growing conditions in the fields.

Evaporation

The clarified juice is then boiled in a series of vacuum evaporators. Each successive evaporator has a lower vacuum pressure than the one before, so the syrup is boiled at a lower temperature than in the evaporator before. This process is known as **vacuum distillation** and concentrates the juice by further evaporation of water into a syrup with 50 to 60% sugar content, or 35% water content from approximately 85%, at low temperature. It is important to use low temperatures to prevent caramelisation of the sugars in the syrup, which would lead to loss of sugar.

Crystallisation

The thick dark gold-coloured syrup is then transferred into a vacuum pan where further evaporation of water occurs. This is done until a saturated syrup is obtained.

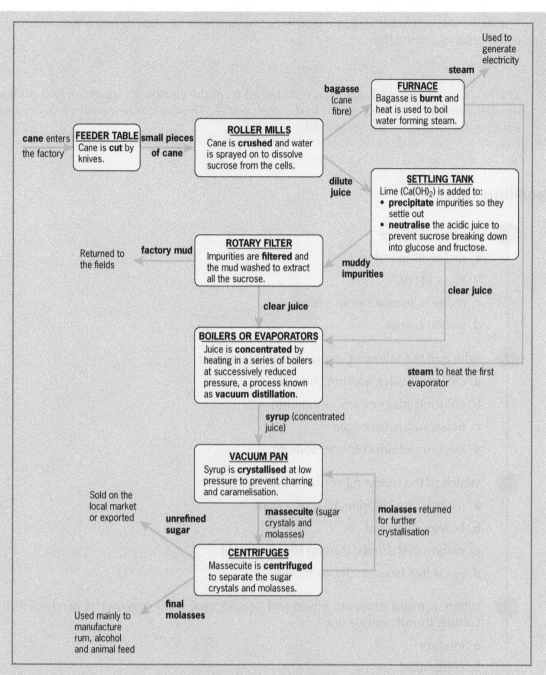

cane enters the factory → **FEEDER TABLE** Cane is **cut** by knives. → **small pieces of cane** → **ROLLER MILLS** Cane is **crushed** and water is sprayed on to dissolve sucrose from the cells.

bagasse (cane fibre) → **FURNACE** Bagasse is **burnt** and heat is used to boil water forming steam.

steam → Used to generate electricity

dilute juice → **SETTLING TANK** Lime (Ca(OH)$_2$) is added to:
• **precipitate** impurities so they settle out
• **neutralise** the acidic juice to prevent sucrose breaking down into glucose and fructose.

ROTARY FILTER Impurities are **filtered** and the mud washed to extract all the sucrose.

factory mud → Returned to the fields

muddy impurities

clear juice

clear juice → **BOILERS OR EVAPORATORS** Juice is **concentrated** by heating in a series of boilers at successively reduced pressure, a process known as **vacuum distillation**.

steam to heat the first evaporator

syrup (concentrated juice)

VACUUM PAN Syrup is **crystallised** at low pressure to prevent charring and caramelisation.

massecuite (sugar crystals and molasses)

molasses returned for further crystallisation

Sold on the local market or exported

unrefined sugar

CENTRIFUGES Massecuite is **centrifuged** to separate the sugar crystals and molasses.

final molasses

Used mainly to manufacture rum, alcohol and animal feed

Figure 2.15 *A flow chart showing how sucrose is extracted from sugar cane*

'Seed crystals', which are small grains of sugar crystals, are added to the saturated syrup, resulting in the sugar **crystals** being drawn out of solution, converting the syrup into sugar crystals. This seeded syrup continues to boil in the vacuum pan, allowing more water to evaporate. The sugar crystals continue to grow and form a viscous paste. This paste consists of molasses and sugar crystals and is called massecuite.

Centrifugation

The sugar crystals are then separated from the molasses by transferring the massecuite to a **centrifuge**. The centrifuge contains a basket which has many holes in it and rotates at very high speed. The molasses escape through the holes and the sugar crystals stay in the basket.

The molasses are channelled into a storage tank and can be used to manufacture animal feed or for ethanol production.

Dryer

The raw wet sugar crystals are then transferred from the centrifuge baskets into a drying mechanism which uses heated air to dry the crystals. The dry crystals are then packaged and sold on the local market or exported.

Recalling facts

1 A pure substance

    a dissolves in water

    b has a pH of 7

    c melts at an exact temperature

    d has no colour

2 Which of the following contains only elements?

    a chlorine, water, sodium chlorine

    b chlorine, magnesium, aluminium

    c brass, sulfur, hydrogen

    d silicon, sodium chloride, sodium

3 Which of the following contains only mixtures?

    a magnesium chloride, bronze, silicon

    b bronze, brass, air

    c carbonated drinks, sterling silver, ethanol

    d sea water, brass, sodium chloride

4 When iron and sulfur are mixed and heated, they come together to produce iron(II) sulfide. Iron(II) sulfide is a:

    a mixture

    b compound

    c element

    d metal

5 When salt is dissolved in water:

    a a compound is formed

    b a solution is formed

    c salt is the solvent

    d water is the solute

6 What type of colloid is mist?

    a solid aerosol   **b** foam   **c** liquid aerosol   **d** gel

7 A solubility curve can be used to determine all of the following except:

    a the quantity of solute deposited when a solution is cooled

    b a comparison of the solubility of various compounds at the same temperature

    c the melting point of a compound

    d solubilities of different solutes at a particular temperature

8 A mixture of ammonium chloride and sodium chloride can be separated using:

    a distillation

    b crystallisation

    c sublimation

    d chromatography

9 Dyes are separated using the method of paper chromatography because:

    a of the pore size of the chromatography paper

    b of differences in the colour

    c of the solubilities of the dyes

    d the solvent is water

10 Calcium hydroxide is added during the clarification step in sugar production from sugarcane to _____ the cane juice.

    a precipitate

    b decompose

    c neutralise

    d caramelise

11 Define the following terms:

    a solute   **b** solvent   **c** solution   **d** soluble

    e insoluble   **f** saturated

Applying facts

12 **a** What is meant by the following terms:

      i mixtures

      ii solutions

      iii suspensions

      iv colloids

b Classify each of the following substances as pure substances, heterogeneous mixtures, or homogeneous mixtures:

    i canned chicken soup

    ii air

    iii seawater

    iv paint

    v blood

    vi smog

    vii clouds

    viii mayonnaise

    ix cheese

13 **a** Rock salt is a mixture of salt, dirt and sand. Describe how you would separate the salt from the impurities. Your discussion must include labelled diagrams and reference must be made to the principles involved.

    b Scientists have claimed that the Amazon pink orchid has the same colour pigments as the European pink orchid. Describe in detail a procedure to test the scientists' claims. You must explain the principles involved and have labelled diagrams in your answer.

14 **a** Fractional distillation is used to separate:

    i what type of mixtures?

    ii on the basis of what physical properties?

    b Draw a fully labelled diagram of the apparatus that you would use to separate methanol and water. Explain the use of each piece of apparatus.

    c What additional pieces of glassware are needed for fractional distillation as compared to simple distillation?

    d Could 100% separation of the components of the methanol and water mixture be achieved? Explain.

15 State the main steps in manufacturing sugar from sugarcane. Describe fully each of the steps mentioned.

Analysing data

16 The table gives the temperature recorded in °C and the solubility in g/100 ml water of an experiment to determine the solubility of potassium nitrate.

Temperature °C	86	73	67	62	57	51	48
Solubility g/100 ml water	154	130	108	95	85	76	70

    a Plot the points given in the table and draw a curve of best fit.

    b What is the solubility of potassium nitrate at 80 °C?

    c A potassium nitrate solution containing 275 g of water is saturated at 65 °C. What mass of potassium nitrate will crystallise out of this solution if it is cooled to 44 °C?

    d At what temperature will 92 g of potassium nitrate saturate 125 g of water?

3 Atomic structure

Learning objectives

- Describe the **structure of the atom** with the aid of a **shell diagram**.
- State the properties of the **subatomic particles**.
- Define the terms **atomic number** and **mass number**.
- Represent and interpret atoms by **nuclear annotation**.
- Define the term **isotope**.
- Discuss the term **radioisotope**.
- List and describe the **uses of radioisotopes**.
- Define the term **relative atomic mass**.

The concept of the atom was born out of the philosophy of Ancient Greece. Democritus, in the fifth century BCE, suggested that matter was not continuous but consisted of tiny inseparable entities which were not visible, called atoms. Their philosophy was that, if a piece of matter, for example, a piece of silver metal, was cut into smaller pieces and these smaller pieces were cut into even smaller pieces, there would come a point where the pieces could not be cut into anything smaller. This smallest piece was named *atomos* which means indivisible, and this is the origin of the word **atom**.

John Dalton, a British scientist, published an article in 1803, in which he envisaged the atom as being a small ball which was solid and indivisible. He also postulated that all the atoms of a particular element are the same. For example, all the atoms of the element silver are the same atoms. On the other hand, different elements have different atoms, so the atoms of the element magnesium are different from those of the element gold.

During the late nineteenth century and early twentieth century, due to the invention of new machinery and experimental developments, scientists discovered new experimental findings and conclusions which Dalton's atomic theory could not explain. These scientists made modifications to Dalton's theory to explain the observations and results obtained from their experiments. Ernest Rutherford, in 1908, proposed the atom as having a very small positively charged centre, and negatively charged particles called electrons, circling around it. Niels Bohr, in 1913, proposed further modifications with respect to the arrangement and movement of the electrons in the atom. A new model (Figure 3.1), the Bohr–Rutherford model, was postulated in which the negatively charged electrons move around a tiny positively charged nucleus in specific shells or at specific energy levels.

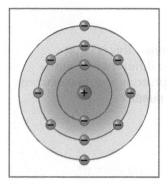

Figure 3.1 *The structure of an atom*

Atoms are the basic building blocks of matter and they are the particles that participate in chemical reactions. They are exceptionally tiny and are not visible with the naked eye. Modern-day technology, the scanning tunnelling microscope, allows scientists to view the atom.

*An **atom** is the smallest particle of an element that can exist by itself and still have the same chemical properties as the element.*

Subatomic particles

As stated in the definition, an atom is the smallest particle of an element that can exist by itself. The atom is made up of **three** fundamental particles called **subatomic** particles. These fundamental particles are **protons**, **neutrons** and **electrons**.

As can be seen in Figure 3.1, the protons and neutrons reside in a fixed position in the centre, or **nucleus**, of an atom. The electrons are found some distance away from the nucleus, existing around the nucleus in **energy shells** (see page 40). The electrons are the only subatomic particles that take part in a chemical reaction. Electrons are either gained or lost during the reaction (see Unit 5).

These subatomic particles have different characteristic properties, for example, their **relative charges and relative masses**. These are shown in Table 3.1.

Both the protons and electrons have a relative charge of one. The protons have a positive charge (+1) and the electrons have a negative charge (–1). The neutrons do not carry any charge. They are neutral.

In any atom, the number of protons and the number of electrons is the **same**. Atoms therefore have **no overall charge**. In other words, they are said to be electrically neutral.

The mass of the proton is equal to the mass of the neutron, and each has a relative mass of one unit. The mass of the electron is 1/1840 of the mass of a proton. The electron therefore has very little mass and can be said to have negligible mass.

As seen above, the protons and neutrons contribute to the mass of the atom, and it can be concluded that the mass of the atom is really confined to the nucleus, since the mass of the electrons is insignificant. The electrons exist around the tiny nucleus in empty space, so most of the atom is empty space.

Table 3.1 *Characteristics of the three subatomic particles*

Particle	Relative charge	Relative mass
Proton	+1	1
Neutron	0	1
Electron	–1	$\dfrac{1}{1840}$

Atoms of different elements contain **different numbers** of protons and electrons – this is what makes the elements different. For example, magnesium and nitrogen are two different elements. Magnesium contains 12 protons and 12 electrons, and nitrogen contains 14 protons and 14 electrons. Two numbers can be assigned to any atom: the **atomic number** and the **mass number**.

Atomic number (symbol Z)

__Atomic number__ (or proton number) is the number of protons in the nucleus of one atom of an element.

As the number of electrons in an atom is always equal to the number of protons, the number of **electrons** in an atom is equal to the atomic number. Each element has its own **unique** atomic number.

For example, the atomic number of lithium is 3, which means that every lithium atom has 3 protons and 3 electrons. Phosphorus has an atomic number of 15. Therefore every phosphorus atom contains 15 protons and 15 electrons.

Mass number (symbol A)

Mass number (or nucleon number) is the total number of protons and neutrons in the nucleus of one atom of an element.

From the definition:

mass number (nucleon number) = number of protons + number of neutrons

Recall that the mass of an electron is negligible and so it is not used in calculating the mass number.

The number of **neutrons** in an atom can be calculated by **subtracting** the atomic number from the mass number:

number of neutrons = mass number – number of protons

More than one element can have the same mass number, so the number is **not unique** to a particular element.

Sample question

An element has a mass number of 35 and contains 18 neutrons. What is its atomic number?

Number of neutrons = mass number – number of protons (atomic number)

Therefore,

number of protons (atomic number) = mass number – number of neutrons

Atomic number = 35 – 18

= **17**

Nuclear notation

An atom (or ion) of an element can be represented using **nuclear notation**:

$$_{Z}^{A}X$$

where: X = atomic symbol

A = mass number

Z = atomic number

Using the nuclear notation, the number of protons, neutrons and electrons in an atom can be calculated.

Example 1

The nuclear notation for silicon is $_{14}^{28}Si$. From this, the following can be deduced about a silicon atom:

Mass number = 28

Atomic number = 14

Number of protons = 14

Number of neutrons = 28 – 14 = 14

Number of electrons = 14

The nuclear notation for sodium is $^{23}_{11}$Na. From this, the following can be deduced about a sodium atom:

Mass number = 23

Atomic number = 11

Number of protons = 11

Number of neutrons = 23 − 11 = 12

Number of electrons = 11

The nuclear notation for lead is $^{207}_{82}$Pb. From this, the following can be deduced about a lead atom:

Mass number = 207

Atomic number = 82

Number of protons = 82

Number of neutrons = 207 − 82 = 125

Number of electrons = 82

The nuclear notations for all elements can be found in the **periodic table** of elements on page 53.

The arrangement of subatomic particles in an atom

Atoms are composed of **two** parts:

- There is a **nucleus** in the centre containing **nucleons (protons** and **neutrons)** packed tightly together.
- There is one or more **energy shells** surrounding the nucleus which contain a cloud of **electrons** that move at high speeds. The shells are relatively distant from the nucleus, such that most of an atom is empty space. The electrons which surround the nucleus make up the **volume** of an atom.
   - Each energy shell is a **specific distance** from the nucleus.
   - Electrons with the **least energy** occupy the energy shells closest to the nucleus.
   - Electrons **fill up** the energy shells closest to the nucleus **first**.
   - Each energy shell has a **maximum number** of electrons it can hold:
     - The **first** energy shell can hold up to **two** electrons.
     - The **second** energy shell can hold up to **eight** electrons.
     - The **third** energy shell holds a maximum of eighteen electrons.

   Further energy shells can hold more electrons, but it is unnecessary to know their maximum numbers at this level of study.

The arrangement of electrons in an atom is known as its **electronic configuration**. This can be represented in writing using **numbers** or by drawing a **shell diagram**.

Representing atoms

To draw a **shell diagram** of an atom, first determine the number of protons, neutrons and electrons, then write its electronic configuration using **numbers** separated by commas.

Example 2

The lithium atom, $^{7}_{3}Li$

A lithium atom has:

3 protons

4 neutrons (7 – 3)

3 electrons

The electronic configuration is **2,1**.

∴ it has: **2** electrons in the first shell

1 electron in the second shell (Figure 3.2)

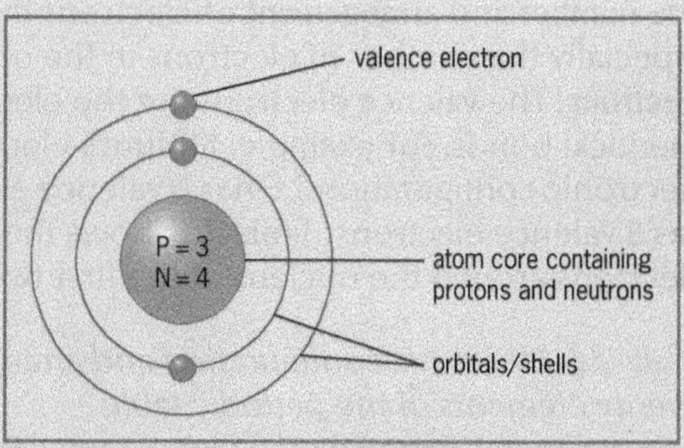

Figure 3.2 *Shell diagram of a lithium atom*

The oxygen atom, $^{16}_{8}O$

An oxygen atom has:

8 protons

8 neutrons (16 – 8)

8 electrons

The electronic configuration is **2,6**.

∴ it has: **2** electrons in the first shell

6 electrons in the second shell (Figure 3.3)

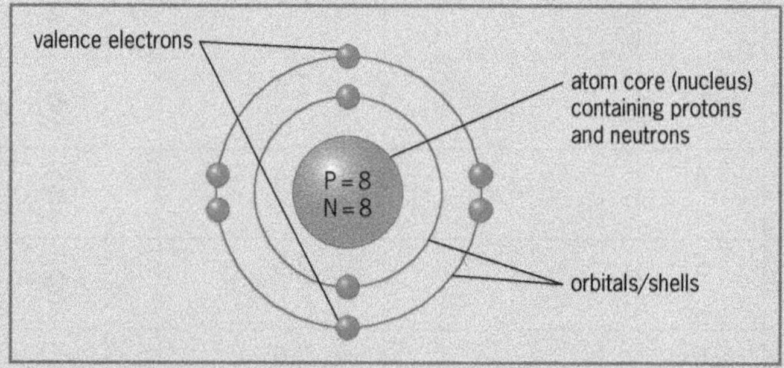

Figure 3.3 *Shell diagram of an oxygen atom*

The phosphorus atom, $^{31}_{15}P$

A phosphorus atom has:

15 protons

16 neutrons (31 – 15)

15 electrons

The electronic configuration is **2,8,5**.

∴ it has: **2** electrons in the first shell

8 electrons in the second shell

5 electrons in the third shell (Figure 3.4)

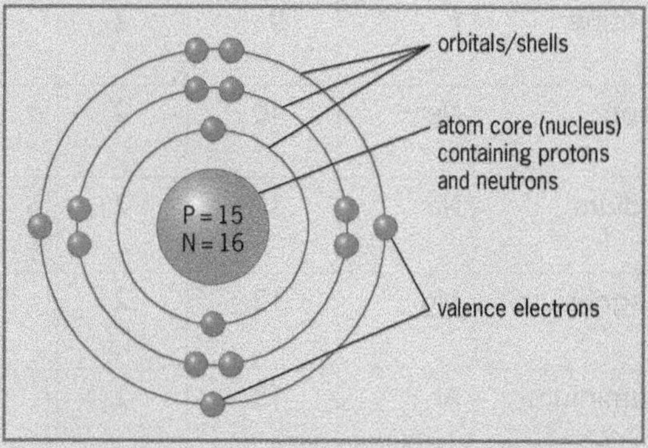

Figure 3.4 *Shell diagram of a phosphorus atom*

Note Electrons are only shown as being paired in the second and third shells when the shells contain five or more electrons.

The **number** and **arrangement** of electrons in an element determine its **chemical properties**, especially the number of electrons in the outermost energy shell, which are known as the **valence electrons**. The valence electrons are the electrons that participate in chemical reactions and form chemical bonds. For example, lithium's electronic configuration 2,1 has 1 valent electron, oxygen's electronic configuration 2,6 has 6 valence electrons and phosphorus' electronic configuration 2,8,5 has 5 valence electrons. Table 3.2 shows the symbols, electronic configuration and arrangements of electrons around the nucleus of the first twenty elements of the periodic table.

Table 3.2 *Electronic configuration and arrangement of elements around the nucleus of the first twenty elements of the periodic table*

| Element | Symbol | Proton number/ atomic number | Number of electrons in | | | | Simplified electronic configuration | Shell diagram |
			1st shell	2nd shell	3rd shell	4th shell		
hydrogen	H	1	1				1	
helium	He	2	2				2	
lithium	Li	3	2	1			2.1	
beryllium	Be	4	2	2			2.2	
boron	B	5	2	3			2.3	
carbon	C	6	2	4			2.4	
nitrogen	N	7	2	5			2.5	
oxygen	O	8	2	6			2.6	
fluorine	F	9	2	7			2.7	
neon	Ne	10	2	8			2.8	
sodium	Na	11	2	8	1		2.8.1	
magnesium	Mg	12	2	8	2		2.8.2	
aluminium	Al	13	2	8	3		2.8.3	
silicon	Si	14	2	8	4		2.8.4	
phosphorus	P	15	2	8	5		2.8.5	
sulfur	S	16	2	8	6		2.8.6	

Element	Symbol	Proton number/ atomic number	Number of electrons in				Simplified electronic configuration	Shell diagram
			1st shell	2nd shell	3rd shell	4th shell		
chlorine	Cl	17	2	8	7		2.8.7	
argon	Ar	18	2	8	8		2.8.8	
potassium	K	19	2	8	8	1	2.8.8.1	
calcium	Ca	20	2	8	8	2	2.8.8.2	

Isotopes

As already mentioned, the proton or atomic number of an element is unique but not its mass number. Atoms of elements that have different mass numbers are said to be **isotopes**. An explanation for an element not having a unique mass number is that the atoms of the element have different numbers of neutrons, since the number of protons cannot be different.

Isotopes are different atoms of a single element that have the same number of protons in their nuclei, but different numbers of neutrons.

Isotopes of an element therefore have the **same** atomic number but **different** mass numbers.

- Isotopes of an element have the **same chemical properties** because the number and arrangement of electrons in them are the same.
- Isotopes of an element have slightly **different physical properties** because they have different numbers of neutrons which give them slightly different masses.

Isotopy is the occurrence of atoms of a single element that have the same number of protons in their nuclei, but different numbers of neutrons.

More than one isotope exists for most elements. It should be noted that some of these isotopes are unstable, and they decay forming other isotopes.

Isotopes can be represented using two notations (boron is used as an example):

- chemical or nuclear notation

  $^{10}_{5}B$ and $^{11}_{5}B$

- name and mass number

  boron-10 or B-10 and boron-11 or B-11.

B-10 or $^{10}_{5}B$ is an isotope with 5 neutrons and mass number 10, whereas B-11 or $^{11}_{5}B$ has 6 neutrons and mass number 11.

Each isotope of an element exists in nature in a specific ratio of other isotope versions of the element, and this is referred to as the **relative abundance** of the isotope. The relative abundance of the isotopes is expressed as a percentage. As mentioned before, boron has two naturally occurring isotopes, B-10 and B-11 (Table 3.3). In a sample, B-11 is the more abundant isotope than B-10, occurring in a ratio of 80% to 20%. In other words, in 100 atoms of the element boron there exist 80 atoms of B-11 and 20 atoms of B-10.

Example 3

Boron

Boron has **two** naturally occurring isotopes: $^{10}_{5}B$ and $^{11}_{5}B$.

Table 3.3 *The isotopes of boron*

Isotope	Percentage of isotope	Mass number	Atomic number	Number of		
				Protons	Electrons	Neutrons
$^{10}_{5}B$	20%	10	5	5	5	5
$^{11}_{5}B$	80%	11	5	5	5	6

Average mass number of naturally occurring boron $= \left[\dfrac{20}{100} \times 10\right] + \left[\dfrac{80}{100} \times 11\right]$

$$= 10.8$$

Chlorine

Chlorine has two naturally occurring isotopes: $^{35}_{17}Cl$ and $^{37}_{17}Cl$ (Table 3.4).

Table 3.4 *The isotopes of chlorine*

Isotope	Percentage of isotope	Mass number	Atomic number	Number of		
				Protons	Electrons	Neutrons
$^{35}_{17}Cl$	75%	35	17	17	17	18
$^{37}_{17}Cl$	25%	37	17	17	17	20

Average mass number of naturally occurring chlorine $= \left[\dfrac{75}{100} \times 35\right] + \left[\dfrac{25}{100} \times 37\right]$

$$= 35.5$$

Carbon

Carbon has **three** naturally occurring isotopes: $^{12}_{6}C$, $^{13}_{6}C$ and $^{14}_{6}C$ (Table 3.5).

Table 3.5 *The isotopes of carbon*

Isotope	Percentage of isotope	Mass number	Atomic number	Number of		
				Protons	Electrons	Neutrons
$^{12}_{6}C$	98.89%	12	6	6	6	6
$^{13}_{6}C$	1.10%	13	6	6	6	7
$^{14}_{6}C$	0.01%	14	6	6	6	8

Average mass number of carbon $= \left[\dfrac{98.89}{100} \times 12\right] + \left[\dfrac{1.10}{100} \times 13\right] + \left[\dfrac{0.01}{100} \times 14\right]$

$$= 12.01$$

Carbon-14 is **radioactive.**

Radioactive isotopes

The nuclei of some isotopes are **unstable** and spontaneously undergo **radioactive decay/decomposition**. These are called **radioactive isotopes** and they eject small particles and **radiation** to achieve a more **stable configuration** during radioactive decay. The types of radiation emitted during radioactive decay are alpha (α) particles, beta (β) particles and gamma (γ) rays. They may produce atoms of one or more different elements at the same time. There are naturally occurring and artificial isotopes. The artificial isotopes do not occur naturally on the Earth and are made by scientists in nuclear accelerators and nuclear reactors. Some examples of naturally occurring isotopes are uranium-235, uranium-238, carbon-14, thorium-234, hydrogen-3 (tritium), radon-222, radium-226, and caesium-137. Examples of artificial isotopes are oxygen-15, iodine-131, cobalt-60, fluorine-18, technetium-97, and plutonium-238. The **time** taken for half of the nuclei in a sample of a radioactive isotope to undergo radioactive decay is called its **half-life**.

*The **half-life** is the time required for one half of any given quantity of isotope to decay.*

The half-life of a radioactive isotope can be as little as 1×10^{-23} seconds or as much as 10^{24} years. Plutonium-239 has a half-life of 24 100 years; technetium-99 has a half-life of 6 hours. Knowledge of the half-life of radioactive isotopes is important when selecting isotopes to be used in industry and in the medical field.

Uses of radioactive isotopes

- **Carbon-14 dating**

  The **age** of plant and animal remains, up to about 60 000 years old, can be determined by **carbon-14 dating**. Living organisms constantly take in carbon from carbon dioxide or food molecules, 0.01% of which is radioactive **carbon-14**. This keeps the percentage of carbon-14 in living organisms constant. When an organism dies, it stops taking in carbon and the percentage of carbon-14 in its body decreases as it undergoes radioactive decay. As the half-life of carbon-14 is **5700 years**, if the percentage of radioactive carbon-14 left in plant and animal remains is measured, it can be used to determine their ages.

  Carbon-14 dating can be used to estimate the age of carbon-bearing materials up to about 58 000 to 62 000 years old. Beyond this, the levels of carbon-14 would not be sufficient to analyse accurately. Carbon-14 dating has been used to determine the age of the mummies (Figure 3.5) found in the Egyptian Pyramids, the Dead Sea Scrolls (Figure 3.6), and mammoth remains.

Figure 3.5 *Egyptian mummy*

- **Cancer treatment (radiotherapy)**

  Cancerous cells in tumours can be destroyed by directing a controlled beam of radiation from radioactive isotopes onto the affected area (Figure 3.7). **Boron-10** is injected into cancer patients and allowed to concentrate in the

Figure 3.6 *One of the Dead Sea Scrolls*

cancerous growth. The area is then irradiated with neutrons, which are strongly absorbed by the boron producing high-energy alpha particles that kill the cancer cells. Alternatively, a radioactive isotope can be injected directly into the cancerous tumour. For example, radioactive **iodine-131** is used to treat thyroid cancer. **Yttrium-90** is also used for the treatment of liver cancer. **Phosphorus-32** is used in the treatment of a disease called polycythaemia vera, which is an excess of red blood cells being produced in the bone marrow.

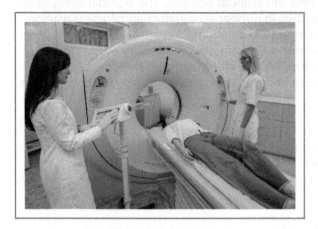

Figure 3.7 *Treatment of cancer patient using radiotherapy*

- **Energy generation**

Electricity is generated in nuclear power stations using radioactive **uranium-235**. If a uranium-235 atom is struck by a fast-moving neutron, it splits into two smaller atoms. As it splits, two or three neutrons and a large amount of heat energy are released. The neutrons can then strike other atoms causing them to split and release more neutrons and energy. This causes a **chain reaction** which releases very large amounts of **heat energy** (Figure 3.8).

If the chain reaction is controlled, the energy can be used to **generate electricity**. If the chain reaction is not controlled, a **nuclear explosion** (for example, from an atom bomb) can occur. The United States, France, China, Russia, South Korea and other nations all use electricity generated from nuclear power plants.

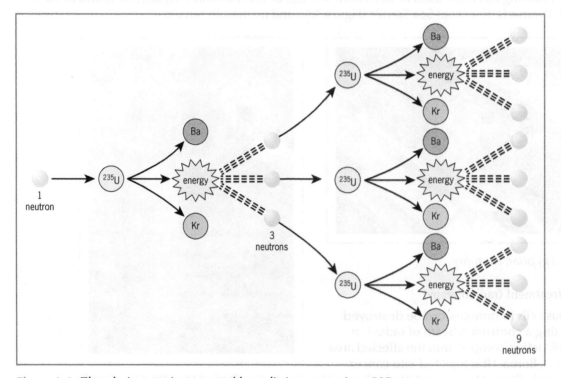

Figure 3.8 *The chain reaction created by splitting a uranium-235 atom*

- **Tracers**

Radioactive tracer compounds are formed by incorporating a short-lived radioactive isotope that emits gamma radiation into a chemical compound. Very tiny quantities of these radioactive tracers are injected into the bloodstream and these are attracted or concentrated by the body system which is being monitored. The gamma radiation being emitted can be studied and traced using special equipment in **medical investigations** and **biological research**. This equipment is very efficient at detecting the gamma radiation emitted and for this reason only very small quantities are injected. The tracers also have a very short half-life, so they are short-lived in the body causing no harm to the patient.

The functioning of the thyroid gland can be examined by injecting radioactive **iodine-131** into patients. **Technetium** (Tc-99m) is a radioactive isotope used as a radioactive tracer for nuclear medicine. This is a form of medical imaging that evaluates how the brain, and other vital organs, are functioning. Radioactive **carbon-14** is used to study carbon dioxide uptake and photosynthesis in plants.

Radioactive tracers can also be injected into natural gas pipelines to detect leaks. **Sodium-24** is an example of a radioisotope used in detecting leaks in pipelines. Beta radiation is emitted by **sodium-24** and would be detected in measurable amounts at the source of the leak. Figure 3.9 shows the instrument used to measure the beta radiation emitted.

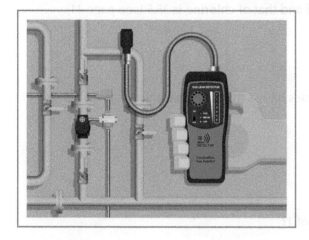

Figure 3.9 *Instrument which measures emitted beta radiation*

- **Heart pacemakers**

A **heart pacemaker** is a tiny battery-powered medical device which is implanted under the skin of a heart patient. This device monitors and identifies irregular heartbeats in the patient. When irregularities are detected, signals are sent to the patient's heart, correcting the pace at which the heart beats and restoring its normal pace. These devices are usually powered by chemical batteries (Figure 3.10) which must be replaced by a surgical procedure about every ten years. Batteries containing **plutonium-238** can power pacemakers for a patient's lifetime without having to be replaced, since the half-life of plutonium-238 is about 87 years.

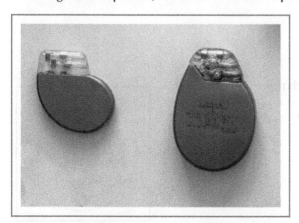

Figure 3.10 *Heart pacemaker batteries*

The mass of atoms

Because an atom of any element is so small, its **absolute mass (actual mass)** is very difficult to measure. For example, the absolute mass of a hydrogen atom is 1.67×10^{-24} g. Consequently, the masses of atoms are usually **compared** using **relative atomic mass**.

Relative atomic mass (A_r) is the average mass of one atom of an element compared to one-twelfth the mass of an atom of carbon-12.

The symbol A_r represents the term relative atomic mass.

$$\text{relative atomic mass } (A_r) = \frac{\text{the average mass of one atom of the element}}{1/12 \times \text{the mass of one atom of carbon-12}}$$

A carbon-12 atom has been assigned a mass of **12.00 atomic mass units** or **amu**. This means that 1/12th the mass of a carbon-12 atom has a mass of **1.00 amu**, and relative atomic mass **compares** the masses of atoms to this value. Being a comparative value, relative atomic mass has **no units**.

When the relative atomic mass of an element is calculated, the **relative abundance** of each **isotope** is taken into account. As a result, relative atomic masses of elements are not usually whole numbers. For example, the relative atomic mass of boron is 10.8 and that of chlorine is 35.5 (see page 44).

Recalling facts

1 Which of the following subatomic particles have a negative charge?

   a electrons only

   b neutrons only

   c protons only

   d protons and electrons

2 Which subatomic particles have a mass of 1?

   a protons and nucleus

   b electrons and neutrons

   c protons and neutrons

   d protons and electrons

3 An atom has atomic number 12. What is the electronic configuration of this atom?

   a 12

   b 2,10

   c 2,8,2

   d 2,2,8

Questions 4 to 6 refer to the diagram which represents an atom.

4 What is the atomic number of this atom?

   a 12

   b 11

   c 22

   d 23

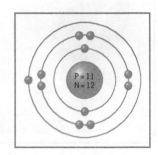

5 What is the mass number of this atom?

    a 12   **b** 22   **c** 23   **d** 34

6 What is the electronic configuration of this atom?

    a 2,9   **b** 2,10   **c** 2,8,1   **d** 2,8,2

7 An element, X, contains 15 protons and 18 neutrons, its nuclear notation is:

    a $^{30}_{15}X$ **b** $^{36}_{18}X$ **c** $^{33}_{15}X$ **d** $^{33}_{18}X$

8 What is the half-life of a radioactive isotope?

    a the time taken for the nuclei to increase

    b the time taken for half the nuclei to decay

    c the time taken for the nucleus to decay

    d the time taken for the nucleus to become unstable

9 Which of the following isotopes is used to generate electricity in nuclear power stations?

    a cobalt-60

    b technetium-99

    c uranium-235

    d palladium-103

10 Which of the following radioactive isotopes would be most suitable as a tracer to monitor the functioning of the thyroid gland?

    a carbon-14

    b plutonium-238

    c iodine-131

    d uranium-235

11 Define the following terms:

    a atom

    b atomic number

    c mass number

    d relative atomic mass

12 **a** Draw the structure of the atom and label the diagram showing all the essential components. On your diagram you should state the charges and relative masses for each of the named particles.

    b The atom is said to be electrically neutral. Explain what is meant by this statement.

Applying facts

 13   **a**   Write the nuclear notation and electronic configuration for each of the following:

     i   sulfur

     ii   argon

     iii calcium

     iv phosphorus

     v   beryllium

     vi oxygen

   b   Draw shell diagrams for each of the elements in part a.

 14   What is meant by the term 'radioactive isotope'? Give three examples of radioactive isotopes and explain how these are used in industry and medicine.

Analysing data

 15   **a**   What is meant by the term isotope?

   b   Three isotopes of potassium (atomic number 19) are K-39, K-40 and K-41 with natural abundances of 93.26%, 0.01% and 6.73% respectively.

     i   Write the nuclear notation for each of the isotopes of potassium, stating the atomic and mass numbers.

     ii   State the number of protons, neutrons and electrons in each of the isotopes of potassium.

     iii Draw the shell diagrams of each of the isotopes of potassium, representing the subatomic particles.

     iv How many valence electrons does a potassium atom have?

     v   Calculate the average mass number of naturally occurring potassium.

     vi Explain why this mass is not a whole number.

 16   A contractor was excavating a site to build a hotel and found some large bones that did not resemble those of humans nor any animals that he knew. He contacted an archaeologist, who gathered the bones and after a few months told him that those bones belonged to a species that lived 10,000 years ago. Explain how the archaeologist determined the age of the bones.

4 The periodic table and periodicity

Learning objectives

- Discuss briefly the **historical development of the periodic table.**
- Describe how elements are classified in the **modern periodic table**.
- Explain the main features of the periodic table, identifying the **metals**, **metalloids** and **non-metals**, giving similarities in the **electronic configuration of elements in the groups** and **periods**.
- Explain how the **physical** and **chemical properties** of elements change as the **group is descended** and **the period traversed.**
- Identify and explain the **trends in Group II.**
- Identify and explain the **trends in Group VII.**
- Identify and explain the **trends in Period 3.**

The periodic table is a **classification** of all elements. The information assists not only chemistry students but chemists in their professional lives. At a glance, information such as the name, symbols, atomic number, mass number and metallic nature of the elements can be obtained. The elements in the periodic table show **periodicity**.

Periodicity is the recurrence of similar chemical and physical properties at regular intervals that is seen in the elements in the periodic table.

Therefore, the chemical and physical properties of individual elements can be predicted from the general trends of the elements in the groups and periods. As will be seen in the next section, Mendeleev was able to predict the properties of elements not yet discovered from trends in his periodic table. Chemists can do the same from the general trends in the periods and groups without learning everything about an individual element. The periodic table contains a wealth of information about the elements, making it a very powerful tool for chemists to use.

The historical development of the periodic table

Scientists started attempting to **classify** elements early in the nineteenth century.

- **Johann Döbereiner**

  Between 1817 and 1829, Johann Döbereiner proposed the **Law of Triads**. He noticed that certain groups of **three** elements, which he called **triads**, showed similar chemical and physical properties. If the elements in any triad were arranged in increasing relative atomic mass, the relative atomic mass of the middle element was close to the average of the first and third elements. The same trend was observed for densities of the middle element. For example, calcium, strontium and barium have relative atomic masses of 40.0, 88.0 and 137.0. The average atomic mass of all three is 88.5, which is approximately the atomic mass of strontium, the middle element. The densities of the three respectively are 1.55 g/cm^3, 2.54 g/cm^3 and 3.59 g/cm^3 with an average of 2.56 g/cm^3 which follows the trend. Compare the triad chlorine, bromine and iodine; does the atomic mass and density follow the same trend?

- **John Newlands**

  In 1865, John Newlands proposed the **Law of Octaves**. He arranged the elements that had been discovered at the time in order of increasing relative atomic mass and found that each element exhibited similar chemical and physical properties to the element **eight** places ahead of it in the list. For example, beryllium (relative atomic mass 4) was eight places ahead of magnesium (relative atomic mass 12) and the two exhibited similar properties. Other examples are carbon (6) and silicon (14), nitrogen (7) and phosphorus (15). He then placed the similar elements into vertical columns called groups. He formed 8 of these groups but no **gaps** were left for the elements which had not been discovered at the time.

- **Dmitri Mendeleev**

  In 1869, Dmitri Mendeleev published his **Periodic Classification of Elements** in which he:

  - arranged elements in **increasing relative atomic mass**
  - placed elements with similar chemical and physical properties together in **vertical** columns (groups)
  - left **gaps** when it appeared that elements had not yet been discovered
  - occasionally ignored the order suggested by relative atomic mass and **exchanged** adjacent elements so they were better classified into chemical families.

  On the basis of the trends used in classifying elements, Mendeleev was able to predict the properties of elements not yet discovered at that time. One such element was scandium which he had named "eka-boron". Others were gallium and germanium.

  Mendeleev is credited with creating the first version of the periodic table.

- **Henry Moseley**

  In 1914, Henry Moseley placed the elements in increasing **atomic number** which resulted in all elements with similar properties falling in the same groups.

The modern periodic table

The modern periodic table includes all the 118 known elements in vertical columns called **groups**, and horizontal rows called **periods**. The design of the periodic table is such that it can include new elements being discovered (Figure 4.1). These new artificial atoms are continuously being produced within thermonuclear reactors. The elements are organised on the basis of:

- **Increasing atomic or proton number.** As the periods are traversed, the atomic number increases; as the groups are descended, the atomic number increases.
- The **electronic configuration** of their atoms. The elements are found in vertical columns called **groups**. From an element's electronic configuration, the group and period it belongs to can be determined. The number of valence electrons is known, and since the outer electrons take part in chemical reactions, this influences **chemical reactivity**. Using electronic configuration, the elements are placed not only into groups and periods but also into blocks.
- Their **chemical properties**. How do they react with other elements? How reactive or non-reactive are the elements? For example, the inert (noble) gases are unreactive.

In Figure 4.2, there is a red line which resembles a flight of stairs. **Metals** are found on the left-hand side of that line and **non-metals** are found on the right-hand side. Hydrogen lies on the left-hand side of the red line even though it is classified as a non-metal. The metals which occupy the flight of stairs display both metallic and non-metallic characteristics and are known as metalloids. Examples of metalloids are boron, silicon, arsenic, tellurium and polonium.

Groups

Groups are **vertical columns** of elements. There are 18 groups, eight of which are numbered using Roman numerals from **I** to **VII**, and the last group is Group **0**. Some of the groups have special names, such as **Group I** or **alkali metals**, **Group II** or **alkaline earth metals**, **Group VII** or **halogens** and **Group 0** or **noble gases**. The following are similarities within a group:

- All elements in the same group have the **same number** of **valence electrons** (electrons in their outermost electron shell). All the elements of Group III, boron (B), aluminium (Al), gallium (Ga), indium (In), tin (Sn) and lead (Pb), have three electrons in their outer shells.

The periodic table of elements

relative atomic mass

atomic (proton) number

	Group I (alkali metals)	Group II (alkaline earth metals)		Group III	Group IV	Group V	Group VI	Group VII (halogens)	Group 0 (noble gases)
Period 1	**H** 1 hydrogen								4 **He** 2 helium
Period 2	7 **Li** 3 lithium	9 **Be** 4 beryllium		11 **B** 5 boron	12 **C** 6 carbon	14 **N** 7 nitrogen	16 **O** 8 oxygen	19 **F** 9 fluorine	20 **Ne** 10 neon
Period 3	23 **Na** 11 sodium	24 **Mg** 12 magnesium	transition metals	27 **Al** 13 aluminium	28 **Si** 14 silicon	31 **P** 15 phosphorus	32 **S** 16 sulphur	35.5 **Cl** 17 chlorine	40 **Ar** 18 argon

Period 4	39 **K** 19 potassium	40 **Ca** 20 calcium	45 **Sc** 21 scandium	48 **Ti** 22 titanium	51 **V** 23 vanadium	52 **Cr** 24 chromium	55 **Mn** 25 manganese	56 **Fe** 26 iron	59 **Co** 27 cobalt	59 **Ni** 28 nickel	64 **Cu** 29 copper	65 **Zn** 30 zinc	70 **Ga** 31 gallium	73 **Ge** 32 germanium	75 **As** 33 arsenic	79 **Se** 34 selenium	80 **Br** 35 bromine	84 **Kr** 36 krypton
Period 5	85 **Rb** 37 rubidium	88 **Sr** 38 strontium	89 **Y** 39 yttrium	91 **Zr** 40 zirconium	93 **Nb** 41 niobium	96 **Mo** 42 molybdenum	98 **Tc** 43 technetium	101 **Ru** 44 ruthenium	103 **Rh** 45 rhodium	106 **Pd** 46 palladium	108 **Ag** 47 silver	112 **Cd** 48 cadmium	115 **In** 49 indium	119 **Sn** 50 tin	122 **Sb** 51 antimony	128 **Te** 52 tellurium	127 **I** 53 iodine	131 **Xe** 54 xenon
Period 6	133 **Cs** 55 caesium	137 **Ba** 56 barium	139 **La** 57 lanthanum *	178.5 **Hf** 72 hafnium	181 **Ta** 73 tantalum	184 **W** 74 tungsten	186 **Re** 75 rhenium	190 **Os** 76 osmium	192 **Ir** 77 iridium	195 **Pt** 78 platinum	197 **Au** 79 gold	201 **Hg** 80 mercury	204 **Tl** 81 thallium	207 **Pb** 82 lead	209 **Bi** 83 bismuth	210 **Po** 84 polonium	210 **At** 85 astatine	222 **Rn** 86 radon
Period 7	223 **Fr** 87 francium	226 **Ra** 88 radium	227 **Ac** 89 actinium **															

Lanthanum series

140 **Ce** 58 cerium	141 **Pr** 59 praseodymium	144 **Nd** 60 neodymium	147 **Pm** 61 promethium	150 **Sm** 62 samarium	152 **Eu** 63 europium	157 **Gd** 64 gadolinium	159 **Tb** 65 terbium	162 **Dy** 66 dysprosium	165 **Ho** 67 holmium	167 **Er** 68 erbium	169 **Tm** 69 thulium	173 **Yb** 70 ytterbium	175 **Lu** 71 lutetium

** *Actinium series*

232 **Th** 90 thorium	231 **Pa** 91 protactinium	238 **U** 92 uranium	237 **Np** 93 neptunium	242 **Pu** 94 plutonium	243 **Am** 95 americium	247 **Cm** 96 curium	249 **Bk** 97 berkelium	251 **Cf** 98 californium	254 **Es** 99 einsteinium	253 **Fm** 100 fermium	256 **Md** 101 mendelevium	254 **No** 102 nobelium	257 **Lr** 103 lawrencium

non-metals

metals

Figure 4.1 *The periodic table*

- For elements in Groups I to VII, the **number of valence electrons** is the same as the **group number**. For example, sodium is in Group I of the periodic table and has one electron in its outer shell; magnesium is in Group II and has two electrons in its outer shell.

- All elements in Group 0 have a **full** outer electron shell. Helium (He) has two electrons in its outer shell, which is the first shell, and can hold a maximum of two. Neon (Ne), argon (Ar) and krypton (Kr) have eight electrons, or a full octet, in their outer shells.

- Moving **down** any group, each element has **one more electron shell** than the element directly above it. In Group III, for example, gallium (Ga) has four shells, which is one more than aluminium (Al) which has three shells.

- All elements in the same group have **similar chemical properties**. Group I elements all react with water and oxygen.

- Moving **down** a group, the **metallic nature** of the elements **increases** and the **non-metallic nature decreases**.

Between Groups II and III there are ten groups of elements called the **transition elements** or **transition metals**. Transition metals usually have **two** valence electrons. Examples of these elements are iron (Fe), cobalt (Co), copper (Cu) and zinc (Zn).

Periods

Periods are **horizontal rows** of elements. There are seven periods, numbered using Arabic numerals from **1** to **7**. The following are the similarities within a period:

- All the elements in the same period have the **same number** of **occupied electron shells**. They therefore have their valence electrons in the same shell. For example, the elements of period 2, lithium (Li), beryllium (Be), boron (B), carbon (C), nitrogen (N), oxygen (O), fluorine (F) and neon (Ne) have two occupied shells with electrons.

- The **number of occupied electron shells** is the same as the **period number**. Period 2 has two occupied shells, Period 3 has three occupied shells, Period 4 has four occupied shells.

- Moving **along** any period from left to right, each element has **one more valence electron** than the element directly before it. In Period 2 boron (B) has one more electron than beryllium (Be).

- Moving **along** any period from left to right, the **metallic nature** of the elements **decreases** and the **non-metallic nature increases**.

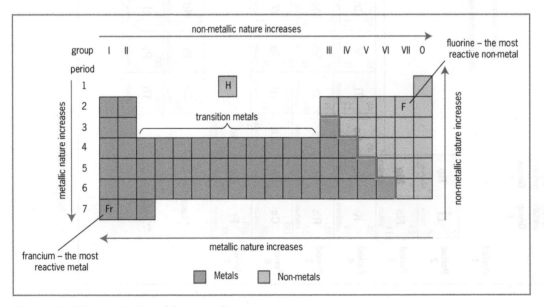

Figure 4.2 *The periodic table in outline*

The periodic table and the electronic configuration of atoms

If the **group number** and **period number** of an atom are known, its electronic configuration can be determined. And if the **electronic configuration** of an atom is known, the group number and period number can be determined using the following:

* The **group number** and the **number of valence electrons** are the same.
* The **period number** and the **number of occupied electron shells** are the same.

Example 1

Magnesium

Magnesium is in **Group II** and **Period 3**.

A magnesium atom has: **2** valence electrons

3 occupied electron shells

Therefore, the **electronic configuration** of a magnesium atom is **2,8,2**.

Phosphorus

The **electronic configuration** of a phosphorus atom is **2,8,5**.

A phosphorus atom has: **5** valence electrons

3 occupied electron shells

Therefore, phosphorus is **Group V** and **Period 3**

Potassium

The **electronic configuration** of a potassium atom is **2,8,8,1**.

A potassium atom has: **1** valence electron

4 occupied shells

Therefore, potassium is in **Group I** and **Period 4**.

Trends in Group II – the alkaline earth metals

Group II elements are extremely reactive and for this reason they do not exist in their free state but exist as compounds in the Earth's crust. The general properties of the Group II metals include them being relatively soft metals which are good conductors of heat and electricity. Being highly reactive, they quickly combine with oxygen in the atmosphere to form a lustreless oxide layer on the metal's surface. For this reason, the metal quickly loses its shiny, silvery-white look shortly after being cut. The atoms of the Group II metals all have two valence electrons. When the atom loses these two electrons, a metal cation with a +2 charge is formed, for example, Mg^{2+} and Ba^{2+} (see page 65). Group II metals have stronger metallic bonding because of the +2 charge and as such have quite high melting and boiling points (see page 82). The atomic radii of the elements of Group II increases as the group is descended, making it easier for the two valence electrons to be lost.

The elements in Group II all have similar chemical properties because their atoms all have **two** valence electrons. They react by **losing** these valence electrons to form positively charged ions called **cations** (see page 65). When they lose these electrons, they are said to **ionise**. The easier an element ionises, the more reactive it is. The **ease of ionisation** increases moving **down** Group II. The **reactivity** of the elements therefore increases moving **down** the group.

How do we explain these trends mentioned above? All the Group II elements have two electrons in their valence shell. As mentioned above, the atomic radii of the elements increases going down the group. Each element descending the group has an additional shell compared with the one above. Each additional inner filled shell offers more 'shielding' to the valence electrons (Figure 4.3). This causes the valence electrons to have a significantly smaller pull by the positively charged nuclear centre. The more filled inner shells there are, the greater the shielding that occurs and the further away the valence shell can spread out, resulting in the atomic radii increasing. The shielding effect also explains why these valence electrons are easier to remove. Since the pull by the positively charged nucleus is weaker, these valence electrons are not as strongly attached to the nucleus and can be lost more easily. The ease of ionisation therefore increases as the group is descended.

Beryllium is the least reactive element in Group II, having only one inner nuclear shell to effect shielding. Radium on the other hand is most reactive because there are six inner shells, resulting in more shielding and thus leading to an increased atomic radius and therefore it can ionise more easily. The electronic structures of Group II elements are given in Table 4.1.

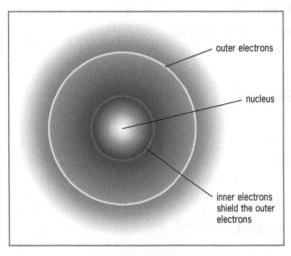

Figure 4.3 *Shielding by inner shells*

Table 4.1 *Summary of the trends in Group II – the alkaline earth metals*

Element	Number of occupied electron shells	Atomic radius	Ease of ionisation	Reactivity with oxygen, water and dilute hydrochloric acid
Be	2	Increases moving **down** due to the increase in the number of **occupied electron shells**.	Increases moving **down**. As the atomic radii **increase**, the attractive pull of the positive nucleus on the valence electrons decreases, and the more easily the atoms **lose** their valence electrons to form cations.	Increases moving **down** due to the increase in the **ease of ionisation**.
Mg	3			
Ca	4			
Sr	5			
Ba	6			
Ra	7			

———▶ Indicates that the property **increases** in the direction of the arrow

Reactions of Group II elements

The Group II elements are metals and their reactions are characteristic of metals. They react with water, oxygen and hydrochloric acid. Their reactivity, shown in Table 4.1, increases on going down the group. This is due to the **ease of ionisation**, which increases on going down the group.

Reaction with water

All the Group II elements, except beryllium, react with water with increasing vigour to produce the metal hydroxide and hydrogen gas on descending the group. Beryllium does not react with water or steam. Very clean magnesium reacts very slowly with cold water. Calcium, strontium and barium react with increasing vigour. Barium, being at the lower end of the group, reacts most vigorously.

An example of the chemical equation of the Group II metal and water is:

$$Sr(s) + 2H_2O(l) \longrightarrow Sr(OH)_2(aq) + H_2(g)$$

Reaction with oxygen

The alkaline earth metals (Group II elements) react with oxygen to produce basic oxides. Beryllium reacts very slowly with oxygen, and as the group is descended, the reactions become more rapid. The reaction of barium and oxygen is the most rapid. All the metal oxides of the Group II elements are white solids.

An example of the chemical equation between a Group II metal and oxygen is:

$$2Sr(s) + O_2(g) \longrightarrow 2SrO(s)$$

Reaction with hydrochloric acid

The Group II metals react with dilute hydrochloric acid to produce salts, known as metal chlorides, and hydrogen gas. As you go down the group, there is an increase in reaction between the metals and the acid. Beryllium is prevented from reacting with the acid because it is coated with a thin non-reactive oxide layer. Magnesium also has a coating of magnesium oxide and when the acid is first added, there is no visible reaction. After some time, the acid penetrates the magnesium oxide layer, the reaction with the magnesium will start and bubbles of hydrogen gas will be noticed. Barium reacts violently, being at the bottom of the group.

An example of the chemical equation with hydrochloric acid is:

$$Sr(s) + 2HCl(aq) \longrightarrow SrCl_2(aq) + H_2(g)$$

Trends in Group VII – the halogens

The elements of Group VII are all non-metals and exist as solids, liquids and gases. As the group is descended, the state of the element moves from gaseous to liquid to solid and its colour also becomes darker (Table 4.2). Elements in Group VII exist as **diatomic molecules**: F_2, Cl_2, Br_2 and I_2. They all have similar chemical properties because their atoms all have **seven** valence electrons. They have a high inclination to draw one extra electron to obtain a full octet achieving stability. They react by **gaining** one valence electron to form negatively charged ions called **anions** (see page 65). When they gain this electron, they are said to **ionise**. The **ease of ionisation** increases moving **up** Group VII. The **reactivity** of the elements therefore increases moving **up** the group. The reason is that, as you ascend the group, the number of occupied shells becomes smaller. There is less shielding of the valence electrons and therefore the pull on these valence electrons is increased, leading to a decrease in the atomic radius. Since there is less shielding, the positive nuclear centre has a greater attraction on the valence electron and can attract an electron much more easily to form an anion. Astatine is the least reactive element in Group VII because it is large, making it harder for the nucleus to attract an electron to form an anion. Fluorine, being the smallest, readily attracts an electron, making it the most reactive non-metal known.

The Group VII elements react with metals to form ionic compounds and other non-metals to form covalent compounds.

Table 4.2 *Summary of the trends in Group VII – the halogens*

Element	Appearance and state at room temperature	Number of occupied electron shells	Atomic radius	Ease of ionisation	Reactivity	Strength of oxidising power	Displacement
F	Pale yellow gas	2	Increases moving **down** due to the increase in number of **occupied electron shells**.	Increases moving **up**. As the atomic radii **decrease**, the attractive pull of the positive nucleus on the electron to be gained increases and the more easily the atoms **gain** this electron to form anions.	Increases moving **up** due to the increase in **ease of ionisation**.	Increases moving **up** due to the increase in **ease of ionisation**. The more easily the element ionises, the more easily it **takes** electrons from another reactant.	An element is displaced from its compounds by an element **above** it in the group.
Cl	Yellow-green gas	3					
Br	Red-brown liquid	4					
I	Grey-black solid	5					

⟶ Indicates that the property **increases** in the direction of the arrow

---

Example 2

Fluorine reacts with sodium to form sodium fluoride.

$$\text{fluorine} + \text{sodium} \longrightarrow \text{sodium fluoride}$$
$$F_2(g) + 2Na(s) \longrightarrow 2NaF(s)$$

Fluorine reacts with hydrogen gas to produce hydrogen fluoride gas:

$$\text{fluorine} + \text{hydrogen} \longrightarrow \text{hydrogen fluoride}$$
$$F_2(g) + H_2(g) \longrightarrow 2HF(g)$$

Displacement reactions and strength of oxidising power

In a **displacement reaction** an element in its free state takes the place of another element in a compound. A **more reactive** element will displace a **less reactive** element. **Chlorine** will displace bromine and iodine, and **bromine** will displace iodine from their compounds. **Iodine** cannot displace bromine, chlorine or fluorine, nor can bromine displace chlorine or fluorine.

For example, chlorine displaces iodine from potassium iodide to produce potassium chloride and iodine:

$$Cl_2(g) + 2KI(aq) \longrightarrow 2KCl(aq) + I_2(aq)$$

When a displacement reaction occurs, a resulting colour change is observed. The halide solutions are all colourless and when the displacement reaction occurs and a different halogen forms, a distinctive colour is observed (see Table 4.3).

Table 4.3 *Halogen displacement reactions showing colour changes*

Halogen added	Potassium chloride solution	Potassium bromide solution	Potassium iodide solution
Chlorine	Very pale green solution. No displacement reaction.	Orange-reddish brown solution. $Cl_2(aq) + 2KBr(aq) \longrightarrow$ $2KCl(aq) + Br_2(aq)$ (orange-reddish brown)	Brown solution/black precipitate. $Cl_2(aq) + 2KI(aq) \longrightarrow$ $2KCl(aq) + I_2(aq)$ (brown solution/black precipitate)
Bromine	Orange-reddish brown solution. No displacement reaction.	Orange-reddish brown solution. No displacement reaction.	Brown solution/black precipitate. $Br_2(aq) + 2KI(aq) \longrightarrow$ $2KBr(aq) + I_2(aq)$ (brown solution/black precipitate)
Iodine	Dark brown solution. No displacement reaction.	Dark brown solution. No displacement reaction.	Dark brown solution. No displacement reaction.

Displacement reactions can be explained by looking at the relative **strength of oxidising power** of the elements. This is determined by how easily one substance **takes electrons** from another substance. The strength of oxidising power of Group VII elements increases moving **up** the group because the ability to **ionise** and **take electrons** from another reactant increases moving upwards. **Chlorine** will take electrons from bromide (Br^-) and iodide (I^-) ions and **bromine** will take electrons from iodide (I^-) ions.

For example:

$$Br_2(g) + 2KI(aq) \longrightarrow 2KBr(aq) + I_2(aq)$$
$$Br_2(g) + 2I^-(aq) \longrightarrow 2Br^-(aq) + I_2(aq)$$

Bromine has oxidised the potassium iodide to form potassium bromide and iodine. Based on the trends in the group, fluorine would be a stronger oxidising agent than chlorine, bromine, iodine or astatine. Astatine, which is lower than iodine in the group, would be a weaker oxidising agent than iodine.

Trends in Period 3

As we move along Period 3 from left to right, the **metallic** nature of the elements **decreases** and the **non-metallic** nature **increases**. As can be seen in Table 4.4, the electronic configuration of the elements of Period 3 have the same number of shells, which is three. There are two fully occupied shells and the third is the valence shell. Going across Period 3, the atomic number of the elements increases by one and the number of protons in the nucleus and the number of valence electrons also increase by one. In other words, the valence electrons of the first three elements – sodium, magnesium and aluminium – have one, two and three valence electrons, classifying them as metals. Typical non-metals have four or more valence electrons.

The physical properties of the elements in Period 3 are reflective of the change in the metallic to non-metallic nature of the elements. Sodium, magnesium and aluminium have high melting and boiling points and are good conductors of heat and electricity. Silicon in Group IV has high boiling and melting points. Silicon is a **semi-metal** or **metalloid**, having both metallic and non-metallic properties. The elements phosphorus, sulfur and chlorine are on the right-hand side of the periodic table and are non-metals with low boiling and melting points and are poor conductors of heat and electricity. Argon is a noble gas.

As can be seen in Table 4.4, as we move across the period, the number of valence electrons increases by one in the third outer shell. The number of protons also increases by one in the nucleus for each successive element in the period. Recall that the number of filled inner shells is the same: two, therefore the shielding would be the same for all the elements in the period. A nucleus with one more proton and the same shielding would have a greater pull on the valence electrons. The atomic radii (as seen in Table 4.4) would also decrease due to the greater pull exhibited by the more positive proton-rich nuclear centre. Thus it becomes easier for the atoms to gain electrons and harder to lose electrons as the period is traversed.

The **ease of ionisation** and **reactivity** of the **metals** sodium, magnesium and aluminium **decreases** moving along the period. This is because ionisation occurs in metal atoms by losing electrons. It would be easier for a sodium atom with its larger atomic radius to lose an electron than an aluminium atom with a smaller atomic radius.

The **ease of ionisation** and **reactivity** of the **non-metals** phosphorus, sulfur and chlorine **increase** moving along the period. This is because in the non-metals the atoms ionise by gaining electrons. It is easier for the chlorine atom with a highly positive nucleus and a smaller atomic radius to capture an electron than sulfur with its larger atomic radius.

Silicon does not usually ionise; it usually reacts by sharing electrons with other non-metal atoms. Argon has a full octet in its valence shell, making it stable. For this reason, this element does not ionise and is chemically unreactive.

Table 4.4 *Summary of the trends in Period 3*

Element	Na	Mg	Al	Si	P	S	Cl	Ar
Electronic configuration	2,8,1	2,8,2	2,8,3	2,8,4	2,8,5	2,8,6	2,8,7	2,8,8
Metal/ non-metal	Metal	Metal	Metal	Semi-metal	Non-metal	Non-metal	Non-metal	Non-metal
Electrical conductivity	Good conductors			Semi-conductor	Non-conductors (insulators)			
Electrons lost, gained or shared	Loses 1e$^-$	Loses 2e$^-$	Loses 3e$^-$	Shares 4e$^-$	Gains 3e$^-$	Gains 2e$^-$	Gains 1e$^-$	None
Atomic radius	**Decreases** moving from **left to right** due to the increase in number of **positive protons** causing the attractive pull of the positive nucleus on the valence electrons to get stronger.							
Ease of ionisation	Increases moving from **right to left**. As the atomic radii **increase** and the number of positive protons decreases, the more easily the atoms **lose** electrons to form positive cations.			Does not usually ionise.	Increases moving from **left to right**. As the atomic radii **decrease** and the number of positive protons increases, the more easily the atoms **gain** electrons to form negative anions.			Does not ionise.
Reactivity	Increases moving from **right to left** due to the increase in ease of ionisation.				Increases moving from **left to right** due to the increase in ease of ionisation.			Unreactive

⟶ Indicates that the property **increases** in the direction of the arrow.

Recalling facts

1 What is the name of the scientist who proposed the Law of Triads?

   a Dimitri Mendeleev

   b Henry Moseley

   c Johann Döbereiner

   d John Newlands

2 Elements are arranged in the periodic table based on:

   a reactivity with water

   b density

   c increase in number of neutrons

   d increasing atomic number

3 The alkaline earth metals belong to:

   a Group 0

   b Group I

   c Group II

   d Group VII

4 The most reactive Group II element is:

   a barium

   b calcium

   c strontium

   d beryllium

5 The period number is:

   a number of valence electrons

   b number of occupied shells

   c total number of electrons

   d total number of protons

6 Which statement is TRUE with regards to the halogens?

   a Ease of ionisation increases on moving up the group.

   b Reactivity decreases as the group is ascended.

   c The atomic radius decreases as the group is descended.

   d The oxidising power decreases as the group is ascended.

7 Which of the following elements is a member of Group III of the periodic table?

   a boron

   b calcium

   c sodium

   d sulfur

8 The most electronegative element in the periodic table is:

    a sodium   **b** oxygen   **c** chlorine   **d** fluorine

9 Which one of the following halogens would iodine displace from the halides in solution?

    a bromine   **b** chlorine   **c** fluorine   **d** astatine

10 What colour change is expected when chlorine displaces bromine from potassium bromide solution?

    a pale green

    b dark brown

    c black

    d orange-reddish brown

11 Give a historical account of how the elements are classified in the modern periodic table. In your answer you must include three scientists and their contributions.

12 What is meant by these terms?

    a groups

    b periods

    c electron shells

    d valence shells

    e valence electrons

    f ease of ionisation

Applying facts

13 **a** Write the electronic configuration of barium, chlorine, silicon, nitrogen and sulfur. State the groups and periods to which each of the elements belongs.

    b Deduce from the electronic configurations from part a, which elements are metals and which are non-metals. Explain your answers.

14 The elements in the table belong to Group II of the periodic table.

Element	Electronic configuration
Beryllium	2,2
Magnesium	2,8,2
Calcium	2,8,8,2
Strontium	2,8,18,8,2
Barium	2,8,18,18,8,2

    a Give the symbol of each of the elements.

    b Write the chemical symbol and charge for the calcium ion.

    c The atomic radius of the element increases as the group is descended. Explain why this occurs.

d Explain why the ease of ionisation increases on going down the group.

e Which element reacts most rapidly with oxygen? Write the equation for the reaction.

f Which element reacts slowly with water? Write the equation for the reaction.

g Which element reacts vigorously with hydrochloric acid? Write the equation for the reaction.

15 **a** List the elements of Group VII.

b Give the physical state and colour of each of the elements named in part a.

c When chlorine is added to potassium bromide, the chlorine displaces the bromide from the potassium bromide.

    i Write the equation for the displacement reaction stated above.

    ii Explain in terms of strength of oxidising power why the displacement occurs.

Analysing data

16 Write the electronic configuration of the elements of Period 3.

a List the elements of Period 3 which are metals, non-metals and metalloids.

b A trend identified in Period 3 is that the atomic radius of the elements decreases moving from left to right. Explain why there is a decrease in atomic radius of the elements.

c The ease of ionisation decreases from sodium to magnesium to aluminium. Explain this statement.

d From the non-metals identified, state which element is the most reactive and explain why this element is the most reactive.

e Which element in Period 3 is unreactive. Explain why this element is unreactive.

17 The table shows the boiling points and properties of some of the elements in Group VII.

Element	Boiling point (°C)	Colour in aqueous solution
Fluorine	−188	Colourless
Chlorine	−35	Pale green
Bromine	X	Orange
Iodine	184	Brown

a Predict the boiling point of bromine.

b Aqueous chlorine is added to potassium iodide solution. What is the colour of the final solution in this reaction?

18 Francium (Fr) is a very rare element and it is estimated that there is only 25 g of francium in the Earth's crust. Francium is a radioactive element and has a half-life of approximately 20 minutes. Use your knowledge of periodicity and the periodic table to answer the following.

a Mendeleev predicted the existence of francium in the 1870s, but the element was not discovered until 1939. Explain why Mendeleev was able to predict the existence of francium in 1870.

b If you could react francium with water, what would you expect to happen?

19 Argon is an inert gas in Period 3.

    a How many electrons does argon have in its outer shell?

    b Explain how the electron arrangement of argon affects its reactivity.

20 The boiling point of xenon is −108 °C. Predict with reasoning whether krypton will be a solid, liquid or gas at this temperature.

5 Structure and bonding

Learning objectives

- Explain why atoms **bond**.
- Explain the formation of **ionic bonds**.
- Explain how **covalent bonds** are formed.
- Write **chemical formulae** representing **ions**, **molecules** and **formula units**.
- Illustrate ionic and covalent compounds using **dot and cross diagrams**.
- Explain **metallic bonding** and relate the **properties of metals** to the bonding in metals.
- Relate the structure of **ionic** and **covalent compounds** to their properties.
- Distinguish between **ionic** and **simple molecular solids**.
- Describe the **structure of diamond** and **graphite** and relate their properties and uses to their structure.
- Define and explain what is meant by **allotropy**.

Atoms of elements in **Group 0** (the **noble** gases of the periodic table) are **stable** and **unreactive** and exist in nature as individual atoms because they have **full** outer electron shells or valence shells. A helium atom has two electrons in its valence shell, which is the maximum number of electrons that the first shell can hold. The other noble gases, for example, neon and argon, have eight electrons in their valence shells or a full octet. Atoms of all other elements are **not stable** because they do not have full valence shells. These atoms attempt to obtain full valence shells and become **stable** by **bonding** with each other to achieve the noble gas configuration closest to them in the periodic table. To form these bonds, atoms use their **valence electrons** or outermost electrons. They can do this by:

- **Losing valence electrons** to atoms of another element. **Metal** atoms with one, two or three valence electrons usually lose their valence electrons and form positive **cations**.
- **Gaining valence electrons** from atoms of another element. **Non-metal** atoms with five, six or seven valence electrons usually gain electrons into their valence shell and form negative **anions**.
- **Sharing electrons** in their valence shells with other atoms. When **non-metal** atoms with four, five, six or seven valence electrons bond with each other, they share valence electrons and form **molecules**.

There are three main types of **chemical bonding**:

- **Ionic bonding.** This occurs when a metal bonds with a non-metal (see page 69).
- **Covalent bonding.** This occurs when two or more non-metals bond (see page 77).
- **Metallic bonding.** This occurs within metals (see page 81).

These bonds are intramolecular forces of attraction that hold the atoms together. These forces of attraction are set up between the atoms when the electrons of the atoms involved are rearranged. **Chemical compounds** are formed when elements bond by ionic or covalent bonding.

Chemical formulae

Chemical formulae can be used to represent **compounds** formed by ionic or covalent bonding. A chemical formula shows which **elements** are present in a compound and shows the **ratio** between the elements. Chemical formulae can be written in three main ways:

- The **molecular formula.** This gives the actual number of atoms of each element present in one molecule of a compound. Subscripts are used to represent the actual number of each element present in the molecule or compound. For example, the molecular formula of butane is C_4H_{10}, there are four carbon atoms and 10 hydrogen atoms. Sulfur dioxide, SO_2, contains one sulfur atom and two oxygen atoms.

- The **structural formula**. This is a diagrammatic representation of one molecule of the compound. Lines between the atoms are used to represent bonds. For example, the structural formula of butane shows that there is one bond between each carbon atom and one bond between each carbon and each hydrogen atom. Another example is sulfur dioxide, which shows that there are two double bonds between the sulfur and each oxygen atom.

- The **empirical formula**. This gives the simplest whole number ratio between the elements in the compound. For example, the empirical formula of propane C_3H_8. This says that the ratio of carbon to hydrogen is 3 to 8. In sulfur dioxide, SO_2, the sulfur to oxygen ratio is 1 to 2. In aluminium oxide, Al_2O_3, the ratio of aluminium to oxygen is 2 to 3. The formula of glucose is $C_6H_{12}O_6$, so its empirical formula is CH_2O.

How to write empirical formulae of compounds formed from two elements

Empirical formulae of compounds formed from two different elements can be written using the concept of **valence number** or **valency**. Valency is the number of bonds an atom can form when bonding with other atoms. It is determined by the number of valence electrons an atom has, and it can be thought of as the number of electrons an atom has to lose, gain or share when bonding.

Table 5.1 *Valence numbers or valency*

Group number	I	II	Transition metals	III	IV	V	VI	VII	0
Valency	1	2	Variable, often 2	3	4	3	2	1	0

- Elements in Groups **I** to **IV**: valency = the group number
- Elements in Groups **V** to **VII**: valency = 8 – the group number

Therefore, the valency of sodium is 1, the valency of magnesium is 2, the valency of aluminium is 3, the valency of silicon is 4.

The valency of oxygen (Group VI element) is 8 – 6 = 2.

The valency of iodine (Group VII element) is 8 – 7 = 1.

The valency of nitrogen (Group V element) is 8 – 5 = 3.

When forming a compound, both types of atoms must lose, gain or share the **same number** of valence electrons. Consequently, the **sum** of the valencies of each element in the compound must be equal.

Example 1

The empirical formula of barium nitride is **Ba$_3$N$_2$**:

- Number of atoms of each element from the formula: Ba = 3
  $\qquad\qquad\qquad\qquad\qquad\qquad\qquad\qquad\qquad$ N = 2
- Valency of each element: Ba = 2 (Group II)
  $\qquad\qquad\qquad\qquad\quad$ N = 3 (Group V)
- Sum of the valencies: Ba = 3 × 2 = 6
  $\qquad\qquad\qquad\qquad\quad$ N = 2 × 3 = 6

This shows that the **sum** of the valencies of the two elements is equal. Here they are both **6**.

Example 2

The empirical formula of calcium bromide is **CaBr$_2$**:

- Number of atoms of each element from the formula: Ca = 1
  $\qquad\qquad\qquad\qquad\qquad\qquad\qquad\qquad\qquad$ Br = 2
- Valency of each element: Ca = 2 (Group II)
  $\qquad\qquad\qquad\qquad\quad$ Br = 8 – 7 = 1 (Group VII)
- Sum of the valencies: Ca = **1** × 2 = 2
  $\qquad\qquad\qquad\qquad\quad$ Br = 2 × 1 = 2

This shows that the **sum** of the valencies of the two elements is equal. Here they are both **2**.

To **write the empirical formula** of a compound formed from two elements:

- Determine the valencies of each element in the compound.
- Write the **symbol** of the first element. If a metal is present, always write its symbol first.
- Write the **valency** of the second element immediately after the symbol of the first element in **subscript**.
- Write the **symbol** of the second element immediately after the subscript.
- Write the **valency** of the first element immediately after the symbol of the second element in **subscript**.

Note If a valency is **1**, then no number is written as a subscript (see **point 1** on page 68).

Example 3

Aluminium sulfide

- Valency of each element: Al = **3** (Group III)
  $\qquad\qquad\qquad\qquad\quad$ S = **2** (Group VI)
- Symbol of the first element followed by the valency of the second element in subscript: Al$_2$
- Symbol of the second element followed by the valency of the first element in subscript: Al$_2$S$_3$

The empirical formula of aluminium sulfide is **Al$_2$S$_3$**

Points to note:

1 Some transition metals have **more than one** valency. The valency is indicated by a Roman numeral placed in brackets after the **name** of the metal, for example:

Phosphorus(V) chloride

Valency of each element: P = **5** (given in the name)

Cl = **1** (Group VII)

Empirical formula of phosphorus(V) chloride is **PCl$_5$**.

Iron(III) sulfide

Valency of each element: Fe = **3** (given in the name)

S = **2** (Group VI)

Empirical formula of iron(III) sulfide is **Fe$_2$S$_3$**.

2 If the ratio of the subscripts is not in its simplest form, then cancel to its **simplest form**, for example:

Calcium oxide

Valency of each element: Ca = **2** (Group II)

O = **2** (Group VI)

Empirical formula of calcium oxide is **CaO** (Ca$_2$O$_2$ is cancelled to its simplest ratio).

Aluminium nitride

Valency of each element: Al = **3** (Group III)

N = **3** (Group V)

Empirical formula of aluminium nitride is **AlN** (Al$_3$N$_3$ is cancelled to its simplest ratio).

Alternatively, the following steps can be used to write the empirical formula of a compound formed from two elements:

- Determine the valencies of each element in the compound.
- Write the symbol of the first element. If a metal is present, always write the symbol first.
- Write the valency of each element as superscripts.
- Draw a diagonal arrow from the element to the valency of the next element.
- Rewrite the formulae, inserting the valencies as subscripts.
- Reduce all subscripts to the lowest whole number ratio.

We will use examples from earlier to demonstrate this alternative method.

Example 4

Iron(III) sulfide

Valency of each element: Fe = **3** (given in the name)

S = **2** (Group VI)

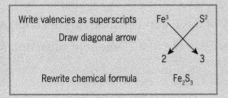

Empirical formula of iron(III) sulfide is **Fe$_2$S$_3$**.

Section A: Principles of chemistry

Calcium oxide

Valency of each element: Ca = 2 (Group II)

O = 2 (Group VI)

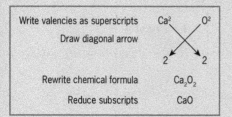

Write valencies as superscripts	Ca^2 O^2
Draw diagonal arrow	
	2 2
Rewrite chemical formula	Ca_2O_2
Reduce subscripts	CaO

Empirical formula of calcium oxide is CaO (Ca_2O_2 is cancelled to its simplest ratio).

Ionic bonding

Ionic bonding occurs between a **metal** and a **non-metal**. Valence electrons are **transferred** from the metal atom (or atoms) to the non-metal atom (or atoms). When this occurs the atoms are no longer neutral, they form **ions**. The metal atom loses valence electrons forming **positive ions** known as **cations**. The charge on the ion is positive: Na^+, Ca^{2+}. The non-metal atoms form **negative ions** known as **anions,** by gaining electrons. The charge on the ion is negative: Cl^-, O^{2-}. Both types of ions have full outer electron shells (and therefore a new electronic configuration of the nearest noble gas in the periodic table) and are now stable. Strong **electrostatic forces of attraction** hold the oppositely charged particles together and this force of attraction is known as the **ionic bond**. The compounds formed are ionic compounds. The ionic bond is strong. The properties associated with ionic compounds are due to the strength of the ionic bond.

*An **ionic bond** is the link formed from the electrostatic attraction between oppositely charged ions in a compound.*

Examples of ion formation

1 Potassium, a Group I metal, has *one* electron in its valence shell. It loses the one valence electron when it undergoes bonding with a non-metal. Therefore, it has one more proton than electrons and carries a single positive, +, charge. The potassium ion or K^+ is formed.

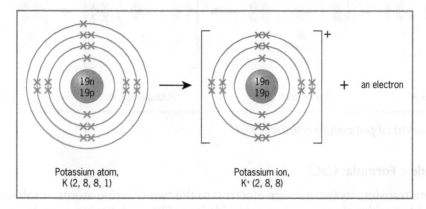

Potassium atom,
K (2, 8, 8, 1)

Potassium ion,
K^+ (2, 8, 8)

2 Beryllium belongs to Group II and has *two* valence electrons. It loses two valence electrons when bonding with a non-metal to form the beryllium ion, which has two more protons than electrons. Therefore, it carries a double positive charge, 2+, and is represented by Be^{2+}.

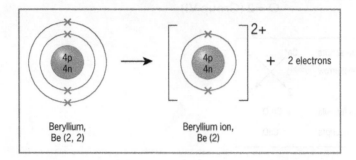

Beryllium,
Be (2, 2)

Beryllium ion,
Be (2)

3 Oxygen belongs to Group VI of the periodic table and has *six* valence electrons. It gains two electrons when bonding with a metal to form the oxide ion. It therefore has two more electrons than protons and carries a double negative charge, 2–, and is represented by O^{2-}, or the oxide ion.

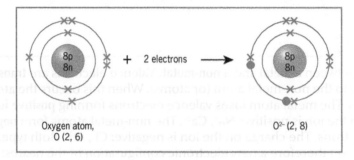

Oxygen atom,
O (2, 6)

O^{2-} (2, 8)

Examples of ionic bonding

Potassium chloride   Formula: KCl

The potassium atom transfers its valence electron to the chlorine atom. A **potassium ion (K⁺)**, which has a single **positive** charge, and a **chloride ion (Cl⁻)**, which has a single **negative** charge are formed (Figure 5.1).

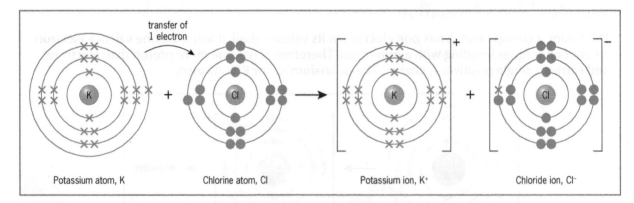

Potassium atom, K   Chlorine atom, Cl   Potassium ion, K⁺   Chloride ion, Cl⁻

Figure 5.1 *Formation of potassium chloride, KCl*

Calcium chloride   Formula: CaCl₂

The calcium atom transfers its two valence electron to the two chlorine atoms. A **calcium ion (Ca²⁺)**, which has a double **positive** charge, and two **chloride ions (Cl⁻)**, each having a single **negative** charge, are formed (Figure 5.2).

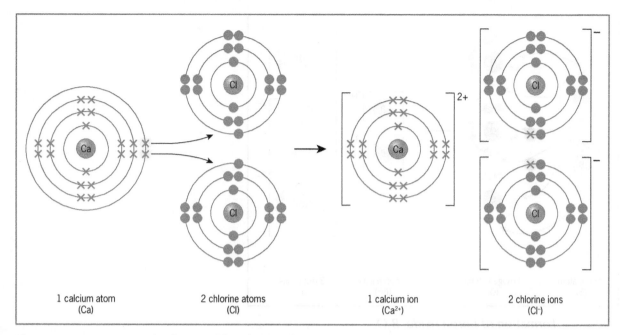

Figure 5.2 *Formation of calcium chloride, CaCl$_2$*

Note Diagrams to show the formation of ionic compounds can be simplified by showing only the **valence electrons**.

Magnesium iodide   Formula: MgI$_2$

The magnesium atom transfers its two valence electron to the two iodine atoms. A **magnesium ion (Mg^{2+})**, which has a double **positive** charge, and two **iodide ions (I$^-$)**, each having a single **negative** charge, are formed (Figure 5.3).

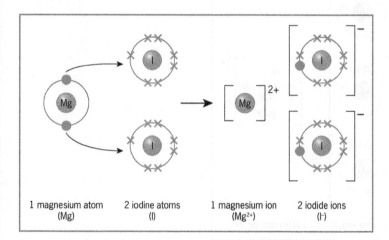

Figure 5.3 *Formation of magnesium iodide, MgI$_2$*

Boron oxide   Formula: B$_2$O$_3$

The boron atom transfers its three valence electrons to the three oxygen atoms. A **boron ion (B^{3+})**, loses three electrons and has a triple **positive** charge, and an oxygen atom gains two electrons forming an oxide **ion (O^{2-})**. Since each boron atom has to lose three electrons and each oxygen has to gain two electrons, two boron atoms would have to lose a total of six electrons to three oxygen atoms, which would need to gain six electrons to form boron oxide, **B$_2$O$_3$** (Figure 5.4).

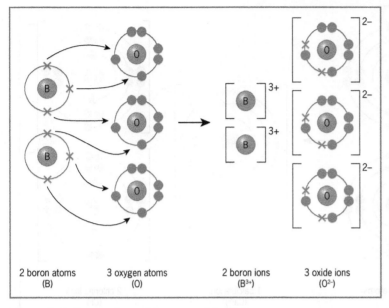

| 2 boron atoms (B) | 3 oxygen atoms (O) | 2 boron ions (B³⁺) | 3 oxide ions (O²⁻) |

Figure 5.4 *Formation of boron oxide, B₂O₃*

Aluminium fluoride   Formula: AlF₃

The aluminium atom transfers its three valence electrons to the three fluorine atoms. An aluminium **ion (Al³⁺)**, loses three electrons and has a triple **positive** charge, and each fluorine atom gains one electron to form a fluoride **ion (F⁻)**. As each boron atom has to lose three electrons, three fluorine atoms are needed to form aluminium fluoride, **AlF₃** (Figure 5.5).

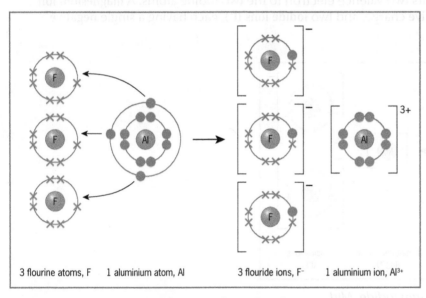

| 3 flourine atoms, F | 1 aluminium atom, Al | 3 flouride ions, F⁻ | 1 aluminium ion, Al³⁺ |

Figure 5.5 *Formation of aluminium fluoride, AlF₃*

The crystalline structure of ionic compounds

At room temperature, the ions formed from the transfer of electrons between metals and non-metals are arranged in an orderly fashion to form a giant crystal lattice. In other words, the ionic compounds exist as **crystalline solids**. Strong **electrostatic forces** of attraction between the ions, called **ionic bonds**, hold the oppositely charged ions together in a regular, repeating, three-dimensional arrangement throughout the crystal. This forms a structure known as a **crystal lattice**.

Example 5

Sodium chloride

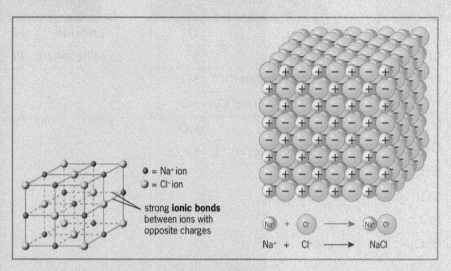

- ● = Na⁺ ion
- ◯ = Cl⁻ ion

strong **ionic bonds** between ions with opposite charges

$$Na^+ + Cl^- \longrightarrow NaCl$$

Figure 5.6 *The sodium chloride crystal lattice*

The crystal lattice of sodium chloride contains millions of Na^+ and Cl^- ions. Each sodium ion, Na^+, is bonded to six chloride ions, Cl^-. Each Cl^- ion is bonded to six Na^+ ions. This can be seen by looking at the Na^+ ion in the centre of the cube. The ionic bond accounts for the properties of sodium chloride (see Table 5.6 on page 85).

Formulae and names of ionic compounds

Ionic compounds can be composed of ions formed from **single atoms** called **monatomic ions** (see page 71), or ions formed from small **groups of atoms** that are bonded together and called **polyatomic ions**, for example, the ammonium ion, NH_4^+, dichromate(VI) ion, $Cr_2O_7^{2-}$ and the sulfate ion, SO_4^{2-}.

Table 5.2 *Common cations*

Monovalent		Divalent		Trivalent	
Hydrogen	H⁺	Magnesium	Mg²⁺	Iron(III)	Fe³⁺
Lithium	Li⁺	Calcium	Ca²⁺	Aluminium	Al³⁺
Sodium	Na⁺	Barium	Ba²⁺		
Potassium	K⁺	Iron(II)	Fe²⁺		
Copper(I)	Cu⁺	Copper(II)	Cu²⁺		
Silver	Ag⁺	Zinc	Zn²⁺		
Ammonium	NH₄⁺	Tin(II)	Sn²⁺		
		Lead(II)	Pb²⁺		

Table 5.3 *Common anions*

Monovalent		Divalent		Trivalent	
Fluoride	F⁻	Oxide	O^{2-}	Nitride	N^{3-}
Chloride	Cl⁻	Sulfide	S^{2-}	Phosphate	PO_4^{3-}
Bromide	Br⁻	Sulfite (sulfate(IV))	SO_3^{2-}		
Iodide	I⁻	Sulfate (sulfate(VI))	SO_4^{2-}		
Hydride	H⁻	Carbonate	CO_3^{2-}		
Hydroxide	OH⁻	Dichromate(VI)	$Cr_2O_7^{2-}$		
Nitrite (nitrate(III))	NO_2^-				
Nitrate (nitrate(V))	NO_3^-				
Hydrogen carbonate	HCO_3^-				
Hydrogen sulfate	HSO_4^-				
Manganate(VII)	MnO_4^-				
Ethanoate	CH_3COO^-				

To **name anions**:

- The name of an anion formed from a **single atom** is derived from the name of the element, with the ending '-ide'. For example, S^{2-} is the sulf**ide** ion, H⁻ is the hydr**ide** ion and I⁻ is the iod**ide** ion.
- When **oxygen** is present in a **polyatomic anion** the name of the ion is derived from the element combined with the oxygen, with the ending '-**ite**' or '-**ate**'. For example, SO_3^{2-} is the sulf**ite** ion and SO_4^{2-} is the sulf**ate** ion. Alternatively, the ending '-**ate**' is used with the **oxidation number** of the element given in brackets. For example, SO_3^{2-} is the sulf**ate(IV)** ion and SO_4^{2-} is the sulf**ate(VI)** ion (see page 166).

When **writing formulae** of ionic compounds, the **sum** of the **positive charges** and the **sum** of the **negative charges** must be **equal**. This is because the **total number** of electrons lost by one type of atom or group of atoms must be the **same** as the total number gained by the other type of atom or group of atoms. Formulae of ionic compounds are **empirical formulae** as they represent the **ratio of ions** present. They are also known as **formula units**.

Example 6

The chemical formula of boron sulfide is **B_2S_3**:

- Number of atoms of each element from the formula: **B = 2**

    S = 3

- Charge on each ion: **B^{3+} = +3**

    S^{2-} = −2

- Sum of the charges: **B = 2 × +3 = +6**

    S = 3 × −2 = −6

This shows the **sum** of the positive charges and the **sum** of the negative charges are equal.

To **write the chemical formula** of an ionic compound:

- Write down the formulae of the two ions present using Tables 5.2 and 5.3.
- Rewrite the **formula** of the cation without its charge.

- Write the **magnitude of the charge** on the anion immediately after the formula of the cation in **subscript**.
- Write the **formula** of the anion immediately after the subscript without its charge.
- Write the **magnitude** of the charge on the cation immediately after the formula of the anion in **subscript**.

Note If the magnitude of the charge is **1**, then no number is written as a subscript (see following examples).

Example 7

Calcium nitride

- Ions present: Ca^{2+} N^{3-}
- Formula of the cation without its charge: **Ca**
- Magnitude of the charge on the anion written after the cation in subscript: Ca_3
- Formula of the anion without its charge: **N**
- Magnitude of the charge on the cation written after the anion in subscript: Ca_3N_2

The empirical formula of calcium nitride is Ca_3N_2.

Barium bromide

- Ions present: Ba^{2+} Br^-
- Formula of the cation without its charge: **Ba**
- Magnitude of the charge on the anion written after the cation in subscript: **Ba**
- Formula of the anion without its charge: **Br**
- Magnitude of the charge on the cation written after the anion in subscript: $BaBr_2$

The empirical formula of barium bromide is $BaBr_2$.

Silver nitrate

- Ions present: Ag^+ NO_3^-
- Magnitude of the charges: $Ag^+ = 1$
                              $NO_3^{1-} = 1$
- Empirical formula of silver carbonate is $AgNO_3$.

Points to note:

1 If either ion is a **polyatomic ion** and **more than one** is required, place the polyatomic ion in **brackets** and write the required subscript outside the bracket, for example:

Copper(II) nitrite

Ions present: Cu^{2+} NO_2^-

Magnitude of the charges: $Cu^{2+} = 2$
                            $NO_2^- = 1$

Empirical formula of copper(II) nitrite is $Cu(NO_2)_2$.

NO_2 is placed in brackets with the subscript of **2** outside showing that two NO_2^- ions are required.

2 Iron(III) dichromate

Ions present: Fe^{3+} $Cr_2O_7^{2-}$

Magnitude of the charges: $Fe^{3+} = 3$

$$Cr_2O_7^{2-} = 2$$

Empirical formula of iron(III) dichromate is $Fe_2(Cr_2O_7)_3$.

Cr_2O_7 is placed in brackets with the subscript of 3 outside showing that three $Cr_2O_7^{2-}$ ions are required.

3 If the ratio of the subscripts is not in its simplest form, then cancel to its **simplest form**, for example:

Lead(II) sulfate

Ions present: Pb^{2+} SO_4^{2-}

Magnitude of the charges: $Pb^{2+} = 2$

$$SO_4^{2-} = 2$$

Empirical formula of lead sulfate is **$PbSO_4$**.

$Pb_2(SO_4)_2$ is cancelled to its simplest ratio.

Alternatively, the following steps can be used to write the chemical formula for an ionic substance:

- Write down the chemical formula of the two ions present using Tables 5.2 and 5.3.
- Rewrite the **ions with the magnitude** of the charge as superscripts of each chemical formula.
- Draw a diagonal arrow from each chemical formula to the numerical value of the charge of the next ion.
- Rewrite the **chemical formula**, inserting the numerical values as subscripts.
- Reduce all subscripts to the lowest whole number ratio.

Note If the magnitude of the charge is **1**, then no number is written as a subscript (see examples below).

When there are polyatomic ions present, the entire polyatomic ion is placed in round brackets.

We will now demonstrate this alternative method by using two examples from earlier.

Examples

Barium bromide

Ions present: **Ba^{2+} Br^-**

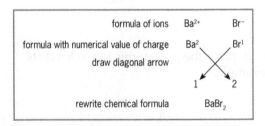

The empirical formula of barium bromide is **$BaBr_2$**.

Iron(III) dichromate

Ions present: Fe^{3+} $Cr_2O_7^{2-}$

Magnitude of the charges: $Fe^{3+} = \mathbf{3}$

$$Cr_2O_7^- = \mathbf{2}$$

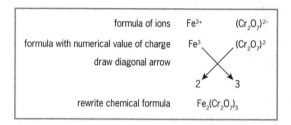

formula of ions	Fe^{3+}	$(Cr_2O_7)^{2-}$
formula with numerical value of charge	Fe^3	$(Cr_2O_7)^2$
draw diagonal arrow		
	2	3
rewrite chemical formula	$Fe_2(Cr_2O_7)_3$	

Empirical formula of iron(III) dichromate is $Fe_2(Cr_2O_7)_3$.

Cr_2O_7 is placed in brackets with the subscript of 3 outside showing that three $Cr_2O_7^{2-}$ ions are required.

Covalent bonding

Covalent bonding occurs when two or more **non-metal** atoms bond. Unpaired valence electrons are **shared** between the atoms which results in the formation of **molecules**. The shared electrons orbit around both atoms, sharing them. This forms strong **covalent bonds** which hold the atoms together. Each shared pair of electrons forms one covalent bond.

Covalent bonding can occur between atoms of the **same element**, for example, chlorine (Cl_2). It can also occur between atoms of two or more **different elements**, for example, sulfur dioxide (SO_2). **Seven** common elements are composed of **diatomic molecules** in their free state:

hydrogen (H_2), oxygen (O_2), nitrogen (N_2), fluorine (F_2), chlorine (Cl_2), bromine (Br_2) and iodine (I_2).

The formula of a covalent substance represents **one molecule** of the substance. Therefore, it is the **molecular formula**. In many covalent compounds, the molecular and empirical formulae are the same, for example, carbon dioxide (CO_2) and ammonia (NH_3). In some they are not the same. For example, the molecular formula of glucose is $C_6H_{12}O_6$ but its empirical formula is CH_2O.

Examples

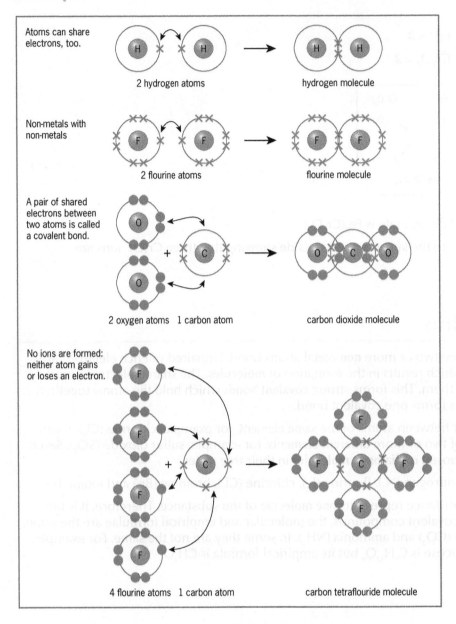

Atoms can share electrons, too.

2 hydrogen atoms → hydrogen molecule

Non-metals with non-metals

2 flourine atoms → flourine molecule

A pair of shared electrons between two atoms is called a covalent bond.

2 oxygen atoms   1 carbon atom → carbon dioxide molecule

No ions are formed: neither atom gains or loses an electron.

4 flourine atoms   1 carbon atom → carbon tetraflouride molecule

Note Like the ionic bonding diagrams, the diagrams to show the formation of covalent substances are simplified by showing only the **valence electrons.**

Nitrogen   Formula N_2

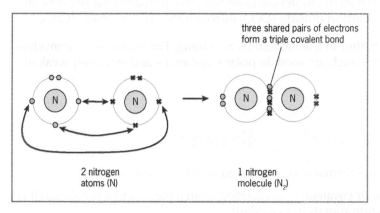

three shared pairs of electrons form a triple covalent bond

2 nitrogen atoms (N)

1 nitrogen molecule (N_2)

Structural formulae can also be used to represent molecules. Each covalent bond is shown by a line between the two atoms (Figure 5.7).

$$H - H$$

$$F - F$$

$$O = C = O$$

$$F - \overset{\displaystyle \overset{F}{|}}{\underset{\displaystyle \underset{F}{|}}{C}} - F$$

$$N \equiv N$$

Figure 5.7 *Structural formulae of hydrogen, fluorine, carbon dioxide, carbon tetrafluoride and nitrogen*

The structure of covalent substances

Covalent substances are composed of **individual molecules**, which can be either **polar** or **non-polar** due to the **electronegativity** of the atoms present. Electronegativity is a measure of how strongly atoms attract bonding electrons. Fluorine, oxygen, chlorine and nitrogen are the most electronegative elements.

- In a **polar molecule**, one type of atom has a **partial positive charge (δ+)** and another type has a **partial negative charge (δ−)** because the atoms at either side of the covalent bond differ in electronegativity and attract the shared electrons with different strengths. Examples are water (H_2O), ammonia (NH_3), hydrogen fluoride (HF), carbon tetrachloride (CCl_4), formaldehyde (CH_2O) and ethanol (C_2H_5OH) (Figure 5.8).

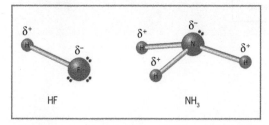

HF

NH_3

Figure 5.8 *A polar hydrogen fluoride and ammonia molecule*

- In a **non-polar molecule**, the electronegativity of the atoms is similar or the same and they attract the shared electrons with equal strengths so the molecule does not have partially charged regions. Examples are hydrogen (H_2), iodine (I_2), carbon dioxide (CO_2), nitrogen (N_2) and methane (CH_4).

The **covalent bonds** holding the atoms together in the molecules are **strong**. The molecules themselves are held together by **intermolecular forces**, which are **weak** in polar substances and **extremely weak** in non-polar substances.

Drawing dot and cross bonding diagrams

To **draw** dot and cross diagrams to show the formation of ionic and covalent compounds:

- Decide whether the compound is **ionic** or **covalent**. If it is formed from a metal and a non-metal it is ionic. If it is formed from two or more non-metals it is covalent.
- Determine the **formula** of the compound using the formulae of the ions, or valency.
- Draw **each atom** in the formula, showing either all the electron shells or just the valence electrons. Use different symbols for electrons of each different type of atom, such as o and x.
- Draw **arrows** to indicate electrons which are transferred or shared.
- Redraw the **ions** formed after electrons have been transferred, or the **molecule** formed after electrons have been shared. Do not forget to put the **charges** on all ions.

Sample questions

Draw a dot and cross diagram to show how each of the following compounds is formed:

a ammonia

b lithium nitride

a Ammonia

Type of compound:	**covalent** since it is formed from two non-metals
Valencies:	N = 3, H = 1
Formula:	**NH$_3$**

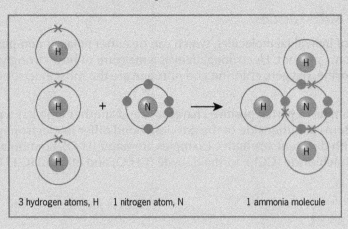

3 hydrogen atoms, H 1 nitrogen atom, N   1 ammonia molecule

b Lithium nitride

Type of compound: **ionic** since it is formed from a metal and a non-metal

Ions present: Li^+ N^{3-}

Formula: **Li_3N**

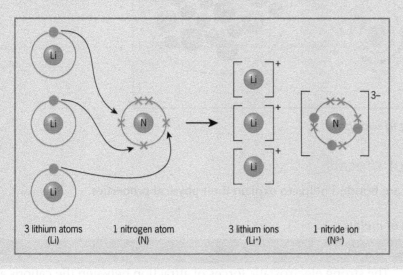

| 3 lithium atoms (Li) | 1 nitrogen atom (N) | 3 lithium ions (Li⁺) | 1 nitride ion (N³⁻) |

Metallic bonding

Metallic bonding occurs in **metals**. Most metals on Earth exist in the solid state; the atoms of the metals are packed tightly together in rows to form a **metal lattice** (Figure 5.9), in which valence electrons become **delocalised**. This means that the valence electrons are no longer associated with any specific atom and are free to move. They therefore form positive **cations.** These cations are tightly packed together in rows and are surrounded by a **'sea' of mobile valence electrons**. The metal lattice is held together by the electrostatic forces of attraction between the delocalised electrons and the cations, known as the **metallic bond**, which is strong (Figure 5.10). It is important to note that metallic bonding occurs in metals and must not be confused with ionic bonding.

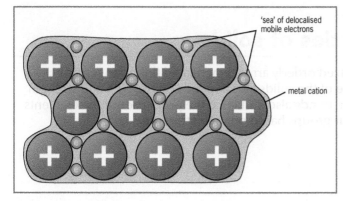

Figure 5.9 *A metal lattice*

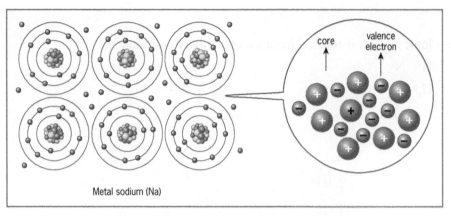

Figure 5.10 *Metallic bonding in sodium*

Physical properties of metals

The way the atoms in metals are bonded helps to explain their **physical properties**.

Table 5.4 *Physical properties of metals*

Physical property	Explanation
High melting points and boiling points	The strong electrostatic forces of attraction between the cations and delocalised electrons require large amounts of heat energy to break.
Solid at room temperature (except mercury)	Room temperature is not high enough to break the strong electrostatic forces of attraction between the cations and delocalised electrons.
High density	The atoms are packed very closely together.
Conduct electricity	The delocalised electrons are free to move and carry electricity through the metal.
Conduct heat	The delocalised electrons move and carry heat through the metal.
Malleable and ductile	The atoms of each metal are all of the same type and size. If force is applied, the atoms can slide past each other into new positions without the metallic bonds breaking.

The structure and properties of solids

The particles in a solid are tightly packed in a fixed orderly arrangement, and this arrangement impacts on the **structure** of solids. The structure of the solids also depends on the type and strength of bonds that hold the particles together. These bonds also influence the properties of the elements and compounds. Solids can be divided into **four** groups based on their structure.

- **ionic** crystals
- **simple molecular** crystals
- **giant molecular** crystals
- **metallic** crystals (see 'Metallic bonding' above).

Ionic crystals

An **ionic crystal** is made of an **ionic lattice** in which strong electrostatic forces of attraction called **ionic bonds** hold the **cations** and **anions** together in a regular, repeating, three-dimensional arrangement. Ionic crystals are represented by **empirical formulae** or **formula units**.

Example 8

- **Sodium chloride**, empirical formula **NaCl**. Made of Na⁺ ions and Cl⁻ ions (see page 73).
- All other **ionic compounds**.

Simple molecular crystals

A **simple molecular crystal** is made of a **molecular lattice** in which weak forces of attraction called **intermolecular forces** hold **small molecules** together in a regular, three-dimensional arrangement. The atoms within each molecule are bonded together by strong covalent bonds. Simple molecular crystals are represented by **molecular formulae**.

Example 9

- **Ice**, molecular formula H_2O. Made of water molecules.
- **Dry ice**, molecular formula CO_2. Made of carbon dioxide molecules.
- **Phosphorus**, molecular formula P_4. Made of phosphorus molecules.
- **Sulfur**, molecular formula S_8. Made of sulfur molecules.
- **Iodine**, molecular formula I_2. Made of iodine molecules.
- **Glucose**, molecular formula $C_6H_{12}O_6$. Made of glucose molecules.

Table 5.5 *Distinguishing between ionic and simple molecular solids*

Property	Ionic solids	Simple molecular solids
Structure	Composed of **ions** held together by strong ionic bonds.	Composed of **molecules** with strong covalent bonds between the atoms in the molecules and weak intermolecular forces between molecules.
Melting point	**High** – the strong ionic bonds between the ions require large amounts of heat energy to break.	**Low** – the weak intermolecular forces between the molecules require little heat energy to break.
Solubility	Most are **soluble** in **water**, a polar solvent, but are insoluble in non-polar organic solvents such as kerosene, gasoline and tetrachloromethane.	Most are **soluble** in **non-polar organic solvents**, but are insoluble in water. Polar compounds are soluble in water, e.g. glucose.
Conductivity	**Do not** conduct electricity when **solid** – the ions are held together by strong ionic bonds and are not free to move. **Do** conduct electricity when **molten** (melted) or **dissolved in water** – the ionic bonds have broken and the ions are free to move and carry electricity.	**Do not** conduct electricity in any state – they do not have any charged particles which are free to move.

Giant molecular crystals

A **giant molecular crystal** is composed of a **giant molecular lattice** in which strong **covalent bonds** hold non-metal atoms together in a regular, three-dimensional arrangement throughout the lattice. Giant molecular crystals are represented by **empirical formulae**.

Example 10

- **Diamond**, empirical formula **C**. Made of carbon atoms.
- **Graphite**, empirical formula **C**. Made of carbon atoms.
- **Silicon dioxide**, silica, empirical formula **SiO₂**. Made of silicon and oxygen atoms.

Diamond and graphite are known as **allotropes** of carbon. Sulfur also exists as allotropes.

Allotropes are different structural forms of a single element in the same physical state.

- Allotropes have the same **chemical properties** because they are both composed of the **same** element.
- Allotropes have different **physical properties** because the atoms are **bonded differently**.

Allotropy is the existence of different structural forms of a single element in the same physical state.

Diamond

In **diamond**, each carbon atom is bonded covalently to **four** others, which are arranged in a **tetrahedron** around it (Figure 5.11). This creates a three-dimensional arrangement of carbon atoms throughout the crystal. In addition to the uses mentioned in Table 5.6, diamonds can be used to make jewellery.

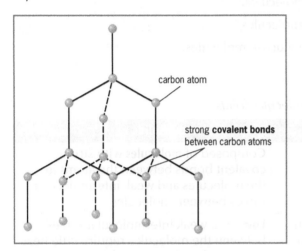

Figure 5.11 *The structure of diamond*

Figure 5.12 *Polished diamonds being used as jewellery*

Graphite

In **graphite**, each carbon atom is bonded covalently to **three** others to form **hexagonal rings** of atoms, which are bonded together to form **layers** (Figure 5.13). The layers have weak forces of attraction between them which hold them together. The fourth electron from each atom becomes **delocalised** and can move within the lattice.

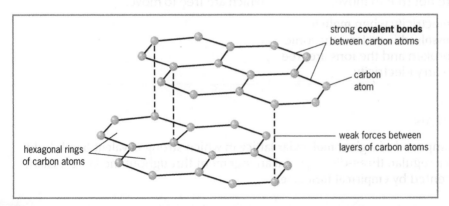

Figure 5.13 *The structure of graphite*

Table 5.6 *A comparison of the properties and uses of sodium chloride, diamond and graphite*

Property	Sodium chloride	Diamond	Graphite
Melting point	**Fairly high** (801 °C) – strong ionic bonds between the ions need a lot of heat energy to break.	**Very high** (3550 °C) – strong covalent bonds between the atoms need large amounts of heat energy to break.	**Very high** (3600 °C) – strong covalent bonds between the atoms need large amounts of heat energy to break. Used to make **crucibles** to hold molten metals.
Solubility in water	**Soluble** – the partial negative ends of polar water molecules attract the positive Na$^+$ ions and the partial positive ends attract the negative Cl$^-$ ions. This pulls the ions out of the lattice causing the crystal to dissolve.	**Insoluble** – polar water molecules do not attract the carbon atoms out of the lattice.	**Insoluble** – polar water molecules do not attract the carbon atoms out of the lattice.
Conductivity	**Only** conducts electricity when **molten** or **dissolved** in water – the ionic bonds have broken and the ions are free to move. **Does not** conduct electricity in the **solid** state – the ionic bonds hold the ions together so they cannot move.	**Does not** conduct electricity – all the valence electrons are shared between carbon atoms and none are free to move.	**Does** conduct electricity in the **solid** state – the fourth valence electron from each carbon atom is delocalised and free to move. Used to make **electrodes** for use in electrolysis.
Hardness	**Hard** – strong ionic bonds exist between the ions throughout the structure. **Brittle** – if pressure is applied, the layers of ions are displaced slightly and ions with the same charges then repel each other and break the lattice apart.	**Extremely hard** – strong covalent bonds exist between the carbon atoms throughout the structure. Used in the tips of **cutting tools** and **drill bits**.	**Soft and flaky** – weak forces exist between the layers of carbon atoms allowing the layers to flake off. Used as the 'lead' in pencils – the layers slip off and leave dark marks on the paper.
Lubricating power	**None** – the ions are in layers, but ionic bonds hold the layers together so they cannot slide over each other.	**None** – the atoms are bonded covalently throughout the structure and cannot slide over each other.	**Extremely good** – weak forces between the layers of atoms allow the layers to slide over each other. Used as a **lubricant**.

Other examples of allotropes are non-metals such as sulfur, phosphorous, oxygen, nitrogen and silicon.

Recalling facts

1 What is the empirical formula of this compound: P_4O_{10}?

   a P_4O_{10}

   b P_2O_5

   c P_8O_{20}

   d P_4O_{20}

2 Which pair of elements forms bonds in a compound by transferring electrons?

   a chlorine and carbon

   b sulfur and oxygen

   c chlorine and sulfur

   d bromine and lithium

3 Which one of the solids listed below contains covalent bonds?

   a copper

   b diamond

   c barium chloride

   d sodium oxide

4 Which of the following conducts electricity?

   a diamond

   b solid sodium chloride

   c molten sodium chloride

   d methane

5 Which of these is NOT a use of graphite?

   a crucibles

   b lubricant

   c drill bit

   d electrode

6 Which is NOT an example of a simple molecular crystal?

   a iodine

   b ice

   c glucose

   d sodium chloride

7 Which of the following is NOT a polar molecule?

   a water

   b carbon dioxide

   c ethanol

   d ammonia

8 What is the formula of a compound formed between elements Y and Z, with atomic numbers 11 and 17?

a YZ

b YZ_7

c Y_7Z

d $Y_{17}Z_{11}$

9 Aluminium is in the same group of the periodic table as boron. The formula for its sulfate is:

a $AlSO_4$

b Al_2SO_4

c $Al(SO_4)_3$

d $Al_2(SO_4)_3$

10 Metals have all the properties listed below except:

a they conduct heat and electricity.

b they have high melting points.

c they are ductile.

d they possess weak bonds.

11 Define the following terms giving an example of each:

a cations

b anions

c molecular formula

d structural formula

e empirical formula

12 Solids can be divided into four groups based on their structure. Name the four groups. State four differences between an ionic solid and a simple molecular solid.

13 Explain the difference between a polar and a non-polar molecule. Give three examples of each.

Applying facts

14 Write a chemical formula for each of the following:

a calcium hydride

b silver(I) oxide

c barium fluoride

d phosphorus(V) oxide

e iron(III) nitride

f lead(IV) oxide

g ammonium sulfate

h zinc hydrogen carbonate

15 Draw dot and cross diagrams for the following compounds and indicate the type of bonding in each.

   a boron trifluoride

   b carbon monoxide

   c copper(I) sulfide

   d iodine pentafluoride

   e methane

   f lithium oxide

   g aluminium oxide

16 **a** What is meant by the term allotrope? Give two examples of allotropes.

   b Draw the structure of diamond and graphite.

   c Using your diagrams explain why graphite conducts electricity and diamond does not.

   d Using your diagrams, explain why diamond can be used as a bit when drilling for oil.

   e Give two other uses of graphite and diamond.

Analysing data

17 **a** The diagram represents the element zinc which is a metal.

     i What type of bonding occurs in zinc?

     ii Using the diagram, explain the type of bonding in part **i**.

     iii Using the structure given, explain why zinc has a high melting point.

     iv Using the structure, explain why zinc is a good conductor of heat.

     v State two other properties of zinc.

   b Zinc reacts with bromine to produce zinc bromide.

     i Write the chemical formulae for the elements and product in part **b**.

     ii What type of bond is formed when the zinc and bromine react? Explain your answer.

     iii What type of structure is zinc bromide?

18 The electronic configuration of 8 elements is given in the table.

Element	Electronic configuration
A	2,1
B	2,7
C	2,8,2
D	2,8,4
E	2,8,6

Element	Electronic configuration
F	2,8,8
G	2,8,8,1
H	2,8,8,2

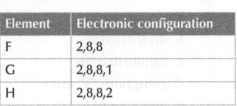

a List all the elements which are metals. Explain why these elements are metals.

b List the elements which are non-metals. Explain why these elements are non-metals.

c Which element(s) is a metalloid?

d What do you mean by the term 'metalloid'?

e Which element(s) belong to the noble gases?

f Which element(s) belong to Group 1 of the periodic table?

g Choose two elements that would bond to give a covalent compound. Draw a dot and cross diagram to illustrate this covalent compound.

h Choose two elements that would bond to give an ionic compound. Draw a dot and cross diagram to illustrate this ionic compound.

6 Chemical equations

Learning objectives

- Construct **balanced chemical equations**, with **state symbols**.
- Construct **ionic equations**, with **state symbols**.

Chemists working in the chemical industry have to do calculations to determine how much raw material is necessary to produce a determined amount of product. For example, how much nitrogen and hydrogen are necessary to manufacture 1000 tonnes of ammonia?

How do you think a chemist would do these calculations? They would have to use **chemical formulae** and **equations**.

The simplest way of representing a chemical reaction is in the form of a **word equation**. It displays the names of the substances that react (the **reactants**) with those new substances that are produced (the **products**).

$$\text{reactants} \longrightarrow \text{products}$$

It should be noted that a word equation only gives some information about a chemical reaction, that is, the chemical substances involved in the reaction.

For example:

$$\text{aluminium} + \text{sulfuric acid} \longrightarrow \text{aluminium sulfate} + \text{hydrogen}$$

A more useful form is to write the equation as a chemical equation using chemical formulae.

*A **chemical equation** uses symbols and chemical formulae instead of words to describe a chemical reaction.*

Reactants and products are shown using symbols and formulae. **Reactants**, separated by plus signs, are shown on the **left**. **Products**, also separated by plus signs, are shown on the **right**. The reactants and products are separated by an **arrow** and any **conditions** required for the reaction, such as a particular temperature, catalyst or pressure, may be given on the arrow. A physical state must be represented by the state symbol after the formulae of each reactant and product. The state symbols are represented by (s) – solid, (l) – liquid, (g) – gas and (aq) – aqueous solution. An aqueous solution is one in which water is the solvent.

The earlier word equation written as a chemical equation is:

$$Al(s) + H_2SO_4(aq) \longrightarrow Al_2(SO_4)_3(aq) + H_2(g)$$

The chemical equation can be read as follows:

solid aluminium reacts with aqueous sulfuric acid to produce aqueous aluminium sulfate and hydrogen gas. (Note the equation is not balanced).

Now you can see how much more information is obtained from a chemical equation than a word equation.

The Law of Conservation of Matter governs chemical reactions.

*The **Law of Conservation of Matter** states that the total mass of all the products of a chemical reaction is equal to the total mass of all the reactants.*

In other words, the Law of Conservation of Matter states that matter is neither created nor destroyed, but rearranged. In a chemical reaction all the atoms that make up the reactants are rearranged to form the products. Therefore, the exact same number and type of atoms need to be present on both sides of the equation.

During a chemical reaction, some bonds between atoms of the reactants are broken and new ones are formed between atoms to form products. During the reaction, atoms do not disappear nor are they changed into atoms of another element, but simply rearranged to form products. Therefore, when a chemical equation is written this law must **not** be ignored.

Writing balanced equations

When writing a chemical equation, it must **balance** so that the **total number** of atoms of **each** element on each side of the arrow is the **same**. When the reactants and products are written for some simple reactions the equations are balanced, while in others they have to be balanced.

$$Fe(s) + S(s) \longrightarrow FeS(s)$$

The equation above is balanced by simply converting it from the word equation to the chemical equation.

The following steps can be used to write a balanced chemical equation:

Step 1: Ensure that you know what the reactants and products are and write out a **word equation**. List all the reactants on the left of the arrow, and all the products on the right.

Step 2: From the word equation write the equation using the **chemical formulae** of the elements and compounds. The elements in their free state must be represented by the atomic symbol of the element, for example, K, Ca, C, Pb. The molecular formula must be written for gases. Some common gases exist as diatomic molecules and hence these must be used, for example, H_2, O_2, N_2, F_2, Cl_2, Br_2 and I_2.

Step 3: Show the **physical state** of each of the reactants and product by placing a **state symbol (s)**, **(l)**, **(g)** and **(aq)** after each formula.

Step 4: Write down the **total number of atoms** of each element in the reactants and in the products.

Step 5: Balance the equation by inserting **simple whole numbers** (or '**coefficients**') in front of the formulae to alter the **proportions** of the reactants and products. Never alter the **formulae**.

Let us look at some reactions to show how to write chemical equations.

Example 1

The reaction between aluminium metal and iodine to produce aluminium iodide.

Step 1: Restate the sentence and write out as a word equation:

$$\text{aluminium} + \text{iodine} \longrightarrow \text{aluminium iodide}$$

Step 2: Write the **chemical formula** for each reactant and product:

$$Al + I_2 \longrightarrow AlI_3$$

Step 3: Show the **physical state** of each reactant and product by placing a **state symbol** after each formula:

$$Al(s) + I_2(s) \longrightarrow AlI_3(s)$$

Step 4: Write down the **total number atoms** of each element in the **reactants** and in the **products**:

$$Al(s) + I_2(s) \longrightarrow AlI_3(s)$$

reactants	products
Al = 1	Al = 1
I = 2	I = 3

Step 5: **Balance** the equation. Do this by placing **simple whole numbers** (or **'coefficients'**) in front of formulae to alter the **proportions** of the reactants and products. **Never alter formulae:**

I does not balance. **Balance** by placing a 3 in front of the I_2 and a 2 in front of the AlI_3:

$$Al(s) + 3I_2(s) \longrightarrow 2AlI_3(s)$$

reactants	products
Al = 1	Al = ~~1~~ 2
I = ~~2~~ 6	I = ~~3~~ 6

Al does not balance. Balance by placing a 2 in front of the Al:

$$2Al(s) + 3I_2(s) \longrightarrow 2AlI_3(s)$$

reactants	products
Al = ~~1~~ 2	Al = 2
I = 6	I = 6

The equation now **balances.**

Example 2

The reaction between potassium metal and water to produce potassium hydroxide and hydrogen gas.

Step 1: potassium + water $\longrightarrow$ potassium hydroxide + hydrogen

Step 2: $K + H_2O \longrightarrow KOH + H_2$

Step 3: $K(s) + H_2O(l) \longrightarrow KOH(aq) + H_2(g)$

Step 4: $K(s) + H_2O(l) \longrightarrow KOH(aq) + H_2(g)$

Reactants	Products
K = 1	K = 1
O = 1	O = 1
H = 2	H = 1 + 2 = 3

Step 5: H does not balance. **Balance** by placing a **2** in front of H_2O and a **2** in front of **KOH**:

$$K(s) + 2H_2O(l) \longrightarrow 2KOH(aq) + H_2(g)$$

Reactants	Products
K = 1	K = ~~1~~ 2
O = ~~1~~ 2	O = ~~1~~ 2
H = ~~2~~ 4	H = ~~3~~ 2 + 2 = 4

K now does not balance. **Balance** by placing a **2** in front of **K**:

$$2K(s) + 2H_2O(l) \longrightarrow 2KOH(aq) + H_2(g)$$

Reactants	Products
K = ~~1~~ 2	K = 2
O = 2	O = 2
H = 4	H = 4

The equation now **balances.**

Example 3

Lead(II) nitrate and potassium iodide react to produce lead(II) iodide and potassium nitrate.

Step 1: lead(II) nitrate + potassium iodide $\longrightarrow$ lead(II) iodide + potassium nitrate

Step 2: $Pb(NO_3)_2 + KI \longrightarrow PbI_2 + KNO_3$

Step 3: $Pb(NO_3)_2(aq) + KI(aq) \longrightarrow PbI_2(s) + KNO_3(aq)$

Step 4: $Pb(NO_3)_2(aq) + KI(aq) \longrightarrow PbI_2(s) + KNO_3(aq)$

Reactants	Products
Pb = 1	Pb = 1
N = 2	N = 1
O = 6	O = 3
K = 1	K = 1
I = 1	I = 2

Step 5: **O, N and I do not balance. Balance by placing a 2 in front of KI and KNO₃:**

$$Pb(NO_3)_2(aq) + 2KI(aq) \longrightarrow PbI_2(s) + 2KNO_3(aq)$$

Reactants	Products
Pb = 1	Pb = 1
N = 2	N = ̶1̶ 2
O = 6	O = ̶3̶ 6
K = ̶1̶ 2	K = ̶1̶ 2
I = ̶1̶ 2	I = 2

The equation now **balances**.

Useful tips for writing and balancing equations

- For an element in its **free state**, if it is one of the seven common elements that exist as **diatomic molecules**, use its **formula** (H_2, N_2, O_2, F_2, Cl_2, Br_2 and I_2). For any other element in its free state, use its **atomic symbol**.
- Metals should be balanced first.
- Balance the elements in the product **immediately after** the arrow first.
- Balance any **polyatomic** ion which appears unchanged from one side to the other as a unit. For example, if SO_4^{2-} appears on both sides, consider it as a single unit.
- If hydrogen or oxygen is present in any compound, balance **hydrogen** second from last and balance **oxygen** last.
- Leave elements in their **free state** until the very last to balance, e.g. Mg, Cu, Cl_2, H_2, O_2.
- Check the coefficients to make sure they are in the **lowest** possible ratio.

Example 4

Balance the following equation:

$$Mg(s) + H_3PO_4(aq) \longrightarrow Mg_3(PO_4)_2(aq) + H_2(g)$$

Reactants	Products
Mg = 1	Mg = 3
H = 3	H = 2
PO$_4$ = 1	PO$_4$ = 2

Start with product immediately after the arrow. **Mg** does not balance. **Balance** by placing a **3** in front of the **Mg**. **PO$_4$** does not balance. **Balance** by placing a **2** in front of the **H$_3$PO$_4$**:

$$3Mg(s) + 2H_3PO_4(aq) \longrightarrow Mg_3(PO_4)_2(aq) + H_2(g)$$

Reactants	Products
Mg = $\cancel{1}$ 3	Mg = 3
H = $\cancel{2}$ 6	H = 2
PO$_4$ = $\cancel{1}$ 2	PO$_4$ = 2

H now does not balance. **Balance** by placing a **3** in front of the **H$_2$**:

$$3Mg(s) + 2H_3PO_4(aq) \longrightarrow Mg_3(PO_4)_2(aq) + 3H_2(g)$$

Reactants	Products
Mg = $\cancel{1}$ 3	Mg = 3
H = $\cancel{2}$ 6	H = $\cancel{2}$ 6
PO$_4$ = $\cancel{1}$ 2	PO$_4$ = 2

The equation is now **balanced**.

To determine state symbols of ionic compounds

In equations, if the compound is **soluble**, it would usually be given the state symbol **(aq)**. If it is **insoluble** it would always be given the state symbol **(s)**. Most **ionic compounds** *are* **soluble** in water; however, some are insoluble. It is extremely important to learn the rules to determine the solubility of ionic compounds. These rules are given in Tables 6.1 and 6.2.

Table 6.1 *Common ionic compounds which are soluble in water*

Compounds	Solubility in water	Exceptions
Potassium, sodium and **ammonium** compounds	Soluble	None
Nitrates	Soluble	None
Chlorides	Soluble	**Silver chloride (AgCl)** is insoluble.
		Lead(II) chloride (PbCl$_2$) is insoluble in cold water but moderately soluble in hot water.
Sulfates	Soluble	**Lead(II) sulfate (PbSO$_4$)** and **barium sulfate (BaSO$_4$)** are insoluble.
		Calcium sulfate (CaSO$_4$) is slightly soluble.
Ethanoates	Soluble	None
Hydrogencarbonates	Soluble	None

Table 6.2 *Common ionic compounds which are insoluble in water*

Compounds	Solubility in water	Exceptions
Carbonates	Insoluble	Potassium carbonate (K_2CO_3), sodium carbonate (Na_2CO_3) and ammonium carbonate (($NH_4)_2CO_3$) are soluble.
Phosphates	Insoluble	Potassium phosphate (K_3PO_4), sodium phosphate (Na_3PO_4) and ammonium phosphate (($NH_4)_3PO_4$) are soluble.
Hydroxides	Insoluble	Potassium hydroxide (KOH), sodium hydroxide (NaOH) and ammonium hydroxide (NH_4OH) are soluble. Calcium hydroxide ($Ca(OH)_2$) is slightly soluble.
Metal oxides	Insoluble	Potassium oxide (K_2O), sodium oxide (Na_2O) and calcium oxide (CaO) react with water to form the equivalent soluble hydroxides.

Ionic equations

Ionic equations show only the atoms or ions which **change** during a reaction. These are the atoms or ions which actually **take part** in the reaction and include the following:

- Two ions in solution may join to form a **precipitate** (an insoluble compound within the solution).
- Two ions may form a **covalent** compound (a compound composed of molecules).
- An ion may be **discharged** (converted to an atom).
- An atom of an element in its free state may be **ionised** (converted to an ion).

Ions which remain **unchanged** during a reaction are known as **spectator ions** and are not included in an ionic equation. Spectator ions remain **in solution** during the reaction. Ionic equations are useful to represent redox reactions, double displacement reactions, acid–base neutralisation reactions, displacement of halogens and displacement of metals.

Writing ionic equations

The four steps given below should be followed when writing ionic equations.

Step 1: Write the **balanced equation** for the reaction showing state symbols for each of the reactants and products.

Step 2: Rewrite the equation showing any **ions** in **solution** as individual ions. In other words, the aqueous ionic compounds. That is, all strong electrolytes are to be written in ionic form. Weak electrolytes, elements and covalent compounds must be written as they appear in step 1. Also make sure that the number of each type of atom and/or polyatomic ions are equal in number on both sides of the equation.

Step 3: Delete the ions which remain **unchanged**, that is, the spectator ions.

Step 4: Rewrite the **ionic equation** showing the ions which **change**, ensuring that only the ions which have undergone change are included and the net charges on both sides of the equation are equal. The coefficients must be in the simplest ratio, and this is achieved by cancelling until the lowest simple ratio is achieved.

Example 5

The reaction between barium nitrate and sodium carbonate

Step 1: Write the **balanced equation** for the reaction:

$$Ba(NO_3)_2(aq) + Na_2CO_3(aq) \longrightarrow BaCO_3(s) + 2NaNO_3(aq)$$

Step 2: Rewrite the equation showing any **ions** in **solution** as individual ions:

$$Ba^{2+}(aq) + 2NO_3^-(aq) + 2Na^+(aq) + CO_3^{2-}(aq) \longrightarrow BaCO_3(s) + 2Na^+(aq) + 2NO_3^-(aq)$$

Step 3: Delete the **Na⁺(aq)** and **NO₃⁻(aq)** ions:

$$Ba^{2+}(aq) + \cancel{2NO_3^-(aq)} + \cancel{2Na^+(aq)} + CO_3^{2-}(aq) \longrightarrow BaCO_3(s) + \cancel{2Na^+(aq)} + \cancel{2NO_3^-(aq)}$$

Step 4: Ionic equation:

$$Ba^{2+}(aq) + CO_3^{2-}(aq) \longrightarrow BaCO_3(s)$$

Example 6

Reaction between silver nitrate and barium chloride

Step 1: $2AgNO_3(aq) + BaCl_2(aq) \longrightarrow 2AgCl(s) + Ba(NO_3)_2(aq)$

Step 2: $2Ag^{2+}(aq) + 2NO_3^-(aq) + Ba^{2+}(aq) + 2Cl^-(aq) \longrightarrow 2AgCl(s) + Ba^{2+}(aq) + 2NO_3^-(aq)$

Step 3: Delete the **Ba²⁺(aq)** and **NO₃⁻(aq)**

$$2Ag^{2+}(aq) + \cancel{2NO_3^-(aq)} + \cancel{Ba^{2+}(aq)} + 2Cl^-(aq) \longrightarrow 2AgCl(s) + \cancel{Ba^{2+}(aq)} + \cancel{2NO_3^-(aq)}$$

Step 4: $2Ag^{2+}(aq) + 2Cl^-(aq) \longrightarrow 2AgCl(s)$

Note If the coefficients are not in the lowest ratio, cancel to the **lowest possible ratio**:

$$2Ag^{2+}(aq) + 2Cl^-(aq) \longrightarrow 2AgCl(s)$$

This cancels to:

$$Ag^{2+}(aq) + Cl^-(aq) \longrightarrow AgCl(s)$$

Recalling facts

1 The reactants in a chemical equation are:

   a on the right-hand side of the arrow

   b on the left-hand side of the arrow

   c unbalanced

   d separated by a minus sign

2 In an equation the symbol (s) means:

   a aqueous

   b insoluble

   c soluble

   d salt

3 All sulfates are soluble except:

    a potassium sulfate

    b sodium sulfate

    c barium sulfate

    d ammonium sulfate

4 Which of the following phosphates is insoluble?

    a potassium phosphate

    b iron(III) phosphate

    c sodium phosphate

    d ammonium phosphate

5 Which is not a step in writing a balanced equation?

    a Write the word equation.

    b Write the state symbol after each formula.

    c Alter the chemical formula when balancing the equation.

    d Use simple whole numbers in front of the formula when balancing the equation.

6 Ionic equations show:

    a the ions which join to form precipitate

    b the ions which form covalent bonds

    c spectator ions

    d an ion which may be discharged

7 Which of the following ionic equations is correctly written?

    a $Ag^+(aq) + Cl^-(aq) \longrightarrow AgCl(s)$

    b $CO_3^{2-}(aq) + 2H^+(aq) \longrightarrow CO_2(g) + H_2O(l)$

    c $Cu^{2+}(aq) + Fe(s) \longrightarrow Fe^{3+}(aq) + Cu(s)$

    d $OH^-(aq) + H^+(aq) \longrightarrow H_2O(l)$

Applying facts

8 Balance EACH of the following equations, giving the state symbol of the compounds:

    a $Al(\ ) + O_2(\ ) \longrightarrow Al_2O_3(\ )$

    b $Fe(\ ) + O_2(\ ) \longrightarrow Fe_2O_3(\ )$

    c $Al(\ ) + HCl(\ ) \longrightarrow AlCl_3(\ ) + H_2(\ )$

    d $C_4H_{10}O(\ ) + O_2(\ ) \longrightarrow CO_2(\ ) + H_2O(\ )$

    e $Pb(NO_3)_4(\ ) + (NH_4)_2SO_4(\ ) \longrightarrow NH_4NO_3(\ ) + Pb_2(SO_4)_4(\ )$

9 Write a balanced chemical equation with state symbols for EACH of the following reactions:

a the reaction between silver nitrate and sodium carbonate to produce sodium nitrate and silver carbonate

b the reaction between ammonium carbonate and calcium chloride to form ammonium chloride and calcium carbonate

c the reaction between sodium phosphate and silver nitrate to form sodium nitrate and silver phosphate

d the reaction between sodium phosphate and calcium chloride to form calcium phosphate and sodium chloride

e the reaction between copper and sulfuric acid to form copper(II) sulfate and water and sulfur dioxide

10 Write the ionic equation stating the spectator ions for the reactions in questions 8e, and 9a to 9e.

11 State whether EACH of the following compounds is soluble or insoluble:

a lead(II) oxide

b iron(III) bromide

c silver chloride

d magnesium hydroxide

e ammonium iodide

7 Types of chemical reaction

Learning objectives

- Differentiate between the types of **chemical reactions**.
- Predict the **products** of a chemical reaction.
- Construct **balanced equations** to represent the different types of chemical reactions.

Chemical reactions are continuously occurring within and around us. These chemical reactions may occur slowly or quickly. Respiration and photosynthesis are chemical reactions that occur within plants and animals. Rusting, combustion and the natural decomposition of waste involve chemical reactions that occur in our surroundings. Humans create and use many chemical reactions in the manufacture of products and in generating energy. These products can be used as medicine, food and energy.

When a chemical reaction occurs, existing bonds in the molecules of reactants are broken and their atoms reorganised to form new bonds, which results in the creation of new chemical products. When a chemical reaction occurs, one or more of the following are observed: a colour change, gas is given off, a temperature change, a change in state, energy changes, and the formation of a precipitate.

As mentioned, there are many different reactions occurring around us and chemists have classified these chemical reactions into **seven** main types. It is important to classify chemical reactions so that chemists can predict the products of chemical reactions and therefore design reactions to produce vital products.

The **seven** main types of reactions are:

- synthesis
- decomposition
- single displacement
- ionic precipitation
- oxidation–reduction
- neutralisation
- reversible.

Synthesis reactions

During a **synthesis reaction**, two or more substances combine chemically to produce a **single product**:

$$A + B \longrightarrow AB$$

The letters on the left-hand side of the general equation, A and B represent the reactants which unite to synthesise a single product AB on the right-hand side of the arrow. Examples of synthesis reactions are:

- when two elements combine to synthesise a compound

$$4Fe(s) + 3O_2(g) \longrightarrow 2Fe_2O_3(s)$$

- when an element and a compound combine to synthesise a compound

$$2CO(g) + O_2(g) \longrightarrow 2CO_2(g)$$

- when two compounds combine to synthesise a new compound

$$MgO(s) + CO_2(g) \longrightarrow MgCO_3(s)$$

Decomposition reactions

During a **decomposition reaction**, a single reactant is **broken down** into two or more products. This can be carried out by heating the compound (**thermal decomposition**), by exposing the compound to light (**photolysis**), or by passing an electric current through the compound in the liquid state or dissolved in aqueous solution (**electrolysis**). The reacting conditions which are required must be written above the arrow as seen in the examples below.

$$AB \longrightarrow A + B$$

- Thermal decomposition:

$$2Fe(OH)_3(s) \xrightarrow{\text{heat}} Fe_2O_3(s) + 3H_2O(g)$$

- Electrolytic decomposition:

$$2NaCl \xrightarrow{\text{electricity}} 2Na + Cl_2$$

- Photolytic decomposition:

$$2AgBr(s) \xrightarrow{\text{sunlight}} 2Ag(s) + Br_2(g)$$

light yellow   grey

Single displacement reactions

During a **single displacement reaction** (see Chapter 11, page 179), an element in its **free** (or **unbonded**) **state** takes the place of (displaces) another element in the compound. A **more reactive** element always displaces a less reactive element. There are two types:

- A **metal** may displace the hydrogen from an acid or another less reactive metal from a compound.

$$A + BY \longrightarrow AY + B$$

For example:
$$2Al(s) + 6HCl(aq) \longrightarrow 2AlCl_3(aq) + 3H_2(g)$$
$$2Al(s) + 6H^+(aq) \longrightarrow 2Al^{3+}(aq) + 3H_2(g)$$
$$Mg(s) + Cu(NO_3)_2(aq) \longrightarrow Mg(NO_3)_2(aq) + Cu(s)$$
$$Mg(s) + Cu^{2+}(aq) \longrightarrow Mg^{2+}(aq) + Cu(s)$$

Aluminium is above hydrogen in the reactivity series (see page 295) and magnesium is more reactive than copper.

- A **more reactive non-metal** may displace another less reactive non-metal from a compound.

$$X + AY \longrightarrow AX + Y$$

For example:
$$Cl_2(g) + 2NaBr(aq) \longrightarrow 2NaCl(aq) + Br_2(aq)$$
$$Cl_2(s) + 2Br^-(aq) \longrightarrow 2Cl^-(aq) + Br_2(aq)$$

Chlorine is more reactive than bromine (see Chapter 4, p. 58).

Ionic precipitation reactions

During an **ionic precipitation** reaction, two compounds in solution **exchange ions** to form an **insoluble precipitate** and another soluble compound. These reactions are sometimes called **double displacement reactions.**

$$AX + BY \longrightarrow AY + BX$$

For example:

$FeSO_4(aq)$	$+$	$2NaOH(aq)$	$\longrightarrow$		$Fe(OH)_2(s) + Na_2SO_4(aq)$
$Fe^{2+}(aq)$	$+$	$2OH^-(aq)$	$\longrightarrow$		$Fe(OH)_2(s)$
green solution		colourless solution			green precipitate
$KCl(aq)$	$+$	$AgNO_3(aq)$	$\longrightarrow$		$KNO_3(aq) + AgCl(s)$
$Cl^-(aq)$	$+$	$Ag^+(aq)$	$\longrightarrow$		$AgCl(s)$
colourless solution		colourless solution			white precipitate

Oxidation–reduction reactions

During an **oxidation–reduction reaction**, one reactant is **oxidised** and the other is **reduced**. Oxidation and reduction are reactions in which electrons are gained or lost. These reactions are also called **redox reactions** (see Chapter 10, page 163).

For example:

$$H_2(g) + F_2(g) \longrightarrow 2HF(g)$$

$$Zn(s) + CuSO_4(aq) \longrightarrow ZnSO_4(aq) + Cu(s)$$

(see Chapter 19, page 296, displacement of metals)

Neutralisation reactions

During **neutralisation reactions**, a **base** reacts with an **acid** to produce a salt and water (see page 150). Heat is also produced in this reaction.

For example:

$$LiOH(aq) + HNO_3(aq) \longrightarrow LiNO_3(aq) + H_2O(l)$$

$$OH^-(aq) + H^+(aq) \longrightarrow H_2O(l)$$

$$HBr(aq) + KOH(aq) \longrightarrow KBr(aq) + H_2O(l)$$

$$OH^-(aq) + H^+(aq) \longrightarrow H_2O(l)$$

Reversible reactions

During a **reversible reaction**, the direction of the chemical change can be easily **reversed**. The products can react to produce the original reactants again. To indicate that the reaction is reversible $\rightleftharpoons$ is used.

$$A + B \rightleftharpoons C + D$$

For example:

$$N_2(g) + 3H_2(g) \rightleftharpoons 2NH_3(g)$$

The equation above shows the production of ammonia. This reaction occurs in a closed vessel. As the reaction proceeds, only the product ammonia is formed. As the quantity of the ammonia (the product) increases, some of the ammonia breaks down to produce the reactants nitrogen and hydrogen. The reaction can therefore occur in both directions and so is **reversible**.

For example: $NH_4Cl(s) \rightleftharpoons NH_3(g) + HCl(g)$

If ammonium chloride is **heated**, it decomposes into ammonia gas and hydrogen chloride gas:

$$NH_4Cl(s) \longrightarrow NH_3(g) + HCl(g)$$

If the ammonia gas and hydrogen chloride gas are **cooled**, or mixed at room temperature, they react to form ammonium chloride:

$$NH_3(g) + HCl(g) \longrightarrow NH_4Cl(s)$$

The reaction is, therefore, **reversible**.

Another example of a reversible reaction is the formation of esters (see page 270). An example is butanoic acid and methanol:

$$C_3H_7COOH(aq) + CH_3OH(aq) \rightleftharpoons C_3H_7COOCH_3(aq) + H_2O(l)$$

In many reversible reactions, the reaction contains a **mixture** of reactants and products because it proceeds in **both directions** at the same time. Most reactions can only proceed in one direction, so they are not reversible.

Recalling facts

1   In what type of reaction is the reactivity series used to predict the products formed?

   a decomposition reaction

   b ionic precipitation

   c single displacement

   d synthesis reaction

2   Ions are exchanged in solutions in what type of reaction?

   a redox reaction

   b reversible reaction

   c synthesis reaction

   d ionic precipitation

3   When water and a salt is produced the reaction is said to be:

   a neutralisation

   b ionic precipitation

   c reversible

   d decomposition

4   When two or more substances combine to form a single product, what type of reaction occurs?

   a single displacement

   b synthesis

   c neutralisation

   d all of the above

5 A decomposition reaction involves:

a heating a compound

b passing an electric current through a solid substance

c adding an acid to a base

d replacing a less reactive metal with a more reaction metal

6 A reaction in which a soluble compound and an insoluble compound are formed after two aqueous compounds react is called:

a synthesis

b ionic precipitation

c single displacement

d decomposition

7 $H_2O_2(aq) \longrightarrow H_2O(g) + O_2(g)$
represents what type of chemical reaction?

a synthesis

b decomposition

c single displacement

d redox

8 List the seven different types of chemical reactions and give a brief description of each.

9 Write the generic form of the following chemical reaction:

a synthesis

b single displacement

c ionic displacement

Applying facts

10 Complete the following chemical equations and classify EACH of the reactions.

a $2Na(s) + Cl_2(g) \longrightarrow$

b $HCl(aq) + NaOH(aq) \longrightarrow$

c $Zn(s) + 2HCl(aq) \longrightarrow$

Analysing data

11 Write balanced equations with state symbols and where applicable ionic equations and classify EACH of the following reactions:

a When carbonic acid (H_2CO_3) is heated it produces water and carbon dioxide.

b Barium chloride reacting with magnesium sulfate to form magnesium chloride and barium sulfate.

c The reaction between acetic acid (CH_3COOH) and sodium hydrogencarbonate ($NaHCO_3$) to produce sodium acetate (CH_3COONa), carbon dioxide and water.

d Potassium chloride reacts with oxygen to produce $KClO_3$.

e Magnesium reacting with water to produce magnesium hydroxide and hydrogen gas.

f Hydrogen is manufactured in a closed vessel by reacting carbon and steam. If the temperature is increased more hydrogen is produced, whereas if the temperature is decreased there would be more carbon and steam.

8 The mole concept

Learning objectives

- Define the terms **relative atomic mass**, **relative molecular mass** and **relative formula mass**.
- Perform calculations to find **relative molecular** and **formula mass**.
- Define the terms **mole** and **molar mass**.
- Give **Avogadro's constant**.
- Quantify numbers of atoms, molecules or ions in moles.
- Perform calculations using molar mass to find the amounts of moles and the **mass of a substance**.
- State **Avogadro's law**.
- Define **molar volume**.
- Perform calculations involving gases using Avogadro's law and molar volume.

Atoms, molecules and formula units (see Chapter 5, page 65) are extremely small and cannot be counted directly. The **mole** is the **unit of amount** used in Chemistry to provide a link between atoms, molecules or formula units and the amount of chemical substances that can be worked with in the laboratory. The **mole** represents a **specific number** of particles (atoms, molecules and formula units), just as a pair, dozen or gross represent specific numbers of objects. The mole represents a very large number and for this reason it is used to represent particles such as atoms, molecules and formula units.

Relative atomic, molecular and formula masses

Because the mass of atoms is extremely small, **relative atomic mass** is used to **compare** their masses.

A carbon-12 atom has been assigned a mass of **12.00 atomic mass units** or **amu**. This means that 1/12th the mass of a carbon-12 atom has a mass of **1.00 amu**. Relative atomic mass **compares** the masses of atoms to this value.

*Relative atomic mass (A_r) is the average mass of **one atom of an element** compared to one-twelfth the mass of an atom of carbon-12.*

The word 'average' is used in the definition because relative atomic mass takes into account the relative abundance of each **isotope**. Relative atomic mass has **no units** because it is a comparative value.

The masses of covalent and ionic compounds are also compared to the carbon-12 atom:

- The term **relative molecular mass** is used when referring to **covalently bonded** elements or compounds.

*Relative molecular mass (M_r) is the average mass of **one molecule of an element or compound** compared to one-twelfth the mass of an atom of carbon-12.*

- The term **relative formula mass** is used when referring to **ionic compounds**.

*Relative formula mass is the average mass of **one formula unit of an ionic compound** compared to one-twelfth the mass of an atom of carbon-12.*

Calculating relative atomic, molecular and formula masses

The **relative atomic mass** of each element, to the nearest whole number, can be found in the **periodic table** on page 53. Using relative atomic mass, we can calculate the relative masses of ionic compounds and molecules.

Relative molecular mass and **relative formula mass** are calculated by **adding** together the relative atomic masses of all the elements present in the compound.

Example 1

Relative atomic masses:

- Magnesium, **Mg = 24**
- Potassium, **K = 39**
- Copper, **Cu = 64**
- Zinc, **Zn = 65**
- Iodine, **I = 127**
- Lead, **Pb = 207**

Relative molecular masses:

- Nitrogen, **N$_2$**

  N$_2$ consists of two N atoms.

  ∴ relative molecular mass of N$_2$ = (2 × 14) = **28**

- Carbon dioxide, **CO$_2$**

  CO$_2$ consists of one C atom and two O atoms.

  ∴ relative molecular mass of CO$_2$ = 12 + (2 × 16) = **44**

- Perchloric acid, **HClO$_4$**

  HClO$_4$ consists of one H, one Cl and four O atoms.

  ∴ relative molecular mass of HClO$_4$ = 1 + 35.5 + (4 × 16) = **100.5**

- Phosphorus tribromide, **PBr$_3$**

  PBr$_3$ consists of one P atom and three Br atoms.

  ∴ relative molecular mass of PBr$_3$ = 31 + (3 × 80) = **271**

- Sucrose, **C$_{12}$H$_{22}$O$_{11}$**

  Relative molecular mass of C$_{12}$H$_{22}$O$_{11}$ = (12 × 12) + (22 × 1) + (11 × 16) = **342**

Relative formula masses:

- Potassium nitrate, **KNO$_3$**

  Relative formula mass of KNO$_3$ = 39 + 14 + (3 × 16) = **101**

- Calcium bromide, **CaBr$_2$**

  Relative formula mass of CaBr$_2$ = 40 + (2 × 80) = **200**

- Iron(III) sulfate, **Fe$_2$(SO$_4$)$_3$**

  Relative formula mass of Fe$_2$(SO$_4$)$_3$ = (2 × 56) + (3 × 32) + (4 × 3 × 16) = **400**

The mole

In our daily routine we might purchase a pair of shoes, a dozen red roses, or a ream of copying paper. Terms like a pair, a dozen and a ream are standard terms that everyone understands and can associate with a specific number. A pair refers to 2 items, a dozen is 12 and a ream of paper is 500 sheets. Chemists deal with matter in their daily practice and matter is composed of very tiny particles that are too small to count. Therefore, chemists had to devise a method of counting and representing these tiny particles. Rather than counting individual particles of matter, the term **the mole** (symbol **mol**) was devised to represent a very large number of atomic particles.

A **mole** is the amount of a substance that contains the **same number** of **particles** as there are atoms in 12.00 g of carbon-12. It was found that 12.00 g of carbon-12 contains **6.0×10^{23} atoms** of carbon-12, therefore, **a mole** represents **6.0×10^{23}**.

A mole is the amount of a substance that contains 6.0×10^{23} particles of the substance.

In the above definition:

- 'Amount' can be the **mass** of a substance, or the **volume** of a substance if it is a **gas**.
- 'Particles' can be **atoms**, **molecules**, **formula units** or **ions**.

The number **6.0×10^{23}** is known as **Avogadro's constant**, or N_A.

The mole and mass

Just as it was found that 12.00 g of carbon-12 contains 6.0×10^{23} carbon-12 atoms, it was also found that:

- **64 g** of copper (Cu) contains 6.0×10^{23} Cu atoms.
- **271 g** of phosphorus tribromide (PBr_3) contains 6.0×10^{23} PBr_3 molecules.
- **200 g** of calcium bromide ($CaBr_2$) contains 6.0×10^{23} $CaSO_4$ formula units.

Looking at the **masses** given above:

- Each mass has the same numerical value as the relative atomic, molecular or formula mass of the element or compound.
- Each is the mass of **6.0×10^{23}** particles, or **one mole** of particles of the substance.

It therefore follows that **one mole** of a substance has a mass equal to the relative atomic, molecular or formula mass expressed in **grams**.

Molar mass (M) is the mass, in grams, of one mole of a chemical substance.

The molar mass of an element or compound is given the unit **grams per mole** or **g mol⁻¹**. For example, the molar mass of carbon is **12 g mol⁻¹**.

Therefore, the **molar mass** of an element or compound is the relative atomic, molecular or formula mass amount expressed in **grams per mole**.

> **Example 2**
>
> Molar mass of **NO_2** = 14 + (2 × 16) g mol⁻¹ = **46 g mol⁻¹**
>
>   Or $M(NO_2)$ = 46 g mol⁻¹
>
> Molar mass of **KNO_3** = 39 + 14 + (3 × 16) g mol⁻¹ = **101 g mol⁻¹**
>
>   Or $M(KNO_3)$ = 101 g mol⁻¹

Molar mass of $Mg_3(PO_4)_2 = (3 \times 24) + (2 \times 31) + (2 \times 4 \times 16)$ g mol^{-1} = **262 g mol^{-1}**

  Or $M(Mg_3(PO_4)_2) = 262$ g mol^{-1}

Molar mass (mass of one mole) can be used to convert a given mass of an element or compound to number of moles, or to convert a given number of moles of an element or compound to mass.

Two conversions

a Given mass of element or compound to number of moles:

$$\text{number of moles} = \frac{\text{given mass}}{\text{mass of one mole (molar mass)}}$$

b Given number of moles to mass:

mass = **given number of moles** × mass of one mole (molar mass)

Sample questions

1 How many moles are there in 126 g of nitric acid?

Mass of 1 mol $HNO_3 = 1 + 14 + (3 \times 16)$ g = **63 g**

∴ number of moles in 126 g $HNO_3 = \dfrac{126}{63}$ mol (using conversion equation **a**)

$$= \underline{\textbf{2.0 mol}}$$

2 What is the mass of 0.34 mol of copper (I) sulfate?

Mass of 1 mol $Cu_2SO_4 = (2 \times 64) + 32 + (4 \times 16)$ g = **224 g**

∴ mass of **0.34 mol Cu_2SO_4** = 0.34 × 224 g (using conversion equation **b**)

$$= \underline{\textbf{76.16 g}}$$

The mole and number of particles

The fact that the number of particles in one mole is always **6.0 × 10^{23}** can be used to convert a given number of particles in a substance to number of moles, or to convert a given number of moles to the number of particles.

Two conversions

c Given number of particles to number of moles:

$$\text{number of moles} = \frac{\text{given number of particles}}{6.0 \times 10^{23}}$$

d Given number of moles to number of particles:

number of particles = **given number of moles** × 6.0 × 10^{23}

Section A: Principles of chemistry

The **type** of particle in a substance depends on the nature of the substance:

- If the substance is an **element**, for example, a metal or a noble gas, the particles are individual **atoms**.
- If the substance is a **molecular element**, for example, oxygen, O_2, or a **covalent compound**, for example, sulfur dioxide, SO_2, the particles are **molecules** made up of **atoms**.
- If the substance is an **ionic compound**, for example, copper(II) oxide, CuO, the particles are **formula units** made up of **ions**.

Sample questions

1 How many moles are in 2.4×10^{23} molecules of oxygen?

1 mol O_2 contains 6.0×10^{23} O_2 molecules

$\therefore$ number of moles in 2.4×10^{23} O_2 molecules $= \dfrac{2.4 \times 10^{23}}{6.0 \times 10^{23}}$ mol (using conversion equation **c**)

$= \textbf{0.4 mol}$

2 Calculate the number of copper oxide formula units in 0.46 mol of magnesium oxide.

1 mol CuO contains 6.0×10^{23} CuO formula units

$\therefore$ **0.46 mol CuO** contains $0.46 \times 6.0 \times 10^{23}$ CuO formula units (using conversion equation **d**)

$= \textbf{2.76} \times \textbf{10}^{\textbf{23}}$ **CuO formula units**

3 How many bromide ions are there in 0.32 mol of phosphorus tribromide?

1 mol PBr_3 contains 6.0×10^{23} PBr_3 formula units

$\therefore$ **0.32 mol PBr_3** contains $0.32 \times 6.0 \times 10^{23}$ PBr_3 formula units (using conversion equation **d**)

$= \textbf{1.92} \times \textbf{10}^{\textbf{23}}$ **PBr_3 formula units**

1 PBr_3 formula unit contains 3 Br⁻ ions

$\therefore$ **1.92×10^{23} PBr_3 formula units** contain $3 \times 1.92 \times 10^{23}$ Br⁻ ions

$= \textbf{5.76} \times \textbf{10}^{\textbf{23}}$ **Br⁻ ions**

The mole, mass and number of particles

The calculation of moles and mass, and moles and number of particles can be combined.

Combined conversions

$$\text{mass of element or compound} \underset{b}{\overset{a}{\rightleftharpoons}} \text{number of moles} \underset{d}{\overset{c}{\rightleftharpoons}} \text{number of particles}$$

1 How many water molecules are there in 5.46 g of water?

Mass of 1 mol H_2O = $(2 \times 1) + 16$ g = **18 g**

$\therefore$ number of moles in 5.46 g H_2O = $\dfrac{5.46}{18}$ mol (using conversion equation **a**)

$$= \textbf{0.30 mol}$$

1 mol H_2O contains 6.0×10^{23} H_2O molecules

$\therefore$ **0.30 mol H_2O** contains $0.30 \times 6.0 \times 10^{23}$ H_2O molecules (using conversion equation **d**)

$$= \textbf{1.8} \times \textbf{10}^{\textbf{23}} \ \textbf{H}_\textbf{2}\textbf{O molecules}$$

2 Calculate the mass of 3.1×10^{22} copper carbonate formula units.

1 mol $CuCO_3$ contains 6.0×10^{23} $CuCO_3$ formula units

$\therefore$ number of moles in 3.1×10^{22} $CuCO_3$ formula units = $\dfrac{3.1 \times 10^{22}}{6.0 \times 10^{23}}$ mol (using conversion equation **c**)

$$= \textbf{0.052 mol}$$

Mass of 1 mol $CuCO_3$ = $64 + 12 + (3 \times 16)$ g = **124 g**

$\therefore$ mass of **0.052 mol $CuCO_3$** = 0.052×124 g (using conversion equation **b**)

$$= \textbf{6.45 g}$$

The mole and volumes of gases

We have already learnt that one of the properties of gases is that they have very low densities and for this reason when expressing the amount of a gas, volume would be a better way of stating this rather than mass.

Avogadro's law states that equal volumes of all gases, under the same conditions of temperature and pressure, contain the same number of molecules.

If the number of molecules in each gas is $\textbf{6.0} \times \textbf{10}^{\textbf{23}}$ (**1 mol**) it follows that one mole of all gases, at the same temperature and pressure, occupy the **same volume**.

Molar volume (V$_m$) is the volume occupied by one mole (6.0×10^{23} molecules) of a gas.

Molar volume depends on temperature and pressure:

- At **standard temperature and pressure** (**stp**), where temperature is 0 °C (273 K) and pressure is 101.3 kPa (1 atmosphere), the volume of one mole of a gas is **22.4 dm³** or **22 400 cm³**. (Note that one decimetre is one tenth of a metre (equivalent to 10 cm). A cubic decimetre is equivalent to 1 litre.)

- At **room temperature and pressure** (**rtp**), where temperature is 25 °C (298 K) and pressure is 101.3 kPa (1 atmosphere), the volume of one mole of a gas is **24.0 dm³** or **24 000 cm³**.

Molar volume can be used to convert a given volume of a gas to number of moles, or to convert a given number of moles of a gas to volume.

Two conversions

e Given volume of gas to number of moles:

$$\text{number of moles} = \frac{\textbf{given volume of gas}}{\text{volume of one mole at stp or rtp (molar volume)}}$$

f Given number of moles to volume of gas:

volume of gas = **given number of moles** × volume of one mole at stp or rtp (molar volume)

Sample questions

1 How many moles are there in 1.94 dm^3 of sulfur dioxide at rtp?

Volume of 1 mol SO_2 at rtp = 24.0 dm^3

$\therefore$ number of moles in 1.94 dm^3 $SO_2 = \frac{1.94}{24.0}$ mol (using conversion equation **e**)

$= \mathbf{0.08\ mol}$

2 What volume is occupied by 0.07 mol of bromine gas at stp?

Volume of 1 mol Br_2 at stp = 22.4 dm^3

$\therefore$ volume of **0.07 mol Br_2** = 0.07 × 22.4 dm^3 (using conversion equation **f**)

$= \mathbf{1.57\ dm^3}$

The mole, mass, number of particles and gas volume

The calculations of moles and mass, moles and number of particles, and moles and gas volumes can be combined.

Combined conversions

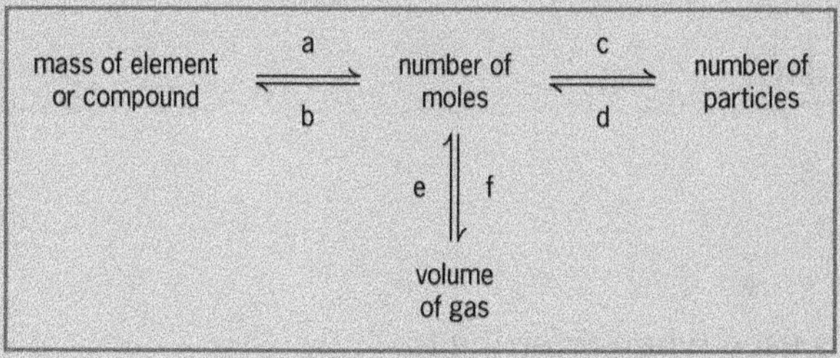

Sample questions

1 What is the volume of 19.4 g of fluorine at rtp?

Mass of 1 mol F_2 = (2 × 19) g = **38 g**

$\therefore$ number of moles in 19.4 g $F_2 = \frac{19.4}{38}$ mol (using conversion equation **a**)

$= \mathbf{0.51\ mol}$

Volume of 1 mol F_2 at rtp = 24.0 dm^3

$\therefore$ volume of **0.51 mol F_2** = 0.51 × 24.0 dm^3 (using conversion equation **f**)

$= \mathbf{12.24\ dm^3}$

2 What is the mass of 943 cm^3 of nitrogen dioxide, NO_2, at stp.

Volume of 1 mol NO_2 at stp = 22 400 cm^3

$\therefore$ number of moles in 943 $cm^3 = \frac{943}{22\ 400}$ mol (using conversion equation **e**)

$= \mathbf{0.042\ mol}$

Mass of 1 mol NO_2 = 14 + (2 × 16) = 46 g

∴ mass of 0.042 mol of NO_2 = 0.042 × 46 g (using conversion equation **b**)

$$= \underline{1.9 \text{ g}}$$

---

3 How many hydrogen sulfide molecules are there in 972 cm³ of hydrogen sulfide gas at rtp?

Volume of 1 mol H_2S at rtp = 24 000 cm³

∴ number of moles in **972** cm³ H_2S = $\dfrac{972}{24\,000}$ mol (using conversion equation **e**)

$$= \textbf{0.04 mol}$$

1 mol H_2S contains 6.0×10^{23} H_2S molecules

∴ **0.04 mol** H_2S contains $0.04 \times 6.0 \times 10^{23}$ H_2S molecules (using conversion equation **d**)

$$= \underline{\textbf{2.4} \times \textbf{10}^{\textbf{22}} \textbf{ H}_2\textbf{S molecules}}$$

---

4 What volume is occupied by 3.8×10^{21} molecules of nitrogen monoxide gas at stp?

1 mol of NO at stp contains 6.0×10^{23} molecules

∴ number of moles in 3.8×10^{21} molecules NO = $\dfrac{3.8 \times 10^{21}}{6.0 \times 10^{23}}$ mol

$$= \textbf{0.006 mol}$$

Volume of 1 mol NO = 22.4 dm³

∴ volume of 0.006 mol NO at stp = 0.006 × 22.4 dm³

$$= \underline{\textbf{0.13 dm}^{-3}}$$

Recalling facts

1 The term relative molecular mass is used when referring to:

a ionic compounds

b covalent compounds

c atoms

d none of the above

2 The unit for relative atomic mass is:

a milligrams

b grams

c kilograms

d no units

3 Avogadro's constant is the amount of a substance that contains 6.0×10^{23} particles of a substance. Particles refer to all except:

a atoms

b formula units

c protons

d ions

4 Which of the following statements is correct?

a rtp is measured at 0 °C and 1 atmosphere

b rtp is 22.4 dm³

c rtp is measured at 273 K and 101.3 kPa

d rtp is 24 000 cm³

5 Molar mass has units:

a g mol⁻¹

b kg mol⁻¹

c mol

d N$_a$

6 Define the term 'mole' and state Avogadro's constant.

Applying facts

7 Explain why stp and rtp are important as standard units.

8 Calculate the mass of and the number of particles contained in each of the following:

a 0.32 moles of bromine gas

b 12 moles of calcium carbonate

c 3.2 moles of ammonium phosphate

d 0.73 moles of iron(II) hydroxide

9 Determine the number of moles in:

a 39 g of aluminium

b 429 g of zinc

c 92 g of calcium hydroxide

d 29 g of sodium sulfate

10 a Define the term 'molar volume' and state Avogadro's law.

b Calculate the volume occupied by 44 g of oxygen at rtp.

c How many nitrogen dioxide molecules are contained in a small steel canister of volume 12.13 dm³ at stp?

d Calculate the number of moles present in 973 cm³ of methane gas.

Analysing data

11 **a** Distinguish between the terms 'relative molecular mass' and 'relative formula mass'.

 b Write the chemical formula for the following compounds and calculate the relative molecular mass or relative formula mass, stating which of these terms apply to each compound:

   i   ozone

   ii ethanol

   iii calcium phosphate

   iv iron(III) chloride

   v   hydrogen chloride

   vi iron(II) sulfide

   vii lead(VI) dichromate

12 **a** A compound containing lead has a relative molecular mass of 391 and formula $Pb(NO_3)_z$. What is the value of z?

 b A compound containing calcium has a relative molecular mass of 239 and formula $Ca(ClO_4)_y$. What is the value of y?

The mole and chemical formulae

Learning objectives

* Distinguish between the terms **empirical** and **molecular formulae**, and **percentage composition**.
* Perform calculations involving empirical and molecular formulae from pertinent data.
* Perform calculations involving the percentage by mass of an element or compound.
* Define the term **standard solution**.
* State that concentrations of solutions can be quantified in **mol dm⁻³** and **g dm⁻³**.
* Perform calculations involving the **concentrations of solutions**.

When considered in terms of moles, a **chemical formula** shows how many **moles of each element** are combined to form one mole of a compound. For example, SO_3 represents 1 mol of sulfur atoms combined with 3 mol of oxygen atoms.

Chemical formulae can be written in two main ways:

* The **empirical formula**. This gives the simplest **whole number mole ratio** between the atoms or ions present in the compound. **Ionic compounds** are always represented by **empirical formulae**.
* The **molecular formula**. This gives the **actual number of moles** of atoms of each element present in one mole of the compound. **Covalent compounds** are represented by **molecular formulae**.

The empirical and molecular formulae of **covalent compounds** may be the same, for example, sulfur trioxide and SO_3, water and H_2O, and nitrogen dioxide and NO_2. However, in some compounds, the molecular formula is a simple **whole number multiple** of the empirical formula, for example, the molecular formula of stearic acid is $C_{18}H_{36}O_2$, ribose is $C_5H_{10}O_5$ and ethane is C_2H_6 and their empirical formulae are $C_9H_{18}O$, CH_2O and CH_3 respectively.

If the **proportions** of the elements, by mass, in a compound are known, then its empirical formula can be determined. If the molecular formula is different from the empirical formula and the relative molecular mass or molar mass is known, the molecular formula can be determined.

1 When analysed, a compound of mass 75.0 g was found to contain an unknown mass of sodium, 8.48 g of carbon and 33.98 g of oxygen. Determine the empirical formula of the compound.

Mass of **sodium** in the compound = 75.0 – (8.48 + 33.98) g = **32.54 g**

Element	Na	C	O
Mass	32.54 g	8.48 g	33.98 g
Mass of 1 mole	23 g	12 g	16 g
Number of moles	$\dfrac{32.54}{23}$ mol = 1.415 mol	$\dfrac{8.48}{12}$ mol = 0.707 mol	$\dfrac{33.98}{16}$ mol = 2.124 mol
Simplest mole ratio (dividing by the smallest number of moles)	2 mol	1 mol	3 mol

Empirical formula is <u>**Na_2CO_3**</u>

2 On analysis, a compound was found to contain 26.7% carbon, an unknown percentage of hydrogen and 71.1% oxygen. Determine the molecular formula of this compound if its relative molecular mass is 90.

Percentage hydrogen in compound = 100 – (26.7 + 71.1)

$$= 2.2\%$$

Element	C	H	O
Percentage	26.7%	2.2%	71.1%
Mass in 100 g	24.03 g	1.98 g	63.99 g
Mass of 1 mole	12 g	1 g	16 g
Number of moles	$\dfrac{24.03}{12}$ mol = 2.00 mol	$\dfrac{1.98}{1}$ mol = 1.98 mol	$\dfrac{63.99}{16}$ mol = 4.00 mol
Simplest mole ratio	1 mol	1 mol	2 mol

Empirical formula is **CHO_2**

To determine the **molecular formula:**

Relative molecular mass of CHO_2 = 12 + 1 + (2 × 16) = 45

Relative molecular mass of compound = **90**

and ratio between relative molecular masses = $\dfrac{90}{45}$ = 2

∴ the molecular formula is **2** × the empirical formula

Molecular formula of the compound is <u>**$C_2H_2O_4$**</u>

Percentage composition

Percentage composition is the percentage, by mass, of each element in a compound. This can be calculated once the formula of a compound is known.

Sample questions

1 Calculate the percentage, by mass, of copper in copper(II) oxide, CuO.

Mass of 1 mol CuO = 64 + 16 = **80 g**

Mass of **copper** in 1 mol CuO = **64 g**

∴ percentage of copper in CuO = $\dfrac{64}{80} \times 100\%$

$$= \underline{80\%}$$

2 Calculate the percentage, by mass, of hydrogen in ammonium sulfate, $(NH_4)_2SO_4$.

Mass of 1 mol $(NH_4)_2SO_4$ = $(2 \times 14) + (2 \times 4 \times 1) + 32 + (4 \times 16)$ g = **132 g**

Mass of **hydrogen** in 1 mol $(NH_4)_2SO_4$ = $(2 \times 4 \times 1)$ g = **8 g**

∴ percentage of hydrogen in $(NH_4)_2SO_4$ = $\dfrac{8}{132} \times 100\%$

$$= \underline{6.06\%}$$

The mole and solutions

We are accustomed to seeing the words "concentrated" or "made from juice concentrate" on the packaging of juices on the supermarket shelves. These phrases are telling us about the concentrations of the juices we are buying. The concentration of solutions is also encountered by chemists in industry and is very important in manufacturing because the concentration is a direct indication of how much of an ingredient is needed. Knowing the concentration of a juice, that is, the amount of concentrate needed, can help to keep quality, for example, taste and colour, consistent. What does concentration mean?

The **concentration of a solution** is a measure of how much solute is dissolved in a fixed volume of the **solution**. The volume usually used is **1 dm³** (1000 cm³). Concentration can be expressed in two ways:

- **Mass concentration** gives the **mass** of solute dissolved in 1 dm³ of solution. The unit is **grams of solute per cubic decimetre** of solution or **g dm⁻³**.

- **Molar concentration** gives the **number of moles** of solute dissolved in 1 dm³ of solution. The unit is **moles of solute per cubic decimetre** of solution (**mol dm⁻³**).

*A **standard solution** is a solution whose concentration is known accurately.*

A standard solution is made in a **volumetric flask**.

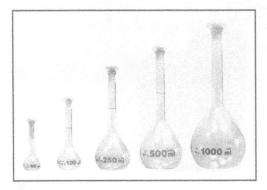

Figure 8.1 *Different sizes of volumetric flasks*

The flask has an accurate volume which is not always 1 dm³ as can be seen in Figure 8.1. The solute is weighed out, added to the flask and water is added to the mark on the neck of the flask. A measuring cylinder can be used to measure and pour the water into the flask. When the meniscus is close to the mark a dropper can be used to fill the volume of water to the mark. The dropper is used to ensure that the volume of water does not pass the mark; otherwise the concentration would be wrong. The concentration of the solution can then be calculated as shown in the following example.

Example 3

A magnesium chloride solution contains 12.7 g of magnesium chloride dissolved in 1 dm³ of solution.

$\therefore$ **mass concentration** of the solution = **12.7 g dm⁻³**

And mass of 1 mole $MgCl_2$ = 24 + (2 × 35.5) g = **95 g**

$\therefore$ number of moles in 12.7 g $MgCl_2$ = $\dfrac{12.7}{95}$ mol (using equation **a**)

$$= 0.13 \text{ mol}$$

$\therefore$ **molar concentration** of the solution = **0.13 mol dm⁻³**

Sample questions

1 500 cm³ of nitric acid solution contains 9.12 g of nitric acid. What are the mass and molar concentrations of this solution?

500 cm³ $HNO_3(aq)$ contains 9.12 g HNO_3

$\therefore$ 1 cm³ $HNO_3(aq)$ contains $\dfrac{9.12}{500}$ g HNO_3

and **1000 cm³ HNO_3(aq)** contains $\dfrac{9.12}{500}$ × 1000 g HNO_3

$$= 18.24 \text{ g } HNO_3$$

Mass concentration of the solution = **18.24 g dm⁻³**

Mass of 1 mol HNO_3 = 1 + 14 + (3 × 16) g = **63 g**

$\therefore$ number of moles in 18.24 g HNO_3 = $\dfrac{18.24}{63}$ mol (using equation **a**)

$$= 0.29 \text{ mol}$$

Molar concentration of the solution = **0.29 mol dm⁻³**

2 How many moles of potassium sulfate are present in 100 cm³ of a solution which has a molar concentration of 0.28 mol dm⁻³?

1 dm³ $K_2SO_4(aq)$ contains 0.28 mol K_2SO_4

that is, 1000 cm³ $K_2SO_4(aq)$ contains 0.28 mol K_2SO_4

$\therefore$ 1 cm³ $K_2SO_4(aq)$ contains $\dfrac{0.28}{1000}$ mol K_2SO_4

and **100 cm³ K_2SO_4(aq)** contains $\dfrac{0.28}{1000}$ × 100 mol K_2SO_4

$$= 0.028 \text{ mol } K_2SO_4$$

3 What mass of sodium chloride would be needed to produce 550 cm³ of sodium chloride solution with a concentration of 0.35 mol dm⁻³?

1000 cm³ NaCl(aq) contains 0.35 mol NaCl

$\therefore$ **550 cm³ NaCl(aq)** contains $\dfrac{0.35}{1000} \times 550$ mol

$= \textbf{0.193 mol NaCl}$

Mass of 1 mol NaCl = 23 + 35.5 g = **58.5 g**

$\therefore$ mass of **0.193 mol NaCl** = 0.193 × 58.5 g (using equation **b**)

$= \textbf{11.29 g}$

Mass of sodium chloride required = **11.29 g**

Recalling facts

13 The apparatus in which a standard solution is made is called a:

   a measuring cylinder

   b burette

   c pipette

   d volumetric flask

14 Which of the following does NOT represent an empirical formula?

   a NO

   b CH_2O

   c NO_2

   d $C_6H_{12}O_6$

15 Which of the following is a TRUE statement concerning empirical and molecular formulae?

   a The empirical formula of a compound can be 4 times its molecular formula.

   b The empirical and molecular formula cannot be the same.

   c Several compounds can have the same molecular formula but different empirical formulae.

   d The molecular formula of a compound can be a whole number multiple of its empirical formula.

16 What is the percent of sulfur in the compound $ZnSO_4 \cdot 7H_2O$?

   a 11.1

   b 22.3

   c 22.6

   d 43.9

17 The unit for mass concentration is:

a mol dm^{-3}

b mol dm^3

c g dm^3

d g dm^{-3}

18 Explain the meaning of the terms empirical formula and molecular formula.

Applying facts

19 a Find the empirical formula of the compound containing 44.4% carbon, 6.21% hydrogen, an unknown percentage of sulfur and 9.86% oxygen.

b Find the empirical and molecular formula of a compound of relative molecular mass 545, containing an unknown mass of carbon, 12 g of hydrogen and 424 g of chlorine.

20 What mass of $KMnO_4$ is required to make 500 cm^3 of a solution with concentration 1.32 M?

21 Calculate the molarity in mol/dm^3 of a solution that contains 0.0345 mol NH_4Cl in 200 cm^3 of water.

22 A bottle of 9.0 M HCl has 23.5 cm^3 remaining. If exactly 500 cm^3 of water is added to the bottle what is the resulting concentration of HCl?

23 5.8 g of solid potassium hydroxide (KOH) is dissolved in 350 cm^3 to make a potassium hydroxide solution. What is the mass concentration in g dm^{-3} and molarity mol dm^{-3} of the solution?

Analysing data

24 Discuss the differences and similarities between the following terms: the mole, mass concentration (g dm^{-3}) and molar concentration (mol dm^{-3}).

25 Outline how you would prepare a 250 ml standard solution of sodium chloride using 3 g of the salt. In your discussion include the apparatus needed, the steps used in the preparation, and calculate the number of moles of sodium chloride in your standard solution.

26 Briefly discuss the use of molarity in the food and beverage industry as a means of maintaining consistent quality.

The mole and chemical reactions

Learning objectives

- State the law of **Conservation of Matter**.
- Perform calculations based on chemical equations involving the mole and reacting masses and volume of gases.

The Law of Conservation of Matter states that matter can neither be created nor destroyed during a chemical reaction.

In any chemical reaction, the total mass of the products is the **same** as the total mass of the reactants. When considered in terms of moles, the **coefficients** (the multiplying number in front of the element/chemical symbol) in a balanced chemical equation show the number of **moles** of each reactant and product.

Example 4

$$4Fe(s) + 3O_2(g) \longrightarrow 2Fe_2O_3(s)$$

This means:

$$\textbf{4 mol} \text{ of Fe} + \textbf{3 mol} \text{ of } O_2 \longrightarrow \textbf{2 mol} \text{ of } Fe_2O_3$$

Converting moles to mass, it means:

$$4(56) \text{ g of Fe} + 3(2 \times 16) \text{ g of } O_2 \longrightarrow 2((2 \times 56) + (3 \times 16)) \text{ g of } Fe_2O_3$$

$$\textbf{224 g} \text{ of Fe} + \textbf{96 g} \text{ of } O_2 \longrightarrow \textbf{320 g} \text{ of } Fe_2O_3$$

The total mass of the original reactants, iron and oxygen, is **320 g** which is the same as the mass of the product, iron(III) oxide.

Applying the Law of Conservation of Matter, if the quantity of one reactant or product is known, the quantities of any of the other reactants and products can be calculated.

Steps to follow when answering questions:

Step 1: Write the **balanced chemical equation** for the reaction if it has not been given. If the question refers to ions, then write the balanced **ionic equation.**

Step 2: Write the **quantity** of the reactant or product which has been given underneath its formula in the equation and place a **question mark** under the reactant or product whose quantity is being calculated.

Step 3: Convert the **given quantity** of reactant or product to **moles**. This is the **known** reactant or product.

Step 4: Use the balanced equation to determine the **mole ratio** between the known and the unknown reactant or product. The **unknown** reactant or product is the one whose quantity is being calculated.

Step 5: Use the **number of moles** of the known reactant or product found in **step 3** and the **mole ratio** found in **step 4** to calculate the **number of moles** of the unknown.

Step 6: Use the **number of moles** of the unknown reactant or product found in **step 5** and its molar mass or volume to determine its **quantity.**

Example 5

To determine the maximum mass of iron(III) chloride that can be produced when 13.5 g of iron(III) oxide reacts with excess hydrochloric acid.

Steps 1 and **2:** $Fe_2O_3(aq) + 6HCl(aq) \longrightarrow 2FeCl_3(aq) + 3H_2O(l)$

13.5 g   ? mass

Mass of Fe_2O_3 is known, mass of **$FeCl_3$** is unknown.

Step 3: Find the **number of moles** of the known reactant, i.e. Fe_2O_3, using its molar mass and given mass:

$$Mass\ of\ 1\ mol\ Fe_2O_3 = (2 \times 56) + (3 \times 16)\ g$$

$$= 160\ g$$

$$\therefore number\ of\ moles\ in\ 13.5\ g\ Fe_2O_3 = \frac{13.5}{160}\ mol$$

$$= 0.08\ mol$$

Step 4: Use the balanced equation to determine the **mole ratio** between Fe_2O_3 and the unknown product, i.e. $FeCl_3$:

1 mol Fe_2O_3 form 2 mol $FeCl_3$

Step 5: Use the number of moles of Fe_2O_3 from **step 3** and the mole ratio from **step 4** to calculate the **number of moles** of $FeCl_3$ produced:

0.08 mol Fe_2O_3 forms 2×0.08 mol $FeCl_3$

$$= 0.16\ mol\ FeCl_3$$

Step 6: Use the number of moles of $FeCl_3$ from **step 5** and its molar mass to determine the **mass** produced:

$$Mass\ of\ 1\ mol\ FeCl_3 = 56 + (3 \times 35.5)\ g$$

$$= 162.5\ g$$

$$\therefore mass\ of\ \mathbf{0.16\ mol\ FeCl_3} = 0.16 \times 162.5\ g$$

$$= 26.0\ g$$

Mass of iron(III) chloride produced = **26.0 g**

---

1 What volume of carbon dioxide, measured at stp, will be produced when 65.5 g of aluminium carbonate reacts with excess hydrochloric acid?

Steps 1 and **2:**

$$Al_2(CO_3)_3(aq) + 6HCl(aq) \longrightarrow 2AlCl_3(aq) + 3H_2O(g) + 3CO_2(g)$$

65.5 g   ? volume at stp

Mass of $Al_2(CO_3)_3$ is known, volume of **CO_2** is unknown.

Step 3: Mass of 1 mol $Al_2(CO_3)_3$ = **234 g**

$$\therefore number\ of\ moles\ in\ 65.5\ g\ Al_2(CO_3)_3 = \frac{65.5}{234}\ mol$$

$$= 0.28\ mol$$

Step 4: 1 mol $Al_2(CO_3)_3$ form **3 mol CO_2**

Step 5: 0.28 mol $Al_2(CO_3)_3$ forms 3×0.28 mol CO_2

$$= 0.84\ mol\ CO_2$$

Step 6: Volume of 1 mol CO_2 at stp = 22.4 dm^3

$\therefore$ volume of **0.84 mol CO_2** = 0.84 × 22.4 dm^3

= **18.8 dm^3**

Volume of carbon dioxide produced = **18.8 dm^3**

---

2 What is the minimum mass of magnesium oxide that must be added to 450 cm^3 of hydrochloric acid with a concentration of 0.18 mol dm^{-3} to exactly neutralise the acid?

Steps 1 and **2:**

$$MgO(s) + 2HCl(aq) \longrightarrow MgCl_2(aq) + H_2O(l)$$

? mass   **450 cm^3**

0.18 mol dm^{-3}

Volume and concentration of **HCl(aq)** are known, mass of **MgO** is unknown.

Step 3: 1 dm^3 HCl(aq) contains 0.18 mol HCl

i.e. 1000 cm^3 HCl(aq) contains 0.18 mol HCl

$\therefore$ **450 cm^3 HCl(aq)** contains $\dfrac{0.18}{1000} \times 450$ mol HCl

= **0.081 mol HCl**

Step 4: **1 mol MgO** reacts with **2 mol HCl**

Step 5: $\dfrac{1}{2} \times 0.081$ mol **MgO** reacts with **0.081 mol HCL**

= **0.0405 mol MgO**

Step 6: Mass of 1 mol MgO = 24 + 16 g = **40 g**

$\therefore$ mass of **0.0405 mol MgO** = 0.0405 × 40 g

= **1.62 g**

Mass of magnesium oxide required = **1.62 g**

---

3 What mass of zinc(II) hydroxide would be produced when a solution containing 12.3 g of OH^- ions reacts with a solution containing excess Zn^{2+} ions?

Steps 1 and **2:**

$$Zn(aq) + 2OH^-(aq) \longrightarrow Zn(OH)_2(s)$$

12.3 g   **? mass**

Mass of **OH^- ions** is known, mass of **$Zn(OH)_2$** is unknown.

Step 3: Mass of 1 mol OH^- ions = 16 + 1 g

= **17 g**

$\therefore$ number of moles in **12.3 g OH^- ions** = $\dfrac{12.3}{17}$ mol

= **0.72 mol**

Step 4: **2 mol OH^- ions** form **1 mol $Zn(OH)_2$**

Step 5: **0.72 mol OH^- ions** forms $\dfrac{1}{2} \times 0.72$ mol $Zn(OH)_2$

= **0.36 mol $Zn(OH)_2$**

Step 6: Mass of 1 mol $Zn(OH)_2$ = 65 + (2 × 16) + (2 × 1) g

= **99 g**

∴ mass of **0.36 mol $Zn(OH)_2$** = 0.36 × 99 g

= **35.64 g**

Mass of zinc hydroxide produced = **35.64 g**

Recalling facts

27. During a chemical reaction matter cannot be:

    a destroyed only

    b transferred only

    c created only

    d destroyed or created

28. Which of the following steps is NOT used when answering questions involving masses of reactants and products?

    a Calculate the number of moles of the known reactant and products using its given mass and its molar mass.

    b Write a balanced equation for the chemical reaction.

    c The balanced chemical equation is used to determine the mole ratio.

    d Equate the number of moles of the unknown reactant.

29. What volume of hydrogen is required to react with 50 cm³ of nitrogen to form ammonia?

    a 50 cm³　　　b 100 cm³　　　c 150 cm³　　　d 16.7 cm³

30. In the equation

    $3Cl_2(g) + 8NH_3(aq) \longrightarrow N_2(g) + 6NH_4Cl(aq)$

    How many moles of ammonium chloride (NH_4Cl) are produced?

    a 3　　　b 8　　　c 2　　　d 6

31. In the reaction below

    $2Li(s) + 2H_2O(l) \longrightarrow 2LiOH(aq) + H_2(g)$

    How many moles of lithium react to form how many moles of hydrogen molecules?

    a 2 lithium react to form 2 hydrogen molecules

    b 1 lithium reacts to form 2 hydrogen molecules

    c 2 lithium reacts to form 1 hydrogen molecule

    d 1 lithium reacts to form 1 hydrogen molecule

32. State the Law of Conservation of Matter.

Applying facts

33   Sodium burns in oxygen to produce sodium oxide. Write a balanced equation for the reaction and explain why the economy of the atoms is 100%. If 483 g of sodium is placed in a container with 5.8 mol of oxygen gas, calculate the mass of sodium oxide that can be produced.

34   What mass of precipitate will be produced when 2.27 dm³ of 0.0820 M silver nitrate solution is reacted with 3.06 dm³ of potassium sulfate solution? Name the precipitate formed.

35   Calcium carbonate reacts with hydrochloric acid to produce calcium chloride, water and carbon dioxide. Write a balanced equation for this reaction. Using this equation, calculate the volume of carbon dioxide gas, measured at stp, which will be produced when excess calcium carbonate is reacted with 25.0 cm³ of 0.75 M HCl.

9 Acids, bases and salts

Acids and **bases** have **opposite** properties and have the ability to neutralise each other. When an acid reacts with a base, the reaction always forms a **salt**. Acids, bases and salts are found everywhere, and we use these in all aspects of our lives. In industry, we use acids, such as sulfuric acid in the manufacture of fertilisers, paints, dyes, synthetic fabrics and in the petroleum industry. Bases, such as sodium hydroxide, are used to manufacture paper, cleaning agents and fabrics. Not only are acids and bases important in industry but also for the survival of all living organisms. Organisms must be able to maintain the pH levels required for enzymes to function. Cells therefore secrete acids and bases to maintain these pH levels.

There are many different types of salts found in nature, for example, in the Earth's crust and the sea. Salts are made when an acid is neutralised by a base. The first part of the salt's name is given by the metal, the metal oxide, or the metal carbonate. The second part of the salt's name comes from the acid. For example, in the name of one of the best-known salts, sodium chloride, sodium is the metal and chloride is the part of the acid left after the salt's creation. Examples of salts include sodium chloride, magnesium sulfate, calcium carbonate and magnesium sulfate. Salts perform a vital role in our daily lives. Salts are used in the agricultural sector as fertilisers and pesticides, in the medical field and in the food and manufacturing industries.

Acids

Learning objectives

- Define acids in terms of the ions they liberate in aqueous solutions.
- Describe the characteristic properties of acids in both general and chemical reactions including those with metals, and with the bases, hydrogen carbonate and carbonate.
- Illustrate the various approaches to classifying acids.
- Define **acid anhydride** and give examples of acid anhydrides.
- State some uses of acids in everyday life and in living systems.

The term 'acid' has its origins from the Latin word 'acere' meaning sour. All acids have this property. An **acid** that is not dissolved in water is composed of **covalent molecules** and can be a solid, liquid or gas at room temperature. Maleic acid, oxalic acid, tartaric acid and ascorbic acid (vitamin C) are all examples of solid acids. Liquid acids include nitric acid, sulfuric acid and phosphoric acid. Acids that are gases in nature include hydrogen fluoride, hydrogen chloride and formic acid.

All acid molecules contain **hydrogen**, such as hydrochloric acid, HCl, phosphoric acid, H_3PO_4, and ethanoic acid, CH_3COOH. Only when acids are dissolved in water do they display their acidic traits.

When added to water, the acid molecules **ionise**, forming positive **hydrogen ions (H^+ ions)** and negative anions:

for example: $HNO_3(l) + water \longrightarrow H^+(aq) + NO_3^-(aq)$

The hydrogen ions give acids their characteristic acid attributes and reactions. The oxygen in the polar water molecule attracts the **H^+ ion** forming a bond resulting in the formation of a **hydronium** or **hydroxonium ion (H_3O^+)**:

$$H^+(aq) + H_2O(l) \longrightarrow H_3O^+(aq)$$
$$\text{hydronium ion}$$

Therefore, the overall reaction for the above example is:

$$HNO_3(aq) + H_2O \longrightarrow H_3O^+(aq) + NO_3^-(aq)$$

The ionisation of an acid in water is normally represented as follows:

$$HNO_3(aq) \longrightarrow H^+(aq) + NO_3^-(aq)$$

Other examples of acids ionising in water are:

$$HCl(g) \longrightarrow H^+(aq) + Cl^-(aq)$$

$$H_3PO_4(aq) \longrightarrow 3H^+(aq) + PO_4^{3-}(aq)$$

$$CH_3CH_2COOH(aq) \rightleftharpoons CH_3CH_2COO^-(aq) + H^+(aq)$$

$$CH_3CH_2CH_2COOH(aq) \rightleftharpoons CH_3CH_2CH_2COO^-(aq) + H^+(aq)$$

An acid may be defined in **two** ways.

- *An **acid** is a substance containing **hydrogen** which can be replaced directly or indirectly by a metal to form a salt.*

For example: $Zn(s) + 2HCl(aq) \longrightarrow ZnCl_2(aq) + H_2(g)$

The zinc replaces the hydrogen to form a salt called zinc chloride.

- *An **acid** is a **proton donor.***

H⁺ ions, present in aqueous acids, are **single protons**. This is because each H⁺ ion is a hydrogen nucleus containing a single proton which is formed by a hydrogen atom, ^1_1H, losing its valence electron (Figure 9.1).

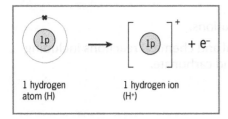

Figure 9.1 *Hydrogen atom in aqueous solution*

When an acid reacts it can **give** ('**donate**') its H⁺ ions or protons to the other reactant. For example, when aqueous nitric acid reacts with potassium hydroxide, the nitric acid donates its H⁺ ions, or **protons,** to the OH⁻ ions, forming water:

$$H^+(aq) + OH^-(aq) \longrightarrow H_2O(l)$$

Another example. When magnesium carbonate reacts with hydrochloric acid, the acid **donates** its H⁺ ions, or **protons,** to the CO_3^{2-} ions, forming carbon dioxide and water:

$$CO_3^{2-}(aq) + 2H^+(aq) \longrightarrow CO_2(g) + H_2O(l)$$

donated

General properties of acids in aqueous solution

The presence of **H⁺ ions** in aqueous solutions of acids gives them their characteristic properties. These solutions are described as being **acidic** and they have the following properties:

- They have a **sour** taste.
- They are **corrosive.** They cause metals to degenerate and cause skin to redden and burn.

- They change blue litmus to **red.** This is a very simple test for an acid.
- They have a pH value of **less than 7.**
- They conduct an electric current, that is, they dissolve in water to form ions. In other words they are **electrolytes.**

Chemical reactions of acids in aqueous solution

When acids react, the H^+ **ions** in the acid are replaced by metal or ammonium ions to form a **salt.** Salts therefore contain metal or ammonium cations and negative anions from the acid. Aqueous acids undergo the following reactions:

- **Acids react with reactive metals**

  Acids, except nitric acid, react with metals above hydrogen in the reactivity series (see page 295), to form a **salt** and **hydrogen.** Copper, silver, mercury and gold do not react. When the reaction occurs, effervescence is observed because hydrogen gas is produced. Heat is also given off in this reaction so the reaction vessel would feel hot when touched.

$$\boxed{\text{reactive metal + acid} \longrightarrow \text{salt + hydrogen}}$$

For example: $Ca(s) + 2HCl(aq) \longrightarrow CaCl_2(aq) + H_2(g)$

Ionically: $Ca(s) + 2H^+(aq) \longrightarrow Ca^{2+}(aq) + H_2(g)$

$Mg(s) + H_2SO_4(aq) \longrightarrow MgSO_4(aq) + H_2(g)$

Ionic equation: $Mg(s) + 2H^+(aq) \longrightarrow Mg^{2+}(aq) + H_2(g)$

Note Nitric acid is an oxidising agent (see page 172) which releases **oxides of nitrogen,** for example, nitrogen dioxide (NO_2), and not hydrogen, when it reacts with metals.

Test for hydrogen gas

To prove that hydrogen gas is generated during the reaction, a burning splint is put near the mouth of the test tube. Hydrogen will extinguish the flame and a popping sound will be heard. See Figure 9.2.

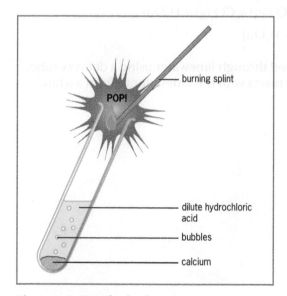

burning splint

POP!

dilute hydrochloric acid

bubbles

calcium

Figure 9.2 *Test for hydrogen gas*

- **Acids react with bases**

  Acids react with bases, which are mainly metal hydroxides and metal oxides (see page 131), to form a **salt** and **water**:

$$\text{base + acid} \longrightarrow \text{salt + water}$$

  For example: sodium hydroxide reacts with sulfuric acid to produce sodium sulfate and water:

$$2NaOH(aq) + H_2SO_4(aq) \longrightarrow Na_2SO_4(aq) + 2H_2O(l)$$

  Ionically: $\quad\quad\quad OH^-(aq) + H^+(aq) \longrightarrow H_2O(l)$

  Copper(II) oxide reacts with nitric acid to produce copper(II) nitrate and water:

$$CuO(s) + 2HNO_3(aq) \longrightarrow Cu(NO_3)_2(aq) + H_2O(l)$$

  Ionically: $\quad\quad\quad CuO(s) + 2H^+(aq) \longrightarrow Cu^{2+}(aq) + H_2O(l)$

- **Acids react with metal carbonates and metal hydrogencarbonates**

  Acids react with metal carbonates and metal hydrogencarbonates to form a **salt**, **carbon dioxide** and **water**. The reaction is effervescent because carbon dioxide is evolved:

$$\text{metal carbonate + acid} \longrightarrow \text{salt + carbon dioxide + water}$$

  For example: calcium carbonate reacts with sulfuric acid to form calcium sulfate, carbon dioxide and water:

$$CaCO_3(s) + H_2SO_4(aq) \longrightarrow CaSO_4(s) + CO_2(g) + H_2O(l)$$

  Ionically: $\quad\quad\quad CO_3^{2-}(aq) + 2H^+(aq) \longrightarrow CO_2(g) + H_2O(l)$

$$\text{metal hydrogencarbonate + acid} \longrightarrow \text{salt + carbon dioxide + water}$$

  For example: potassium hydrogencarbonate reacts with nitric acid to produce potassium nitrate, carbon dioxide and water:

$$KHCO_3(aq) + HNO_3(aq) \longrightarrow KNO_3(aq) + CO_2(g) + H_2O(l)$$

  Ionically: $\quad\quad\quad HCO_3^-(aq) + H^+(aq) \longrightarrow CO_2(g) + H_2O(l)$

To prove that carbon dioxide is evolved, the gas is passed through limewater using a delivery tube. The limewater turns milky because the carbon dioxide reacts with the limewater to form a white precipitate of calcium carbonate. See Figure 9.3.

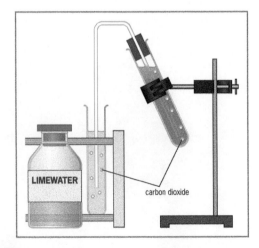

Figure 9.3 *Test for carbon dioxide*

There are several classifications of acids and these include:

- inorganic or organic
- strong or weak
- concentrated and dilute
- centred on basicity.

Inorganic or organic acids

Inorganic acids or mineral acids have origins from inorganic compounds and form hydrogen ions when dissolved in water. Examples of common inorganic acids include hydrochloric acid (HCl), sulfuric acid (H_2SO_4), nitric acid (HNO_3), phosphoric acid (H_3PO_4), sulfurous acid (H_2SO_3) and carbonic acid (H_2CO_3).

Organic acids are derived from living organisms. These acids consist mainly of carbon, hydrogen and oxygen and they dissolve in water to liberate H^+ ions from their carboxyl group ($-COOH$). Examples of these are tartaric acid, which is found in tamarind, citric acid present in citrus, lactic acid, methanoic acid and ascorbic acid. We will learn more about these acids in the Organic Chemistry section of this book (see page 269).

Strong and weak acids

Strong acids totally dissociate in water to form their ions. Examples of these are hydrochloric acid, sulfuric acid and phosphoric acid.

For example, hydrochloric acid: $HCl(aq) \longrightarrow H^+(aq) + Cl^-(aq)$

Weak acids only partially dissociate into their ions in aqueous solution. Examples of these are carbonic acids and organic acids such as methanoic acid, ethanoic acids, and citric acid.

For example, ethanoic acid: $CH_3COOH(aq) \rightleftharpoons H^+(aq) + CH_3COO^-(aq)$

The reversible arrows $\rightleftharpoons$ denote incomplete ionisation.

Dilute and concentrated acids

Dilute acids have a low concentration of acid in aqueous solution, that is, they contain a large quantity of water. For example, 0.05 mol dm^{-3} sulfuric acid is dilute.

Concentrated acids have a high concentration of acid and a small quantity of water. Examples of these are commercially available hydrochloric and sulfuric acid. A 10 mol dm^{-3} hydrochloric acid is concentrated.

The basicity of acids

Acids can also be **classified** according to their **basicity**.

Basicity is the number of H$^+$ ions produced per molecule of acid when the acid dissolves in water.

- **Monobasic acids** produce **one** H^+ ion per molecule. Examples of these are hydrochloric acid, nitric acid, ethanoic acid and lactic acid.

  For example: $HCl(aq) \longrightarrow H^+(aq) + Cl^-(aq)$

  $HNO_3(aq) \longrightarrow H^+(aq) + NO_3^-(aq)$

  Monobasic acids can only form **normal salts** (see page 141).

- **Dibasic acids** produce **two** H^+ ions per molecule. Examples are sulfuric acid, ethanedioic acid and tartaric acid.

  For example: $\quad H_2SO_4(aq) \longrightarrow 2H^+(aq) + SO_4^{2-}(aq)$

  Dibasic acids can form both **normal salts** and **acid salts** (see page 141).

- **Tribasic acids** produce **three** H^+ ions per molecule. Examples are phosphoric acid and citric acid.

  For example: $\quad H_3PO_4(aq) \longrightarrow 3H^+(aq) + PO_4^{3-}(aq)$

  Tribasic acids can form both **normal salts** and **acid salts**.

Acid anhydrides

An acid anhydride is a compound that reacts with water to form an acid.

Many acid anhydrides are **acidic oxides** of non-metals. Examples include carbon dioxide (CO_2), sulfur dioxide (SO_2), sulfur trioxide (SO_3) and nitrogen dioxide (NO_2).

$$CO_2(g) + H_2O(l) \rightleftharpoons H_2CO_3(aq)$$
carbonic acid

$$SO_2(g) + H_2O(l) \rightleftharpoons H_2SO_3(aq)$$
sulfurous acid

$$SO_3(g) + H_2O(l) \longrightarrow H_2SO_4(aq)$$
sulfuric acid

$$N_2O_5(g) + H_2O(l) \longrightarrow 2HNO_3(aq)$$
nitric(V) acid

$$2NO_2(g) + H_2O(l) \longrightarrow HNO_2(aq) + HNO_3(aq)$$
nitrous   nitric
acid   acid

Acids in living systems

Acids can be found naturally in living organisms and some are used in everyday activities.

Table 9.1 *Acids in living organisms and everyday activities*

Acid	Where found	Notes
Ascorbic acid or vitamin C ($C_6H_8O_6$)	In many fruits and vegetables, e.g. West Indian cherries, citrus fruit, raw green vegetables	• Vitamin C is essential in a healthy diet. A shortage can lead to **scurvy**. • When exposed to heat during cooking, vitamin C is **oxidised** which destroys it. • Sodium hydrogencarbonate is occasionally added to fruits and vegetables to improve appearance and texture. This **neutralises** any vitamin C in the foods which reduces its content.
Citric acid ($C_6H_8O_7$)	In citrus fruit, e.g. limes and lemons	• Lime juice can be used to **remove rust stains** from clothing. The acid in the juice reacts with the iron(III) oxide (Fe_2O_3) in the rust stains. This makes a **soluble** compound which washes out of the clothes removing the rusty yellow Fe^{3+} ions: $Fe_2O_3(s) + 6H^+(aq) \longrightarrow 2Fe^{3+}(aq) + 3H_2O(l)$ iron(III) oxide in the wash out i.e. rust acid of clothes

Acid	Where found	Notes
Methanoic acid (HCOOH)	In the venom of ants	• Methanoic acid can cause itching, swelling, redness and pain around the sting. • Ant stings can be treated by applying a paste of sodium hydrogencarbonate or calamine lotion which contains zinc oxide. Both compounds **neutralise** the acid.
Lactic acid ($C_3H_6O_3$)	Produced in the cells of muscles during strenuous activity.	• A person **collapses** if too much lactic acid builds up in the **muscles** because it prevents the muscles from contracting.
Ethanoic acid (CH_3COOH)	In vinegar	• Vinegar can be used to **preserve** food items. Its low pH denatures (destroys) enzymes that cause decay and prevents the growth of microorganisms, i.e. bacteria and fungi.

Other uses of acids

Acids have many uses in industry:

- Hydrochloric acid is used as a rust remover from metals. For example, the bodies of cars are dipped in hydrochloric acid before painting.
- Sulfuric acid is used in manufacturing fertilisers, detergents and car batteries.
- Nitric acid is used to manufacture fertilisers.
- Some tablets, when added to water, fizz because the tablets contain solid citric acid and solid sodium hydrogencarbonate. When added to water, the solid acid produces H^+ ions that react with the sodium hydrogencarbonate giving off carbon dioxide which causes the fizz.
- Soft drinks contain carbonic acid.
- Acids are used in the manufacture of antacids, which are used to raise the pH of stomach acid. A small amount of acid is added to this product. The acid serves two purposes: to start the reaction of the antacid tablet, and to add flavour to the tablet.

Bases

Learning objectives

- Define the terms **base** and **alkali** and distinguish between the two.
- Describe the characteristic properties of bases both generally and in chemical reactions with acids (**neutralisation**) and **ammonium compounds.**
- Give uses of bases.

Bases are chemically opposite to acids. Bases include **metal oxides**, for example, sodium oxide (Na_2O), copper(II) oxide (CuO) and **metal hydroxides**, for example, sodium hydroxide (NaOH), calcium hydroxide ($Ca(OH)_2$), copper(II) hydroxide ($Cu(OH)_2$), iron(II) hydroxide ($Fe(OH)_2$) and **ammonia** (NH_3).

A base is a proton acceptor.

When a **base** reacts with an **acid**, the O^{2-} ions or OH^- ions in the base **accept** the H^+ ions, or **protons**, from the acid, forming water. For example, when calcium hydroxide reacts with hydrochloric acid:

$$Ca(OH)_2(s) + 2HCl(aq) \longrightarrow CaCl_2(aq) + 2H_2O(l)$$

The ionic equation is as follows:

$$OH^-(aq) + H^+(aq) \longrightarrow H_2O(l)$$

accepted

Alkalis

An alkali is a base that dissolves in water to form a solution that contains OH⁻ ions.

Since most bases are **insoluble** in water, most bases are **not** alkalis. Therefore, sodium oxide, calcium oxide, copper(II) oxide, iron(III) oxide, copper(II) hydroxide, iron(II) oxide and iron(III) oxide are bases because they do not dissolve in water.

Alkalis include:

- potassium hydroxide (KOH) and sodium hydroxide (NaOH), which are soluble in water, and calcium hydroxide ($Ca(OH)_2$) which is slightly soluble:

  for example: $NaOH(s) + water \longrightarrow Na^+(aq) + OH^-(aq)$

- ammonia gas (NH_3), potassium oxide (K_2O), lithium oxide (Li_2O) and rubidium oxide (Rb_2O) which react with water to form a solution containing hydroxide ions:

  for example: $NH_3(g) + H_2O(l) \rightleftharpoons NH_4^+(aq) + OH^-(aq)$

  $K_2O(s) + H_2O(l) \longrightarrow 2K^+(aq) + 2OH^-(aq)$

General properties of aqueous solutions of alkalis

The presence of **OH⁻ ions** in aqueous solutions of alkalis gives them their characteristic properties. These solutions are described as being **alkaline** and they have the following properties:

- They have a **bitter** taste.
- They are **corrosive** when concentrated and can burn skin. In the dilute form they are irritants.
- They feel **slippery or soapy**. They react with the natural oils in the skin making soap.
- They change red litmus to **blue**. This is a simple test for an alkali.
- They have a pH value **greater than 7**.
- They conduct an electric current, that is, they are **electrolytes,** since they dissociate into their ions in water.

Chemical reactions of bases

- **Bases react with acids**

  Bases react with acids to produce a **salt** and **water** (see p. 128). The general word equation is as follows:

  base + acid ⟶ salt and water

  for example: potassium hydroxide and dilute nitric acid reacts to form potassium nitrate and water:

  $$KOH(aq) + HNO_3(aq) \longrightarrow KNO_3(aq) + H_2O(l)$$

  Ionic equation:

  $$OH^-(aq) + H^+(aq) \longrightarrow H_2O(l)$$

For example: copper(II) oxide and dilute hydrochloric acid react to produce copper(II) chloride and water:

$$CuO(s) + 2HCl(aq) \longrightarrow CuCl_2(aq) + H_2O(l)$$

Ionic equation:

$$CuO(s) + 2H^+(aq) \longrightarrow Cu^{2+}(aq) + H_2O(l)$$

Heat is produced during this reaction. Hence the reacting vessels feels warm when touched.

- **Bases react with ammonium salts**

When heated, bases react with ammonium salts to produce a **salt**, **ammonia** and **water**.

$$\boxed{\text{base} + \text{ammonium salt} \longrightarrow \text{salt} + \text{ammonia} + \text{water}}$$

For example:

$$Ba(OH)_2(s) + (NH_4)_2SO_4(s) \longrightarrow BaSO_4(s) + 2NH_3(g) + 2H_2O(l)$$
$$MgO(s) + 2NH_4Cl(s) \longrightarrow MgCl_2(s) + 2NH_3(g) + H_2O(l)$$

Test for ammonia gas

In addition to detecting ammonia gas by its pungent smell, it can be identified by holding a piece of moist litmus paper in the vicinity of the mouth of the test tube. The gas will turn the red litmus paper blue. This is one of the few gases that you would encounter at this level to turn red litmus blue! The ammonia gas is alkaline and dissolves in the water on the moist litmus paper to form aqueous ammonia, which is a weak alkali, hence the observation.

Uses of bases

- Bases are used as antacid tablets to neutralise excess stomach acids to prevent acid stomach, for example, aluminium hydroxide and sodium hydrogen carbonate.
- Hydroxides of potassium and sodium are used in the manufacture of soaps and detergents.
- Bases are used in the manufacture of window cleaners, for example, ammonia, to remove grease and dirt from glass.
- Sodium hydroxide is used in oven cleaners.
- Calcium carbonate and aluminium hydroxide are used in toothpaste to neutralise acids produced by bacteria in the mouth.
- Bases are used to correct soil acidity by adding calcium carbonate or calcium hydroxide which neutralises acidic soil. Acidic soil does not allow some plants to grow properly.

Distinguishing between acids and alkalis

Learning objectives

- Give the colours of some **common indicators** in acidic and alkaline solutions.
- Describe the differences between **strong and weak acids and alkalis**.
- Describe the **pH scale** as a gauge of relative acidity and alkalinity.
- Define the term **amphoteric substances**.
- Classify **oxides** centred around their metallic and non-metallic traits as **acidic, basic, amphoteric** or **neutral**.

Indicators are used to distinguish between **acids** and **alkalis** in aqueous solutions. These are dyes, or mixtures of dyes, which display one colour in an acidic solution and another colour in an alkaline solution.

Table 9.2 *Common indicators*

Indicator	Colour in an acidic solution	Colour in an alkaline solution
Litmus	Red	Blue
Universal	Red	Violet
Methyl orange	Red	Yellow
Screened methyl orange	Red	Green
Phenolphthalein	Colourless	Pink
Bromothymol blue	Yellow	Blue

There are many brightly coloured vegetables and flowers that can be used as indicators. For example, the coloured juice extracted from purple cabbage can be used as an indicator. It turns red when mixed with something acidic and green when in an alkali solution. Imagine – you can make an indicator at home and test solutions to determine which are acidic and which are alkaline.

The strength of acids and alkalis

The strength of an acid or alkali depends on the **degree of ionisation** that occurs when they dissolve in water.

- A **strong acid** is **fully ionised** when dissolved in water. All of the acid molecules ionise and the concentration of H^+ ions in the solution is **high**. Hydrochloric acid (HCl), sulfuric acid (H_2SO_4), nitric acid (HNO_3) and phosphoric acid (H_3PO_4) are strong acids.

  For example: $$H_2SO_4(aq) \longrightarrow 2H^+(aq) + SO_4^{2-}(aq)$$

- A **weak acid** is only **partially ionised** when dissolved in water. The solution contains a mixture of acid molecules and H^+ ions, and the concentration of H^+ ions in the solution is **low**, for example, ethanoic acid (CH_3COOH) and carbonic acid (H_2CO_3):

$$CH_3COOH(aq) \rightleftharpoons CH_3COO^-(aq) + H^+(aq)$$
$$\text{ethanoate ion}$$

$$H_2CO_3(l) \rightleftharpoons 2H^+(aq) + CO_3^{2-}(aq)$$

Other examples of weak acids include sulfurous acid (H_2SO_3), citric acid ($C_6H_8O_7$) and all other organic acids such as carboxylic acids.

Strong acids are strong electrolytes because they fully ionise. Weak acids do not fully ionise and so have very few ions to migrate towards the electrodes, making them weak electrolytes.

- A **strong alkali** is **fully ionised** when dissolved in water. The concentration of OH^- ions in the solution is **high**. Potassium hydroxide (KOH) and sodium hydroxide (NaOH) are strong alkalis.

  For example: $$KOH(aq) \longrightarrow K^+(aq) + OH^-(aq)$$

- A **weak alkali** is only **partially ionised** when dissolved in water. The concentration of OH^- ions in the solution is **low**, for example, ammonia (NH_3):

$$NH_3(g) + H_2O(l) \rightleftharpoons NH_4^+(aq) + OH^-(aq)$$

Measuring the strength of acids and alkalis

pH is an abbreviation which denotes the **power of the hydrogen** and is a scale of numbers of values between 0 and 14 that tells the **strength** of an acid or alkali. **pH 7** on the scale is neutral. The pH of pure water is 7.

A solution with a pH of less than 7 is acidic and the smaller the pH value the more acidic the solution and the higher the concentration of hydrogen ions it contains. A solution of pH 4 or 5 is a weak acid, for example, ethanoic acid, whereas a solution of pH 1 is a strong acid, for example, sulfuric acid.

A solution with a larger pH than 7 is alkaline. The higher the pH the more hydroxide ions are present and the more alkaline the solution. A solution of pH 9 or 10 is a weak alkali, for example, aqueous ammonia, and one with pH 14 is a strong alkali such as potassium hydroxide.

The **strength** of an aqueous acid or alkali can be measured on the **pH scale** by using **universal indicator**. Simple indicators, litmus for example, only tell if a solution is acidic or alkali. However, universal indicator, which is a mixture of several indicators, can not only tell whether the solution is acidic or alkaline but also whether it is a strong or weak acid or alkali. Universal indicator not only changes colour from red to violet but also changes to colours in-between red and violet: orange, yellow, green, blue and indigo. Each of these colours is associated with a particular pH value (Figure 9.4) and thus the colours obtained indicate the strength of the acid or alkali.

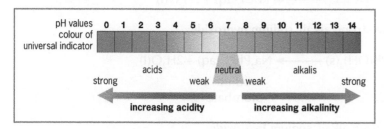

Figure 9.4 *The pH scale*

Note None of the indicators named in Table 9.2 measures pH.

Another method of measuring pH is to use a pH meter. Figure 9.5 shows a pH meter. When the probe is dipped into the solution, the pH is either digitally displayed or shown on a scale. The pH meter gives accurate values unlike universal indicator, which gives approximate pH values.

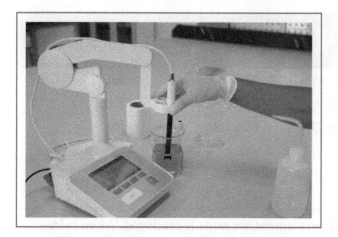

Figure 9.5 *A pH meter*

Amphoteric oxides and hydroxides

*An **amphoteric oxide** or **hydroxide** can react with both **acids** and **strong alkalis** to form a salt and water.*

These oxides and hydroxides display both acidic and basic characteristics and so are referred to as **amphoteric oxides or hydroxides.**

The general word equations for the reactions of these amphoteric oxides and hydroxides with an acid and a base respectively are given below:

> amphoteric oxide or hydroxide + acid ⟶ salt + water

> strong alkali + amphoteric oxide or hydroxide ⟶ salt + water

The oxides and hydroxides of **aluminium**, **zinc** and **lead** are amphoteric.

Example 1

- **Lead(II) hydroxide** reacts with the acid, **hydrochloric acid:**

$$Pb(OH)_2(s) + 2HCl(aq) \longrightarrow PbCl_2(aq) + 2H_2O(l)$$

- **Lead(II) hydroxide** reacts with the strong alkali, **sodium hydroxide:**

$$2NaOH(aq) + Pb(OH)_2(s) \longrightarrow Na_2PbO_2(aq) + 2H_2O(l)$$
$$\text{sodium}$$
$$\text{plumbate}$$

- **Zinc hydroxide** reacts with the strong alkali, **sodium hydroxide:**

$$2NaOH(aq) + Zn(OH)_2(s) \longrightarrow Na_2ZnO_2(aq) + 2H_2O(l)$$
$$\text{sodium}$$
$$\text{zincate}$$

Table 9.3 *Amphoteric oxides and hydroxides*

Amphoteric oxide	Amphoteric hydroxide	Salts formed when reacting with a strong alkali	Anion present in the salt
Aluminium oxide (Al_2O_3)	Aluminium hydroxide ($Al(OH)_3$)	**Aluminates**	AlO_2^-
Zinc oxide (ZnO)	Zinc hydroxide ($Zn(OH)_2$)	**Zincates**	ZnO_2^{2-}
Lead(II) oxide (PbO)	Lead(II) hydroxide ($Pb(OH)_2$)	**Plumbates**	PbO_2^{2-}

Classification of oxides

During a reaction in which oxygen combines with an element, an oxide is produced. When oxides are dissolved in water they display different characteristics. Based on their characteristics, oxides are classified into **four** groups:

- **Acidic oxides**

  *Acidic oxides are oxides of some **non-metals** that react with **alkalis** to form a salt and water.*

  Acidic oxides dissolve in water to form acids and therefore turn moist blue litmus paper red.

Examples include carbon dioxide (CO_2), sulfur dioxide (SO_2), sulfur trioxide (SO_3), nitrogen dioxide (NO_2), phosphorous(V) oxide (P_2O_5) and silicon dioxide (SiO_2).

Potassium hydroxide reacts with carbon dioxide to produce potassium carbonate and water:

$$2KOH(aq) + CO_2(g) \longrightarrow K_2CO_3(aq) + H_2O(l)$$

Most acidic oxides also react with **water** to form an acid, that is, they are acid anhydrides (see page 130).

Carbon dioxide and water produces carbonic acid, which is a weak acid:

$$CO_2(g) + H_2O(l) \longrightarrow H_2CO_3(aq)$$

- **Basic oxides**

  Basic oxides *are oxides of* metals *which react with* acids *to form a salt and water.*

  These basic oxides if soluble in water produce alkalis and therefore turn damp red litmus paper blue.

  Examples include magnesium oxide (MgO), iron(III) oxide (Fe_2O_3) and copper(II) oxide (CuO).

  For example: $\quad MgO(s) + 2HNO_3(aq) \longrightarrow Mg(NO_3)_2(aq) + H_2O(l)$

  Potassium oxide (K_2O), sodium oxide (Na_2O) and calcium oxide (CaO) are basic oxides which are also classified as **alkalis** because they react with **water** to form a solution containing OH^- ions.

  For example: $\quad CaO(s) + H_2O(l) \longrightarrow Ca(OH)_2(aq)$

- **Amphoteric oxides**

  Amphoteric oxides *are oxides of some* metals *which react with both* acids *and* strong alkalis *to form a salt and water.*

  There are three common amphoteric oxides, aluminium oxide (Al_2O_3), zinc oxide (ZnO) and lead(II) oxide (PbO) (see page 136).

  Lead oxide can react with sulfuric acid to produce lead sulfate and water:

  $$PbO(s) + H_2SO_4(aq) \longrightarrow PbSO_4(aq) + H_2O(l)$$

  Lead oxide can also react with potassium hydroxide to form potassium plumbate and water:

  $$2KOH(aq) + PbO(s) \longrightarrow K_2PbO_2(aq) + H_2O(l)$$

- **Neutral oxides**

  Neutral oxides *are oxides of some* non-metals *which do not react with* acids *or* alkalis.

  Examples include carbon monoxide (CO), nitrogen monoxide (NO), dinitrogen monoxide (N_2O) and hydrogen oxide, H_2O (water).

Recalling facts

1   Which of the following is NOT true about an acid?

a turns red litmus blue

b has a pH less than 7

c ionises forming H^+ ions

d corrosive

2 A dibasic acid produces:

   a one H⁺ ion in solution

   b two H⁺ ions in solution

   c three H⁺ ions in solution

   d none of the above

3 A metal and an acid form:

   a salt only

   b hydrogen only

   c salt and water

   d salt and hydrogen

4 A metal carbonate and an acid react to produce:

   a salt only

   b carbon dioxide and water only

   c salt and water only

   d salt, water and carbon dioxide

5 The colour of screened methyl orange in dilute hydrochloric acid is:

   a blue

   b yellow

   c red

   d pink

6 Which of the following is the weakest acid?

   a 0.3 M HCl

   b 0.3 M H_2SO_4

   c 0.3 M H_3PO_4

   d 0.3 M CH_3COOH

7 The following are properties of bases except:

   a pH greater than 7

   b turns blue litmus red

   c produces OH⁻ ions in solution

   d conducts an electric current

8 The pH of a solution is 9. Therefore this solution is:

   a less basic than one of pH 8

   b less basic than one of pH 11

   c more acidic than water

   d more acidic than CH_3COOH

9   Potassium hydroxide is a strong alkali, therefore its pH is expected to be:

a   2

b   6

c   9

d   13.5

10   A strong alkali:

a   partially ionises

b   fully ionises

c   fully unionises

d   is dilute

11   What is meant by the term basicity of an acid? Give an example of a monobasic, a dibasic and a tribasic acid.

12   Describe a test to prove that the following gases are given off when a reaction occurs:

a   hydrogen gas

b   ammonia gas

c   carbon dioxide gas

13   Define the term acid anhydride. Name three examples of acid anhydrides and write equations to represent their reactions with water.

14   List five general properties of bases.

15   List three uses of bases.

16   Distinguish between a strong acid and a weak acid, giving two examples of each.

Applying facts

17   Explain the following.

a   Why do HCl, H_2SO_4 and CH_3COOH show acidic properties in water.

b   Why do KOH and $NaOH$ show alkali properties in water.

c   Why does an aqueous solution of acids and bases conduct electricity.

d   Why does dry HCl gas does not change the colour of dry litmus paper but a colour change from blue to red is observed when the litmus paper is moistened.

18   Name three different types of chemical substances which react with acids to produce salts. For each type give a named example and write a balanced chemical reaction and the corresponding ionic equation to represent the reaction.

19   Discuss how three acids which are found in living organisms can benefit a person in their everyday activities.

20   Discuss two methods of distinguishing between the strengths of acids and alkalis.

21 Describe what happens if you add a drop of litmus on a small amount of yoghurt, window cleaner, dishwashing liquid, apple cider vinegar, oven cleaner and a cut piece of lime.

22 a Link the metallic and non-metallic attributes of oxides to their classification as acidic, basic or amphoteric.

b Give an example of each of these oxides: acidic, basic, amphoteric and neutral.

c For the example given for an amphoteric oxide in part b, write a balanced chemical equation to represent its reaction with:

i an acid

ii an alkali.

Salts

Learning objectives

- Define the term **salt**.
- Classify salts as **normal** or **acidic**.
- Describe the techniques used in the **preparation** and **separation of salts**.
- Recommend a method of **salt preparation** given the suitable starting raw materials and other appropriate data.
- Explain the uses of salts in everyday life.
- Give some of the dangers of salts.

A salt is a compound formed when some or all of the hydrogen ions in an acid are replaced by metal or ammonium ions.

In other words, a salt is formed when an acid neutralises a base or an alkali, and also when an acid and a metal or metal carbonate react. Salts are ionic compounds and are made up of two components: a cation and an anion. The **cation** is a positively charged ion that originates from the metal itself, a base, a carbonate, or a hydrogen carbonate. The **anion** is a negatively charged ion, originating from the acid.

For example, copper oxide reacts with hydrochloric acid to produce copper chloride and water. In this example, the salt is copper chloride, the copper cation is derived from the base, copper oxide, and the chloride anion is derived from the acid, hydrochloric acid.

base part

$$CuO(s) + 2HCl(aq) \longrightarrow CuCl_2(aq) + H_2O(l)$$

acid part

Classification of salts

It has already been discussed (see page 126) that the hydrogen atom of an acid is replaced by a metal to form the cation in a salt, and that when an acid dissolves in water at least one hydrogen ion is liberated. The amount of hydrogen liberated depends on the basicity of the acid. Therefore a monobasic acid, such as nitric acid (HNO_3) produces one hydrogen ion per molecule, sulfuric acid (H_2SO_4), a dibasic acid produces two hydrogen ions per molecule, and phosphoric acid (H_3PO_4), a tribasic acid produces three hydrogen ions per molecule. The dibasic and tribasic acids therefore, have more hydrogen atoms to be replaced by the metal. Therefore, the nature of the salt depends on how many hydrogen atoms are replaced. This is discussed below.

Salts can therefore be **classified** into **two** groups:

Acid salts are formed when the H^+ ions in an acid are only **partially replaced** by metal or ammonium ions. Only **dibasic** and **tribasic** acids can form acid salts as seen below.

For example: using a dibasic acid

$$NaOH(aq) + H_2SO_4(aq) \longrightarrow NaHSO_4(aq) + H_2O(l)$$

Sodium hydrogensulfate is an acidic salt – only one H^+ ion is replaced.

The **relative quantity** of each reactant determines the **type** of salt formed by the dibasic acid.

A **normal salt** is produced when **2 mol** of sodium hydroxide react with **1 mol** of sulfuric acid.

An **acidic salt** is produced when **1 mol** of sodium hydroxide reacts with **1 mol** of sulfuric acid.

For example: using a tribasic acid

$$NaOH(aq) + H_3PO_4(aq) \longrightarrow NaH_2PO_4(aq) + H_2O(l)$$
$$2NaOH(aq) + H_3PO_4(aq) \longrightarrow Na_2HPO_4(aq) + 2H_2O(l)$$

Sodium dihydrogenphosphate (only one H^+ ion is replaced) and sodium hydrogenphosphate (two H^+ ions are replaced) are acidic salts.

A **normal salt** is produced when **3 mol** of sodium hydroxide reacts with **1 mol** of phosphoric acid.

An **acidic salt** is produced when **2 mol** of sodium hydroxide react with **1 mol** of phosphoric acid.

Another **acidic salt** is produced when **1 mol** of sodium hydroxide reacts with **1 mol** of phosphoric acid.

Table 9.4 *Salts formed by some common acids*

Acid	Salts formed	Anion present	Type of salt	Name of the sodium salt	Formula
hydrochloric acid (HCl)	Chlorides	Cl^-	Normal	sodium chloride	$NaCl$
nitric acid (HNO_3)	Nitrates	NO_3^-	Normal	sodium nitrate	$NaNO_3$
ethanoic acid (CH_3COOH)	Ethanoates	CH_3COO^-	Normal	sodium ethanoate	CH_3COONa
sulfuric acid (H_2SO_4)	Sulfates	SO_4^{2-}	Normal	sodium sulfate	Na_2SO_4
	hydrogensulfates	HSO_4^-	acid	sodium hydrogensulfate	$NaHSO_4$
carbonic acid (H_2CO_3)	carbonates	CO_3^{2-}	normal	sodium carbonate	Na_2CO_3
	hydrogencarbonates	HCO_3^-	acid	sodium hydrogencarbonate	$NaHCO_3$
phosphoric acid (H_3PO_4)	Phosphates	PO_4^{3-}	normal	sodium phosphate	Na_3PO_4
	hydrogenphosphates	HPO_4^{2-}	acid	disodium hydrogenphosphate	Na_2HPO_4
	Dihydrogenphosphates	$H_2PO_4^-$	acid	sodium dihydrogenphosphate	NaH_2PO_4

Water of crystallisation

Some salts may contain **water of crystallisation**. This is a fixed proportion of water molecules held within their crystal lattice. Salts containing water of crystallisation are said to be **hydrated** and the water of crystallisation can be shown in the formula, for example, $CuSO_4 \cdot 5H_2O$ represents hydrated copper(II) sulfate, $CoCl_2 \cdot 6H_2O$ represents hydrated cobalt chloride and $ZnSO_4 \cdot 7H_2O$ represents hydrated zinc sulfate.

In some compounds, water of crystallisation is responsible for the **shape**, and sometimes the **colour**, of the crystals. If removed by heating, the salt becomes **anhydrous**; it loses its crystalline structure and its colour may change (Figure 9.6).

For example:
$$CoCl_2 \cdot 6H_2O(s) \xrightarrow{\text{heat}} CoCl_2(s) + 6H_2O(g)$$

pink crystals   blue colour
hydrated   anhydrous

Figure 9.6 *Hydrated and anhydrous cobalt chloride crystals*

Methods used to prepare salts

Salts are utilised in the agricultural, medical, research, food, chemical and construction industries. In other words, salts perform a vital role in our daily lives. It is therefore important to know how to prepare these salts, which are so essential for our existence. When preparing any salt, the following must be considered:

• the **solubility** of the **salt** being prepared
• the **solubility** of the **reactants** being used to prepare the salt.

The solubility of ionic compounds is summarised in Tables 6.1 and 6.2 on pages 94 and 95. The method chosen to prepare soluble salts is different from the method for insoluble salts.

Preparation of a soluble salt

There are three main methods for preparing soluble salts:

• direct combination
• reactions with acids
• neutralisation reactions of acid and alkali.

Direct combination

Some soluble salts are prepared through the direct reaction between a metal and a non-metal. Recall that a salt is made up of two parts – the cation and the anion. In this method of salt preparation, the cation is derived from the metal and the anion from the non-metal, preparation of anhydrous iron chloride and anhydrous aluminium chloride.

Let us look at the method of preparation of anhydrous iron chloride. Figure 9.7 illustrates the set-up for the preparation.

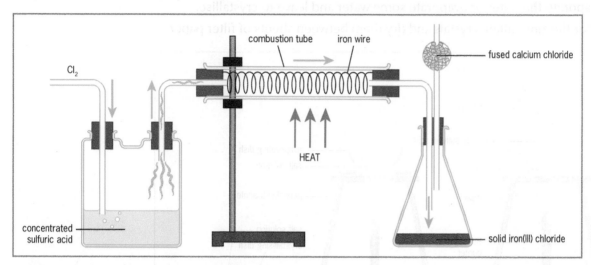

Figure 9.7 *Preparation of iron chloride*

Iron wire is placed in a combustion tube as seen on the diagram. Chlorine gas is dried by bubbling it through concentrated sulfuric acid. The dry chlorine gas is then passed through the combustion tube. The iron and chlorine react in the combustion tube to produce iron chloride.

$$2Fe(s) + 3Cl_2(g) \longrightarrow 2FeCl_3(s)$$

heated   dry   black solids in anhydrous form

Heat is given off in this reaction, so the iron chloride vaporises when formed and then solidifies in the collecting vessel. Iron chloride is deliquescent (it tends to absorb moisture from the air and dissolve in it), so moisture is kept away by using fused calcium chloride. Iron chloride in the anhydrous form is black and in the hydrated form a yellow colour develops.

Reactions with acids

Soluble salts can be prepared by the reaction of an acid with a metal, an insoluble base or an insoluble carbonate.

Reacting an acid with a metal

This method is only suitable for metals that react moderately with a dilute acid, for example magnesium, aluminium, iron and zinc.

Experiment 9.1

Aim: to prepare zinc sulfate (soluble salt) crystals by reacting zinc (metal) and sulfuric acid (acid).

1 Add zinc with stirring to 50 cm³ hot dilute sulfuric acid.
2 Keep adding zinc until effervescence (bubbling) stops and the metal is present in excess.
3 Dip a piece of blue litmus paper into the solution; it should remain blue.
4 Filter to remove the excess zinc metal, collect the filtrate.
5 Evaporate the water or evaporate some water and leave to crystallise.
6 Filter the zinc sulfate crystals and dry them between sheets of filter paper.

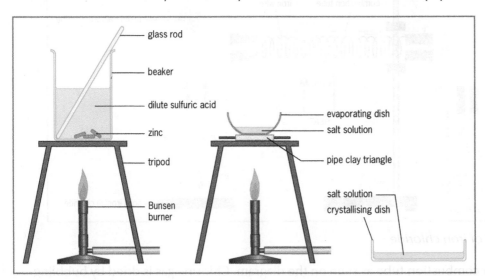

Figure 9.8 *Preparation of zinc sulfate*

Reacting an acid with an insoluble base

This method involves reacting insoluble metal oxides with acids. This method is like that of reacting an acid with a metal.

For example, the preparation of copper(II) sulfate:

$$CuO(s) + H_2SO_4(aq) \longrightarrow CuSO_4(aq) + H_2O(l)$$

Experiment 9.2

Aim: to prepare copper(II) sulfate (soluble salt) crystals by reacting copper(II) oxide (insoluble base) with sulfuric acid (acid).

1 Add copper(II) oxide to 50 cm³ warm sulfuric acid in a beaker.
2 Keep adding copper(II) oxide until it is present in excess, that is, until effervescence stops.
  Dip a piece of **blue litmus** paper into the solution, it should remain **blue**.
3 **Filter** to remove the excess copper(II) oxide, collect the filtrate.
4 **Evaporate** the water or evaporate some water.
5 Leave to **crystallise**.
6 Filter the copper(II) sulfate crystals.
7 Dry the copper(II) sulfate crystals between sheets of filter paper.

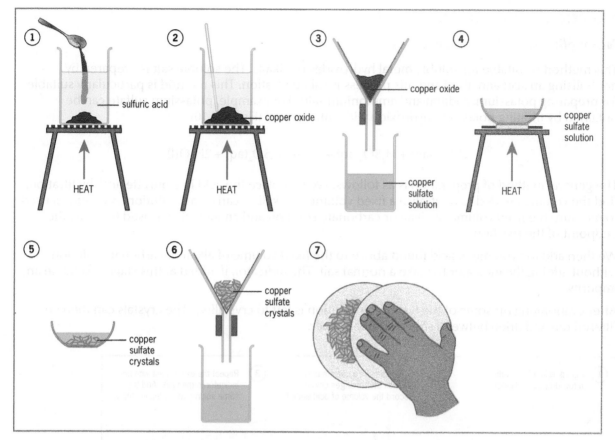

Figure 9.9 *Preparing copper(II) sulfate crystals by the action of acid on insoluble bases*

Reacting an acid with an insoluble carbonate

This method is like that involved in the action of acids on insoluble bases, except heating is not necessary. In this reaction, the carbonate bubbles and carbon dioxide gas is evolved. The general equation for this type of reaction is

$$\text{metal carbonate + acid} \longrightarrow \text{salt + water + carbon dioxide}$$

Copper(II) carbonate, calcium carbonate and zinc carbonate can be used to prepare salts using this method.

An example of this reaction is zinc carbonate reacting with nitric acid to produce zinc nitrate, water and carbon dioxide:

$$ZnCO_3(s) + 2HNO_3(aq) \longrightarrow Zn(NO_3)_2(aq) + H_2O(l) + CO_2(g)$$

Soluble zinc nitrate can be prepared by first adding zinc carbonate to about 25 cm³ of nitric acid in a beaker. We keep adding until the zinc carbonate is present in excess, that is, until effervescence stops.

To check that there is no acid remaining, we can dip a piece of blue litmus paper into the solution; it should remain blue.

We then filter the mixture to remove the excess zinc carbonate and collect the filtrate. After evaporating some of the water, the solution is left to crystallise. The zinc nitrate crystals can then be filtered out and dried between sheets of filter paper.

Reaction with a soluble base

Neutralisation of acids and alkalis

This method is suitable for soluble metal hydroxides or alkalis. The soluble salt is prepared by neutralising an acid and alkali and this process is called titration. This method is particularly suitable for preparing potassium, sodium and ammonium salts. For example, potassium sulfate can be obtained by titrating potassium hydroxide with sulfuric acid (Figure 9.10)

$$2KOH(aq) + H_2SO_4(aq) \longrightarrow K_2SO_4(aq) + 2H_2O(l)$$

The general method of preparation is as follows. We first place the acid in a burette and, by titration, find the volume needed to neutralise a fixed volume of alkali or carbonate solution. A pipette is used to measure the fixed volume of alkali or carbonate solution and an indicator is used to signal the endpoint of the reaction.

We then add the volume of acid found above to the fixed volume of alkali or carbonate solution without adding the indicator to make a normal salt. The indicator, if added at this stage, would be an impurity.

After evaporating off some of the water, the solution is left to crystallise. The crystals can then be filtered out and dried between sheets of filter paper.

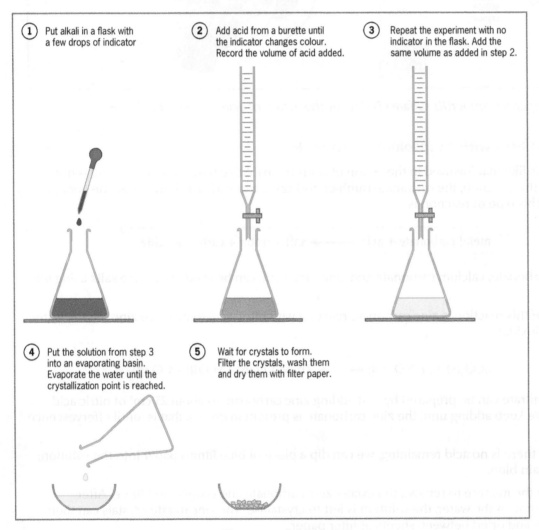

(1) Put alkali in a flask with a few drops of indicator

(2) Add acid from a burette until the indicator changes colour. Record the volume of acid added.

(3) Repeat the experiment with no indicator in the flask. Add the same volume as added in step 2.

(4) Put the solution from step 3 into an evaporating basin. Evaporate the water until the crystallization point is reached.

(5) Wait for crystals to form. Filter the crystals, wash them and dry them with filter paper.

Figure 9.10 *Preparing potassium sulfate crystals by titration*

Ionic precipitation

Preparation of an insoluble salt

As can be seen in Figure 9.11, an insoluble salt can be made by **precipitation.** This involves mixing aqueous solutions of two suitable salts, one containing its positive ions with another solution containing its negative ions. Insoluble salts such as lead(II) chloride, lead(II) sulfate, barium sulfate and copper(II) carbonate can be prepared using this method.

For example, lead(II) sulfate can be prepared by reacting lead(II) nitrate with sodium sulfate:

$$Pb(NO_3)_2(aq) + Na_2SO_4(aq) \longrightarrow PbSO_4(s) + 2NaNO_3(aq)$$

This reaction can be carried out in this way. Lead(II) nitrate is dissolved in 50 cm³ of distilled water in a beaker. In another beaker sodium sulfate is dissolved using 50 cm³ of distilled water.

The two solutions are then mixed together to form a precipitate. The mixture is then filtered and the residue washed with distilled water. The lead(II) sulfate crystals can now be air dried or dried between two sheets of filter paper.

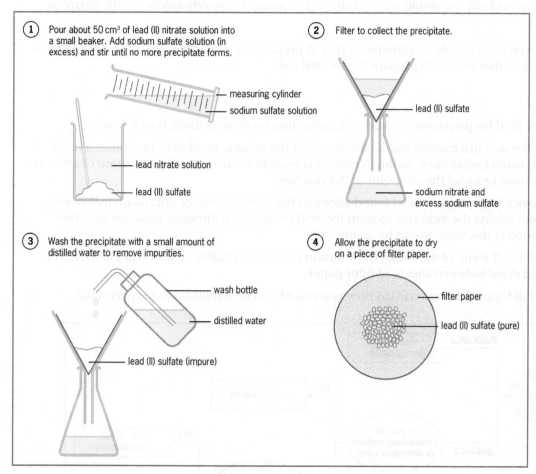

(1) Pour about 50 cm³ of lead (II) nitrate solution into a small beaker. Add sodium sulfate solution (in excess) and stir until no more precipitate forms.
- measuring cylinder
- sodium sulfate solution
- lead nitrate solution
- lead (II) sulfate

(2) Filter to collect the precipitate.
- lead (II) sulfate
- sodium nitrate and excess sodium sulfate

(3) Wash the precipitate with a small amount of distilled water to remove impurities.
- wash bottle
- distilled water
- lead (II) sulfate (impure)

(4) Allow the precipitate to dry on a piece of filter paper.
- filter paper
- lead (II) sulfate (pure)

Figure 9.11 *Preparation of an insoluble salt*

Preparation of acid salt

It was discussed earlier that when reacting dibasic or tribasic acids with bases, there are two or three possible salts produced respectively, a normal salt or an acidic salt.

Look at the reaction between potassium hydroxide and sulfuric acid. Two possible salts can be derived:

The formation of a normal salt:

$$2KOH(aq) + H_2SO_4(aq) \longrightarrow K_2SO_4(aq) + 2H_2O(l)$$

The formation of an acidic salt:

$$KOH(aq) + H_2SO_4(aq) \longrightarrow KHSO_4(aq) + H_2O(l)$$

When we examine the stoichiometric equation for the reactions above, we can conclude that:

- To prepare a normal salt, a 2:1 mol ratio of the reactants potassium hydroxide to sulfuric acid is necessary.
- To prepare an acidic salt, a 1:1 mol ratio of the reactants potassium hydroxide to sulfuric acid is necessary.

Let us now use the same concentrations of potassium hydroxide and sulfuric acid, then we can use the ratios mentioned above to volumes of these solutions. For example, if we use a 0.2 mol dm^{-3} potassium hydroxide solution and 0.2 mol dm^{-3} sulfuric acid solution then:

- To prepare a normal salt, we would react 50 cm^3 of potassium hydroxide solution with 25 cm^3 of sulfuric acid.
- To produce an acid salt, we would react 50 cm^3 of potassium hydroxide solution with 50 cm^3 of sulfuric acid.

It can be deduced from the above statements that to prepare the acid salt we would need to **double** the volume of acid that we use to prepare the normal salt.

Method

The general method for preparing the acid salt, potassium hydrogensulfate, is as follows.

We first place the acid in a burette and by titration find the volume needed to neutralise a fixed volume of potassium hydroxide solution. A pipette is used to measure the fixed volume of alkali and an indicator is used to signal the endpoint of the reaction.

We then add twice the volume of acid found above to the fixed volume of potassium hydroxide solution without adding the indicator to form the acid potassium hydrogencarbonate salt. The indicator, if added at this stage would be an impurity.

After evaporating off some of the water, the solution is left to crystallise. The crystals can then be filtered out and dried between sheets of filter paper.

The flow chart in Figure 9.12 summarises how you would choose a method to prepare a salt.

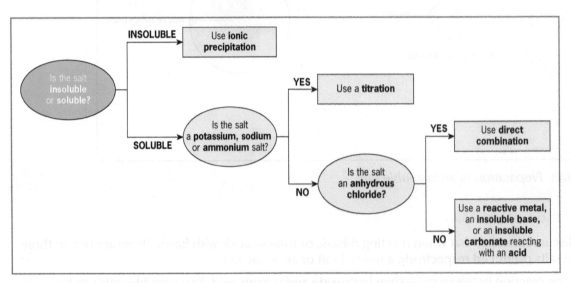

Figure 9.12 *A flow diagram summarising the methods to prepare salts*

Salts in everyday life

Salts are important in everyday life, though some can be dangerous. Tables 9.5 and 9.6 give uses of salts in everyday life and the dangers associated with using some of these salts.

Table 9.5 *Uses of salts in everyday life*

Salt	Use	Notes
Sodium hydrogencarbonate ($NaHCO_3$)	A component of baking powder used to make cakes rise.	Baking powder also contains a weak acid and when mixed with the liquid in the cake mixture, the two active components react and form **carbon dioxide**: $$HCO_3^-(aq) + H^+(aq) \longrightarrow CO_2(g) + H_2O(l)$$ Carbon dioxide forms bubbles in the cake. These bubbles cause the cake to rise as they expand on heating.
Sodium benzoate (C_6H_5COONa)	To preserve food.	Used to preserve foods which have a **low pH**, e.g. fruit juices and fizzy drinks. At a low pH it is converted to benzoic acid which prevents the growth of microorganisms.
Sodium chloride ($NaCl$)	To preserve food.	Used to preserve and also flavour food such as **meat** and **fish** (see page 7).
Sodium nitrate ($NaNO_3$) and **sodium nitrite** ($NaNO_2$)	To preserve food.	Used to preserve **meat**, e.g. bacon and ham. They destroy bacteria which cause food poisoning, slow the oxidation of fats and oils which causes rancidity, give an attractive red colour to the meat and add flavour. They are often used together with sodium chloride.
Calcium carbonate (limestone) ($CaCO_3$)	To manufacture cement used in the construction industry.	When heated in a kiln, it decomposes to form **calcium oxide**: $$CaCO_3(s) \longrightarrow CaO(s) + CO_2(g)$$ Calcium oxide is blended with the other materials in the kiln to form **clinker** which is then ground with calcium sulfate to make cement.
Calcium sulfate (gypsum) ($CaSO_4 \cdot 2H_2O$)	To manufacture plaster of Paris used as a building material and for setting broken bones.	Plaster of Paris is made of anhydrous calcium sulfate. When water is added, heat is given off and a **paste** forms. The paste is used to coat walls and ceilings, and bandages impregnated in it are used to make orthopaedic casts.
Magnesium sulfate (Epsom salt) ($MgSO_4 \cdot 7H_2O$)	For various medicinal purposes.	Has numerous **health benefits**. Added to bath water it relieves stress, eases aches and pains, reduces inflammation and helps cure skin problems. Taken orally it works as a laxative.
	In agriculture.	Improves **plant growth**.

Table 9.6 *Dangers of salts*

Salt	Dangers of the salt
Sodium benzoate (C_6H_5COONa)	May increase the risk of developing **cancer** (may be **carcinogenic**). May increase **hyperactivity** and **asthma** in children.
Sodium chloride (NaCl)	Can lead to **hypertension** (high blood pressure) if consumed in excess.
Sodium nitrate ($NaNO_3$) and **sodium nitrite** ($NaNO_2$)	May increase the risk of developing **cancer** (may be **carcinogenic**). May cause **brain damage** in infants.

Neutralisation reactions

Learning objectives

- Describe **neutralisation** as a reaction between hydrogen ions and hydroxide ions to produce water.
- Describe how to perform neutralisation reactions using an indicator and temperature changes.
- Describe applications of neutralisation in our daily lives.

*A **neutralisation reaction** is a reaction between a base and an acid to form a salt and water.*

A neutralisation reaction involves the transfer of a hydrogen ion, H^+, from one chemical species to another. During a neutralisation reaction, the acid and the base cancel one another's chemistry to produce a salt and water as stated above. The general reaction is:

$$\text{acid} + \text{base} \longrightarrow \text{salt and water}$$

Such reactions are of crucial importance to numerous biological, environmental and industrial processes. These extend from the biochemical changes that occur in our cells and in the marine environment, to the manufacturing of fertilisers, pharmaceuticals and other materials vital to our survival.

In a neutralisation reaction between an aqueous alkali and an aqueous acid, for example, potassium hydroxide and hydrochloric acid forming potassium chloride and water:

$$KOH(aq) + HCl(aq) \longrightarrow KCl(aq) + H_2O(l)$$

the **OH^- ions** of the alkali react with the **H^+ ions** of the acid and this is represented by the ionic equation:

$$OH^-(aq) + H^+(aq) \longrightarrow H_2O(l)$$

Remember that the K^+ and Cl^- ions remain as spectator ions in solution and are not included in the ionic equation.

The **neutralisation point** or **end point** occurs when the OH^- ions have fully reacted with the H^+ ions and neither ion is present in excess. In a reaction between a **strong alkali** and a **strong acid**, the solution at this point is neutral, **pH 7**. Neutralisation reactions are **exothermic** as they produce heat energy. This characteristic of an acid–base reaction can be used when obtaining the **neutralisation point** of reactions.

To determine the neutralisation point in an acid–alkali reaction

The **neutralisation point** of a reaction between an aqueous alkali and an aqueous acid is determined by performing a **titration** using an **indicator** (see Table 9.2, page 134) or **temperature change**.

- **Using an indicator**

  A fixed volume of alkali (for example, 25 ml) is measured using a pipette and transferred into a conical flask. A few drops of **indicator** are added and the acid is added from a burette. The neutralisation point is determined when the **colour** of the solution changes on the addition of a **single drop** of acid from the burette. Some common indicators are given in Table 9.2. The experiment is repeated three times and the average volume is calculated from the results.

- **Using temperature change (a thermometric titration)**

  A fixed volume of alkali is placed into an insulated container and its temperature is recorded. The acid is added in small quantities, for example, 2 cm^3, from a burette and the temperature is recorded after each addition until several successive drops in temperature have been recorded. A **graph** is drawn showing temperature against volume of acid added. Two straight lines of **best fit** are drawn and the **point of intersection** of the lines is the neutralisation point.

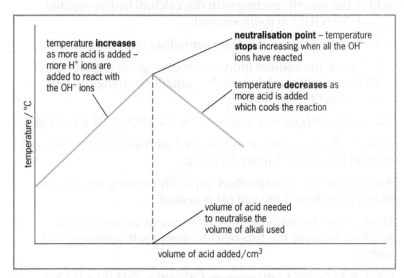

Figure 9.13 *Graph showing temperature against volume of acid added to a fixed volume of alkali*

Sodium chloride crystals can be prepared by thermometric titration. The chemical equation below shows the formation of sodium chloride:

$$NaOH(aq) + HCl(aq) \longrightarrow NaCl(aq) + H_2O(l)$$

This reaction can be carried out in this way. We first rinse the burette with 0.5 M hydrochloric acid solution and fill it with the acid. A pipette is then used to transfer 25 cm^3 of 0.5 M sodium hydroxide solution into a plastic cup. The temperature of the sodium hydroxide is checked and recorded using a thermometer. We then keep the thermometer in the sodium hydroxide solution and add 5 cm^3 of the 0.5 M hydrochloric acid, stirring the mixture with the thermometer and recording the highest temperature reached. We then promptly add another 5 cm^3 0.5 M hydrochloric acid, stirring the mixture and recording the highest temperature reached. This is repeated until 50 cm^3 of hydrochloric acid has been used.

The volumes of 0.5 M hydrochloric acid added and temperatures obtained are recorded in a table and a graph of temperature against the total volume of acid added is plotted. We then draw two best fit straight lines as shown in Figure 9.13, and where the two lines intersect is the neutralisation point.

We then add the exact amount of hydrochloric acid, which was found on the graph at the neutralisation point, to 25 cm³ of sodium hydroxide solution.

After evaporating off some of the water, the solution is left to crystallise. The sodium chloride crystals can then be filtered out and dried between sheets of filter paper.

Using neutralisation reactions in everyday life

As discussed earlier, neutralisation reactions are important to our survival and Table 9.7 gives some examples of neutralisation reactions which we use in our daily lives.

Table 9.7 *Neutralisation reactions in everyday life*

Use	Active compounds	Explanation
Toothpaste	Sodium hydrogencarbonate and sodium monofluorophosphate (Na_2FPO_3)	Toothpaste helps **reduce tooth decay** which is caused by **acid** in the mouth reacting with the calcium hydroxyapatite ($Ca_{10}(PO_4)_6(OH)_2$) in tooth enamel: • Sodium hydrogencarbonate **neutralises** any acid present. • F⁻ ions in the sodium monofluorophosphate **displace** the OH⁻ ions in the calcium hydroxyapatite forming calcium fluoroapatite ($Ca_{10}(PO_4)_6F_2$): $$Ca_{10}(PO_4)_6(OH)_2(s) + 2F^-(aq) \longrightarrow Ca_{10}(PO_4)_6F_2(s) + 2OH^-(aq)$$ Calcium fluoroapatite does not react with acid, therefore tooth enamel is protected from decaying.
Soil treatment	'Lime' in the form of calcium oxide (CaO) or calcium hydroxide ($Ca(OH)_2$)	Adding lime to soil **neutralises** any acids present, since most plants grow best if the soil pH is **neutral.** Lime cannot be added at the same time as an ammonium fertiliser because the two react to form a salt, ammonia and water: e.g. $CaO(s) + 2NH_4^+(aq) \longrightarrow Ca^{2+}(aq) + 2NH_3(g) + H_2O(l)$ The lime and the NH_4^+ ions are no longer available in the soil, so the benefits of both are lost.
Antacids	Sodium hydrogencarbonate ($NaHCO_3$), magnesium hydroxide ($Mg(OH)_2$), aluminium hydroxide ($Al(OH)_3$) or magnesium carbonate ($MgCO_3$)	Antacids are used to treat **indigestion** and **acid reflux**. They do this by **neutralising** excess hydrochloric acid in the stomach.

Volumetric analysis

Learning objectives

- Describe **volumetric analysis**.
- Perform volumetric analysis experiments.
- Perform calculations using the concept of **concentrations** and data obtained from volumetric experiments to determine mass and molar concentrations of the reactant in a **titration**.

Volumetric analysis, as the name suggests, involves the measurement of volumes of acids and alkalis, by performing a **titration** and using the results **quantitatively** in one of two ways:

- To calculate the **mole ratio** in which the two reactants combine.
- To calculate the **molar concentration** or **mass concentration** of one of the reactants used.

Titration involves the addition of an acid, which is usually dispensed from a burette, to an alkali, which is usually contained in a conical flask. The exact volume of the alkali is measured using a pipette. Prior to starting titration, a suitable indicator is added to the conical flask so that the end point or neutralisation point of the titration can be observed. If the solution is coloured, then there is no need to add an indicator because the colour change which occurs in the coloured solution will indicate when the endpoint is reached. The titration volume is the final volume minus the initial volume. To find the average titration volume, the values are added together and divided by the number of readings that were taken. The rough volume is not used to calculate the average (see examples below).

Volumetric analysis is a vital tool used by chemists in analysing chemicals in the manufacturing, food, pharmaceutical and agricultural industries. It is also used when analysing samples acquired from crime scenes to help solve crimes.

Using a titration to determine mole ratios

If **both** reactants are **standard solutions** (their mass or molar concentrations are known) the **mole ratio** in which they combine can be determined.

A titration was carried out to determine the mole ratio of unknown acid X and an unknown alkali Y. 25.0 cm³ of 0.2 mol dm⁻³ Y was measured using a pipette and dispensed into a conical flask. X, of concentration 0.5 mol dm⁻³, was placed in a burette and a titration carried out. The results are given in the table.

	Titration number		
	Rough	1	2
Final burette reading/cm³	20.10	40.10	20.50
Initial burette reading/cm³	0.00	20.10	0.50
Volume of acid added/cm³	20.10	20.00	20.00

Volume of X needed to neutralise 25.0 cm³ of Y = **20.0 cm³**

Determine the **number of moles** of Y that reacted:

     1 dm³ of Y(aq) contains 0.2 mol Y

     i.e. 1000 cm³ of Y(aq) contains 0.2 mol Y

     $\therefore$ **25.0 cm³ of Y(aq) contains** $\dfrac{0.2}{1000} \times 25.0$ mol Y

              = **0.005 mol Y**

Determine the **number of moles** of X that reacted:

    1 dm³ of acid X(aq) contains 0.5 mol X

    i.e. 1000 cm³ of X(aq) contains 0.5 mol X

    $\therefore$ **20.0 cm³ of X(aq)** contains $\dfrac{0.5}{1000} \times 20.0$ mol X

        = **0.01 mol X**

Determine the **mole ratio** in which the reactants combine:

    0.005 mol Y reacts with 0.01 mol X

    $\therefore$ **1 mol Y reacts with 2 mol X**

Therefore, the mole ratio in which the reactants combine is 1 mol alkali Y to 2 mol acid X.

Using a titration to determine concentration

If **one** reactant is a **standard solution** (its mass or molar concentration is known), the **concentration** of the other reactant can be determined by following the same **six** steps used on page 120.

the same **six** steps used on page 120.

Example 3

To determine the molar concentration of a solution of sulfuric acid, 25.0 cm³ of potassium hydroxide solution of concentration 0.2 mol dm⁻³ was measured in a pipette and dispensed into a conical flask. The sulfuric acid was placed in a burette and a titration was performed. The results are given in the table:

	Titration number		
	Rough	1	2
Final burette reading/cm³	30.10	50.30	30.00
Initial burette reading/cm³	0.00	20.30	0.00
Volume of acid added/cm³	30.10	30.00	30.00

Volume of sulfuric acid needed to neutralise 25.0 cm³ of sodium hydroxide solution = **30.0 cm³**

Steps 1 and **2:**

$$2NaOH(aq) \quad + \quad H_2SO_4(aq) \quad \longrightarrow \quad Na_2SO_4(aq) + 2H_2O(l)$$

    25.0 cm³   **30.0 cm³**

    0.2 mol dm⁻³   **? concentration**

Volume and concentration of **NaOH(aq)** are known, concentration of **H₂SO₄(aq)** is unknown.

Step 3: Find the **number of moles** of the known reactant, i.e. NaOH, using its volume and concentration:

    1 dm³ NaOH(aq) contains 0.2 mol NaOH

    i.e. 1000 cm³ NaOH(aq) contains 0.2 mol NaOH

    $\therefore$ **25.0 cm³ NaOH(aq)** contains $\dfrac{0.2}{1000} \times 25.0$ mol NaOH

        = **0.005 mol NaOH**

Step 4: Use the balanced equation to determine the **mole ratio** between the NaOH and the H_2SO_4:

2 mol NaOH react with 1 mol H_2SO_4

Step 5: Use the number of moles of NaOH from **step 3** and the mole ratio from **step 4** to calculate the **number of moles** of H_2SO_4 that reacted:

0.005 mol NaOH reacts with $\frac{1}{2}$ × 0.005 mol H_2SO_4

= 0.0025 mol H_2SO_4

Step 6: Use the number of moles of H_2SO_4 from **step 5** and the volume used in the titration to determine the **molar concentration** of the H_2SO_4(aq):

Since 30.0 cm³ H_2SO_4 was used:

30.0 cm³ H_2SO_4(aq) contains 0.0025 mol H_2SO_4

∴ 1000 cm³ H_2SO_4(aq) contains $\frac{0.0025}{30.0}$ × 1000 mol H_2SO_4

= 0.08 mol H_2SO_4

Molar concentration of H_2SO_4(aq) = **0.08 mol dm⁻³**

---

1 During a titration it was found that 12.5 cm³ of hydrochloric acid of concentration 0.4 mol dm⁻³ neutralised 25.0 cm³ of potassium carbonate solution of unknown concentration. Determine the mass concentration of the potassium carbonate solution.

Steps 1 and **2:**

$$K_2CO_3(aq) \quad + \quad 2HCl(aq) \quad \longrightarrow \quad 2KCl(aq) + H_2O(l) + CO_2(g)$$

      25.0 cm³   **12.5 cm³**

   ? concentration   **0.4 mol dm⁻³**

Volume and concentration of **HCl(aq)** are known, concentration of **K_2CO_3(aq)** is unknown.

Step 3: 1 dm³ HCl(aq) contains 0.4 mol HCl

i.e. 1000 cm³ HCl(aq) contains 0.4 mol HCl

∴ **12.5 cm³ HCl(aq) contains $\frac{0.4}{1000}$ × 12.5 mol HCl**

= 0.005 mol HCl

Step 4: **1 mol K_2CO_3 reacts with 2 mol HCl**

Step 5: $\frac{1}{2}$ × 0.005 mol **K_2CO_3 reacts with 0.005 mol HCl**

= 0.0025 mol K_2CO_3

Step 6: Since 25.0 cm³ K_2CO_3 was used:

25.0 cm³ K_2CO_3(aq) contains 0.0025 mol K_2CO_3

∴ 1000 cm³ K_2CO_3(aq) contains $\frac{0.0025}{25.0}$ × 1000 mol K_2CO_3

= 0.10 mol K_2CO_3

i.e. molar concentration of K_2CO_3(aq) = **0.10 mol dm⁻³**

Mass of 1 mol K_2CO_3 = (2 × 39) + 12 + (3 × 16) g

= 138 g

$\therefore$ mass of **0.10 mol K_2CO_3** = 0.10×138 g

$$= 13.8 \text{ g}$$

Mass concentration of K_2CO_3(aq) = <u>**13.8 g dm^{-3}**</u>

---

2 25.0 cm^3 of phosphoric acid of concentration 0.25 mol dm^{-3} exactly neutralised 32.5 cm^3 of sodium hydroxide solution of unknown concentration. Determine the mass concentration of the sodium hydroxide solution.

Steps 1 and **2:**

$$3NaOH(aq) \quad + \quad H_3PO_4(aq) \longrightarrow Na_3PO_4(aq) + 3H_2O(l)$$

32.5 cm^3	25.0 cm^3
? concentration	**0.25 mol dm^{-3}**

Volume and concentration of **H_3PO_4(aq)** are known, concentration of **NaOH(aq)** is unknown.

Step 3: 1 dm^3 H_3PO_4(aq) contains 0.25 mol H_3PO_4

i.e. 1000 cm^3 H_3PO_4(aq) contains 0.25 mol H_3PO_4

$\therefore$ **25.0 cm^3 H_3PO_4 (aq)** contains $\dfrac{0.25}{1000} \times 25$ mol H_3PO_4

$$= 0.00625 \text{ mol } H_3PO_4$$

OR we could have simply used the following formulae:

$$\text{concentration} = \frac{\text{number of moles}}{\text{volume}} \times 1000$$

$$\text{number of moles} = \frac{\text{concentration}}{1000} \times \text{volume}$$

Concentration of H_3PO_4 is 0.25 mol dm^{-3}

Number of moles in 25 cm^3 of H_3PO_4(aq) $= \dfrac{0.25}{1000} \times 25$

$$= 0.00625 \text{ mol } H_3PO_4$$

Step 4: **3 mol NaOH** reacts with **1 mol H_3PO_4**

Step 5: 3×0.00625 mol **NaOH** reacts with **0.00625 mol H_3PO_4**

$$= 0.01875 \text{ mol NaOH}$$

Step 6: Since 32.5 cm^3 NaOH was used:

32.5 cm^3 NaOH(aq) contains 0.01875 mol NaOH

$\therefore$ **1000 cm^3 NaOH(aq)** contains $\dfrac{0.01875}{32.5} \times 1000$ mol NaOH

$$= 0.58 \text{ mol NaOH}$$

i.e. molar concentration of NaOH(aq) = **0.58 mol dm^{-3}**

Mass of 1 mol NaOH = $23 + 16 + 1$ g

$$= 40 \text{ g}$$

$\therefore$ mass of **0.58 mol NaOH** = 0.58×40 g

$$= 23.2 \text{ g}$$

Mass concentration of NaOH(aq) = <u>**23.2 g dm^{-3}**</u>

Thermometric titrations can be used to determine the concentration of a solution of unknown concentration.

Example 4

A student conducted a thermometric titration to determine the volume of hydrochloric acid of an unknown concentration that is required to neutralise 25 cm³ of 0.5 M sodium hydroxide. The results are given in the table

a Using the data, plot a graph of the volume of the hydrochloric acid added against temperature. Use your graph to determine the volume of hydrochloric acid that corresponds to the highest temperature.

b Use your answer from **a** and the fact that the concentration of the sodium hydroxide is 0.5 mol/dm³ to find the concentration of the hydrochloric acid.

Volume of HCl added/cm³	Temperature/°C
0.00	30.0
5.00	32.0
10.00	34.5
15.00	36.0
20.00	38.0
25.00	40.0
30.00	39.0
35.00	37.0
40.00	35.0

The chemical equation for the reaction is: $NaOH(aq) + HCl(aq) \longrightarrow NaCl(aq) + H_2O(l)$

a Plot the graph using the data in the table, drawing two lines of best fit. Where the two lines intersect is the neutralisation point.

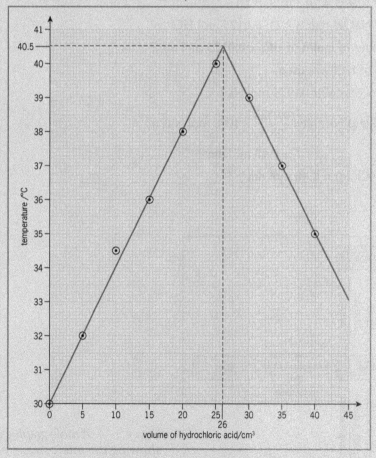

Figure 9.14 *Graph showing temperature against volume of hydrochloric acid added to 25 cm³ of sodium hydroxide solution*

From the graph, the volume of hydrochloric acid that corresponds to the highest temperature of 40.5 °C is 26.0 cm³.

b The concentration of sodium hydroxide is 0.5 mol dm⁻³

1 dm³ of NaOH(aq) contains 0.5 mol NaOH

1000 cm³ of NaOH(aq) contains 0.5 mol NaOH

$\therefore$ 25 cm³ of NaOH contains $\dfrac{0.5}{1000} \times 25$

= **0.0125 mol NaOH**

OR we could have simply used the following formulae:

$$\text{concentration} = \dfrac{\text{number of moles}}{\text{volume}} \times 1000$$

$$\text{number of moles} = \dfrac{\text{concentration}}{1000} \times \text{volume}$$

Concentration of NaOH(aq) is 0.5 mol

Number of moles in 25 cm³ of NaOH(aq) $= \dfrac{0.5}{1000} \times 25$

= **0.0125 mol NaOH**

Using the balanced chemical equation

1 mol of NaOH reacts with 1 mol of HCl

$\therefore$ 0.0125 mol of **NaOH** reacts with **0.0125 mol HCl**

$\therefore$ **number of moles of HCl = 0.0125 mol dm⁻³**

From the graph 26.0 cm³ of HCl was used.

26.0 cm³ HCl(aq) contains 0.0125 mol HCl

$\therefore$ **1000 cm³ HCl(aq) contains** $\dfrac{0.0125}{26.0} \times 1000$ **mol NaOH**

= **0.48 mol dm⁻³**

Molar concentration of HCl(aq) = 0.48 mol dm⁻³

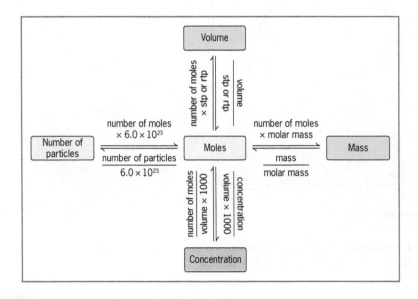

Figure 9.15 *A mole graphic organiser showing the interconversion of the mole into mass, concentration, number of particles and volume of gases*

It must be noted that the mole is at the centre of any computation concerning quantity of substance in chemistry. At a glance, the conversion factors necessary to interconvert the mole into mass, concentrations, number of particles and volumes of gases (page 158) can be found in a mole map or mole graphic organiser as shown in Figure 9.15. The mole map or mole graphic organiser can therefore be used to assist when performing moles calculations.

Recalling facts

23 Which of the following acids reacts with a base to form an acid salt?

   a HCl

   b HNO_3

   c H_3PO_4

   d CH_3COOH

24 A salt is prepared by reaction between all of the following except:

   a reactive metal and an insoluble carbonate

   b an alkali and an acid

   c a reactive metal and an acid

   d two acids

25 Calcium carbonate is a salt used:

   a to make cake rise

   b to make cement

   c to make plaster of Paris

   d to preserve foods

26 The neutralisation point of a titration is determined by using all of the following except:

   a indicator

   b spectator ion

   c pH meter

   d temperature

27 In a titration 25 cm³ of a base is accurately measured in a:

   a conical flask

   b beaker

   c pipette

   d measuring cylinder

28 An insoluble salt can be prepared by:

   a direct combination

   b ionic precipitation

   c reaction between an alkali and an acid

   d reaction between an insoluble carbonate and a reactive metal

29 Phenolphthalein changes from pink to _____ when hydrochloric acid is added to sodium hydroxide solution:

 a yellow

 b colourless

 c purple

 d red

30 22 cm^3 of 0.5 M sodium hydroxide solution would neutralise:

 a 44 cm^3 of 0.25 M hydrochloric acid solution

 b 22 cm^3 of 0.25 M hydrochloric acid solution

 c 22 cm^3 of 0.5 M sulfuric acid solution

 d 22 cm^3 of 0.5 M phosphoric acid solution

31 20 cm^3 of 0.1 mol dm^{-3} sulfuric acid reacts exactly with 30 cm^3 of aqueous sodium hydroxide. What is the concentration of the sodium hydroxide in g dm^{-3}?

 a 0.125

 b 0.100

 c 0.133

 d 0.145

32 25 cm^3 of 0.25 mol dm^{-3} of phosphoric acid completely neutralises 25 cm^3 of potassium hydroxide. What is the concentration of the potassium hydroxide?

 a 0.25

 b 0.50

 c 0.75

 d 1.00

33 Name three salts that are dangerous and unhealthy and explain why these salts are described in this way.

Applying facts

34 Using a named acid, discuss how a normal salt and an acid salt can be produced using the same reagents. You must include in your discussion a definition of each type of salt, chemical equations, and the role of the mole ratios, volumes and concentrations of the reagents.

35 Name the method used to prepare anhydrous aluminium chloride. Describe briefly but include all essential experimental details and a relevant equation, how you would prepare a pure, dry sample of it.

36 Salts are important in our everyday lives. Discuss this statement by referring to three named examples of salts. Write chemical equations where applicable to explain their importance.

37 a What is a neutralisation reaction?

 b What is the neutralisation point?

 c Outline two methods which can be used to determine the neutralisation point.

38 25.0 cm³ of nitric acid of concentration 0.25 mol dm⁻³ exactly neutralised 35.0 cm³ of potassium hydroxide solution. Determine the molar concentration and mass concentration of the potassium hydroxide solution.

39 Describe two applications of neutralisation reactions in our everyday lives.

Analysing data

40 A student was given a beaker of aqueous sodium chloride and another beaker of lead(II) nitrate and was asked to prepare lead(II) chloride.

   a Outline how the student would obtain a sample of pure dry crystals of lead(II) chloride.

   b State the name of the method used by the student to prepare the salt.

   c Write a balanced chemical equation and ionic equation for the reaction between the sodium chloride and lead(II) nitrate.

   d Name the other product formed in the reaction besides lead(II) chloride.

41 A student conducted a thermometric titration to determine the volume of sulfuric acid of unknown concentration required to neutralise 25 cm³ of a 0.25 mol dm⁻³ sodium hydroxide solution. The results are given in the table.

Volume of H_2SO_4 added/cm³	Temperature/°C
0.0	30.0
5.0	32.5
10.0	35.0
15.0	37.0
20.0	40.0
25.0	38.0
30.0	36.0
35.0	35.0
40.0	33.0

   a Using the tabulated data, plot a graph showing the volume of the sulfuric acid added against the temperature. Draw two straight lines of best fit.

   b Use your graph to determine the volume of sulfuric acid needed to neutralise 25 cm³ of sodium hydroxide solution.

   c Use your answer from part b and the fact that the concentration of the sodium hydroxide is 0.25 mol/dm³ to find the concentration of the sulfuric acid.

   d Using an ionic equation, explain why the temperature of the solution increases.

   e You can use the volume obtained from the experiment in the preparation of sodium chloride. Briefly describe how you would use the volume and the solutions at your disposal to prepare a dry sample of sodium chloride.

42 To prove that a brand of homemade vinegar was 'stronger', that is, had a higher concentration of ethanoic acid, than a commercial brand, a student titrated each brand of vinegar with 25 cm³ of 0.5 M sodium hydroxide using methyl orange indicator. The burette was filled with the brand of vinegar and a pipette was used to measure the 25 cm³ sodium hydroxide. The results are given in the tables.

Results for commercial vinegar

	Rough	1	2
Final burette reading/cm³	8.60	17.30	25.90
Initial burette reading/cm³	0.00	8.60	17.30
Volume of vinegar used/cm³	8.60		

Results for homemade brand

	Rough	1	2
Final burette reading/cm³	35.50	45.20	9.5
Initial burette reading/cm³	25.90	35.70	0.00
Volume of vinegar used/cm³			

a Complete the tables by calculating the final volumes of the vinegar used.

b For each brand calculate the average volume of vinegar used in the titration.

c Write a balanced equation for the reaction. The acid in vinegar is ethanoic acid CH_3COOH.

d Calculate for the commercial brand the number of moles of sodium hydroxide in the conical flask.

e Use the balanced equation to determine the mole ratio between the sodium hydroxide and acid.

f Use the number of moles of sodium hydroxide found in part d and the mole ratio to calculate the number of moles of vinegar used in the titration.

g Use the number of moles calculated in part f and the average volume of vinegar calculated in part a to determine the molarity of the vinegar

h Now calculate the molarity of the homemade vinegar.

i Compare the concentrations for each brand of vinegar and determine which vinegar contains a higher concentration of ethanoic acid. Was it proven that the homemade vinegar was stronger?

j Would you use your rough reading in your calculation of average volume of vinegar used?

k Why do you use an indicator in titrations?

l Do you use indicators in all titrations? When do you not use an indicator and why?

10 Oxidation–reduction reactions

Learning objectives

- Define **oxidation** and **reduction** in terms of gain or loss of **hydrogen** or **oxygen, electron transfer** and **change in oxidation number.**
- Identify oxidation and reduction in terms of gain or loss of hydrogen or oxygen, electron transfer or changes in oxidation number.
- Explain **redox** in terms of oxidation and reduction taking place at the same time.
- Define the terms **oxidising** and **reducing agents** in terms of electron transfer and changes in oxidation number.
- Identify oxidising and reducing agents.
- Give examples of chemical compounds which can act as both oxidising and reducing agents.
- Describe the use of colour changes that occur in chemical tests to distinguish between oxidising and reducing agents.
- Give examples of common everyday oxidation and reduction activities.

Oxidation and reduction reactions occur constantly around us. These reactions are important in our daily lives. These reactions can be as simple as the burning of organic material to obtain energy for transport, commercial and domestic purposes and as intricate as the extraction of reactive metals and non-metals by electrolysis, the generation of energy using electrochemical cells and the oxidation of glucose.

Oxidation and **reduction** are **opposite** processes that occur **together** in certain reactions. These are known as **redox reactions**. Oxidation and reduction were first defined in terms of gain and loss of oxygen. The definitions of these terms were later developed to include the loss and gain of hydrogen, loss and gain of electrons and using the notion of increase and decrease of oxidation number. These will now be discussed.

Oxygen–reduction reactions in terms of oxygen

Oxidation is the **gain** of **oxygen** by a substance in a chemical reaction. When this occurs, the substance is said to have been **oxidised.**

When magnesium burns in oxygen to produce magnesium oxide, magnesium is said to have been oxidised because it gains oxygen:

$$2Mg(s) + O_2(g) \longrightarrow 2MgO(s)$$

When oxygen is removed from a substance, as in the reaction of zinc oxide and carbon to produce zinc and carbon monoxide, the zinc oxide loses oxygen and is said to have been **reduced**:

$$ZnO(s) + C(s) \longrightarrow Zn(s) + CO(s)$$

Reduction is therefore defined as the **loss** of **oxygen** by a substance in a chemical reaction.

It can be seen in the reaction with zinc oxide that zinc oxide loses oxygen and is therefore **oxidised**, whereas the carbon gains oxygen and is **reduced**. **Oxidation** and **reduction** have therefore occurred in the same chemical reaction and this is an example of a **redox reaction**.

Oxidation–reduction reactions in terms of hydrogen

Loss or gain of hydrogen is another way of defining oxidation and reduction.

Oxidation is the **loss** of **hydrogen** by a substance in a chemical reaction.

Reduction is the **gain** of **hydrogen** by a substance in a chemical reaction.

Let us look at the following reaction:

Hydrogen sulfide and chlorine react to produce hydrogen chloride and sulfur:

$$H_2S(g) + Cl_2(g) \longrightarrow 2HCl(g) + S(s)$$

The hydrogen sulfide **loses hydrogen** and becomes **oxidised** to sulfur.

In the reaction between nitrogen and hydrogen to form ammonia in the Haber process, the nitrogen is reduced to ammonia because it gains hydrogen.

$$2N_2(g) + 3H_2(g) \longrightarrow 2NH_3(g)$$

In the reaction with hydrogen sulfide, as stated, the hydrogen sulfide loses hydrogen and is **oxidised** and the chlorine gains hydrogen and is **reduced**. Here oxidation and reduction occur in the same chemical equation and this represents a **redox** reaction, just like in the case of loss and gain of oxygen.

Oxidation–reduction reactions in terms of electrons

So far, oxidation and reduction have been defined in terms of loss and gain of oxygen and hydrogen. Another definition involves the transfer of electrons: one element **loses** electrons and another **gains** them. Oxidation and reduction can be defined in terms of **electron transfer.**

*Oxidation is the **loss** of electrons by an element in its free state, or an element in a compound.*

*Reduction is the **gain** of electrons by an element in its free state, or an element in a compound.*

To remember these definitions, remember two words, **OIL RIG:**

OIL Oxidation Is Loss	**RIG** Reduction Is Gain

Example 1

In the reaction between zinc and sulfur, zinc sulfide is formed:

$$Zn(s) + S(s) \longrightarrow ZnS(s)$$

Zinc sulfide (ZnS) is an ionic compound composed of Zn^{2+} and S^{2-} **ions.** In the reaction:

- Each zinc atom **loses** two electrons to form a Zn^{2+} ion:

$$Zn - 2e^- \longrightarrow Zn^{2+}$$

This is more correctly written as:

$$Zn \longrightarrow Zn^{2+} + 2e^-$$

Overall: $Zn(s) \longrightarrow Zn^{2+}(s) + 2e^-$

Zinc (Zn) has been **oxidised.**

- The sulfur atom gains two electrons to form an S^{2-} ion:

$$S + 2e^- \longrightarrow S^{2-}$$

Overall: $S(s) + 2e^- \longrightarrow S^{2-}(s)$

Sulfur (S) has been **reduced.**

Section A: Principles of chemistry

In the reaction between copper(II) oxide and magnesium, copper metal and magnesium oxide is formed:

$$CuO(s) + Mg(s) \longrightarrow Cu(s) + MgO(s)$$

The ionic equation for the reaction is:

$$Cu^{2+}(s) + Mg(s) \longrightarrow Cu(s) + Mg^{2+}(s)$$

Each magnesium (Mg) atom has to lose 2 electrons to form a magnesium ion (Mg^{2+}):

$$Mg - 2e^- \longrightarrow Mg^{2+}$$

More correctly, $Mg(s) \longrightarrow 2Mg^{2+}(s) + 2e^-$

Magnesium (Mg) has been **oxidised**.

To make copper atoms, 2 electrons must be added to the copper(II) ion:

$$Cu^{2+}(s) + 2e^- \longrightarrow Cu(s)$$

The copper(II) ion (Cu^{2+}) has been **reduced**.

As seen in the equation with copper(II) oxide and magnesium, **oxidation** and **reduction** have occurred in the same chemical equation but do not involve the loss or gain of hydrogen or oxygen but the loss or gain of electrons. Therefore, this is another example of a **redox** reaction.

Oxidation number

An **oxidation number** can be assigned to **each** atom or ion in a chemical substance. The oxidation number indicates the number of electrons lost, gained or shared as a result of chemical bonding. Oxidation numbers are positive, negative or zero. Unless an oxidation number is zero, a **plus** or **minus** sign is written in front of the number, and the number 1 is always written, e.g. +1, –3. It is important not to confuse the ionic state with formal ionic charges of an atom. For example, the oxidation state of Cu in Cu^{2+} is +2 and the charge is 2+, the oxidation state of the sulfur in the sulfide ion is –2 and the charge is 2–.

Rules to follow when determining oxidation numbers

Rule 1: The oxidation number of each **atom** of an element in its free, uncombined state is **zero.**

For example: In Na: oxidation number of the **Na atom = 0**

In Cl_2: oxidation number of each **Cl atom = 0**

Rule 2: The oxidation number of each **monatomic ion** in an ionic compound is the same as the **charge** on the ion.

For example: In **FeS**: oxidation number of the **Fe^{2+} ion = +2**

oxidation number of each **S^{2-} ion = –2**

Rule 3: The oxidation number of **hydrogen** in a compound or polyatomic ion is always **+1**, except in metal hydrides, where it is –1.

For example: In **HCl**: oxidation number of **hydrogen = +1**

In the **NH_3**: oxidation number of **hydrogen = +1**

In the **NH_4^+**: oxidation number of **hydrogen = +1**

In AlH_3 (aluminium hydride): oxidation number of **hydrogen = –1**

In **$LiAlH_4$** (lithium aluminium hydride): oxidation number of **hydrogen = –1**

Rule 4: The oxidation number of **oxygen** in a compound or polyatomic ion is always **−2**, except in peroxides, where it is −1.

    For example: In **FeO**: oxidation number of **oxygen = −2**

                        In **Li_2O**: oxidation number of **oxygen = −2**

                        In the **CO_3^- ion**: oxidation number of **oxygen = −2**

                        In the **NO_3^-**: oxidation number of **oxygen = −2**

                        In **H_2O_2** (hydrogen peroxide): oxidation number of **oxygen = −1**

Rule 5: With the exception of hydrogen and oxygen, the oxidation numbers of elements in **covalent compounds** and **polyatomic ions** may **vary**. The oxidation number may appear in the **name** of the compound or ion:

    For example: In **phosphorus(III) oxide** (**P_4O_6**): oxidation number of **phosphorus = +3**

                        In the **phosphorus(V) ion** (**PO_4^{3-}**): oxidation number of **phosphorus = +5**

Rule 6: The **sum** of the oxidation numbers of all the atoms or ions in a **compound** is **zero**.

    For example: In **$AlCl_3$**, the sum of the oxidation numbers of all the ions is **zero**:

                (oxidation number of Al) + 3(oxidation number of Cl) = 0

(+3)	+	3(−1)	= 0
(+3)	+	(−3)	= 0

Rule 7: The **sum** of the oxidation numbers of all the atoms in a **polyatomic ion** is equal to the **charge on the ion**.

    For example: In the **CO_3^{2-} ion**, the sum of the oxidation numbers of the two elements is **−2**:

                (oxidation number of C) + (oxidation number of O) = −2

(+4)	+	3(−2)	= −2
(+4)	+	(−6)	= −2

If these rules are followed, it is possible to determine the oxidation number of any element from the **formula** of the compound or polyatomic ion it is in.

Example 2

1 To determine the oxidation number of lead in lead dioxide (**PbO_2**), rules **4** and **6** are applied:

    (oxidation number of Pb) + 2(oxidation number of O) = 0

    (oxidation number of Pb) +   2(−2)   = 0

    (oxidation number of Pb) +   (−4)   = 0

                              oxidation number of Pb = 0 + 4

                                                    = **+4**

Lead dioxide can also be called **lead(IV) oxide**.

2 To determine the oxidation number of nitrogen in nitrogen monoxide (**NO**), rules **4** and **6** are applied:

    (oxidation number of N) + (oxidation number of O) = 0

    (oxidation number of N) +   1(−2)   = 0

    (oxidation number of N) +   (−2)   = 0

                                oxidation number of N = 0 + 2

                                                  = **+2**

Nitrogen monoxide can also be called **nitrogen(II) oxide**.

    Section A: Principles of chemistry

3 To determine the oxidation number of chromium in chromium oxide (Cr_2O_3), rules **4** and **6** are applied:

2(oxidation number of Cr) + 3(oxidation state of O) = 0

2(oxidation number of Cr) +   3(−2)   = 0

2(oxidation number of Cr) +   (−6)   = 0

2(oxidation number of Cr) = 0 + 6

$$\text{Oxidation state of Cr} = \frac{+6}{2}$$

= +3

Chromium oxide can also be called **chromium(III) oxide.**

4 To determine the oxidation number of phosphorus in phosphoric acid (H_3PO_4), rules **4** and **6** are applied:

3(oxidation state of H) + (oxidation number of P) + 4(oxidation state of O) = 0

3(+1)   + (oxidation number of P) +   4(−2)   = 0

+3   + (oxidation number of P) +   (−8)   = 0

Oxidation number of P = 0 − 3 + 8

= +5

The oxidation state of phosphorus in phosphoric acid is **+5.**

5 To determine the oxidation number of sulfur in the sulfate ion (SO_4^{2-}), rules **4** and **7** are applied:

(oxidation number of S) + 4(oxidation number of O) = −2

(oxidation number of S) +   4(−2)   = −2

(oxidation number of S) +   (−8)   = −2

Oxidation number of S = −2 + 8

= +6

The SO_4^{2-} ion can be called the **sulfate(VI) ion.**

6 To determine the oxidation number of manganese in the permanganate ion (MnO_4^-), rules **4** and **7** are applied:

(oxidation number of Mn) + 4(oxidation number of O) = −1

(oxidation number of Mn) +   4(−2)   = −1

(oxidation number of Mn) +   (−8)   = −1

Oxidation number of N = −1 + 8

= +7

The MnO_4^- ion can be called the **manganate(VII) ion.**

Note When naming polyatomic ions using an oxidation number, the name always ends in '**-ate**'.

Oxidation–reduction reactions in terms of oxidation number

In all redox reactions, the oxidation number of one element increases and the oxidation number of another element decreases. Oxidation and reduction can be defined in terms of oxidation number.

Oxidation is the increase in oxidation number of an element in its free state, or an element in a compound.

When a lithium atom loses its valence electron, the lithium atom is oxidised to a lithium ion:

$$Li - e^- \longrightarrow Li^+$$

Oxidation numbers: (0)   (+1)

Similarly, when an iron(II) ion (Fe^{2+}) loses an electron, it is oxidised to an iron(III) ion (Fe^{3+}):

$$Fe^{2+} - e^- \longrightarrow Fe^{3+}$$

Oxidation numbers: (+2)   (+3)

Reduction is the decrease in oxidation number of an element in its free state, or an element in a compound.

When a bromine atom gains an electron, the bromine atom is reduced to the bromide ion:

$$Br_2 + 2e^- \longrightarrow 2Br^-$$

Oxidation numbers: (0)   (−1)

Similarly, when copper(II) ions gain electrons, the copper(II) ions are reduced to copper atoms:

$$Cu^{2+} + 2e^- \longrightarrow Cu$$

Oxidation numbers: (+2)   (0)

Example 3

The displacement reaction between chlorine and sodium iodide:

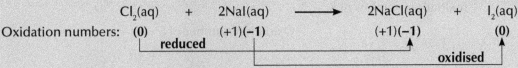

$$Cl_2(aq) \quad + \quad 2NaI(aq) \quad \longrightarrow \quad 2NaCl(aq) \quad + \quad I_2(aq)$$

Oxidation numbers: **(0)**   **(+1)(−1)**   **(+1)(−1)**   **(0)**

reduced / oxidised

During the reaction:

- The oxidation number of each I⁻ ion in the sodium iodide has **increased** from −1 to 0. **Sodium iodide (NaI)** has been **oxidised**.

- The oxidation number of each chlorine atom in the chlorine molecule has **decreased** from 0 to −1. **Chlorine (Cl$_2$)** has been **reduced**.

Using oxidation numbers to recognise redox reactions

Any redox reaction can be recognised using the following steps:

- Write the **balanced chemical equation** for the reaction if it has not been given.
- Write the **oxidation number** of each element below it in brackets. The oxidation numbers of elements in **polyatomic ions** which remain **unchanged** during a reaction need not be determined.
- Decide which element shows an **increase** in oxidation number. This element has been **oxidised**.
- Decide which element shows a **decrease** in oxidation number. This element has been **reduced**.

Note If the oxidation numbers of **all** elements remain **unchanged**, the reaction is **not** a redox reaction.

1 Determine which reactant has been oxidised and which has been reduced when magnesium is burnt to produce magnesium oxide.

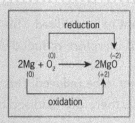

- **Magnesium (Mg)** has been **oxidised** because the oxidation number of each magnesium atom has increased from 0 to +2.

- **Oxygen (O)** has been **reduced** because the oxidation number of each oxygen atom in the oxygen molecules has decreased from 0 to –2.

2 Determine which reactant has been oxidised and which has been reduced in the reaction between copper and silver nitrate to produce silver and copper nitrate.

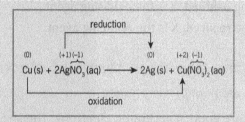

- **Copper (Cu)** has been **oxidised** because the oxidation number of each copper atom has increased from 0 to +2.

- **Silver nitrate (AgNO$_3$)** has been **reduced** because the oxidation number of each Ag$^+$ ion in silver nitrate has been decreased from +1 to 0.

We can write ionic equations and determine spectator ions in a redox reaction.

Example 4

Let us use question 2 to write the ionic equation and identify the spectator ions.

Step 1: Write the balanced equation for the reaction:

$$Cu(s) + 2AgNO_3(aq) \longrightarrow 2Ag(s) + CuNO_3(aq)$$

Step 2: Rewrite the equation showing any ions in solution as individual ions:

$$Cu(s) + 2Ag^+(aq) + 2NO_3^-(aq) \longrightarrow 2Ag(s) + Cu^{2+}(aq) + 2NO_3^-(aq)$$

Step 3: Delete the ions which remain unchanged: that is, NO$_3^-$(aq) ions remain in solution:

$$Cu(s) + 2Ag^+(aq) + 2\cancel{NO_3^-(aq)} \longrightarrow 2Ag(s) + Cu^{2+}(aq) + \cancel{NO_3^-(aq)}$$

Step 4: Rewrite the ionic equation showing the ions which change:

$$Cu(s) + 2Ag^+(aq) \longrightarrow 2Ag(s) + Cu^{2+}(aq)$$

The spectator ion is **NO$_3^-$(aq)**.

Oxidising and reducing agents

During any redox reaction:

- One reactant causes another reactant to be **oxidised**. This is the **oxidising agent**.

  This reactant causes oxidation and is therefore reduced by either gaining electrons or there is a decrease in its oxidation number.

- One reactant causes another reactant to be **reduced**. This is the **reducing agent**.

  This reactant causes reduction and is therefore oxidised by either losing electrons or there is an increase in its oxidation number.

In the following reaction, **X** has been **oxidised** and **Y** has been **reduced**:

oxidised   reduced

X   +   Y   ⟶   Q   +   R

reducing   oxidising
agent   agent

- **Y** must have caused X to be **oxidised**. **Y** is the **oxidising agent**.
- **X** must have caused Y to be **reduced**. **X** is the **reducing agent**.

Oxidising and reducing agents in terms of electrons

*An **oxidising agent** causes an element in its free state, or an element in a compound, to **lose electrons**.*

Non-metals or positive ions are good at accepting electrons. The strongest oxidising agents are highly electronegative elements like the halogens (Group VII). Examples of Group VII elements are chlorine (Cl), bromine (Br) and iodine (I).

*A **reducing agent** causes an element in its free state, or an element in a compound, to **gain electrons**.*

Metals and negative ions are good at donating electrons, the strongest reducing agents are the alkali metals (Group I) as they have low electronegativities and lose electrons very easily. Examples of Group I metals are lithium (Li), sodium (Na) and potassium (K).

Some molecules, such as carbon monoxide (CO), are also used in the chemical industry as reducing agents to help extract metals.

Remember **OIL RIG**.

Example 5

Copper when heated over a flame turns black as the copper metal is reduced by the oxygen in the air, forming copper(II) oxide:

$$2Cu(s) + O_2(g) \longrightarrow 2CuO(s)$$

where: $2Cu(s) \longrightarrow 2Cu^{2+}(s) + 4e^-$ and $O_2(g) + 4e^- \longrightarrow 2O^{2-}(s)$

      (0)   (+2)   (0)   (−2)

          oxidised   **reduced**

- Each copper atom lost two electrons to form a Cu^{2+} ion; copper has been **oxidised**. The oxygen atoms caused this loss by taking away the electrons. **Oxygen (O_2)** is the **oxidising agent**.
- Each oxygen atom in the oxygen molecule gained two electrons to form an O^{2-} ion; oxygen has been **reduced**. The copper atoms caused this gain by donating the electrons. **Copper (Cu)** is the **reducing agent**.

Another example uses an active metal such as lithium. As mentioned already, active metals are strong reducing agents.

Lithium reacts with oxygen to form lithium oxide:

$$4Li(s) + O_2(g) \longrightarrow 2Li_2O(s)$$

where: $4Li(s) \longrightarrow 4Li^+(s) + 4e^-$ and $O_2(g) + 4e^- \longrightarrow 2O^{2-}(s)$

- Each lithium atom lost one electron to form a Li^+ ion; lithium has been **oxidised**. The oxygen atoms caused this loss by taking away the electrons. **Oxygen (O_2)** is the **oxidising agent.**
- Each oxygen atom in the oxygen molecule gained two electrons to form an O^{2-} ion; oxygen has been **reduced**. The lithium atoms caused this gain by donating the electrons. **Lithium (Li)** is the **reducing agent.**

Oxidising and reducing agents in terms of oxidation number

*An **oxidising agent** causes the oxidation number of an element in its free state, or an element in a compound, to **increase**.*

*A **reducing agent** causes the oxidation number of an element in its free state, or an element in a compound, to **decrease**.*

Example 6

When iron is in contact with an open flame and combusts with oxygen air, a brown soot of iron oxide is formed:

$$4Fe(s) + 3O_2(g) \longrightarrow 2Fe_2O_3(s)$$

oxidation numbers: (0)   (0)   (+2) (−2)

- The oxidation number of each iron atom has increased from 0 to +2. The **iron** has been **oxidised. Oxygen** is the reactant that caused this increase in oxidation number. **Oxygen (O_2)** is the **oxidising agent.**
- The oxidation number of each oxygen atom in the oxygen molecule has decreased from 0 to −2. Oxygen has been **reduced.** Iron is the reactant that caused this decrease in oxidation number. **Iron (Fe)** is the **reducing agent.**

Sample question

Determine which reactant is the oxidising agent and which is the reducing agent in the reaction between aluminium and iron(III) oxide.

$$2Al(s) + Fe_2O_3(s) \longrightarrow Al_2O_3(s) + 2Fe(s)$$

(0)   (+3)   (+3)   (0)

- **Iron(III) oxide (Fe_2O_3)** is the **oxidising agent** because it caused the oxidation number of the aluminium atom to increase from 0 to +3.
- **Aluminium (Al)** is the **reducing agent** because it caused the oxidation number of the Fe^{3+} ion in the iron(III) oxide to decrease from +3 to 0.

Common oxidising and reducing agents

Some substances always behave as **oxidising agents** (Table 10.1) and others always behave as **reducing agents** (Table 10.2). A **visible change** may occur when some of these react.

- A **colour change** may occur.
- A **precipitate** may form.
- A particular **gas** may be produced.

Table 10.1 *Common oxidising agents*

Oxidising agent	Visible change when the agent reacts	Reason for the visible change
Acidified potassium manganate(VII) solution, $H^+/KMnO_4(aq)$	Purple to **colourless**	The purple MnO_4^- ion forms the colourless Mn^{2+} **ion.**
Acidified potassium dichromate(VI) solution, $H^+/K_2Cr_2O_7(aq)$	Orange to **green**	The orange $Cr_2O_7^{2-}$ ion forms the green Cr^{3+} **ion.**
Aqueous iron(III) salts, $Fe^{3+}(aq)$	Yellow-brown to **pale green**	The yellow-brown Fe^{3+} ion forms the pale green Fe^{2+} **ion.**
Sodium chlorate(I) solution, $NaClO_3(aq)$	Turns many coloured dyes **colourless** (see Table 10.3, page 174).	The dyes are oxidised to their colourless form.
Hot concentrated sulfuric acid, $H_2SO_4(l)$	A **pungent** colourless gas is evolved.	**Sulfur dioxide** gas (SO_2) is produced.
Dilute or concentrated nitric acid, $HNO_3(aq)$	A **brown** gas is evolved.	**Nitrogen dioxide** gas (NO_2) is produced.

Table 10.2 *Common reducing agents*

Reducing agent	Visible change when the agent reacts	Reason for the visible change
Potassium iodide solution, $KI(aq)$	Colourless to **brown**	**Iodine** (I_2) forms which dissolves forming a brown solution.
Aqueous iron(II) salts, $Fe^{2+}(aq)$	Pale green to **yellow-brown**	The pale green Fe^{2+} ion forms the yellow-brown Fe^{3+} **ion.**
Hydrogen sulfide gas, $H_2S(g)$	A **yellow** precipitate forms.	Solid **sulfur** (S) forms.
Concentrated hydrochloric acid, $HCl(aq)$	A **yellow-green** gas is evolved.	**Chlorine** gas (Cl_2) is produced.

- Other common **oxidising agents** include oxygen, O_2, chlorine, Cl_2, and manganese(IV) oxide, MnO_2.
- Other common **reducing agents** include hydrogen, H_2, carbon, C, carbon monoxide, CO, and reactive metals.

Substances that can behave as both oxidising and reducing agents

Some compounds can act as both oxidising and reducing agents. Their behaviour depends on the other reactant.

Acidified hydrogen peroxide, H^+/H_2O_2

Acidified hydrogen peroxide is usually an **oxidising agent**. If it reacts with a stronger oxidising agent than itself, it acts as a **reducing agent**:

* With **potassium iodide** solution, it acts as an **oxidising agent** and **oxidises** the iodide ions to iodine.
* With both **acidified potassium manganate(VII)** solution and **acidified potassium dichromate(VI)** solution, both stronger oxidising agents than itself, it acts as a **reducing agent**. The acidified hydrogen peroxide **reduces** the purple MnO_4^- ion to the colourless Mn^{2+} ion; and the orange $Cr_2O_7^{2-}$ ion to the green Cr^{3+} ion, respectively.

Sulfur dioxide, SO_2

Sulfur dioxide is usually a **reducing agent**. If it reacts with a stronger reducing agent than itself, it acts as an **oxidising agent**:

* With both **acidified potassium manganate(VII)** solution and **acidified potassium dichromate(VI)** solution, it acts as a **reducing agent** causing the reactions described above.
* With **hydrogen sulfide**, a stronger reducing agent than itself, sulfur dioxide acts as an **oxidising agent** and **oxidises** the hydrogen sulfide to yellow sulfur.

Tests for oxidising and reducing agents

Certain tests can be performed in the laboratory to determine if an unknown substance is an oxidising or reducing agent.

Tests for the presence of an oxidising agent

To test whether a substance is an **oxidising agent**, add it to a known **reducing agent** that gives a visible change when **oxidised**. The reducing agents usually used are **potassium iodide solution** or an aqueous solution of an **iron(II) salt**.

* An oxidising agent causes **potassium iodide** solution to change from colourless to **brown** because it **oxidises** the colourless I^- ion to **iodine** which dissolves forming a brown solution.
* An oxidising agent causes an aqueous solution of an **iron(II) salt**, for example, iron(II) sulfate, to change from pale green to **yellow-brown** because it **oxidises** the pale green Fe^{2+} ion to the yellow-brown **Fe^{3+} ion**.

Tests for the presence of a reducing agent

To test to see whether a substance is a **reducing agent**, add it to a known **oxidising agent** that gives a visible change when it is **reduced**. The oxidising agents usually used are **acidified potassium manganate(VII)** solution or **acidified potassium dichromate(VI)** solution.

* A reducing agent causes **acidified potassium manganate(VII)** solution to change from purple to **colourless** because it **reduces** the purple MnO_4^- ion to the colourless **Mn^{2+} ion** (Figure 10.1).
* A reducing agent causes **acidified potassium dichromate(VI)** solution to change from orange to **green** because it **reduces** the orange $Cr_2O_7^{2-}$ ion to the green **Cr^{3+} ion** (Figure 10.1).

Purple acidified potassium manganate(VII) solution turns colourless

Orange acidified potassium dichromate(VI) solution turns green

Figure 10.1 *Colour changes of reducing agents*

Oxidation–reduction reactions in everyday activities

Oxidation–reduction reactions are encountered and used in everyday activities (Table 10.3).

Table 10.3 *Oxidation and reduction in everyday activities*

Activity	Oxidation–reduction reaction
Bleaches	**Chlorine bleaches** containing sodium chlorate(I) (NaClO) and **oxygen bleaches** containing hydrogen peroxide (H_2O_2) remove coloured stains by **oxidising** the coloured chemicals, or dyes, in the stain to their colourless form: e.g. $ClO^-(aq)$ + coloured dye $\longrightarrow$ $Cl^-(aq)$ + colourless dye
Rusting	When oxygen and moisture come into contact with iron and its alloy, steel, the iron is **oxidised** to form hydrated iron(III) oxide ($Fe_2O_3 \cdot xH_2O$) commonly known as **rust.**
Browning of cut fruits and vegetables	When some fruits and vegetables are peeled or cut, e.g. apples, bananas and potatoes, enzymes in the cells on the cut surfaces are exposed to oxygen in the air. These enzymes **oxidise** certain chemicals in the cells to brown compounds called **melanins** which cause the cut surfaces to turn brown.
Preserving food	**Sodium sulfite** (Na_2SO_3) and **sulfur dioxide** (SO_2) are reducing agents used as **food preservatives**, e.g. to preserve dried fruit, fruit juices, wine and certain shellfish. They prevent spoilage of foods by **preventing oxidation**, e.g. they prevent oxidation of wine to vinegar and oxidation of vitamin C in fruits and fruit juices. They also prevent browning by **reducing** any melanins back to their colourless form.
The breathalyser test	This is a test used to detect the presence and level of alcohol in a driver's breath. The driver blows into a mouthpiece which is connected to a chamber filled with orange crystals of acidified potassium dichromate(IV). Any ethanol vapours present in the driver's breath would cause a chemical reaction resulting in *reduction* and colour change of the *orange* dichromate(VI) ion ($Cr_2O_7^{2-}$) to the *green* chromium(III) ion (Cr^{3+}). The more ethanol present, the greater the extent of green colour produced.

Recalling facts

1 Oxidation and reduction can be defined in terms of the following except:

    a loss or gain of electrons

    b increase and decrease of oxidation number

    c number of neutrons

    d transfer of electrons

2 When iron comes into contact with oxygen and moisture, iron is _____ by the oxygen:

    a reduced

    b oxidised

    c acidified

    d none of the above

3 What is the oxidation number of nitrogen in NO_2^-?

    a +2   **b** −4   **c** +3   **d** −3

4 What is the oxidation number of carbon in the CH_4 molecule?

    a +4   **b** −4   **c** +6   **d** −6

5 Which of the following is NOT a redox reaction?

    a $H_2(g) + F_2(g) \longrightarrow 2HF(g)$

    b $Zn(s) + CuSO_4(aq) \longrightarrow ZnSO_4(aq) + Cu(s)$

    c $BaCl_2(aq) + Na_2SO_4(aq) \longrightarrow BaSO_4(s) + 2NaCl(aq)$

    d $CuO(s) + H_2(g) \longrightarrow Cu(s) + H_2O(g)$

6 Identify the spectator ion(s) in the following redox reaction:

$Mg(s) + H_2SO_4(aq) \longrightarrow MgSO_4(aq) + H_2(g)$

    a $H^+(aq)$

    b $Mg^{2+}(aq)$

    c $Mg^{2+}(aq)$ and $SO_4^{2-}(aq)$

    d $SO_4^{2-}(aq)$

For questions 7 and 8, use the following equation:

$H_2S(g) + Cl_2(g) \longrightarrow 2HCl(g) + S(s)$

7 In the equation, name the oxidising agent:

    a $H_2S(g)$

    b $Cl_2(g)$

    c $HCl(g)$

    d $S(s)$

8 In the equation, name the reducing agent:

    a $HCl(g)$

    b $Cl_2(g)$

    c $S(s)$

    d $H_2S(g)$

9 When an acidified solution of potassium dichromate(VII) is added to a reducing agent, what colour change is observed?

    a green to orange-yellow

    b brown to dark brown

    c purple to colourless

    d orange-yellow to green

10 What colour change is expected when potassium iodide solution ($KI(aq)$) is added to an oxidising agent?

    a pale green to yellow-brown

    b brown to colourless

    c colourless to brown

    d yellow-brown to pale green

11 Define EACH of the following in terms of loss or gain of hydrogen and oxygen:

    a oxidation

    b reduction

12 Define EACH of the following in terms of oxidation number:

    a oxidation

    b reduction

    c oxidising agent

    d reducing agent

13 Explain, by using an example, when an oxidising agent can act as a reducing agent.

Applying facts

14 State, with a reason, whether EACH of the following equations shows oxidation or reduction:

    a $Li \longrightarrow Li^+ + e^-$

    b $Pb^{2+} \longrightarrow Pb + 2e^-$

    c $Sn \longrightarrow Sn^{2+} + 2e^-$

15 Determine the oxidation number of the underlined element:

    a $\underline{V}_2O_5$ **b** $Na\underline{H}$ **c** $\underline{Zn}(OH)_4^{2-}$

16 Determine the oxidation number of:

 a bismuth in: sodium bismuthate ($NaBiO_3$) and bismuth nitrate ($Bi(NO_3)_3$)

 b manganese in: manganese sulfate ($MnSO_4$), manganese nitrate ($Mn(NO_3)_2$), and permanganic acid ($HMnO_4$)

 c chromium in: chromium oxide (Cr_2O_3), chromium sulfate ($CrSO_4$) and sodium dichromate ($Na_2Cr_2O_7$)

17 For each of the following reactions, identify the atom oxidised, the atom reduced, the oxidising agent and the reducing agent:

 a $Si + 2F_2 \longrightarrow SiF_4$

 b $2Fe + 3V_2O_3 \longrightarrow Fe_2O_3 + 6VO$

 c $2Al + 3Cl_2 \longrightarrow 2AlCl_3$

 d $3H_2C_2O_4 + 2K_2MnO_4 \longrightarrow 6CO_2 + 2K_2O_2 + Mn_2O_3 + 3H_2O$

18 Discuss two everyday activities that involve redox reactions.

Analysing data

19 State the change which represents oxidation, reduction or neither:

 a $CuCO_3 \longrightarrow CuO + CO_2$

 b $P_2O_5 \longrightarrow P_4H_{10}$

 c $HClO_4 \longrightarrow HCl + H_2O$

20 Would you use an oxidising agent or reducing agent to effect the following reactions?

 a $SO_4^{2-} \longrightarrow S^{2-}$

 b $Mn^{2+} \longrightarrow MnO_4$

 c $Zn \longrightarrow ZnCl_2$

21 Describe how you would test an unknown substance to determine whether it is an oxidising agent or reducing agent. You need to state the apparatus and reagents to be used and the visual changes which occur.

11 Electrochemistry

Electrochemistry is the study of chemical processes that cause electrons to move. Electrochemical reactions can either produce electrical energy or require electrical energy to proceed. When a chemical reaction is driven by an external applied voltage, as in electrolysis, or if the voltage is created by a chemical reaction, as in a battery, an electrochemical reaction occurs.

Learning objectives

- Use the **electrochemical series** to predict chemical reactions.
- Differentiate between **conductors** and **non-conductors**.
- Distinguish between **metallic** and **electrolytic conductivity**.
- Distinguish between **electrolytes and non-electrolytes**.
- Classify electrolytes as **strong** or **weak** based on their **conductivity**.

Predicting reactions using the electrochemical series of metals

The electrochemical series arranges the metals in the order of decreasing tendency for reduction to occur or power as oxidising agent. In other words, the metals are placed in order of how easily they lose electrons (ionise), and the series can be used to predict certain chemical reactions. The ability of metal atoms to give away (donate) electrons to another reactant increases going up the series. Therefore, the uppermost metals of the table (for example, sodium, calcium and potassium) have full tendency to get oxidised and consequently they will act as good reducing agents. The strength as a reducing agent therefore increases going up the series.

Table 11.1 *The electrochemical series of the common metals*

Metal	Ease of ionisation	Cation
Potassium		K^+
Calcium		Ca^{2+}
Sodium		Na^+
Magnesium		Mg^{2+}
Aluminium		Al^{3+}
Zinc		Zn^{2+}
Iron		Fe^{2+}
Lead		Pb^{2+}
Hydrogen		H^+
Copper		Cu^{2+}
Silver		Ag^+

⟶ Indicates **an increase**

Displacement of metals

A metal displaces a metal **below** it in the series from a compound containing ions of the lower metal. The **higher** metal is a **stronger reducing agent**, so it readily **gives** electrons to the ions of the lower metal. In doing so, the higher metal **ionises** to form cations. The ions of the lower metal **gain** these electrons and are **discharged** to form atoms.

Example 1

$$Mg(s) + CuSO_4(aq) \longrightarrow MgSO_4(aq) + Cu(s)$$

Magnesium is above copper in the series. The magnesium atoms **ionise** and form Mg^{2+} ions. The Cu^{2+} ions are **discharged** and form copper atoms:

$$Mg(s) \longrightarrow Mg^{2+}(aq) + 2e^-$$
$$Cu^{2+}(aq) + 2e^- \longrightarrow Cu(s)$$

Displacement of hydrogen

Metals **above** hydrogen in the series displace the H^+ ions in an **acid**, forming hydrogen gas. Metals **below** hydrogen do not react with acids because they do not displace the H^+ ions. In other words, if the metal is more reactive than hydrogen, hydrogen gas is liberated; if the metal is less reactive than hydrogen, the metal will be formed.

Example 2

Copper is below hydrogen in the series, copper is less reactive than hydrogen, so copper would be formed.

Example 3

Calcium is above hydrogen in the series. The calcium atoms ionise and form Ca^{2+} ions. The H^+ ions are discharged to form hydrogen gas:

$$Ca(s) + 2HCl(aq) \longrightarrow CaCl_2(aq) + H_2(g)$$

The ionic equation is:

$$Ca(s) + 2H^+(aq) \longrightarrow Ca^{2+}(aq) + H_2(g)$$

The ionic half equations show the transfer of electrons:

$$Ca(s) \longrightarrow Ca^{2+}(aq) + 2e^-$$
$$2H^+(aq) + 2e^- \longrightarrow H_2(g)$$

Example 4

If copper metal is added to sulfuric acid, no reaction is observed. Copper is below hydrogen in the electrochemical series, therefore copper metal will not displace hydrogen from the acid.

Example 5

If silver metal is added to sulfuric acid, no reaction is observed because silver like copper is below hydrogen in the electrochemical series. Silver metal will therefore not displace hydrogen from the acid.

Predicting reactions using the electrochemical series of non-metals

The **electrochemical series of non-metals** places non-metals in order of how easily they **gain** electrons, (**ionise**), and can be used to predict **certain** chemical reactions. The ability of non-metal atoms to ionise and take away electrons from another reactant **increases** going **up** the series. Therefore, the **strength as an oxidising agent** increases going up the series (this is opposite to what is observed in the electrochemical series of metals).

Table 11.2 *The electrochemical series of certain non-metals*

Non-metal	Ease of ionisation	Anion
Fluorine	↑	F^-
Chlorine		Cl^-
Bromine		Br^-
Iodine		I^-

Displacement of non-metals

A non-metal displaces a non-metal **below** it in the series from a compound containing ions of the lower non-metal. The **higher** non-metal is a **stronger oxidising agent**, so it readily **takes** electrons from the ions of the lower non-metal. In doing so, the higher non-metal **ionises** to form anions. The ions of the lower non-metal **lose** these electrons and are **discharged** to form atoms.

Example 6

$$Br_2(g) + 2KI(aq) \longrightarrow 2KBr(aq) + I_2(aq)$$

Bromine is above iodine in the series. The bromine atoms **ionise** and form Br^- ions. The I^- ions are **discharged** to form iodine:

The ionic equation is:

$$Br_2(g) + 2I^-(aq) \longrightarrow 2Br^-(aq) + I_2(aq)$$

The ionic half equations show the transfer of electrons:

$$Br_2(g) + 2e^- \longrightarrow 2Br^-(aq)$$
$$2I^-(aq) \longrightarrow I_2(aq) + 2e^-$$

Example 7

If iodine solution is added to a sodium chloride solution, there will be no reaction because iodine is *lower* than chlorine in the electrochemical series.

Electrical conduction

Based on their ability to conduct an electric current, materials can be classified into **two** groups: conductors and non-conductors.

- **Conductors** allow an electric current to pass through them. Examples of conductors are metals, graphite, molten ionic compounds (lead(II) bromide, lead(II) chloride, potassium iodide), aqueous solutions of ionic compounds (aqueous sodium chloride and copper(II) sulfate), acids and alkalis (dilute and concentrated sulfuric acid, hydrochloric acid, nitric acid and potassium hydroxide, sodium hydroxide). All these have charged particles which are necessary for the conduction of electricity. Molten and dissolved ionic compounds have free ions. Metals, because of their bonding, have free electrons that are no longer part of the atom and are mobile.

- **Non-conductors** do not allow an electric current to pass through. Example of non-conductors are non-metals (except graphite), plastics, solid ionic compounds, covalent compounds and aqueous solutions of covalent compounds. These do not have any mobile charge carriers to conduct electricity. These non-conductors can be used as insulators and are used to insulate electrical wire, for example.

Electrolytes

When an ionic compound melts or dissolves in water, the liquid or solution that forms is known as an **electrolyte**. In the solid state, the ions of the compound are held together by strong forces of attraction that do not allow for free movement of ions. For this reason, the lattice structure of the compound has to be broken down by the solid either melting or being dissolved in water to produce the free ions. Because the ionic bonds have broken and the ions are free to move, electrolytes are **conductors**. When an electric current passes through an electrolyte, it **decomposes**. Molten ionic or electrovalent compounds, solutions of acids and alkalis in water, ionic or electrovalent compounds dissolved in water and aqueous solutions of some polar covalent solvents are all examples of electrolytes. Some named examples of electrolytes are aqueous hydrochloric acid, aqueous sodium hydroxide, sodium chloride in water, hydrogen chloride and molten potassium bromide.

Differences between metallic and electrolytic conduction

Differences exist between conduction of electricity in a metal (**metallic conduction**) and conduction in an electrolyte (**electrolytic conduction**). As stated before, metals exhibit metallic bonding (see page 81), that is, because metals are solids, the particles are compact and are very close together. When the metal atoms come together in their metallic structure, they each lose an electron forming a sea of electrons and the atoms become positive ions. When these metals are used as wires in an electric cell, the electromotive force of the electric cell makes this sea of electrons mobile. They move out of the metal (wire) into the cell and the same number of electrons have to move in to replace them, causing an electric current to flow. It must be noted that no chemical change occurs. On the other hand, when the electric current flows through an electrolyte, the electric current is carried by mobile ions, not **electrons** in the solution or liquid. Decomposition of the electrolyte occurs to form these ions, resulting in a chemical change occurring. This chemical change makes electrolytic conduction different from metallic conduction in which there are no chemical changes.

Strength of electrolytes

The **strength** of an electrolyte is determined by the **concentration of ions** present and hence their electrical conductivity.

Electrolytes are therefore categorised as either being strong or weak electrolytes.

- **Strong electrolytes** fully dissociate into their ions in the aqueous or molten state, resulting in a high concentration of free ions. Examples of strong electrolytes are strong acids (sulfuric acid or hydrochloric acid) and bases (sodium hydroxide or potassium hydroxide):

$$HCl\ (aq) \longrightarrow H^+(aq) + Cl^-(aq)$$
$$NaOH(aq) \longrightarrow Na^+(aq) + OH^-(aq)$$

- **Weak electrolytes** only slightly dissociate into ions when dissolved in water, subsequently releasing a few ions in solution. Examples of weak electrolytes are limewater, aqueous ethanoic acid, aqueous carbonic acid, propanoic acid and aqueous ammonia:

$$CH_3CH_2\,COOH(aq) \rightleftharpoons CH_3CH_2\,COO^-(aq) + H^+(aq)$$

Pure water

Pure water is a covalent compound but is an **extremely weak** electrolyte. This is explained by the fact that covalent compounds have a small quantity of ionic character. Pure water has a very small amount of ionic character and therefore a very small proportion of water molecules exist as free ions. Approximately one in every 5.56×10^8 water molecules is ionised into H^+ and OH^- ions at any one time:

$$H_2O(l) \rightleftharpoons H^+(aq) + OH^-(aq)$$

The presence of these ions is important when an electric current passes through an aqueous electrolyte.

Non-electrolytes

Non-electrolytes are substances which remain as molecules in the liquid state or dissolved in water, that is, they do not ionise and therefore they do not contain any free ions to accommodate the flow of electricity. Non-electrolytes are **non-conductors** and include:

- liquids, for example, gasoline, methanol or propanone
- molten covalent substances, for example, molten sulfur, molten wax or naphthalene
- solutions of covalent substances, for example, solutions of glucose, turpentine, tetrachloromethane, trichloromethane or paraffin.

Recalling facts

1 In the electrochemical series of common metals, the higher metals ionise to form:

  a anion   **b** atom   **c** cathode   **d** cations

2 The strongest oxidising agent in the electrochemical series of non-metals is:

  a bromine   **b** chlorine   **c** fluorine   **d** iodine

3 Which of the following are all anions?

  a F^-, Na^+, OH^-

  b F^-, Cl^-, OH^-

  c Mg^{2+}, Na^+, Ca^{2+}

  d F, Na^+, OH^-

4 Which of the following are all cations?

  a K^+, K, K^-

  b K^+, Mg^{2+}, Ca^{2-}

  c K^+, Mg^{2+}, Ca^{2+}

  d K^-, Mg^{2+}, Ca^{2+}

5 Which substance conducts electricity?

  a molten potassium iodide

  b ethanol

  c paraffin wax

  d solid sodium chloride

6 Ethanoic acid is a:

a non-conductor

b non-electrolyte

c weak electrolyte

d strong electrolyte

7 Pure water is a:

a weak electrolyte

b strong electrolyte

c non-conductor

d non-electrolyte

8 Metallic conduction involves:

a mobile electrons

b mobile ions

c chemical change

d none of the above

9 Does the ease of ionisation increase or decrease on ascending the electrochemical series of common metals?

10 Give three examples of non-electrolytes and explain why they are non-conductors.

Applying facts

11 Name any two metals which would displace silver from silver nitrate solution. Write the ionic equations for the displacement for both named metals.

12 Fluorine is above bromine in the electrochemical series of non-metals. Write an ionic equation to show which non-metal is displaced and which one is discharged.

13 Explain how an electrical current passes through a metal and through graphite.

14 Explain why mineral acids are considered to be strong electrolytes and organic acids to be weak electrolytes.

Analysing data

15 Discuss the differences between metallic and electrolytic conduction.

Electrolysis

Learning objectives

- Define **electrolysis, cathode, anode, cation, anion**.
- Identify ions present in electrolytes.
- Predict the electrode to which an ion will drift.
- Predict likely products of **molten binary compounds**.
- Predict using the concepts of **concentration of electrolyte, type of electrode**, and **selective discharge** the likely products of **electrolysis of aqueous solutions**.
- Construct **ionic equations** for the reactions occurring at the electrodes.

*Electrolysis is the **chemical change** occurring when an electric current passes through an **electrolyte**.*

The electrolyte is 'split up' or decomposed with the passage of electricity through it. The process of electrolysis is carried out in an electrolytic cell which consists of two electrodes, an electrolyte and a direct current (DC) power source connected to both electrodes (as can be seen in Figure 11.1).

- The **electrolyte**. This is a molten ionic compound or solution which contains charged **mobile ions** (**cations** and **anions**).
- A **battery** or other DC power supply. This supplies the **electric current**.
- Two **electrodes**. These are connected to the power supply by wires and are placed in the electrolyte so that they can carry the current **into** and **out of** the electrolyte. They are usually made of an inert material, for example, graphite (carbon) or platinum, which can conduct electricity.
- The **anode** is the **positive** electrode, connected to the positive terminal of the power supply.
- The **cathode** is the **negative** electrode, connected to the negative terminal of the power supply.

When an electric current is passed through the circuit, the mobile charged ions are attracted to the oppositely charged electrodes. The cations are attracted to the cathode and the anions migrate towards the anode. The cations are metals, such as sodium (Na^+), lead (Pb^{2+}), copper (Cu^{2+}), silver (Ag^+) or hydrogen (H^+). The anions are typically non-metals ions, such as chloride (Cl^-), hydroxide (OH^-) or sulfate (SO_4^{2-}). As the ions migrate to the respective electrodes, they carry the electric charge through the electrolyte and a current flows through the circuit. An electrochemical reaction occurs, resulting in the process of electrolysis.

Principles of electrolysis

During electrolysis:

- The negative **anions** are attracted to the positive **anode** where they are **discharged** to form atoms by losing electrons to the anode:

$$N^{n-} \longrightarrow N + ne^-$$

- **Oxidation** occurs at the **anode** (Oxidation Is Loss, OIL). The anode behaves as the **oxidising agent**.
- The **electrons** that the anions lose at the anode move through the circuit from the anode to the positive terminal of the battery. The electrons re-enter the circuit from the negative terminal of the battery and move from the battery to the cathode.
- The positive **cations** are attracted to the negative **cathode** where they are **discharged** to form atoms by gaining electrons from the cathode:

$$M^{n+} + ne^- \longrightarrow M$$

- **Reduction** occurs at the **cathode** (Reduction Is Gain, RIG). The cathode behaves as the **reducing agent**.

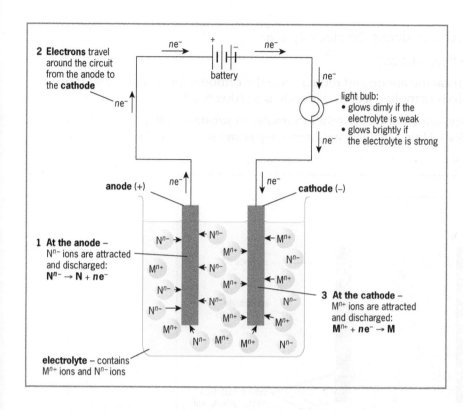

In the diagram:

2 Electrons travel around the circuit from the anode to the **cathode**

ne^-

battery

light bulb:
- glows dimly if the electrolyte is weak
- glows brightly if the electrolyte is strong

anode (+)   cathode (–)

1 At the anode – N^{n-} ions are attracted and discharged:
$N^{n-} \rightarrow N + ne^-$

3 At the cathode – M^{n+} ions are attracted and discharged:
$M^{n+} + ne^- \rightarrow M$

electrolyte – contains M^{n+} ions and N^{n-} ions

Figure 11.1 *Events occurring during electrolysis*

Electrolysis of molten electrolytes

Molten electrolytes contain **two** different ions only, a cation and an anion. Both ions are **discharged** during electrolysis.

Example 8

Electrolysis of molten lead(II) chloride using inert graphite electrodes

The diagram in Figure 11.2 shows how molten lead(II) chloride can be electrolysed in the laboratory. The lead(II) chloride is strongly heated until it melts. Then a current is passed through the molten lead(II) chloride. A liquid (molten lead) forms at the cathode (negative electrode) and bubbles of chlorine gas are visible effervescing at the anode (positive electrode).

- Lead(II) chloride is an ionic compound containing lead ions, Pb^{2+}, and chloride ions, Cl^-. In the solid state the cations and anions are strongly held by electrostatic forces of attraction and are therefore not free to move. However, when molten, the ions become mobile.

- Events at the anode:

  The Cl^- **ions** move towards the anode where each ion loses an electron to the anode to form a chlorine atom (the ions are discharged). As chlorine ions lose electrons, oxidation occurs at the anode. Chlorine atoms immediately bond covalently in pairs to form **chlorine molecules**:

  $$2Cl^-(l) \longrightarrow Cl_2(g) + 2e^-$$

  Chlorine vapour is evolved around the anode.

- Events at the cathode:

  The Pb^{2+} **ions** move towards the cathode where each ion gains two electrons to form a lead atom (the ions are discharged):

  $$Pb^{2+}(l) + 2e^- \longrightarrow Pb(l)$$

  As the lead ions gain electrons, reduction occurs at the cathode. Molten **lead** is formed around the cathode and drips off.

- The overall chemical change during the electrolysis is:

$$PbCl_2(l) \longrightarrow Pb(l) + Cl_2(g)$$

Since oxidation occurs at the anode and reduction at the cathode, the reaction that takes place during electrolysis of molten lead(II) chloride is a redox reaction.

Lead(II) bromide and sodium chloride are other examples of substances that can undergo the process of electrolysis, liberating lead and bromine gas and sodium and chlorine gas respectively.

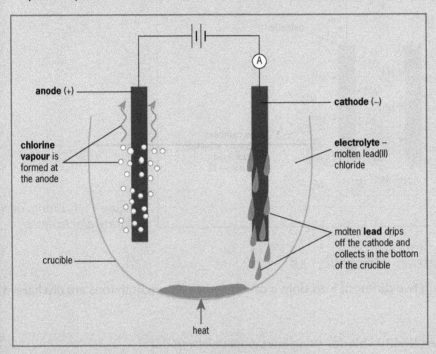

Figure 11.2 *Electrolysis of molten lead(II) chloride*

Electrolysis of aqueous electrolytes

When molten compounds are electrolysed, only two types of ions are present and both are discharged. An **aqueous solution** contains at least **two** different **cations** and **two** different **anions** because it contains ions from the **solute** and **H⁺ ions** and **OH⁻** ions from the ionisation of water molecules. During electrolysis, **one** type of cation and **one** type of anion are discharged in preference to any others present. This is called **preferential discharge** and the factors governing this phenomenon will be discussed now.

When predicting the products of electrolysis of an aqueous electrolytic reaction the following need to be considered:

- The **electrolyte** – the ions present in the electrolyte. Remember that four ions are present; H⁺ and OH⁻ ions are always present because there is water in the system and the concept of preferential discharge must be taken into consideration.
- The **type of electrode** (inert or active) and the reactions that occur.
- The **product** at each electrode and the **type of reaction** that occurs at each (oxidation occurs at the anode and reduction occurs at the cathode).
- The **equations** at each electrode.

Table 11.5 summarises the electrolysis of some aqueous solutions taking these points into consideration.

Factors influencing the preferential discharge of anions

Three main factors influence the preferential discharge of the **anions**:

- **The type of anode**

  An anode that is **not inert**, for example, copper, can take part in the electrolysis process and this affects what happens at the anode. If an **active** anode is used, the reaction occurring is the one which requires the least energy. This usually involves the anode **ionising** instead of an anion being discharged.

  Comparing the electrolysis of copper(II) sulfate solution using an inert anode and an active copper anode demonstrates this (see Table 11.5). The flow diagram in Figure 11.3 indicates what happens at the anode.

- **The concentration of the electrolyte**

  The **greater** the concentration of an ion, the **more likely** it is to be preferentially discharged. This rule applies mainly to solutions containing **halide ions** (Cl^-, Br^- and I^- **ions**).

  Comparing the electrolysis of dilute and concentrated sodium chloride solutions using inert electrodes demonstrates this (see Table 11.5).

- **The position of the ion in the electrochemical series**

  The **lower** the ion in the electrochemical series of anions (Table 11.3), the **more likely** it is to be preferentially discharged. Ions at the **top** of the series are the **hardest to discharge** because they are the most stable. Ions at the **bottom** are the **easiest to discharge** because they are the least stable. Unless affected by the concentration of the electrolyte and/or nature of the anode, ions usually discharge based on their position in the electrochemical series.

The electrolysis of dilute sulfuric acid, dilute sodium chloride solution and copper(II) sulfate solution using inert electrodes all demonstrate this (see Table 11.5).

Table 11.3 The electrochemical series of anions

Anion
F^-
SO_4^{2-}
NO_3^-
Cl^-
Br^-
I^-
OH^-

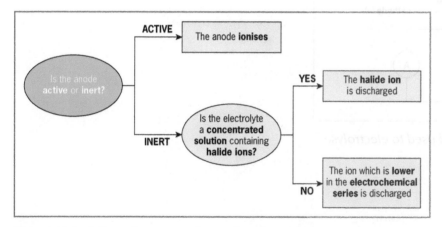

Figure 11.3 A flow diagram to determine the reaction occurring at the anode

Preferential discharge of cations

The **position** of the ion in the **electrochemical series influences** the **preferential discharge** of the cations.

The **lower** the ion in the electrochemical series of cations (Table 11.4), the **more likely** it is to be preferentially discharged. Ions at the **top** of the series are the **hardest to discharge** because they are the most stable. Ions at the **bottom** are the **easiest to discharge** because they are the least stable.

The electrolysis of both dilute and concentrated sodium chloride solutions, and copper(II) sulfate solution demonstrate this (see Table 11.5).

Table 11.4 *The electrochemical series of cations*

Cation
K^+
Ca^{2+}
Na^+
Mg^{2+}
Al^{3+}
Zn^{2+}
Fe^{2+}
Pb^{2+}
H^+
Cu^{2+}
Ag^+

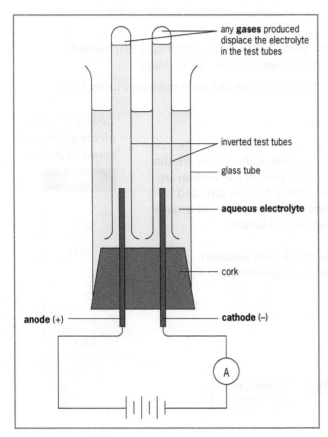

any **gases** produced displace the electrolyte in the test tubes

inverted test tubes

glass tube

aqueous electrolyte

cork

anode (+)

cathode (−)

A

Figure 11.4 *An electrolytic cell used to electrolyse aqueous solutions*

Table 11.5 *The electrolysis of some aqueous solutions*

Electrolyte and ions present	Electrodes	Reactions at the electrodes and nature of the products	How the electrolyte changes
Dilute sulfuric acid, H_2SO_4(aq) From H_2SO_4: H^+(aq), SO_4^{2-}(aq) From H_2O: H^+(aq), OH^-(aq)	**Inert –** carbon or platinum	• **At anode: OH^- ions** are preferentially discharged. They are lower in the electrochemical series than SO_4^{2-}: $4OH^-(aq) \longrightarrow 2H_2O(l) + O_2(g) + 4e^-$ **Effervescence** occurs as **oxygen** gas is evolved. • **At cathode: H^+ ions** are discharged: $2H^+(aq) + 2e^- \longrightarrow H_2(g)$ **Effervescence** occurs as **hydrogen** gas is evolved. • **Relative proportions of gases:** for every 4 mol electrons, 1 mol O_2 and 2 mol H_2 are produced.	Becomes **more concentrated:** H^+ and OH^- ions are removed, leaving H^+ and SO_4^{2-} ions in excess, i.e. water is removed.
Concentrated hydrochloric acid, HCl(aq) From HCl: H^+(aq), Cl^-(aq) From H_2O : H^+(aq), OH^-(aq)	**Inert –** carbon or platinum	• **At anode: Cl^- ions** preferentially discharged instead of OH^- because of their higher concentration. **Effervescence** occurs as **chlorine** gas is evolved. $2Cl^-(aq) - 2e^- \longrightarrow Cl_2(g)$ • **At cathode: H^+ ions** discharged: $2H^+(aq) + 2e^- \longrightarrow H_2(g)$ **Effervescence** occurs as **hydrogen** gas is evolved. • **Relative proportion of gases:** for every 2 electrons 1 mol Cl_2 and 1 mol H_2 is produced.	Becomes **more dilute:** H^+ and Cl^- ions are removed.
Dilute sodium chloride solution, NaCl(aq) From NaCl: Na^+(aq), Cl^-(aq) From H_2O: H^+(aq), OH^-(aq)	**Inert –** carbon or platinum	• **At anode: OH^- ions** are preferentially discharged. They are lower in the electrochemical series than Cl^-: $4OH^-(aq) \longrightarrow 2H_2O(l) + O_2(g) + 4e^-$ **Effervescence** occurs as **oxygen** gas is evolved. • **At cathode: H^+ ions** are preferentially discharged. They are lower in the electrochemical series than Na^+: $2H^+(aq) + 2e^- \longrightarrow H_2(g)$ **Effervescences** occurs as **hydrogen** gas is evolved. • **Relative proportions of gases:** for every 4 mol electrons, 1 mol O_2 and 2 mol H_2 are produced.	**Becomes more concentrated:** H^+ and OH^- ions are removed, leaving Na^+ and Cl^- ions in excess, i.e. water is removed.

(Continued)

Table 11.5 *Continued*

Electrolyte and ions present	Electrodes	Reactions at the electrodes and nature of the products	How the electrolyte changes
Concentrated sodium chloride solution, NaCl(aq) From NaCl: $Na^+(aq)$, $Cl^-(aq)$ From H_2O: $H^+(aq)$, $OH^-(aq)$	**Inert –** carbon or platinum	• **At anode: Cl^- ions** are preferentially discharged. They are halide ions in a concentrated solution: $2Cl^-(aq) \longrightarrow Cl_2(g) + 2e^-$ **Effervescence** occurs as **chlorine** gas is evolved. • **At cathode: H^+ ions** are preferentially discharged. They are lower in the electrochemical series than Na^+: $2H^+(aq) + 2e^- \longrightarrow H_2(g)$ **Effervescence** occurs as **hydrogen** gas is evolved. • **Relative proportions of gases**: for every 2 mol electrons, 1 mol Cl_2 and 1 mol H_2 are produced.	Becomes **alkaline**: H^+ and Cl^- ions are removed leaving Na^+ and OH^- ions in excess, i.e. sodium hydroxide is formed.
Copper(II) sulfate solution, $CuSO_4(aq)$ From $CuSO_4$: $Cu^{2+}(aq)$, $SO_4^{2-}(aq)$ From H_2O: $H^+(aq)$, $OH^-(aq)$	**Inert –** carbon or platinum	• **At anode: OH^- ions** are preferentially discharged. They are lower in the electrochemical series than SO_4^{2-}: $4OH^-(aq) \longrightarrow 2H_2O(l) + O_2(g) + 4e^-$ **Effervescence** occurs as **oxygen** gas is evolved. • **At cathode: Cu^{2+} ions** are preferentially discharged. They are lower in the electrochemical series than H^+: $Cu^{2+}(aq) + 2e^- \longrightarrow Cu(s)$ **Pink** copper is deposited and the cathode **increases** in size.	Becomes **acidic**: Cu^{2+} and OH^- ions are removed, leaving H^+ and SO_4^{2-} ions in excess, i.e. sulfuric acid is formed. Becomes **paler blue**: blue Cu^{2+} ions are removed.
Copper(II) sulfate solution, $CuSO_4(aq)$ From $CuSO_4$: $Cu^{2+}(aq)$, $SO_4^{2-}(aq)$ From H_2O: $H^+(aq)$, $OH^-(aq)$	Anode – **active copper** Cathode – carbon, platinum or copper	• **At anode:** the anode **ionises**. This requires less energy than discharging either anion: $Cu(s) \longrightarrow Cu^{2+}(aq) + 2e^-$ Cu^{2+} ions go into the electrolyte and the anode **decreases** in size. • **At cathode: Cu^{2+} ions** are preferentially discharged. They are lower in the electrochemical series than H^+: $Cu^{2+}(aq) + 2e^- \longrightarrow Cu(s)$ **Pink** copper is deposited and the cathode **increases** in size.	Remains **unchanged**: for every 2 mol electrons, 1 mol Cu^{2+} ions enter the electrolyte at the anode, and 1 mol Cu^{2+} ions is discharged at the cathode.

Recalling facts

16 Which of the following species would be attracted to the anode?

    a H_2O **b** Ca^{2+} **c** Cl^- **d** $NaCl$

17 Which of the following species would be attracted to the cathode?

    a cations

    b anions

    c solid potassium iodide

    d acid

18 Where does oxidation take place?

    a wires

    b anode

    c cathode

    d cations

19 All aqueous solutions ionise to give how many ions?

    a 1   **b** 2   **c** 3   **d** 4

20 Molten compounds ionise to give:

    a 1 ion

    b 2 ions

    c 3 ions

    d 4 ions

21 The cathode behaves as the:

    a oxidising agent

    b reducing agent

    c anion

    d cation

22 When using dilute sodium chloride solution as the electrolyte, what are the ions present?

    a Na^+, Cl^-

    b Na^+, Cl^-, H^+

    c Na^+, Cl^-, H^+, OH^-

    d Cl^-, H^+

23 What are the products of the electrolysis of dilute sulfuric acid using inert electrodes?

    a $S(s)$, $O_2(g)$

    b $H_2(g)$, $O_2(g)$

    c $H^+(g)$, $O_2(g)$

    d $S(s)$, $H_2(g)$

24 Which of the following **does not** occur when copper(II) sulfate is electrolysed using active copper as the anode and inert cathode?

    a anode shrinks in size

    b anode increases in size

    c cathode turns pink

    d cathode increases in size

25 What are the main components of an electrolytic cell? State the importance of each component.

26 What is meant by the term preferential discharge? State the factors which influence the preferential discharge of cations and anions during the process of electrolysis.

Applying facts

27 When dilute sulfuric acid undergoes electrolysis using an inert electrode, what products are formed?

28 Account for the differences in products formed at the electrodes when dilute and concentrated sodium chloride undergoes electrolysis using inert electrodes.

29 Predict the products that would be formed at the anode and cathode when molten **a** lead(II) iodide, PbI_2 and **b** sodium chloride, NaCl, are electrolysed. In your answer for each compound you must include the formulae of the ions in the electrolyte and write ionic half equations for the reactions occurring at the electrodes.

Analysing data

30 What are the products at the anode and cathode when **a**, magnesium chloride and **b**, copper(II) chloride, are electrolysed using carbon electrodes? In your answer you should include for each compound the names of the ions formed in solution and write ionic half equations at the electrodes.

Quantitative electrolysis

Learning objectives

- Define the **Faraday constant.**
- Calculate the masses and volumes of substances liberated during electrolysis.

During electrolysis, the movement of electrons through the external circuit from anode to cathode results in a **flow of electrical charge** since each electron possesses an extremely small electrical charge. The quantity of a substance produced at, or dissolved from, an electrode during electrolysis is directly proportional to the **quantity of electrical charge**, or **quantity of electricity**, which flows through the electrolytic cell.

The quantity of electrical charge (Q) is measured in **coulombs (C)**. The quantity of electrical charge flowing through an electrolytic cell during electrolysis is dependent on **two** factors:

- The **current** (**I**), which is the rate of flow of the electrical charge. Current is measured in **amperes** (known as **amps, A**).
- The length of **time** (**t**) that the current flows for. Time is measured in **seconds** (**s**).

The quantity of electrical charge can be calculated using the formula below.

> quantity of electrical charge (C) = current (A) × time (s)
>
> or $\qquad\qquad\qquad\qquad\qquad Q = I \times t$

One mole of electrons (6.0×10^{23} electrons), has a total charge of **96 500 C**. This value is known as the **Faraday constant**.

*The **Faraday constant** is the size of the electrical charge on one mole of electrons, that is, 96 500 C mol^{-1}.*

The following equations show **that one mole** of electrons is required to discharge **one mole** of an ion with a single charge:

$$M^+ + e^- \longrightarrow M \quad \text{or} \quad N^- \longrightarrow N + e^-$$
$$\textbf{1 mol} \qquad\qquad\qquad\qquad\qquad\qquad \textbf{1 mol}$$

Using the Faraday constant, it follows that **96 500 C** is the quantity of electrical charge required to discharge **one mole** of ions with a **single charge**. The Faraday constant can be used to calculate the masses of substances and volumes of gases formed during electrolysis.

Electrolysis calculations

Information that can be given in electrolysis can be:

- the amount of product formed in moles, mass or volume
- since electrolysis involves ions, their charge
- the current or electric charge utilised.

Any two pieces of the listed information that are identified can be used to calculate the one that is unknown.

To calculate the mass or volume of product produced at the anode or cathode

The following steps can be used.

- Calculate the charge in coulombs by using the formula:

  $Q = IT$

  ○ Using the Faraday constant, calculate the number of moles of electrons:

  one mole of product deposited = Faraday constant

  1 Faraday = Avogadro's constant of electrons = 6×10^{23} electrons
- Write the balanced electrode equation.
- Using the mole ratio, calculate the number of moles of products that can be deposited.
- The number of moles is now converted to either mass or volume depending on what the question asks.

1 Determine the mass of nickel produced at the cathode when a current of 8.5 A flows through molten nickel(II) chloride for 35 minutes and 32 seconds.

Determine the **quantity of electricity (Q)** that flows: current = **8.5 A**

Time in seconds = (35 × 60) + 32 s = **2132 s**

Quantity of electricity (C) = current (A) × time (s)

∴ quantity of electricity = 8.5 × 2132 C

$$= 18\ 122\ \text{C}$$

Write the equation for the reaction at the **cathode**:

$$\underset{\textbf{2 mol}}{Ni^{2+}(l)} + \underset{}{2e^-} \longrightarrow \underset{\textbf{1 mol}}{Ni(l)}$$

From the equation:

2 mol of electrons are required to form **1 mol Ni**

∴ 2 × 96 500 C are required to form 1 mol Ni

i.e. **193 000 C** form 1 mol Ni

∴ 1 C forms 1/193 000 mol Ni

and 18 122 C form $\dfrac{1}{193\ 000}$ × 18 122 mol Ni

$$= \textbf{0.09 mol Ni}$$

Mass of 1 mol Ni = 58.7 g

∴ mass of **0.09 mol Ni** = 0.09 × 58.7 g

$$= \textbf{5.28 g}$$

Mass of nickel produced = **5.28 g**

---

2 Calculate the volume of oxygen produced at the anode at stp if an electric current of 8.0 A is passed through dilute sulfuric acid solution for 4 hours, 31 minutes and 56 seconds.

Quantity of electricity that flows: current = **8.0 A**

Time in seconds = (4 × 60 × 60) + (31 × 60) + 56 s = 16 316 s

∴ quantity of electricity = 8.0 × 16 316 C

$$= \textbf{130 528 C}$$

Equation for the reaction at the anode:

$$4OH^-(aq) \longrightarrow 2H_2O(aq) + \underset{\textbf{1 mol}}{O_2(g)} + \underset{\textbf{4 mol}}{4e^-}$$

From the equation:

4 mol electrons are lost in forming **1 mol O_2**

∴ 4 × 96 500 C form 1 mol O_2

i.e. **386 000 C** form 1 mol O_2

∴ 130 528 C form $\dfrac{1}{386\ 000}$ × 130 528 mol O_2

$$= \textbf{0.34 mol } O_2$$

Volume of 1 mol O_2 at stp = 22.4 dm³

∴ volume of **0.34 mol O_2** = 0.34 × 22.4 dm³

$$= \textbf{7.62 dm}^3$$

Volume of oxygen produced = **7.62 dm³**

To calculate the current or time for the mass of product to be deposited

- Calculate the number of moles of product produced.
- Write the equation occurring at the electrode.
- Calculate the number of moles of electrons being transferred to yield the product.
- Calculate the electric charge.
- Calculate the current if the charge is given, or the time if the current is given.

Sample questions

How long will it take for 33.5 cm³ of oxygen gas to be liberated at the anode at stp, when 7.8 A of electricity is passed through dilute sulfuric acid solution?

Number of moles of oxygen produced at the anode:

Volume of 1 mol of O_2 at stp = 22 400 cm³

Therefore number of moles of 33.5 cm³ $= \dfrac{33.5}{22\,400}$

$= 0.0015$ mol

Equation for the reaction at the anode:

$$4OH^-(aq) \quad - \quad 4e^- \longrightarrow 2H_2O(l) \quad + \quad O_2(g)$$
$$\textbf{4 mol} \qquad\qquad\qquad\qquad\qquad \textbf{1 mol}$$

From the equation:

4 mol electrons are required to form 1 mol of O_2

Therefore 4 × 96 500 C form 1 mol of O_2

i.e. 386 000 C form 1 mol O_2

∴ 0.0015 × 386 000 C form 0.0015 mol of O_2

$= \textbf{579 C}$

i.e. quantity of electricity required = 579 C

Time taken for 579 C to flow using a current of 7.8 A

Quantity of electricity (C) = current (A) × time (s)

579 C = 7.8 A × time

∴ time $= \dfrac{579}{7.8}$

$= \textbf{74.2 s}$

Time taken = **74.2 seconds**

Recalling facts

31 When using the formula $Q = IT$ in electrolysis calculations, the unit for time is:

a milliseconds

b seconds

c minutes

d hours

32 Which of the following metals needs the smallest number of moles of electrons to form one mole of atoms during electrolysis?

    a Aluminium

    b Calcium

    c Magnesium

    d Sodium

33 Calculate the number of coulombs of charge which passes through a cell with a current of 3 A flowing for 3 minutes.

    a 9

    b 90

    c 180

    d 540

34 Determine the number of moles of electrons which is required to produce 0.32 mol of chromium from chromium ions:

    a 0.16

    b 0.32

    c 0.96

    d 3.20

35 What mass of aluminium atoms is formed from the ions by the gain of 0.45 mol of electrons at the cathode?

    a 2.7

    b 4.05

    c 4.50

    d 12.15

Applying facts

36 Calculate the number of moles of electrons required to produce 0.15 mol zinc from zinc ions. What mass of zinc is obtained?

37 Calculate the electric charge required for a current of 3.7 A to flow for 2 hours 22 minutes and 30 seconds.

38 Find the time it takes for 0.035 mol of nickel to deposit from nickel(II) ions with a current flow of 3.7 A.

39 Determine the mass of potassium deposited at the cathode when a current of 5 A passes through molten potassium chloride for 2 hours 25 seconds.

Industrial applications of electrolysis

Learning objectives

- Describe how **metallic extraction** works using electrolysis.
- Describe **electrolysis of aqueous copper(II) sulfate**, with copper electrodes, as a means to purifying copper.
- Describe the **electroplating** of metals.
- Describe **anodising** as a means of protecting metals against **corrosion**.

Electrolysis is used in many ways in industry, for example, extraction of metals from their ores, purifying metals, electroplating and anodising.

Extraction of metals from their ores

Metals are very reactive and for this reason they do not occur in nature in their free or uncombined state. Except for copper, silver and gold, all metals occur bonded to other elements in ionic compounds referred to as minerals. The metallic compound together with impurities are known as ores. For example, bauxite is the ore of aluminium. The metals in the ores are positively charged and the process of extracting the metals from their ores involves reduction of the metal ions to atoms.

$$M^{n+} + ne^- \longrightarrow M$$

Metals that are high in the electrochemical series form very stable ions because they ionise easily. In other words, these metal ions are very difficult to reduce to the metal atoms. A powerful method of reduction is therefore needed to extract these metals from their ores. **Electrolysis** of the **molten ore** is one such method of reduction and this method is used in the extraction of aluminium (page 298) and other metals (e.g. sodium) which are above aluminium in the electrochemical series from their ores.

Summary of aluminium production using electrolysis

Impurities are removed from the ore. The ore is then dissolved in molten cryolite (Na_3AlF_6). Adding the cryolite lowers the melting point of the ore allowing for less energy to be expended during the liquifying process of the ore. Graphite can be used as both cathode and anode.

The reaction at the cathode is as follows:

$$Al^{3+}(l) + 3e^- \longrightarrow Al(l)$$

The aluminium ions gain electrons to become aluminium metal, which is a liquid because of the temperature at which the cell operates.

The reaction at the anode is as follows:

$$2O^{2-}(l) - 4e^- \longrightarrow O_2(g)$$
$$C(s) + O_2(g) \longrightarrow CO_2(g)$$

The oxide ions lose their excess electrons and produce oxygen, which reacts with the graphite electrode to liberate carbon dioxide gas. As carbon dioxide is released, the electrodes are corroded and have to be replaced. For this reason, alloys of titanium can be used as the anode.

Purification of metals (electrorefining)

Metals occur naturally as mixtures and electrolysis can be used to convert an impure metal into the pure metal by a process also known as **electrorefining**.

- The **anode** is the **impure metal**.
- The **cathode** is a very thin strip of the **pure metal**.
- The electrolyte is an aqueous solution containing **ions of the metal** being purified.

Example 9

Purification of copper

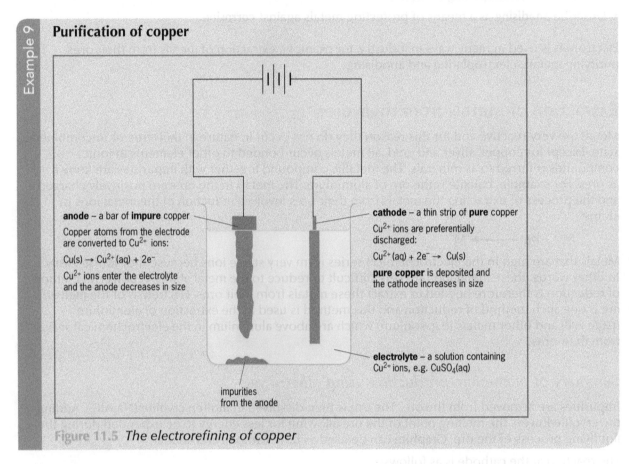

anode – a bar of **impure** copper

Copper atoms from the electrode are converted to Cu^{2+} ions:

$Cu(s) \rightarrow Cu^{2+}(aq) + 2e^-$

Cu^{2+} ions enter the electrolyte and the anode decreases in size

cathode – a thin strip of **pure** copper

Cu^{2+} ions are preferentially discharged:

$Cu^{2+}(aq) + 2e^- \rightarrow Cu(s)$

pure copper is deposited and the cathode increases in size

electrolyte – a solution containing Cu^{2+} ions, e.g. $CuSO_4(aq)$

impurities from the anode

Figure 11.5 *The electrorefining of copper*

Note Electrorefining is only suitable to purify metals whose ions are **below hydrogen** in the electrochemical series.

Electroplating

Electroplating is the process by which a thin layer of one metal is deposited on another metal by electrolysis. It is used to **protect** the original metal from corrosion, to make it look more **attractive** or to make an inexpensive metal object appear more valuable.

Metals such as chromium, tin, silver, gold and nickel can be coated and used as water taps, bicycle parts, tin cans, silver plated knives and forks, electroplated gold jewellery chrome-plated rims (Figure 11.6).

Figure 11.6 *Chrome-plated rims*

The principles of electroplating are as follows:

- The **anode** is a pure sample of the **metal** being used for plating.
- The **cathode** is the **object** to be electroplated.
- The electrolyte is an aqueous solution containing **ions of the metal** being used for plating.

Electroplating using silver

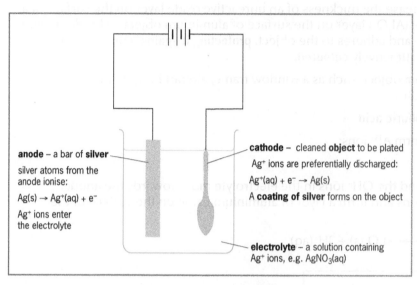

anode – a bar of **silver**

silver atoms from the anode ionise:

$Ag(s) \rightarrow Ag^+(aq) + e^-$

Ag^+ ions enter the electrolyte

cathode – cleaned **object** to be plated

Ag^+ ions are preferentially discharged:

$Ag^+(aq) + e^- \rightarrow Ag(s)$

A **coating of silver** forms on the object

electrolyte – a solution containing Ag^+ ions, e.g. $AgNO_3(aq)$

Figure 11.7 *Electroplating a spoon with silver*

Note Only metals whose ions are **below hydrogen** in the electrochemical series can be used for plating. The object that is being electroplated must be cleaned to eliminate dirt, corrosion and grease.

Electroplating using nickel

The electrolyte could be nickel sulfate.

Reaction at the anode:

- Ni^{2+} is discharged from the anode into solution. The electrode decreases in size.

  $Ni(s) \longrightarrow Ni^{2+}(aq) + 2e^-$

Reaction at the cathode:

- Ni^{2+} which is produced from the anode gains electrons at the cathode and becomes a nickel atom. Nickel is therefore deposited onto the iron object coating it. Hence the object increases in size.

  $Ni^{2+}(aq) + 2e^- \longrightarrow Ni(s)$

Electroplating using copper

The object is made the cathode, for example, a copper coin (an old coin can be resurfaced using copper), and a piece of copper is used as the anode. The electrolyte is copper(II) sulfate solution.

Reaction at the anode:

- Cu^{2+} is discharged from the anode into solution. The electrode decreases in size.

  $Cu(s) \longrightarrow Cu^{2+}(aq) + 2e^-$

Reaction at the cathode:

- Cu^{2+} which is produced from the anode gains electrons at the cathode and becomes a copper atom. Copper is deposited onto the coin, resurfacing it. The copper(II) sulfate solution remains unchanged.

Anodising

Anodising is a process used to increase the thickness of an unreactive oxide layer on the surface of a metal, usually the **aluminium oxide** (Al_2O_3) layer on the surface of aluminium objects. The aluminium oxide layer is relatively unreactive and adheres to the object, **protecting** it against corrosion. It also readily absorbs dyes, so it can be attractively **coloured**.

The **anode** is the cleaned **aluminium** object, such as a window frame, aircraft body, kettle, bottle cap or saucepan (Figure 11.8).

The electrolyte is usually **dilute sulfuric acid**.

The aluminium anode **ionises** to form Al^{3+} ions:

$$Al(s) \longrightarrow Al^{3+}(aq) + 3e^-$$

At the same time, the SO_4^{2-} ions and the OH^- ions in the electrolyte move towards the anode. The Al^{3+} ions react with the OH^- ions and form a layer of aluminium oxide on the surface of the aluminium object:

$$2Al^{3+}(aq) + 3OH^-(aq) \longrightarrow Al_2O_3(s) + 3H^+(aq)$$

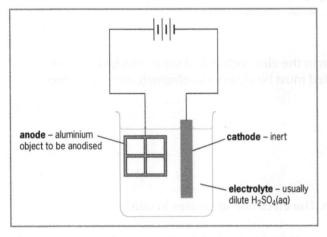

anode – aluminium object to be anodised

cathode – inert

electrolyte – usually dilute H_2SO_4(aq)

Figure 11.8 *Anodising an aluminium window frame*

Recalling facts

 40 A spoon can be gold-plated by the process of electroplating. At the cathode the reaction is shown by which equation:

a $Au(s) - e^- \longrightarrow Au^+(aq)$

b $Au^+(aq) - e^- \longrightarrow Au(s)$

c $Au^+(aq) + e^- \longrightarrow Au(s)$

d $Au^+(s) + e^- \longrightarrow Au(s)$

41 Which of the following is NOT true when an object is anodised?

    a The object is purified.

    b The aluminium oxide coating can readily absorb dyes.

    c The aluminium is made corrosion resistant.

    d The thickness of the aluminium oxide layer is increased.

42 Why is electrolysis of molten compounds important industrially?

    a The production of hydrogen

    b The production of oxygen

    c The extraction of metals from metal ores

    d The purification of metals

43 An object is being electroplated with silver. Which statement is true?

    a The anode is the object.

    b The cathode is the silver bar.

    c Silver dissolves from the anode.

    d Reduction occurs at the anode.

Applying facts

44 The following liquids are electrolysed using inert electrodes. State and explain the products formed and give the reaction half equations at each electrode:

    a concentrated hydrochloric acid

    b molten potassium bromide

    c dilute sodium chloride

45 Electroplating is the coating of an object with a thin layer of a metal by electrolysis. An object can be gold plated to enhance its beauty and value. Explain how this is done. Your answer must include a diagram showing the electroplating cell, the electrodes used, the electrolyte and the reaction half equations at the electrodes.

46 During the electrolysis of lead(II) chloride using a current of 0.7 A, a mass of 0.635 grams of lead was formed at the cathode.

    a Calculate the number of moles of lead formed.

    b Determine the number of moles of electrons needed to liberate the lead.

    c Calculate the electric charge in coulombs used.

    d Calculate the time the current needs to flow through the cell.

Analysing data

47 Copper(II) sulfate solution undergoes the process of electrolysis using two different types of electrodes, either inert carbon electrodes or active copper electrodes. In each case the products and the observations are different. Explain what happens in each electrolysis process of the copper(II) sulfate solutions by giving the ions present in the electrolyte, the relevant half equations that occur at the electrodes and hence the products at the electrodes. State what you observe during the process.

48 Aluminium is extracted from its ore by the process of electrolysis. The electrolyte is a mixture of cryolite and aluminium oxide and the electrodes are made of graphite.

   a Why is a mixture of cryolite and aluminium used instead of aluminium?

   b State what happens at the anode and cathode. Give the reaction half equations that occur at each electrode.

   c Explain why the carbon electrodes have to be replaced periodically and suggest another anode that can be used.

   d State three uses of aluminium and give the properties that make aluminium suitable for these uses.

12 Rates of reaction

Learning objectives

- Define the term **rates of reaction**.
- State **characteristic changes in a reaction system** and describe related **experiments** which can be used to measure the rate of a reaction.
- State **collision theory**.
- Identify and explain the factors that affect the rate of reactions.
- Use the collision theory between reacting particles to explain **speeds of reaction**.
- Plot graphs and interpret data obtained from experiments on speed of reaction.
- Describe the effects of concentration, temperature, surface area, catalyst, light and pressure on the rates of reaction, both graphically and using the collision theory.
- Describe experiments which can be used to determine the effects of **shifting a factor** on the rate of reaction.

When we think of the rate of a chemical reaction, we think of speed or how fast a reaction occurs. The speeds of chemical reactions vary considerably and are very important in the natural environment, manufacturing industry and within living organisms. Some chemical reactions occur extremely slowly. For example, iron rusting takes a few months or even years (Figure 12.1), while fruits take days or even weeks to ripen. Other chemical reactions occur rapidly, such as precipitation, while others are instantaneous and explosive, such as when sodium reacts with water to produce a base and hydrogen gas

Figure 12.1 *Slow reaction rusting of iron pipes*

(Figure 12.2). It is important for chemists to study the rate of chemical reactions so that they can run chemical processes which maximise production and profits, minimise hazards, such as explosions, and detect inefficiencies which would increase the cost of production. Examples of large-scale manufacturing where studying rates is important in maximising profits are in the manufacture of fertiliser, pharmaceuticals and household cleaning chemicals.

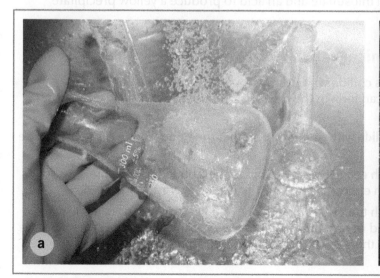

Figure 12.2 *Fast reaction a sodium and water, b showing explosion of sodium on water*

During a chemical reaction, substances (the reactants) react to form substances with new chemical identity (products). As a result, the concentration of the products will increase while that of the reactants will decrease. The measurement of how long it takes for the concentrations of reactants and products to decrease and increase respectively can assist in determining the rate of a chemical reaction.

*The **rate of reaction** is a measured change in the concentration of a reactant or product with time, at a given temperature.*

The rate of a reaction can be determined by using the following formulae:

$$\text{rate of reaction} = \frac{\text{decrease in the concentration of a reactant}}{\text{time taken for the decrease}}$$

or

$$\text{rate of reaction} = \frac{\text{increase in the concentration of a product}}{\text{time taken for the increase}}$$

Measuring rates of reaction

It is usually difficult to measure changes in concentration directly. Other **property changes** may occur which are more easily measured.

- The **volume of gas** produced over time can be measured using a gas syringe if the reaction produces a gas. An example of this is a reactive metal reacting with an acid to give hydrogen gas and a salt.

- The **decrease in mass** of the reaction can be measured over time using a balance if the reaction produces a gas that escapes. An example of this is a carbonate or hydrogen carbonate reacting with an acid, during which carbon dioxide gas is liberated and escapes.

- A change in **colour intensity**, **pressure**, **temperature** or **pH** can be measured over time if any of these properties change during a reaction. An example when monitoring colour intensity is that, when an indicator is used in an acid–base titration, the faster the colour changes the faster the rate of the reaction. Temperature can be used to determine the endpoint of an acid–base titration. pH can be used to indicate the neutralisation point of an acid–base reaction.

- The appearance of a **precipitate** can be measured if one is formed in the reaction. An example of this is the reaction between sodium thiosulfate and an acid to produce a yellow precipitate of sulfur.

The collision theory for chemical reactions

During any chemical reaction, molecules collide with each other and the existing bonds in the **reactants** must **break** so that new bonds can **form** in the **products** producing a new species. In order to **react**:

- The particles of the reactants must **collide** with each other so that the bonds in the reactants can be broken.

- The reactant particles must collide with **enough energy** to break their bonds and enable new bonds to form in the products. This minimum energy is known as **activation energy** (see page 222).

- The reactant particles must collide with the **correct orientation**. They must line up correctly with each other so that bonds can break and reform in the required way. If the collisions of the particles do not occur in the correct alignment, then no product is formed (Figure 12.3).

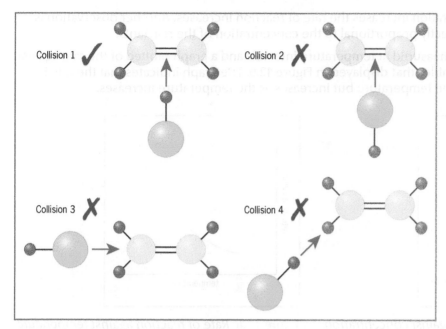

Figure 12.3 *Orientation of particles*

Not all collisions result in a reaction occurring. Some do not occur with the required activation energy, and some do not occur with the correct orientation of particles. Any collision that results in a reaction is known as an **effective collision**. The more effective collisions that occur, the faster the rate of reaction.

For example, for the combustion reaction between methane and oxygen to form carbon dioxide and water, see Figure 12.4.

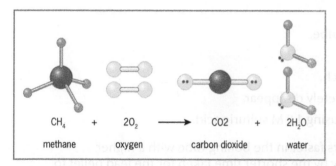

Figure 12.4 *The reaction between methane and oxygen*

There must be collision between the methane (CH_4) and the oxygen (O_2) molecules which has the correct activation energy to break the four C–H covalent bonds in the methane molecules and two O–O covalent bonds in the oxygen molecules. These molecules must also be in the correct orientation, so that the bonds can be broken and reformed in the required way to produce effective collisions forming the products carbon dioxide and water.

Rate curves for reactions

A **rate curve** can be drawn if a measured property, such as concentration, temperature or surface area, is plotted on a graph against time as the reaction proceeds.

When the graph of rate against concentration is plotted for a reaction at different concentrations of one of the reactants, a graph comparable to the one in Figure 12.5 is obtained. It can be deduced from the graph that as the concentration increases the rate of reaction increases. Another observation is that rate of the reaction is directly proportional to the concentration of the reactants.

When the rate of reaction is measured at temperature intervals and a graph plotted of the rate against temperature, the graph resembles that displayed in Figure 12.6. The graph indicates that the rate is not directly proportional to the temperature but increases as the temperature increases.

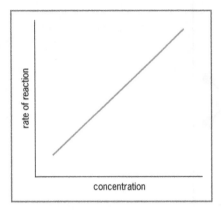

Figure 12.5 *Rate of reaction against concentration*

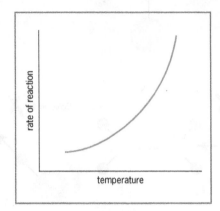

Figure 12.6 *Rate of reaction against temperature*

When studying the speed at which a chemical reaction occurs, the time taken for a reaction to be completed can be measured or the quantity of product produced or quantity of residual/unreacted reactants remaining can be measured in a specific time period. The method which is used to study the reaction's speed depends on the individual reaction.

A simple experiment to measure the rate of a reaction involves the time taken for a lead pellet to completely disappear in a measured volume of sulfuric acid.

- Select two lead pellets of equal mass
- Add 25 cm³ of 0.5 M sulfuric acid to a boiling tube.
- Place one pellet in the boiling tube.
- As soon as the pellet is added, start a stopwatch.
- Time how long it takes for the pellet to completely disappear.
- Repeat the experiment with the other pellet, using 1.0 M sulfuric acid.

As can be seen in Figure 12.7, the reaction occurs faster in the boiling tube with a higher concentration of acid and this was seen not only by the shorter time taken for the lead pellet to dissolve but also by the rapidity of bubbles given off in this boiling tube.

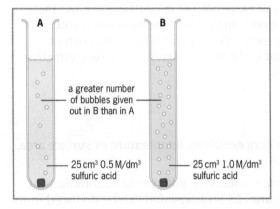

Figure 12.7 *Showing the speeds of reactions between lead pellet and two different concentrations of sulfuric acid*

Measuring the product formed to determine the rate of a reaction

When calcium carbonate is reacted with dilute hydrochloric acid, carbon dioxide is produced as one of the products as seen in the chemical equation (example reaction 2) in Figure 12.8.

- Measure out 100 cm³ of dilute hydrochloric acid into a measuring cylinder and add it to a conical flask.
- Weigh out 25 g of calcium carbonate chips. Add them to the conical flask.
- Immediately stopper the flask with a bung with a syringe attached to it.
- The volume of the carbon dioxide produced can be measured using the markings on the syringe.
- Plot a graph of the volume of carbon dioxide produced against time to determine the rate of the reaction. See Figure 12.8.

As can be seen in Figure 12.8 (example reaction 1), the volume of hydrogen gas can be measured when magnesium reacts with dilute sulfuric acid to produce magnesium sulfate and hydrogen.

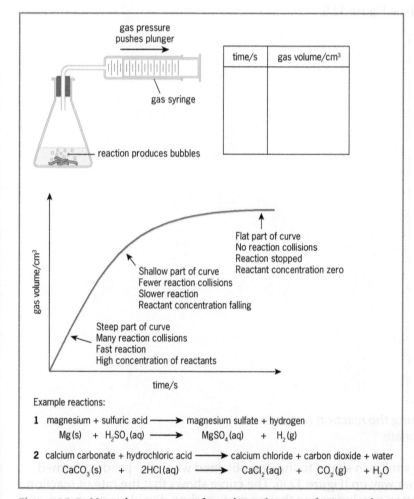

Example reactions:

1 magnesium + sulfuric acid ⟶ magnesium sulfate + hydrogen
   $Mg(s) + H_2SO_4(aq) \longrightarrow MgSO_4(aq) + H_2(g)$

2 calcium carbonate + hydrochloric acid ⟶ calcium chloride + carbon dioxide + water
   $CaCO_3(s) + 2HCl(aq) \longrightarrow CaCl_2(aq) + CO_2(g) + H_2O$

Figure 12.8 *How the amount of product changes during a chemical reaction*

The graph gives several important pieces of information about the rate of the reaction. First, the gradient of the graph is sharpest at the start of the reaction, indicating that the speed of the

becoming less and less sharp, which indicates that the speed of the reaction is decreasing. Third, the gradient of the graph becomes zero, as indicated by the flat part of the curve, and this suggests that the speed of the reaction is now zero. The reaction has now ceased, and no more gas is being produced.

As an alternative to measuring the amount of product formed, the decrease in the mass or concentration of the reactants can be measured.

For the reaction between calcium carbonate and hydrochloric acid, the decrease in mass can be measured. The experiment is carried out in the following way.

- Place an empty conical flask on an electronic balance.
- Reset the balance to zero.
- Add some calcium carbonate chips and measure how much they weigh.
- Add 100 cm³ of dilute hydrochloric acid to the conical flask and calcium carbonate chips on the electronic balance.
- Immediately place cotton wool inside the mouth of the conical flask to avoid spray loss occurring and to allow the carbon dioxide gas produced to escape.
- Record the mass of the conical flask (and its contents) every 30 seconds for 5 minutes.
- Plot a graph of mass against time (see Figure 12.9).

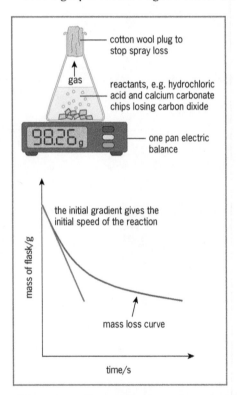

Figure 12.9 *Recording mass loss during the reaction between hydrochloric acid and calcium carbonate*

Note that the graph in Figure 12.9 is similar in shape to the one obtained when the product formed is measured, except that it is the other way up (Figure 12.8). The curve shows that the rate of reaction decreases over time and starts to flatten out, indicating that no more carbon dioxide is produced, and the reaction has ended. The rate of the reaction is fastest at the beginning and, as seen, the gradient of the graph is sharpest.

We refer to the gradient of the graph as being sharp or decreasing and this gives an indication of whether the rate of reaction is increasing or decreasing. The gradient of the tangent to the graph is equal to the rate of reaction at that point and can be found as follows.

Let us use the graph Figure 12.10, which measures the loss in concentration of product with time. This is another method of measuring reactant loss to determine the rate of reaction.

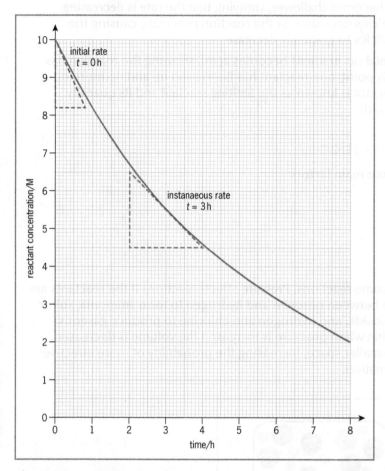

Figure 12.10 *Rate curve showing a decrease in concentration of reactants as reaction proceeds*

The rate of reaction can be calculated at instantaneous time t as follows.

Instantaneous rate at time t = slope of tangent to the line at time t

From the graph (Figure 12.10):

instantaneous rate at time 3 hours = gradient of tangent to the line at 3 hours

$$= \frac{\text{loss in mass of reactant}}{\text{time taken}}$$

$$= \frac{6.5 - 4.5}{4 - 2}$$

$$= \frac{2}{2}$$

$$= 1 \, M \, h^{-1}$$

There are some general points to note from rate curves. All rate curves have a very similar **shape**. This shape shows that the **rate** of a reaction **decreases** as the reaction proceeds.

- At the **beginning** of the reaction the gradient is at its **sharpest**, showing that the rate is at its **highest**. The concentration of the reactant particles is at its highest resulting in the **frequency of collision** between particles being at its **highest**.
- As the **reaction proceeds**, the gradient becomes **shallower**, showing that the rate is **decreasing**. The concentration of the reactant particles decreases as the reaction proceeds, causing the **frequency of collision** between the particles to gradually **decrease**.
- The curve eventually becomes **horizontal** (its gradient becomes **zero**), showing the reaction has **reached completion** and **stopped**. At this point, one reactant has been used up and no more of its particles are left to collide. This reactant is known as the **limiting reactant** and its quantity determines the quantity of products made.

Factors that affect rates of reaction

The rate of a reaction is dependent on **four** main factors:

- **concentration**
- **temperature**
- **surface area** (particle size)
- presence or absence of a **catalyst**.

Pressure and **light** also affect the rate of some reactions. **Pressure** affects reactions if the reactants are in the **gaseous** state, such as the reaction between nitrogen and hydrogen to form ammonia, sulfur dioxide and oxygen to produce sulfur trioxide, and hydrogen and chlorine to produce gaseous hydrogen chloride. Figure 12.11 shows that when pressure is increased the volume is decreased, so the molecules are concentrated in a smaller space, increasing the probability of more effective collisions resulting in more product formation.

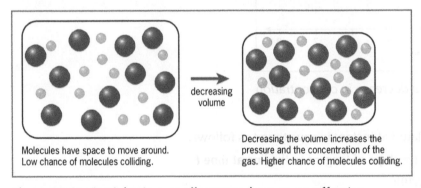

Molecules have space to move around. Low chance of molecules colliding.

decreasing volume

Decreasing the volume increases the pressure and the concentration of the gas. Higher chance of molecules colliding.

Figure 12.11 *Particles in a smaller space have more effective collisions and an increased reaction rate*

Light affects the reaction between methane and chlorine (see page 260), hydrogen and chlorine, and photosynthesis in plants. Light energy is captured by the chlorophyll (implied by the arrow) in the plant cell and converts carbon dioxide and water into glucose and oxygen.

The process of photosynthesis is represented by the chemical equation:

$$6CO_2(g) + 6H_2O(l) \longrightarrow C_6H_{12}O_6(aq) + 6O_2(g)$$

In all these reactions, if pressure or light intensity **increase**, the rate of reaction **increases**.

Concentration of reactants

The higher the concentration of a reactant, the faster the reaction. This applies to reactants in solution. Increasing the concentration of a reactant increases the number of particles in a unit volume of solution. As a result, the particles **collide more frequently**, increasing the chances of effective collisions (Figure 12.12).

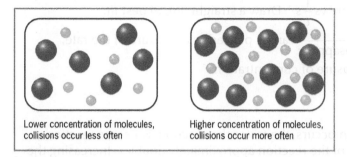

Lower concentration of molecules, collisions occur less often

Higher concentration of molecules, collisions occur more often

Figure 12.12 *More effective collisions when concentration is increased*

The rate of reaction when concentration is increased is graphically represented as shown in Figure 12.13.

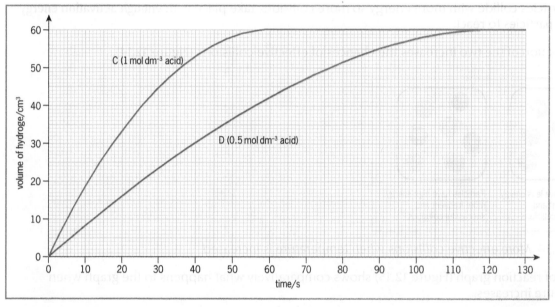

Figure 12.13 *Showing the variation in the total amount of product with time at two different concentrations*

When dilute sulfuric acid and sodium thiosulfate react, a pale-yellow precipitate of sulfur is produced, and this reaction can be used to investigate the effects of varying concentration of the reactants on the rate of a reaction.

A very simple way of measuring the effects of concentration on the rate of reaction is by measuring the time taken for a small, predetermined quantity of precipitate to form. Place a beaker on a white tile with a cross drawn on it, and then look down through the solution until the cross disappears.

- Place a beaker on a tile that has a cross drawn on it in black marker.
- Add 50 cm³ of sodium thiosulfate solution to the beaker.
- Add 50 cm³ of sulfuric acid to the beaker. Start a stopwatch as soon as the acid is added.
- When the cross is observed to disappear from view through the bottom of the beaker, stop the stopwatch and record the time taken.

- Empty the contents of the beaker and rinse it.
- Repeat the experiment using a 5 cm³ reduction in the volume of sodium thiosulfate with the remainder topped up with water. Add 50 cm³ of sulfuric acid as before and start the stopwatch.
- Repeat the experiment until 25cm³ of sodium thiosulfate is used.
- Record your results in a table.

Plot a graph of volume of sodium thiosulfate/cm³ vs $\frac{1}{t}$ s⁻¹. Draw a straight line of best fit.

The quantity $\frac{1}{t}$ or $\frac{1}{\text{time taken for the cross to disappear}}$ can be plotted as a measure of the rate, and the volume of sodium thiosulfate as a measure of concentration.

Temperature

The higher the temperature at which a reaction occurs, the faster the reaction. For some reactions, if the temperature increases by 10 °C, the rate of the reaction approximately doubles. Increasing the temperature of a reaction gives the reactant particles more **kinetic energy**.

As a result:

- The particles move faster so they **collide more frequently**.
- The particles collide with more energy so more collisions take place with **enough activation energy** for the particles to react.

A combination of the two increases the chances of effective collisions (Figure 12.14).

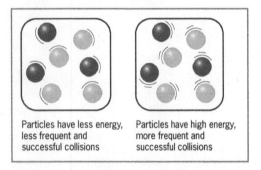

Particles have less energy, less frequent and successful collisions

Particles have high energy, more frequent and successful collisions

Figure 12.14 *More effective collisions when temperature is increased*

The rate of reaction graph (Figure 12.15) shows comparatively what happens to the graph when temperature increases.

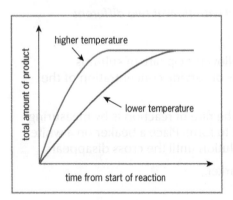

Figure 12.15 *Showing the variation in the total amount of product with time at two different temperatures*

Food is cooked much faster when the temperature is increased. On the other hand, food is prevented from spoiling quickly by lowering the temperature, that is, placing it in a refrigerator or freezer.

Surface area

The smaller the particles of a reactant, the faster the reaction. This applies to reactants in their solid state. The reaction occurs on the surface of a solid. Small solid particles have a larger total **surface area** than large particles with the same mass. Decreasing particle size exposes a greater surface area to the other reactant. As a result, the particles **collide more frequently**, increasing the chances of effective collisions (Figure 12.16). The rate of reaction graph (Figure 12.17) shows comparatively what happens to the graph when the surface area increases. The rate of the reaction increases as the particle size decreases, and this is seen by the sharpness of the red curve compared to the blue curve.

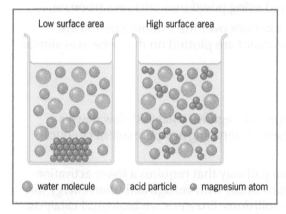

Figure 12.16 *Larger surface area more collision between particles resulting in more product formed*

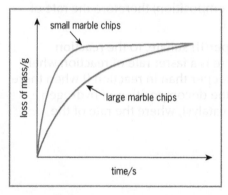

Figure 12.17 *Showing the variation in the total loss of mass of reactant with time using two different particle sizes*

In **flour mills** and **coal mines** the flour and coal dust are extremely flammable. A slight spark can start a reaction with the oxygen in the air, which can be **explosive** because of the large surface area of the finely divided flour and coal particles.

Some medicines work faster when administered in powdered form with warm water, whereas others are administered in capsule form, which allows the drug to be released over a longer period of time.

When calcium carbonate is added to dilute hydrochloric acid, calcium chloride, carbon dioxide and water are formed as shown in the equation below:

$$CaCO_3(s) + 2HCl(aq) \longrightarrow CaCl_2(aq) + CO_2(g) + H_2O(l)$$

To investigate the effects of surface area on the rate of a reaction, we can measure the volume of carbon dioxide produced in the above reaction using powdered calcium carbonate and chips of calcium carbonate in separate experiments.

The experiment is carried out in the following way.

- Measure 100 cm³ of dilute hydrochloric acid in a measuring cylinder and add it to a conical flask.
- Weigh out 20 g of calcium carbonate chips and add them to the flask.
- Immediately stopper the flask with a bung with a syringe.
- Start a stopwatch.
- Measure the volume of gas produced at 30 second intervals for a 5 minute period.
- Repeat the experiment using powdered calcium carbonate.
- The volume of gas collected in the syringe at 30 second intervals over a 5 minute period is measured using a stopwatch. The experiment is repeated using powdered calcium carbonate.
- The volumes of carbon dioxide collected at 30 second intervals over the 5 minute period are recorded for each experiment and graphs of each experiment are plotted on the same axes similar to that shown in Figure 12.8.

Catalyst

Most catalysts **speed up** a reaction. A few catalysts (inhibitors or negative catalysts) **slow down** a reaction. A **catalyst** alters the rate of a reaction without itself undergoing any permanent chemical change.

A catalyst speeds up a reaction by providing an alternative pathway that requires a **lower activation energy** than the normal pathway. As a result, more collisions occur with **enough activation energy** for the particles to react, increasing the chances of effective collisions. Enzymes are biological catalysts. They speed up chemical reactions occurring in living cells.

Tetraethyl lead(IV) $(Pb(C_2H_5)_4)$ is an inhibitor that used to be added to petrol ('leaded petrol') to stop premature ignition ('knocking'). Another example of a negative catalyst is propane-1,2,3-triol (glycerine), which when added to hydrogen peroxide inhibits decomposition; therefore the rate of the reaction of decomposition of hydrogen peroxide is decreased.

Figure 12.18 shows graphically the effect of adding a catalyst, copper(II) sulfate, to the reaction between granulated zinc and hydrochloric acid. For reaction I there is a faster rate of reaction when the catalyst is present. The gradient of the graph of reaction I is steeper than in reaction II when there is no catalyst present. Other examples of catalysed reactions are the decomposition of hydrogen peroxide solution using lead(II) oxide or manganese(IV) oxide as catalyst, where the rate of the reaction increases because this is a positive catalyst.

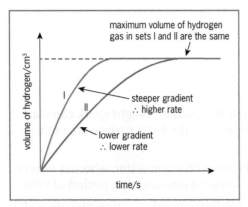

Figure 12.18 *Showing the effect on the rate of reaction with and without the presence of a catalyst*

The effect of changing different factors on rate curves

The effect of changing any factor which alters the rate of a reaction can be shown by the **rate curve** for the reaction.

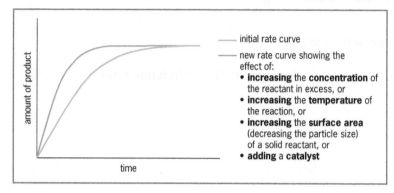

Figure 12.19 *The effect of changing any factor which increases the rate of a reaction*

Points to note from Figure 12.19 and seen above in Figures 12.13, 12.15 and 12.18:

- The new curve has a **sharper gradient**, indicating the reaction is occurring at a **faster rate**.
- The new curve becomes **horizontal sooner**, indicating the reaction reaches completion in **less time**.
- Both curves become horizontal when the **same amount of product** has been made, since the **number of moles** of the limiting reactant is unchanged.
- **Decreasing** the concentration of the reactant in excess, the temperature of the reaction, the surface area of a solid reactant, or adding a negative catalyst would cause the curve to have a **shallower gradient** than the original rate curve, become **horizontal later**, but become horizontal when the **same amount of product** has been made.

Recalling facts

 1 When measuring the speed of a chemical reaction, the following property changes can be observed except:

    a temperature changes

    b changes in colour

    c aroma

    d pH changes

 2 All of the following affects the speed of a chemical reaction except:

    a particle size

    b concentration of reactants

    c temperature

    d colour of the reaction container

3 A single spark from a piece of machinery can cause explosions in a coal mine because:

   a coal dust is inflammable

   b the finely divided coal particles create a large surface area for reaction

   c coal is black in colour

   d there is carbon dioxide present in the air

4 The speed of a reaction is _____ for every 10 °C rise in temperature:

   a halved

   b tripled

   c doubled

   d quadrupled

5 Which of the following best describes a catalyst?

   a It is used up in a chemical reaction.

   b It speeds up a chemical reaction but is not itself used up.

   c It does not affect the speed of a chemical reaction.

   d At the end of the reaction the catalyst transforms into a new substance.

6 A student conducted four separate experiments, by adding 10 g pieces of magnesium ribbon to excess sulfuric acid solution. In which experiment would the student notice hydrogen gas bubbling most rapidly?

Experiment	Volume of sulfuric acid/cm³	Concentration of sulfuric acid/mol dm⁻³
A	25	0.25
B	20	0.75
C	30	0.50
D	15	4.00

7 Which of the following are necessary for effective collisions to occur?

   I   no bond breaking

   II correct orientation of particles

   III sufficient activation energy

   a I only

   b II only

   c II and III only

   d I, II and III

8 The rate of a chemical reaction can be determined by measuring the _____ over time.

   a catalyst

   b collision

   c amount of product

   d density

9 Define rate of reaction.

10 State the factors which affect the rate of a chemical reaction. Explain how light and pressure affect the rate of a chemical reaction. Does light and pressure affect all reactions? Explain.

Applying facts

11 Explain in terms of collision theory for chemical reactions why:

a Finely powdered chalk reacts faster than a large piece with sulfuric acid.

b Doubling the temperature of a reaction results in an increase in the rate of reaction.

c The rate of a reaction decreases as the concentration of the reactants decreases.

12 a When the rate of the reaction is measured at different concentrations, a straight line is obtained through the origin, when a plot of rate against concentration is done. Sketch such a plot and explain what this graph shows.

b Sketch the graph of rate against temperature, when the rate of reaction at different temperatures are measured. What information about the rate of the reaction can be deduced from the sketch?

13 a Define the term 'catalyst'.

b A catalyst can have a positive or negative effect on the rate of reaction. Explain this statement, giving examples of each type.

c Sketch two graphs on the same page showing rate curves for a catalysed and uncatalysed reaction. Label each rate curve.

d Describe each, stating the differences in each curve.

14 The graph shows the volume of hydrogen gas collected against time as some magnesium reacts with dilute sulfuric acid.

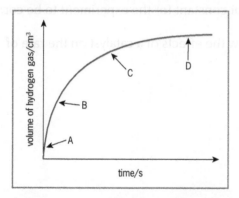

a Account for the shape of the curve at each point A, B, C and D of the graph.

b State at which letter the reaction is fastest and at which it has ceased to occur.

15 Describe in each case an experiment to measure the speed of a reaction by measuring:

a the increase in product formed

b the decrease in reactants

16 The results obtained when an investigation was carried out to compare the effect of concentration of sodium thiosulfate on the rate of reaction between sodium thiosulfate and sulfuric acid are shown.

Experiment no.	Volume of sulfuric acid/cm³	Volume of sodium thiosulfate/cm³	Volume of water/cm³	Time/s	Time/s⁻¹
1	50	50	0	147	
2	50	45	5	159	
3	50	40	10	197	
4	50	35	15	238	
5	50	30	20	322	
6	50	25	25	476	

a What is the purpose of adding water to the mixture?

b In which experiment was the concentration of the sodium thiosulfate **i** highest and **ii** lowest?

c Plot a graph of volume of sodium thiosulfate against time.

d Account for the shape of the graph.

e Describe how you would determine the speed of the reaction at instantaneous time t.

f Determine the rate at instantaneous time **i** $t = 165$ seconds and **ii** $t = 218$ seconds.

g Calculate $\frac{1}{t}$ s⁻¹ for each experiment and plot a graph of volume of sodium thiosulfate against time.

h Account for the shape of the graph and what conclusions can be drawn from the graph.

i Give two factors which must be kept constant for the experiment to be correct.

17 Plan and design an experiment to show the effects of a catalyst on the rate of a reaction.

13 Energetics

Learning objectives

- State the meaning of **enthalpy change** in terms of **endothermic** and **exothermic reactions**.
- Give examples of endothermic and exothermic reactions.
- Explain enthalpy changes in terms of the energy changes involved in **bond making** and **bond breaking**.
- Represent exothermic and endothermic reactions using **energy profile diagrams**, including **activation energies**.
- Define the terms **specific heat capacity**, **heat of solution** and **heat of neutralisation**.
- Use experimental data to calculate heat changes.

All chemical substances contain energy stored in their bonds. When a chemical reaction occurs, there is usually a **change in energy** between the reactants and products. This is normally in the form of **heat energy**, but may also be in the form of light, nuclear or electrical energy. When hydrocarbons undergo combustion in an engine, energy is given out, and this energy is used to power vehicles such as cars. When magnesium ribbon burns in oxygen, energy in the form of heat and light (bright white light) is released, and for this reason magnesium is used in flares and fireworks. It is very important to study energy changes in chemical reactions because it helps to determine whether a particular reaction will occur and if it occurs, whether energy would be absorbed or released.

Exothermic and endothermic reactions

Based on the energy changes occurring, reactions can be of **two** types (Figure 13.1) exothermic and endothermic.

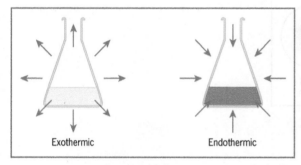

Figure 13.1 *Energy changes which occur during exothermic and endothermic reactions*

- An **exothermic reaction** produces heat which causes the reaction mixture and its surroundings to get **hotter** (it **releases energy** to the surroundings, Figure 13.2). Exothermic reactions include:
  - neutralisation reactions, when acid and bases react, such as potassium hydroxide and sulfuric acid
  - when reactive metals (such as sodium, magnesium and calcium) react with acids (such as hydrochloric acid or sulfuric acid)
  - burning fossil fuels and wood to release energy (to power your motor cars and cook your food, for example)
  - respiration – the biochemical process in which the cells of all organisms release energy from food molecules
  - when certain chemical substances are dissolved in water, such as acids (hydrochloric acid, sulfuric acid), alkalis (sodium hydroxide and potassium hydroxide) and some salts (anhydrous copper(II) sulfate, anhydrous calcium chloride and anhydrous sodium carbonate)

- some soap powders when they are mixed with water release heat
- condensation and freezing (changes of state).

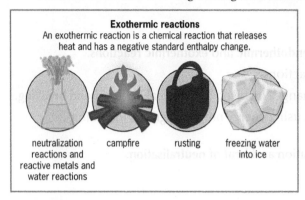

Exothermic reactions
An exothermic reaction is a chemical reaction that releases heat and has a negative standard enthalpy change.

neutralization reactions and reactive metals and water reactions   campfire   rusting   freezing water into ice

Figure 13.2 *Exothermic reactions*

- An **endothermic reaction** absorbs heat which causes the reaction mixture and its surroundings to get **colder** (it **absorbs energy** from the surroundings, Figure 13.3). Endothermic reactions include:
  - dissolving certain salts in water, for example, ammonium nitrate and sodium carbonate crystals, ammonium chloride and potassium nitrate
  - thermal decomposition reactions, for example, copper(II) carbonate to produce copper(II) oxide and carbon dioxide
  - photosynthesis in plants where plants absorb sunlight, water and carbon dioxide to produce sugar molecules and oxygen
  - melting and boiling (changes of state).

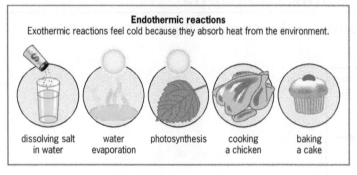

Endothermic reactions
Exothermic reactions feel cold because they absorb heat from the environment.

dissolving salt in water   water evaporation   photosynthesis   cooking a chicken   baking a cake

Figure 13.3 *Endothermic reactions*

Breaking and forming bonds during reactions

During any chemical reaction, existing bonds in the **reactants** are **broken** and new bonds are **formed** in the **products**:

- Energy is **absorbed** when the existing bonds in the reactants are **broken** (Figure 13.4).
  Energy is **released** when new bonds are **formed** in the products (Figure 13.5).

reactants	$\longrightarrow$	products
existing bonds are **broken**		new bonds are **formed**
energy is **absorbed**		energy is **released**

- In an **exothermic reaction**:

  energy **absorbed** to break bonds < energy **released** when forming bonds

The extra energy is **released** to the surroundings causing the **temperature** of the surroundings to **increase**.

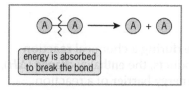

Figure 13.4 *Bond breaking*

- In an **endothermic reaction**:

    energy **absorbed** to break bonds > energy **released** when forming bonds

The extra energy is **absorbed** from the surroundings causing the **temperature** of the surroundings to **decrease**.

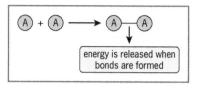

Figure 13.5 *Bond formation*

Enthalpy changes during reactions

The energy content of a substance is called its **enthalpy** (**H**) and cannot be measured directly. However, it is possible to measure the **enthalpy change** (**ΔH**) during a reaction.

The enthalpy change of a reaction is the difference between the enthalpy of the products and the enthalpy of the reactants (Figure 13.6):

    enthalpy change of a reaction = (total enthalpy of products) – (total enthalpy of reactants)

or $\Delta H_{reaction}$ = $H_{products}$ – $H_{reactants}$

ΔH is usually expressed in kilojoules (**kJ**), or kilojoules per mol (**kJ mol⁻¹**).

- In an **exothermic reaction**:

    $H_{products} < H_{reactants}$

The value of ΔH is less than zero. ΔH is **negative** (**–ve**). The extra energy from the reactants is **released** to the surroundings and the environment, so the reaction container feels warm or hot.

- In an **endothermic reaction**:

    $H_{products} > H_{reactants}$

The value of ΔH is greater than zero. ΔH is **positive** (**+ve**). The extra energy gained by the products is **absorbed** from the surroundings and so the surroundings and the container feels cooler or cold.

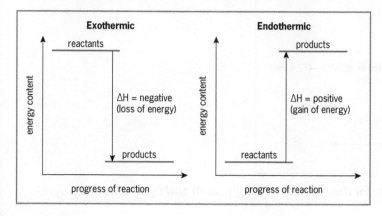

Figure 13.6 *Exothermic and endothermic reactions summarised*

Energy profile diagrams

An **energy profile diagram** can be drawn to illustrate the energy change during a chemical reaction (Figure 13.7). The diagram includes the **enthalpy** of the reactants and products, the **enthalpy change** (ΔH), and the **activation energy**. Activation energy can be thought of as the **energy barrier** of a reaction.

Activation energy is the minimum amount of energy that reactants must be given, in excess of what they normally possess, so that bonds start breaking in the reactants and products start forming.

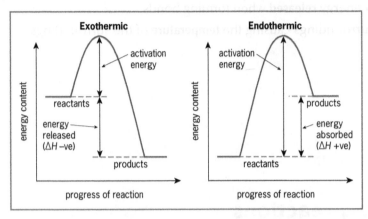

Figure 13.7 *Energy profile diagrams*

An energy profile diagram for a **specific reaction** must include:

- the **formulae** of the **reactants** and the **formulae** of the **products**
- an arrow indicating **activation energy**
- an arrow indicating ΔH with the **value of** ΔH written alongside.

It must be noted that for exothermic reactions the energy of the products is less than that of the reactants and therefore the **value of** ΔH **is negative.** For endothermic reactions the **value of** ΔH **is positive** because the energy of the products is greater than that of the reactants. From the **value of** ΔH the ease or difficulty of a reaction taking place can be determined. A reaction occurs easily when the **value of** ΔH is very negative. If the **value of** ΔH is very positive, then a lot of energy has to be absorbed for the reaction to occur, indicating that the reaction does not occur easily on its own.

Example 1

When **1 mole** of magnesium reacts with **2 moles** of hydrochloric acid, 462 kJ of energy is **lost**, meaning that the reaction is **exothermic** (Figure 13.8):

$$Mg(s) + 2HCl(aq) \longrightarrow MgCl_2(aq) + H_2(g) \qquad \Delta H = -462 \text{ kJ mol}^{-1}$$

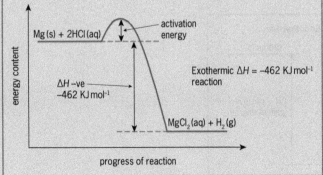

Figure 13.8 *Energy profile diagram for the reaction of magnesium and hydrochloric acid*

When **1 mole** of calcium carbonate decomposes, 222 kJ of heat energy is **absorbed**, meaning that the reaction is **endothermic** (Figure 13.9):

$$CaCO_3(s) \longrightarrow CaO(s) + CO_2(g) \qquad \Delta H = +222 \text{ kJ mol}^{-1}$$

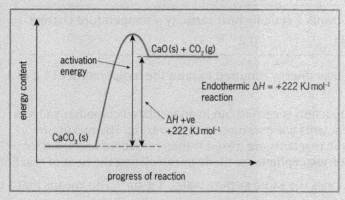

Figure 13.9 *Energy profile diagram for the decomposition of calcium carbonate*

The action of a catalyst

Most **catalysts** increase the rate of a reaction while remaining chemically unchanged at the end of the reaction. A reaction in which a catalyst is used to increase the rate by allowing more frequent successful collisions to occur has a **lower activation energy** than the same reaction without a catalyst (see page 214). The effect of using a catalyst can be shown on energy profile diagrams (Figure 13.10). A catalyst lowers the activation energy but there is no change to the **value of ΔH** because the energy values for the reactants and products remain the same.

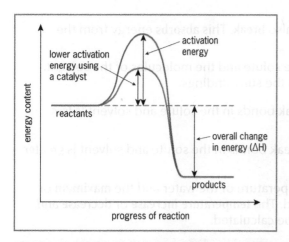

Figure 13.10 *Action of a catalyst on an exothermic reaction*

Calculating enthalpy changes

If the change in **temperature** that occurs during a reaction is measured, the **heat change**, known as the **heat of reaction**, can be determined using the formula given below.

heat change (ΔH) = mass reactants × specific heat capacity × temperature change
(J)   (g)   ($J\,g^{-1}\,°C^{-1}$)   (°C)

Specific heat capacity is the quantity of heat energy required to raise the temperature of 1 g of a substance by 1 °C.

To determine the heat of reaction, the reaction is carried out in an insulated container called a **calorimeter**. The temperatures of the reactants are measured before mixing. The maximum or minimum temperature reached when the reactants are mixed is then measured and used to determine the **temperature change**. Three **assumptions** are made in calculating the heat of reaction:

- The **density** of a dilute aqueous solution is the same as pure water, **1 g cm⁻³**. This means that 1 cm³ of solution has a mass of 1 g.
- The **specific heat capacity** of a dilute aqueous solution is the same as pure water, **4.2 J g⁻¹ °C⁻¹**. This means that it requires 4.2 J to increase the temperature of 1 g of water by 1 °C.
- A **negligible amount of heat** is lost to, or absorbed from, the surroundings during the reaction.

Determining the heat of solution

*The **heat of solution** is the heat change when 1 mol of solute dissolves in such a volume of solvent that further dilution by the solvent produces no further heat change.*

When a solute dissolves in a solvent:

- Bonds **break** between the solute particles; **ionic bonds** between ions break in ionic compounds and **intermolecular forces** between the molecules break in covalent substances. This **absorbs** energy from the surroundings.
- **Intermolecular forces** between the solvent molecules also **break**. This **absorbs** energy from the surroundings.
- Attractions form between the ions or molecules of the solute and the molecules of the solvent. This process is called **solvation**. This **releases** energy to the surroundings.

The reaction is **exothermic** if the energy **absorbed** to break bonds in the solute and solvent is **less** than the energy **released** during solvation.

The reaction is **endothermic** if the energy **absorbed** to break bonds in the solute and solvent is **greater** than the energy **released** during solvation.

When determining the heat of a solution, the **initial** temperature of the water and the **maximum** or **minimum** temperature of the solution must be measured. The **temperature increase** or **decrease** and the **number of moles** of solute that dissolved must then be calculated.

> **Sample questions**
>
> Dissolving 9.85 g of sodium carbonate in 100 cm³ of distilled water resulted in a temperature decrease of 7.2 °C. Calculate the heat of solution of sodium carbonate and draw an energy profile diagram for the solution process.
>
> To determine the **number of moles** of Na_2CO_3 dissolved:
>
> $$\text{Mass of 1 mol } Na_2CO_3 = (23 \times 2) + 12 + (16 \times 3) \text{ g} = \textbf{106 g}$$
>
> $$\therefore \text{number of moles in 9.85 g} = \frac{9.85}{106} \text{ mol}$$
>
> $$= \textbf{0.09 mol}$$

To determine the **heat of solution**:

  Volume of water = 100 cm^3

  $\therefore$ mass of water = **100 g**

  Final mass of solution = 100 g = **100 g**

  Temperature decrease = **7.2 °C**

  Specific heat capacity of the solution = **4.2 J g^{-1} °C^{-1}**

  Heat change = mass of solution × specific heat capacity × temperature change

      (J)   (g)   (J g^{-1} °C^{-1})   (°C)

  $\therefore$ heat absorbed in dissolving **0.09 mol NaCO$_3$** = 100 × 4.2 × 7.2 J

                                   = 3024 J

  and heat absorbed in dissolving **1 mol NaCO$_3$** = $\dfrac{3024}{0.09}$ J

                                   = 33600 J

                                   = **33.6 kJ**

Heat of solution, ΔH = **+33.6 kJ mol^{-1}**

The heat of solution, ΔH, is **positive** because the temperature of the reaction **decreased** indicating that it **absorbed** energy from the surroundings. The reaction was **endothermic**.

The energy profile diagram is shown in Figure 13.11:

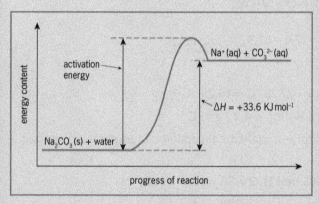

Figure 13.11 *Energy profile diagram for the solution of sodium carbonate*

Determining the heat of neutralisation

The heat of neutralisation is the heat change when 1 mol of water is produced in a neutralisation reaction between an alkali and an acid.

When determining the heat of neutralisation, the temperature of both solutions must be measured and used to determine the **average initial** temperature. The **maximum** temperature of the solution after mixing must then be measured and used to calculate the **temperature increase**. Finally, the **number of moles** of water made in the reaction must be determined.

25 cm³ of a 4 mol dm⁻³ sodium hydroxide solution with a temperature of 27.0 °C are added to 25 cm³ of hydrochloric acid of concentration 2.0 mol dm⁻³ and temperature 27.5 °C. The maximum temperature of the solution after mixing is 40.5 °C. Determine the heat of neutralisation.

To determine the **number of moles of water** made in the reaction:

1000 cm³ NaOH(aq) contains 4.0 mol NaOH

$\therefore$ 25 cm³ NaOH(aq) contains $\frac{4.0}{1000} \times 25$ mol NaOH

= 0.1 mol NaOH

1000 cm³ HCl(aq) contains 2.0 mol HCl

$\therefore$ 25 cm³ HCl(aq) contains $\frac{2.0}{1000} \times 25$ mol HCl

= 0.05 mol HCl

Equation: NaOH(aq) + HCl(aq) $\longrightarrow$ NaCl(aq) + H₂O(l)

i.e. 1 mol NaOH reacts with 1 mol HCl forming 1 mol H₂O(aq)

The NaOH is in excess. Therefore only 0.5 mol NaOH to react with 0.5 mol of HCl

$\therefore$ **0.05 mol NaOH** reacts with **0.05 mol HCl** to form **0.05 mol H₂O**

0.05 mol H₂O is made in the reaction

To determine the **heat of neutralisation**:

Total volume of solution = 25 + 25 = 50 cm³

$\therefore$ mass of solution = **50 g**

Average initial temperature = $\frac{27.0 + 27.5}{2}$ °C = 27.25 °C

Final temperature = 40.5 °C

$\therefore$ temperature increase = 40.5 − 27.25 °C = **13.25 °C**

Specific heat capacity of the solution = **4.2 J g⁻¹ °C⁻¹**

Heat change = mass of solution × specific heat capacity × temperature change
$\qquad$ (J) $\qquad\qquad$ (g) $\qquad\qquad$ (J g⁻¹ °C⁻¹) $\qquad\qquad$ (°C)

$\therefore$ heat evolved in forming **0.05 mol H₂O** = 50 × 4.2 × 13.25 J

= 2782.5 J

and heat evolved in forming **1 mol H₂O** = $\frac{2782.5}{0.05}$ J

= 55650 J

= 55.7 kJ

Heat of neutralisation, $\Delta H =$ **−55.7 kJ mol⁻¹**

The heat of neutralisation, ΔH, is **negative** because the temperature of the reaction **increased**, indicating that it **lost energy** to the surroundings. The reaction was **exothermic**.

When any strong alkali reacts with any strong acid, the heat of neutralisation is always approximately **−57 kJ mol⁻¹**. This is because the energy change is for the common reaction occurring between the **OH⁻ ions** of the alkali and the **H⁺ ions** of the acid:

OH⁻(aq) + H⁺(aq) $\longrightarrow$ H₂O(l) $\qquad \Delta H = -57$ kJ mol⁻¹

Recalling facts

1 Which statement is NOT correct concerning an exothermic reaction?

   a Surroundings get colder.

   b Surroundings get hotter.

   c The enthalpy change is negative.

   d Respiration in cells is an example.

2 When drawing an energy profile diagram for a specific reaction it is important to include all of the following except:

   a the formulae of the reactants

   b the value of ΔH

   c arrows indicating the activation energy and not ΔH

   d the formulae of the products

3 Which statement is not true about a catalyst?

   a it decreases the activation energy

   b it increases the activation energy

   c it increases the speed of the reaction

   d it provides an alternative pathway for the reaction

4 When measuring heats of solutions which of the following is NOT true?

   a A calorimeter is used.

   b The density of a dilute aqueous solution is the same as water, 1 g cm^{-3}.

   c The specific heat capacity of water a dilute aqueous solution is the same as water, $4.2 \text{ J kg}^{-1} \text{ K}^{-1}$

   d Negligible heat is lost to the surroundings.

5 Which statement is NOT true of the enthalpy change of a reaction?

   a Enthalpy change = total enthalpy of reactants – total enthalpy of products

   b Is expressed as kJ per mol

   c Results from bond-breaking and bond-making

   d Cannot be measured directly

6 Which of the following processes is an example of an endothermic reaction?

   a dissolving sodium hydroxide in water

   b dissolving ammonium chloride in water

   c burning of gasoline in a car engine

   d potassium hydroxide reacting with hydrochloric acid

7 In the formula

$$\Delta H = mc\Delta T$$

which is not correct?

a m = mass of reactants, kg **b** $c = 4.2\ J\ g^{-1}\ °C^{-1}$

c ΔT is the change in temperature measured in °C. **d** ΔH is measured in J.

For questions 8 to 10, the energy profile diagram of a chemical reaction is shown:

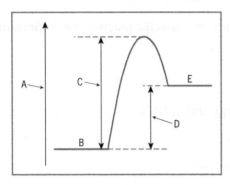

8 The energy profile diagram represents:

a an exothermic reaction

b a catalysed reaction

c an endothermic reaction

d none of the above

9 'A' represents:

a energy content

b energy content of products

c enthalpy

d energy content of reactants

10 'D' is:

a positive

b negative

c course of the reaction

d energy of the reactants

11 State if the changes below are exothermic or endothermic:

a reacting sodium in dilute hydrochloric acid

b change of state of water to ice

c adding sodium hydroxide to water

d rusting

12 Define the term 'activation energy'. Draw a fully labelled energy profile diagram representing a catalysed and uncatalysed reaction. Explain how a catalyst works to speed up a chemical reaction.

Analysing data

13 The equation for the formation of nitrogen oxide in a car engine is:

$$N_2(g) + O_2(g) \longrightarrow 2NO(g) \qquad \Delta H = +18.0 \text{ kJ mol}^{-1}$$

a State whether this reaction is exothermic or endothermic. Explain your answer.

b Using your answer in **a**, explain what happens during the reaction in terms of bonds breaking and bonds forming.

c Draw a fully labelled energy profile diagram for the reaction.

d Judging from the ΔH value, does this reaction occur easily? Explain your answer.

14 To determine the heat of solution of sodium thiosulfate ($Na_2S_2O_3 \cdot 5H_2O$), a student dissolved 24.8 g of the solid in 100 cm^3 of distilled water at 27.0 °C. He stirred the solution in an insulated beaker and recorded a minimum temperature of 19.0 °C.

a Define 'heat of solution'.

b State, with a reason, if the reaction was exothermic or endothermic.

c Calculate the heat of solution of sodium thiosulfate, assuming that the specific heat capacity of the solution is 4.2 J g^{-1} °C^{-1}.

d Draw a fully labelled energy profile diagram for the reaction.

e Why was an insulated beaker used?

15 a Define 'heat of neutralisation'.

b 25 cm^3 of 2 mol dm^{-3} nitric acid was mixed with 25 cm^3 of 2 mol dm^{-3} sodium hydroxide solution in an insulated beaker. The initial temperature of both the acid and the alkali was 30 °C and the maximum temperature attained was 41.5 °C.

  i Determine the heat of neutralisation.

  ii The value given in the data book for the molar heat of neutralisation of a strong acid by an alkali is −57.3 kJ. How does this value compare with your calculated value in **i**? Provide an explanation for any difference observed.

Section B
Organic chemistry

In this section

Organic chemistry – an introduction

- Carbon atoms – single and double bonds; branched, unbranched and ringed compounds of carbon; structural formulae of organic compounds; homologous series; general and molecular formulae for alkanes, alkenes, alcohols and alkanoic acids; isomers

Sources of hydrocarbon compounds

- Natural gas and petroleum; separation of petroleum into useful fractions by fractional distillation; main fractions obtained from the fractional distillation of petroleum and their uses; cracking; thermal and catalytic cracking of alkanes

Reactions of carbon compounds

- Reactions of alkanes and alkenes linked to their functional groups; properties of alkanes and alkenes; production of biogas; use of functional groups to identify alcohols, acids and esters; reactions of ethanol; fermentation process that converts carbohydrates to ethanol; reactions of ethanoic acids; hydrolysis of esters including saponification; comparison of soapy and soapless detergents

Polymers

- Formation of addition and condensation polymerisation; structure of polymers given a monomer; structure of monomers given a polymer; uses of addition and condensation polymers; positive and negative effects of plastics

14 Organic chemistry – an introduction

Learning objectives

- Illustrate that **carbon atoms** can form **single** and **double bonds**.
- Understand that carbon can form **branched**, **unbranched** and **ringed compounds**.
- Write **molecular**, **fully displayed** and **condensed structural formulae** for simple organic compounds.
- Explain what is meant by the term **homologous series**.
- List the general characteristics of a homologous series.
- Write **general** and **molecular formulae** for members of the homologous series **alkanes**, **alkenes**, **alcohols** and **alkanoic acids**.
- Determine the homologous series given the fully displayed and condensed formulae of compounds.
- Name and draw fully displayed branched and unbranched alkanes and unbranched alkenes, alcohols and alkanoic acids.
- Define the term **isomer** and identify isomers.
- Write and name the fully displayed structures of isomers given their molecular formulae.

Organic chemistry is the study of the structure, properties, composition, reactions and preparation of compounds which contain **carbon**. These compounds are known as **organic compounds**. Organic compounds are found everywhere and are produced naturally by living organisms and synthetically by humans. Naturally occurring organic compounds include carbohydrates, fats, proteins and synthetic organic compounds such as plastics.

In addition to carbon, most organic compounds also contain hydrogen, and these are known as **hydrocarbons**. Many organic compounds also contain oxygen, nitrogen, phosphorus, sulfur and halogens.

As indicated above, organic compounds occur in all living organisms and are found everywhere, so they are vital to our existence. These compounds are the key components of many naturally occurring cycles on Earth: for instance, the carbon cycle, where carbon is continuously exchanged during photosynthesis and respiration between plants and animals.

The study of organic chemistry is critical to many economies because organic compounds are converted into consumer and industrial products. Examples of these are agrochemicals, cosmetics, detergents, dyes, food, pharmaceuticals, petrochemicals, fuels and plastics.

The unique nature of carbon

The element carbon combines with itself and other elements to form a vast number of organic and inorganic compounds. No other element forms as many compounds as carbon. The element carbon is described as being unique because carbon:

- has four valence electrons and can form four covalent bonds with itself as well as with atoms of other elements, such as oxygen, nitrogen and sulfur
- can form straight chains, branched chains and ring compounds
- can form single and double bonds with itself
- can form an enormous variety of compounds with different molecular shapes.

Examples of inorganic compounds containing carbon are carbon monoxide, carbon dioxide, carbonate and hydrogen carbonates.

Examples of organic compounds are ethanoic acid, citric acid, methane, polypropylene, ethanol, glucose, sucrose, proteins, carbohydrates and fats.

Bonding in organic compounds

Carbon has an atomic number of 6 with electronic configuration: C 2,4 (page 42). The shell diagram (page 42) is shown in Figure 14.1.

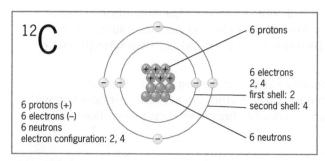

Figure 14.1 *Electronic structure of carbon*

Let us examine the electronic configuration of the carbon atom. It contains six electrons: **two electrons** occupy the inner shell and four occupy the valence shell and these are known as the **four valence electrons**. The four valence electrons can form **four covalent bonds** with other carbon atoms, or atoms of other elements including hydrogen, oxygen, nitrogen and the halogens.

Example 1

Methane   Formula: CH_4

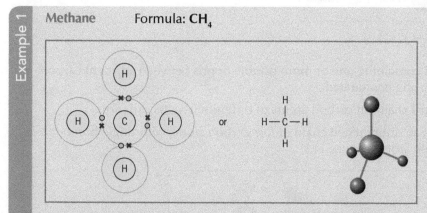

Figure 14.2 *Methane (CH_4)*

In the methane molecule (Figure 14.2), the four hydrogen atoms are arranged in a **tetrahedron** around the central carbon atom and the angle between covalent bonds is 109.5°.

Because carbon has four valence electrons, carbon atoms can bond with other carbon atoms in an almost unlimited way:

• **Single bonds** can form in which adjacent carbon atoms share **one pair** of electrons between them. The three other valence electrons in the carbon atom can bond to other atoms. For example, propane (C_3H_8) has single bonds between each carbon atom, which are represented by single lines (Figure 14.3).

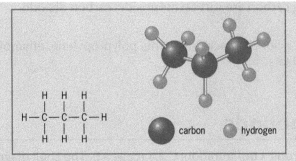

Figure 14.3 *Propane (C₃H₈)*

Any organic compound containing single bonds only between adjacent carbon atoms is referred to as being **saturated**. Saturated hydrocarbons (alkanes) are the simplest of the hydrocarbon species. They are composed entirely of single bonds and are saturated with hydrogen.

- **Double bonds** can form in which adjacent carbon atoms share **two pairs** of electrons between them. The other two electrons in each carbon atom are available for bonding with other atoms. For example, propene (C_3H_6) has a double bond between two carbon atoms represented by two lines (Figure 14.4):

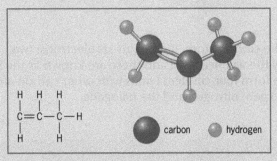

Figure 14.4 *Propene (C₃H₆)*

Any organic compound containing one or more double bonds between adjacent carbon atoms is referred to as being **unsaturated**.

- **Unbranched** and **branched chains** of carbon atoms of different lengths can form.

For example, pentane is an unbranched chain of five carbon atoms with single bonds between adjacent carbon atoms (Figure 14.5):

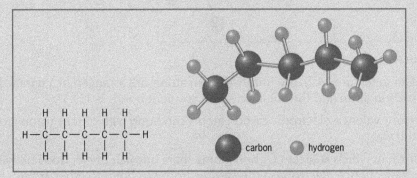

Figure 14.5 *Pentane (C₅H₁₂) unbranched chain*

An example of a branched chain is methylbutane, which consists of a straight chain containing four carbons and a fifth carbon atom branching off from the second carbon atom in the straight chain (Figure 14.6):

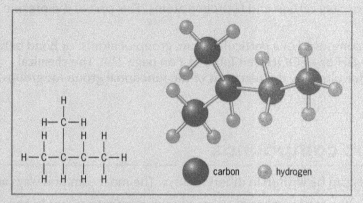

Figure 14.6 *Methylbutane (C_5H_{12}) branched chain*

- **Rings** of carbon atoms can form with single or double bonds between adjacent carbon atoms. Examples of ring organic compounds are cyclobutane (Figure 14.7), cyclopentane (Figure 14.8) and benzene (Figure 14.9):

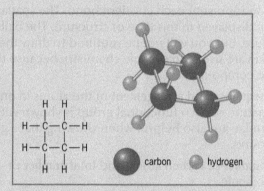

Figure 14.7 *Cyclobutane (C_4H_8)*

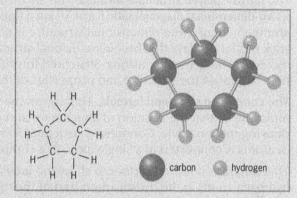

Figure 14.8 *Cyclopentane (C_5H_{10})*

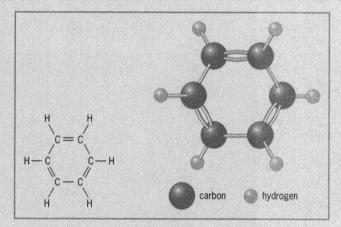

Figure 14.9 *Benzene (C_6H_6)*

Catenation is the ability of carbon atoms to bond covalently with other carbon atoms to form long chains, branched chains and rings of carbon atoms.

The structure of organic molecules

The simplest organic molecules can be thought of as being composed of **two** parts:

- The **hydrocarbon part** composed of only carbon and hydrogen atoms. This part of the organic molecule is fairly unreactive.

- The **functional group** (or **groups**), composed of a particular atom, group of atoms, or bond between adjacent carbon atoms, such as –OH or –COOH (see Table 14.2 on page 239). The **chemical properties** of a compound are determined by the reactions of the functional group (or groups) present.

Formulae of organic compounds

The **formulae** of organic compounds can be written in different ways. The most common ways are:

- The **molecular formula**. This shows the **total number** of atoms of each element present in one molecule of the compound. So, by looking at the molecular formula the number of atoms of each type in the molecule's composition can be determined. The disadvantage is that it does not show how the atoms are linked to each other within the molecule; you therefore cannot tell what the molecule is nor its properties.

- The **fully displayed structural formula**. This shows how the atoms are bonded in one molecule in a **two-dimensional diagrammatic** form, using a line to represent each covalent bond. The spatial arrangement or three-dimensional structure is not displayed in this type of structure. The ball and stick model displays the three-dimensional structure, but you will not be required to draw the molecules in three-dimensions. Structural formulae are useful in organic chemistry because they help to explain the structure and properties of the compound.

- The **condensed structural formula**. This shows the **sequence** and **arrangement** of the atoms in one molecule so that the position of attachment and nature of each functional group is shown without drawing the molecule. Condensed structural formulae are also helpful when showing that a group of atoms is connected to a single atom in a compound.

  This can be condensed further to show the **total number** of **carbon** atoms and **total number** of **hydrogen** atoms in the hydrocarbon part of the molecule.

  It is important to note that, even though the bonds are not displayed in the condensed formulae, the carbon atom always forms four covalent bonds with other carbon atoms or atoms of other elements.

Example 2

Hexane

The functional group of hexane is C–C.

- Its molecular formula is C_6H_{14}.
- Its fully displayed structural formula is:

- Its ball and stick model is:

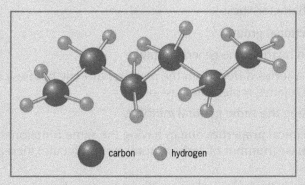

carbon   hydrogen

- Its condensed structural formula is $CH_3CH_2CH_2CH_2CH_2CH_3$.
  This can be further condensed to $CH_3(CH_2)_4CH_3$.

Hexanoic acid

The functional group of hexanoic acid is –COOH.

- Its molecular formula is $C_6H_{12}O_2$.
- Its fully displayed structural formula is:

$$
\begin{array}{c}
\quad\; H \;\; H \;\; H \;\; H \;\; H \\
\quad | \;\;\; | \;\;\; | \;\;\; | \;\;\; | \\
H-C-C-C-C-C-C{\overset{\textstyle O}{\underset{\textstyle OH}{}}} \\
\quad | \;\;\; | \;\;\; | \;\;\; | \;\;\; | \\
\quad\; H \;\; H \;\; H \;\; H \;\; H
\end{array}
$$

- Its ball and stick model is:

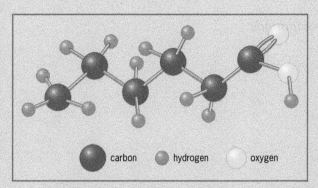

carbon   hydrogen   oxygen

- Its condensed structural formula is $CH_3CH_2CH_2CH_2CH_2COOH$.
  This can be condensed further to $CH_3(CH_2)_4COOH$
  and $C_5H_{11}COOH$.

Homologous series

Many organic compounds exist and can be **classified** into groups known as **homologous series.**
These are based on the functional group which contain the compunds. Each homologous series can
be represented by a **general formula.** For example, the general formula of the alkane series is C_nH_{2n+2}.
Classifying organic compounds helps chemists to understand the chemical behaviours of organic
compounds.

*A **homologous series** is a group of organic compounds that all possess the same functional group and
can be represented by the same general formula.*

The characteristics of a homologous series

Each homologous series has the following characteristics:

* Members of a series all have the same **functional group.**
* Members of a series can all be represented by the same **general formula.**
* The **molecular formula** of each member of a series differs from the member directly before it or directly after it by CH_2 and, therefore, by a relative molecular mass of **14.**
* Members of a series can all be **prepared** using the same general method.
* Members of a series all possess similar **chemical properties** due to having the same functional group but vary in reactivity. As the molar mass (number of carbon atoms per molecule) increases, the reactivity **decreases.**
* Members of a series show a gradual change in their **physical properties** as the number of carbon atoms per molecule increases. Generally, as molar mass increases, the melting point, boiling point and density **increase.** Also, the viscosity increases as relative molecular mass and size increase.

How to name the straight chain members of a homologous series

The International Union of Pure and Applied Chemistry (IUPAC) nomenclature system is a set of consistent rules developed and used by organic chemists to name the progressively huge quantity of organic compounds identified and synthesised daily. Each compound must have a unique name just as they have a distinct molecular structure.

Straight chain members of a homologous series have a name consisting of **two** parts:

* The first part, or **prefix**, which depends on the **total number of carbon atoms** in one molecule (see Table 14.1).

Table 14.1 *Prefixes used to name organic compounds*

Total number of carbon atoms	Prefix
1	meth-
2	eth-
3	prop-
4	but-
5	pent-
6	hex-
7	hept-
8	oct-
9	non-
10	dec-

* The second part, which depends on the **functional group** present in the compound (see Table 14.2).

Section B: Organic chemistry

Table 14.2 *The four main homologous series*

Name of homologous series	General formula	Functional group present	Naming members of the series	Example containing four carbon atoms	Fully displayed structural formula and condensed structural formula
Alkane	C_nH_{2n+2}	carbon–carbon single bond $-\overset{\vert}{\underset{\vert}{C}}-\overset{\vert}{\underset{\vert}{C}}-$	prefix + **ane**	**butane** (but + ane)	H–C–C–C–C–H (with H atoms) or C_4H_{10}
Alkene	C_nH_{2n}	carbon–carbon double bond $\overset{}{\underset{}{}}C=C\overset{}{\underset{}{}}$	prefix + **ene**	**butene** (but + ene)	C=C–C–C–H structure or C_4H_8
Alcohol or alkanol	$C_nH_{2n+1}OH$	hydroxyl group $-O-H$ $(-OH)$	prefix + **anol**	**butanol** (but + anol)	H–C–C–C–C–O–H structure or $CH_3CH_2CH_2CH_2OH$ or C_4H_9OH
Alkanoic acid or carboxylic acid	$C_nH_{2n+1}COOH$	carboxyl group $-C\overset{O}{\underset{O-H}{}}$ $(-COOH)$	prefix + **anoic acid**	**butanoic acid** (but + anoic acid)	H–C–C–C–C(=O)O–H structure or $CH_3CH_2CH_2COOH$ or C_3H_7COOH

Determining the homologous series

The homologous series an organic compound belongs to can be determined given its name or its formula, as follows:

- When given the name:

   The formula of a compound can be determined given its name. The homologous series it belongs to must be determined. This is done by looking at the suffix of the name. The prefix of the name gives the number of carbon atoms it contains. For example, for propene, the suffix of the name is '-ene'. Therefore, it belongs to the alkenes and thus possesses a double bond. It contains three carbon atoms since the prefix is 'prop-'. The general formula of the alkenes is C_nH_{2n}. The formula of propene is therefore C_3H_6.

- When given the structural formula:

   The structural formula needs to be examined and the functional group identified. The functional group in the organic compound determines the homologous series to which the compound belongs. For example, if the functional group identified is C=C, then the organic compound belongs to the alkenes. If a –COOH group is identified, then the organic compound belongs to the alkanoic acids.

- When given the molecular formula:

   The structural formula of the organic compound must be drawn using the molecular formula. The longest chain of carbon atoms must be drawn first and the functional group attached. If the alkene functional group is present, then a double line would be placed to denote the double bond between the carbon atoms based on the position specified in the molecular formula. Any other groups must then be placed in the position specified in the molecular formula and finally all the hydrogen atoms placed as specified in the formula. It must be noted that only the number of each type of atom stated in the formula must be used when drawing the structure and that each carbon atom must have four bonds attached to it. The functional group(s) must be identified and the homologous series named (refer to Table 14.2).

The name of the compound can be determined from its structure by first determining the homologous series it belongs to. Then determine the number of carbon atoms present in the molecule. For example, the formula of a compound is $C_6H_{15}OH$. The homologous series the molecule belongs to is the alcohol or alkanol series and the suffix must be 'anol'. A total of 6 carbons are present, so the prefix must be 'hex-'. The name of the compound is therefore hexanol.

Structural isomerism

One thought-provoking aspect of organic chemistry is that it is three-dimensional. Molecules can differ in the spatial arrangement of their atoms and this can contribute to its properties. Organic compounds can therefore have the same molecular formula but different structural formulae because their atoms are bonded differently. These are called **structural isomers.**

It is worth mentioning that another type of isomerism, called stereoisomerism, is demonstrated by organic compounds. Stereoisomers are molecules with the same arrangement of atoms but different orientations of groups in space. This type of isomerism is beyond the scope of this syllabus, so we will only focus on structural isomerism.

Structural isomers are organic compounds which have the same molecular formula but different structural formulae.

Structural isomerism is the occurrence of two or more organic compounds with the same molecular formula but different structural formulae.

Each different structural isomer has a **different name** and, if they contain the same functional group, they belong to the same homologous series. These isomers are called structural **chain isomers** and they have different physical properties (because the different shapes change the strength of the intermolecular forces), but similar chemical properties.

Structural isomers of straight chain molecules can be formed in two ways:

• by the chain of carbon atoms becoming **branched**

• by the **position** of the functional group changing.

Isomers formed by branching

Carbon chains can have **side branches** composed of one or more carbon atoms. For this to happen, the molecules must have four or more carbon atoms.

Example 3

Isomers of C_4H_{10}

C_4H_{10} has **two** isomers, given below:

$CH_3CH_2CH_2CH_3$

A straight chain isomer

$CH_3CH(CH_3)CH_3$

B branch chain isomer

When drawing the structural formula of any organic compound, the longest continuous chain of carbon atoms should always be drawn **horizontally** and care must be taken not to draw bent versions of the straight chain isomer or mirror images of branched chain isomers.

To check whether two structures are isomers, write the **condensed structural formula** of each. When reading these formulae forwards or backwards, if two formulae are the **same**, then the structures are **not** isomers (see Table 14.5, page 246, isomers of hexane).

C

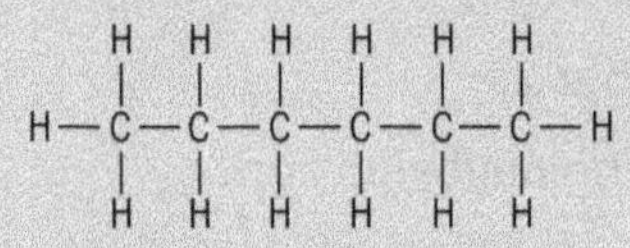

$CH_3CH_2CH_2CH_2CH_2CH_3$

D

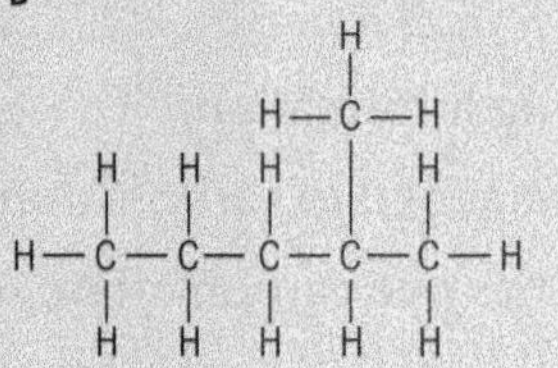

$CH_3CH_2CH_2CH(CH_3)CH_3$

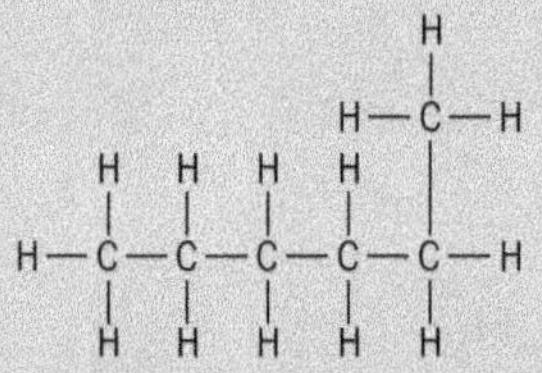

$CH_3CH_2CH_2CH_2CH_2CH_3$

This is a bent version of **C**, it is **not** another isomer

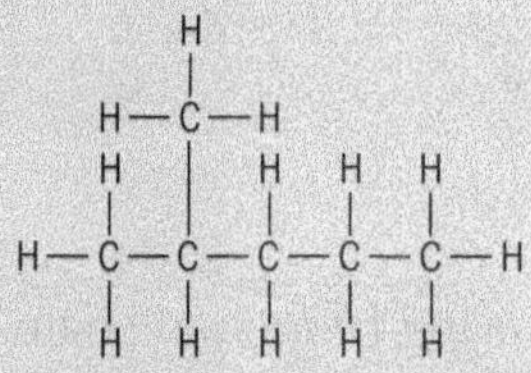

$CH_3CH(CH_3)CH_2CH_2CH_3$

This is a mirror image of **D**, it is **not** another isomer

How to name branched chain isomers

Side chains branching off from the longest chain of carbon atoms are called **alkyl groups**. They have the general formula C_nH_{2n+1} and are named using the appropriate prefix with the ending '-yl'.

Table 14.3 *Naming alkyl groups*

Formula of the alkyl group	Name
$-CH_3$	methyl
$-CH_2CH_3$ or $-C_2H_5$	ethyl
$-CH_2CH_2CH_3$ or $-C_3H_7$	propyl

The **name** of any branched chain molecule has **three** parts:

• The **first** part gives the **number of the carbon atom** to which the alkyl group (side chain) is attached.
• The **second** part gives the **name** of the **alkyl** group (Table 14.3).
• The **third** part gives information about the **longest** continuous chain of carbon atoms. The **number of carbon atoms** in this chain is indicated using the correct **prefix**, and the **homologous series** to which the compound belongs is indicated using the correct **ending**.

Example 4

To determine the name of the following branched chain isomer of C_5H_{12}:

A

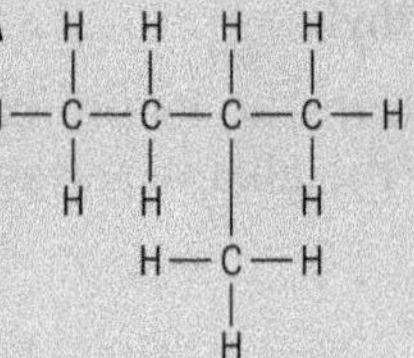

Number the carbon atoms in the longest continuous chain of carbon atoms from the end closest to the alkyl group so that the group is attached to the atom with the **lowest** possible number:

B

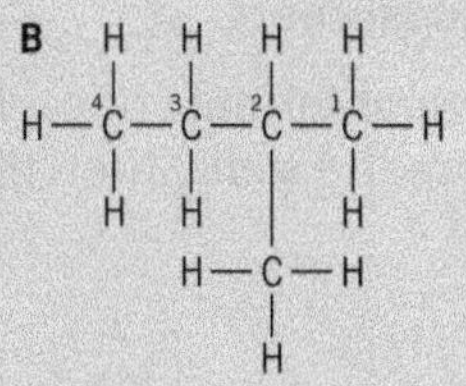

```
      H   H   H   H
      |   |   |   |
H  —  C — C — C — C — H
    4 |  3|  2|  1|
      H   H   |   H
             H—C—H
                |
                H
```

Name the isomer using the following information:

- The **first** part: the alkyl group is attached to carbon atom number **2**.

- The **second** part: the alkyl group has **one** carbon atom, so it is the **methyl** group.

- The **third** part: the longest continuous carbon chain has **four** carbon atoms, so its prefix is 'but-'. The compound has the general formula C_nH_{2n+2}, so it belongs to the **alkane** series which means its name ends in '**-ane**'.

The isomer is called **2-methylbutane**.

Example 5

To determine the name of the following branched chain isomer of C_6H_{14}:

A

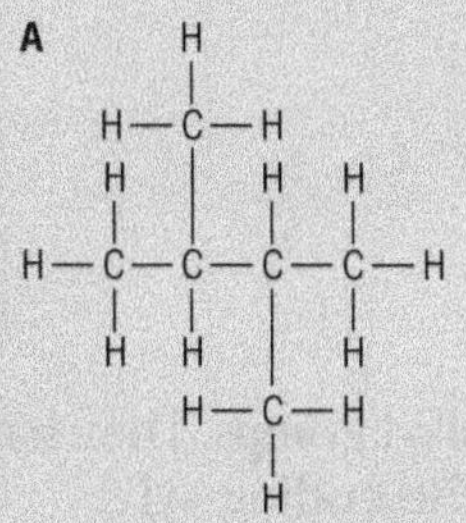

```
          H
          |
      H—C—H
      H   |   H   H
      |   |   |   |
H  —  C — C — C — C — H
      |   |   |   |
      H   H   |   H
             H—C—H
                |
                H
```

Number the carbon atoms in the longest continuous chain of carbon atoms from the end closest to the alkyl group so that the group is attached to the atom with the **lowest** possible number:

B

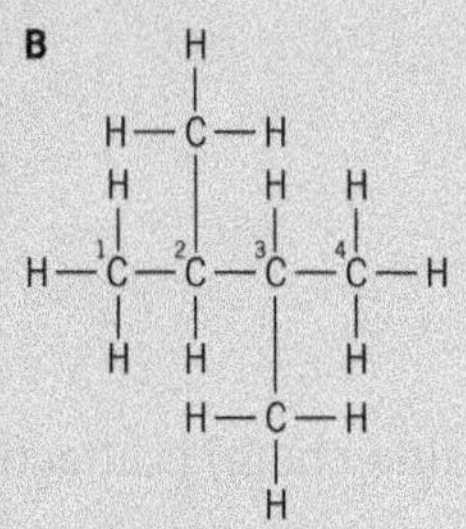

```
          H
          |
      H—C—H
      H   |   H   H
      |   |   |   |
H  —  C — C — C — C — H
    1 |  2|  3|  4|
      H   H   |   H
             H—C—H
                |
                H
```

Name the isomer using the following information:

- The **first** part: there are two alkyl groups one is attached to carbon atom number **2**, the second is attached to carbon atom **3**. When writing the name we write **2,3-** because both side chains are the same, CH_3.

- The **second** part: each alkyl group has **one** carbon atom, so it is the methyl group and because there are two of them the prefix 'di' is used, so we write **dimethyl**.

- The **third** part: the longest continuous carbon chain has **four** carbon atoms, so its prefix is 'but-'. The compound has the general formula C_nH_{2n+2}, so it belongs to the alkane series, which means its name ends in '**-ane**'.

The isomer is called **2,3-dimethylbutane**.

Example 6

To determine the name of the following branched chain isomer of C_6H_{14}:

A

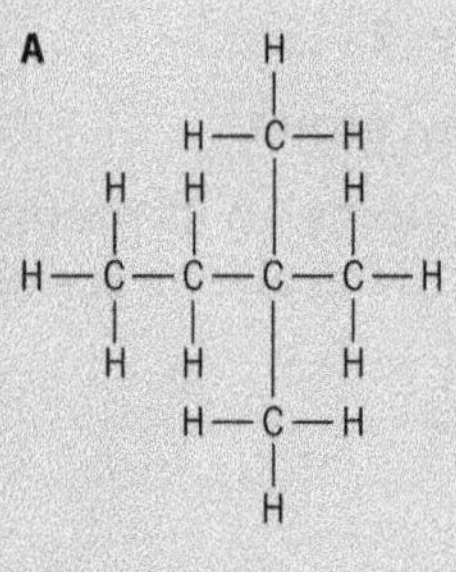

Number the carbon atoms in the longest continuous chain of carbon atoms from the end closest to the alkyl group so that the group is attached to the atom with the **lowest** possible number:

B

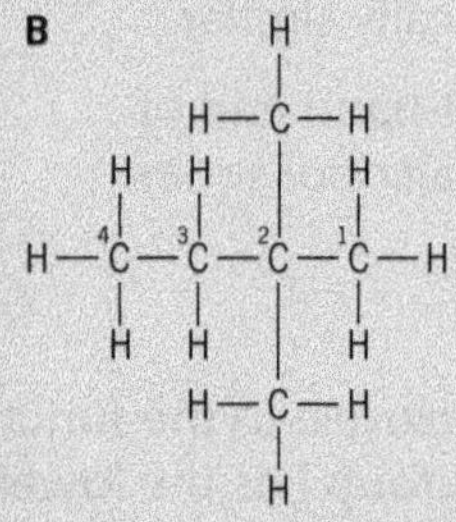

Name the isomer using the following information:

- The **first** part: the alkyl group is attached to carbon atom number **2**. When writing the name we write **2,2-** because both side chains are the same, CH_3.

- The **second** part: each alkyl group has **one** carbon atom, so it is the methyl group and because there are two of them the prefix 'di' is used, so we write **dimethyl**.

- The **third** part: the longest continuous carbon chain has **four** carbon atoms, so its prefix is **'but-'**. The compound has the general formula C_nH_{2n+2}, so it belongs to the alkane series, which means its name ends in **'-ane'**.

The isomer is called **2,2-dimethylbutane**.

Example 7

To determine the name of the following branched chain isomer of C_4H_8:

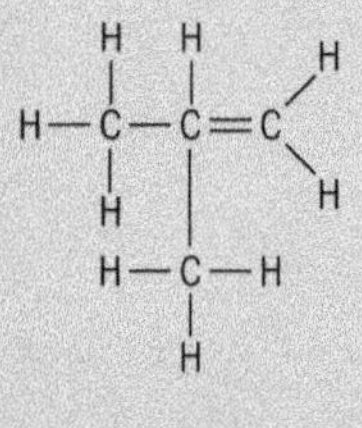

Number the carbon atoms in the longest continuous chain of carbon atoms from the end closest to the sidechain so that the sidechain is attached to the atom with the **lowest** possible number:

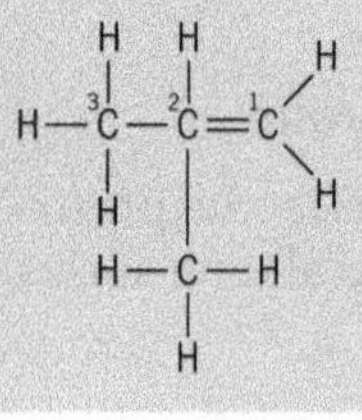

Name the isomer using the following information:

- The **first** part: there is one alkyl group attached to carbon atom number **2**.
- The **second** part: the alkyl group has **one** carbon atom, so it is the **methyl** group.
- The **third** part: the longest continuous carbon chain has three carbon atoms, so its prefix is **'prop-'**. The compound has the general formula C_nH_{2n}, so it belongs to the alkene series, which means its name ends in **'-ene'**.

The isomer is called **2-methylpropene**.

Isomers formed by changing the position of the functional group

Positional isomers are structural isomers in which the functional groups occupy different positions on the same carbon chain. Isomers with the same functional group are chemically similar.

A compound is usually drawn so that its functional group is shown at the right-hand end of the molecule; however, its **position** can change. This is seen in the alkene and alcohol series (Tables 14.6, 14.7 and 14.8, pages 247–248).

When naming the isomers of alkenes and alcohols:

- The carbon atoms from the longest chain must be numbered from the end closest to the functional group (C=C in the alkenes and –OH in the alcohols) so that the functional group has the lowest number and the position of the functional group in the name is shown using the lowest possible number.
- The steps outlined on page 241 for naming branched chain isomers must be followed.

To determine the name of the following branched chain isomer of C_5H_{10}:

Number the carbon atoms in the longest continuous chain of carbon atoms from the end closest to the functional group so that the group is attached to the atom with the **lowest** possible number:

Name the isomer using the following information:

- The functional group C=C is attached to carbon number **1**.
- The **first** part: there is one alkyl group attached to carbon atom number **2**.
- The **second** part: the alkyl group has **one** carbon atom, so it is the **methyl** group.
- The **third** part: the longest continuous carbon chain has four carbon atoms, so its prefix is **'but-'**. The compound has the general formula C_nH_{2n}, so it belongs to the alkene series, which means its name ends in **'-ene'**.

The isomer is called **2-methylbut-1-ene**.

Example 9

To determine the name of the following unbranched chain isomer of C_6H_{12}:

$$H-\underset{\underset{H}{|}}{\overset{\overset{H}{|}}{C}}-\underset{\underset{H}{|}}{\overset{\overset{H}{|}}{C}}-\overset{\overset{H}{|}}{C}=\overset{\overset{H}{|}}{C}-\underset{\underset{H}{|}}{\overset{\overset{H}{|}}{C}}-\underset{\underset{H}{|}}{\overset{\overset{H}{|}}{C}}-H$$

Number the carbon atoms in the longest continuous chain of carbon atoms from the end closest to the functional group, so that the group is attached to the atom with the **lowest** possible number:

$$H-\overset{6}{\underset{\underset{H}{|}}{\overset{\overset{H}{|}}{C}}}-\overset{5}{\underset{\underset{H}{|}}{\overset{\overset{H}{|}}{C}}}-\overset{4}{\overset{\overset{H}{|}}{C}}=\overset{3}{\overset{\overset{H}{|}}{C}}-\overset{2}{\underset{\underset{H}{|}}{\overset{\overset{H}{|}}{C}}}-\overset{1}{\underset{\underset{H}{|}}{\overset{\overset{H}{|}}{C}}}-H$$

Name the isomer using the following information:

- The functional group C=C is attached to carbon number **3**. It should be noted that the functional group is on carbon number 3 no matter which side the longest carbon chain is numbered from.
- The longest continuous carbon chain has six carbon atoms, so its prefix is **'hex-'**. The compound has the general formula C_nH_{2n}, so it belongs to the alkene series, which means its name ends in **'-ene'**.

The isomer is called **hex-3-ene**.

Example 10

To determine the name of the following unbranched chain isomer of $C_5H_{11}OH$:

$$H-\underset{\underset{H}{|}}{\overset{\overset{H}{|}}{C}}-\underset{\underset{H}{|}}{\overset{\overset{H}{|}}{C}}-\underset{\underset{H}{|}}{\overset{\overset{H}{|}}{C}}-\underset{\underset{OH}{|}}{\overset{\overset{H}{|}}{C}}-\underset{\underset{H}{|}}{\overset{\overset{H}{|}}{C}}-H$$

Number the carbon atoms in the longest continuous chain of carbon atoms from the end closest to the functional group, so that the group is attached to the atom with the **lowest** possible number:

$$H-\overset{5}{\underset{\underset{H}{|}}{\overset{\overset{H}{|}}{C}}}-\overset{4}{\underset{\underset{H}{|}}{\overset{\overset{H}{|}}{C}}}-\overset{3}{\underset{\underset{H}{|}}{\overset{\overset{H}{|}}{C}}}-\overset{2}{\underset{\underset{OH}{|}}{\overset{\overset{H}{|}}{C}}}-\overset{1}{\underset{\underset{H}{|}}{\overset{\overset{H}{|}}{C}}}-H$$

Name the isomer using the following information:

- The functional group –OH is attached to carbon number **2**.
- The longest continuous carbon chain has five carbon atoms, so its prefix is **'pent-'**. The compound has the general formula $C_nH_{2n+1}OH$, so it belongs to the alcohol or alkanol series, which means its name ends in **'-anol'**.

The isomer is called **pentan-2-ol** or **2-pentanol**.

The alkanes: C_nH_{2n+2}

Alkanes contain only **single bonds** between carbon atoms. Alkanes with **four** or **more** carbon atoms show **structural isomerism** resulting from their ability to form **branched chains**.

Table 14.4 *The first three alkanes*

Molecular formula	CH_4	C_2H_6	C_3H_8
Structural formula and name	methane	ethane	propane

Table 14.5 *The isomers of alkanes with four, five and six carbon atoms*

Molecular formula	Structural formulae and names of isomers
C_4H_{10}	butane 2-methylpropane
C_5H_{12}	pentane 2-methylbutane 2,2-dimethylpropane
C_6H_{14}	hexane 2-methylpentane 3-methylpentane 2,2-dimethylbutane 2,3-dimethylbutane

The alkenes: C_nH_{2n}

Alkenes contain one double bond between two carbon atoms. Their functional group is this **carbon–carbon double bond**:

$$\diagdown C = C \diagup$$

Alkenes with **four** or **more** carbon atoms show **structural isomerism** resulting from:

- A **change in position** of the carbon–carbon double bond. This bond must always be drawn horizontally.
- **Branching** of the molecule.

To name **unbranched isomers** of alkenes, **number** the carbon atoms in the longest continuous chain from the end closest to the double bond. Indicate the position of the double bond using the lowest possible number of the carbon atom it is attached to (see Tables 14.6 and 14.7). **Branched isomers** are named following the guidelines given on page 241, but using the ending '**-ene**'.

Table 14.6 *The first three alkenes*

Molecular formula	Structural formulae and names
C_2H_4	ethene
C_3H_6	propene
C_4H_8	but-1-ene (or 1-butene) but-2-ene (or 2-butene) 2-methylpropene

Table 14.7 *The unbranched isomers of pentene and hexene*

Molecular formula	Structural formulae and names
C_5H_{10}	pent-1-ene (or 1-pentene) pent-2-ene (or 2-pentene)
C_6H_{12}	hex-1-ene (or 1-hexene) hex-2-ene (or 2-hexene) hex-3-ene (or 3-hexene)

Alcohols: $C_nH_{2n+1}OH$ or R–OH

Alcohols (or **alkanols**) have the **hydroxyl** group (**–OH**) as their functional group.

Alcohols with **three** or **more** carbon atoms show **structural isomerism** resulting from:

- a **change in position** of the hydroxyl (–OH) group.
- **branching** of the molecule.

To name **unbranched isomers** of alcohols, **number** the carbon atoms in the longest continuous chain from the end closest to the –OH group. Indicate the position of the group using the number of the carbon atom it is bonded to (see Table 14.8). **Branched isomers** are named following the guidelines given on page 241, but using the ending '**-anol**'.

Table 14.8 *The unbranched isomers of the first five alcohols*

Condensed formula	Structural formula and name
CH_3OH	 **methanol**
C_2H_5OH	 **ethanol**
C_3H_7OH	 **propan-1-ol** **propan-2-ol** (1-propanol) (2-propanol)
C_4H_9OH	 **butan-1-ol** **butan-2-ol** (or 1-butanol) (or 2-butanol)
$C_5H_{11}OH$	 **pentan-1-ol** **pentan-2-ol** **pentan-3-ol** (or 1-pentanol) (or 2-pentanol) (or 3-pentanol)

Note The unbranched isomers of **hexanol** ($C_6H_{13}OH$) are drawn and named in the same way as those of pentanol.

Alkanoic acids: C$_n$H$_{2n+1}$COOH or R–COOH

Alkanoic acids (or **carboxylic acids**) have the **carboxyl** group (**–COOH**) as their functional group:

Table 14.9 *Names and formulae of the first six alkanoic acids*

Condensed formula	Structural formula and name
HCOOH	methanoic acid
CH$_3$COOH	ethanoic acid
C$_2$H$_5$COOH	propanoic acid

Condensed formula	Structural formula and name
C$_3$H$_7$COOH	butanoic acid
C$_4$H$_9$COOH	pentanoic acid
C$_5$H$_{11}$COOH	hexanoic acid

Recalling facts

1. How many hydrogen atoms are there in pentane?

   a 5

   b 8

   c 10

   d 12

2. Name this compound:

   a 1-hexene

   b 2-hexene

   c 2-methylpropene

   d 3-hexene

3 Name this compound:

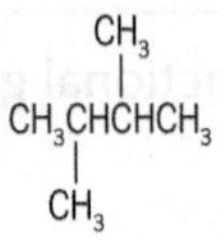

CH₃
|
CH₃CHCHCH₃
|
CH₃

Structure: CH₃CHCHCH₃ with CH₃ groups above and below the middle carbons

a 2-methylpentane

b 3-methylpentane

c 2,2-dimethylbutane

d 2,3-dimethylbutane

4 Name the following compound:

Structure: H₃C—C—C—C—CH₃ with H, OH, H on top and H, H, H on bottom

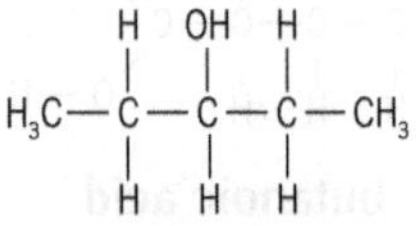

a propan-3-ol

b butan-3-ol

c pentan-3-ol

d hexan-3-ol

5 Name the following compound:

Structure: H—C—C—C—C—C—OH with H's around and O double bonded

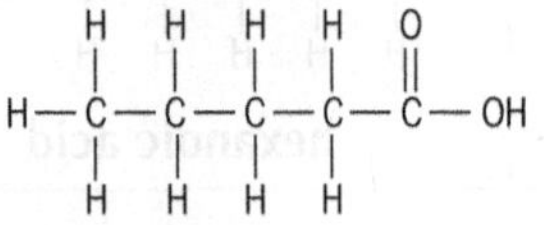

a butanoic acid

b pentanol

c pentanoic acid

d hexanol

6 Which of the following is an unsaturated compound?

a *Structure:* H—C—C—C—C with O double bond and O—C

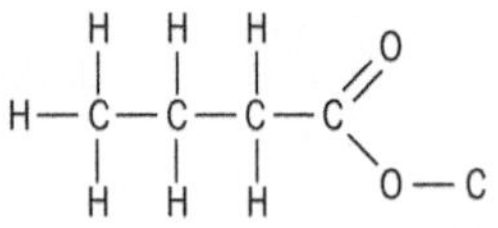

b *Structure:* H—C—C—C—C—C—H with OH group*

c *Structure:* H—C—C—C—C—C—H (all single bonds)*

d *Structure:* H—C—C=C—C—C—H (double bond present)*

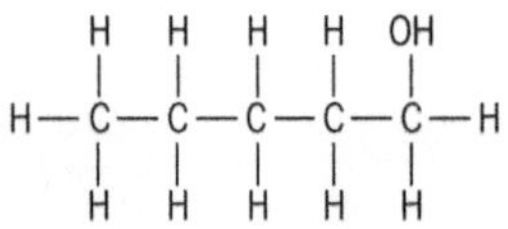

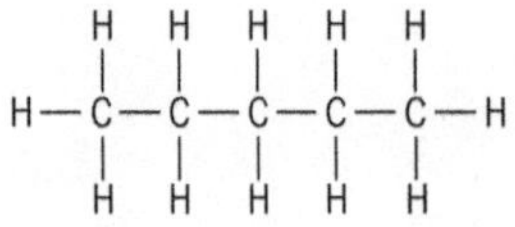

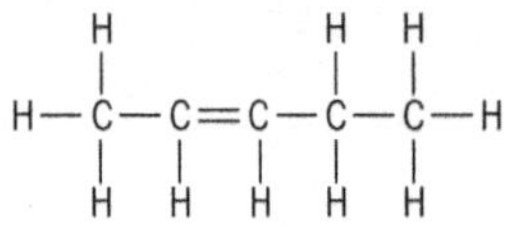

7 Which of the following is an example of a condensed formula?

a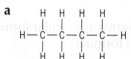

b $CH_3CH_2CH_2CH_3$

c C_nH_{2n+2}

d all of the above

8 Give the name of the following compound C_3H_6:

a pentane

b propane

c propene

d pentene

9 Give the name of the following compound C_3H_7COOH:

a butanol

b propanoic acid

c butanoic acid

d propanol

10 Which homologous series does the compound C_3H_8O belong to:

a alkane series

b alkene series

c alkanoic acid series

d alkanol series

11 Discuss the different types of bonds a carbon atom can form with another carbon atom.

12 What is the meaning of the term 'catenation'? Name the different types of chains formed when carbon atoms bond and give one example of each.

13 Explain what is meant by the term 'homologous series'. State three general characteristics of homologous series. Give the names of four homologous series you have learnt. State their general formulae and their functional group.

14 Name and draw the fully displayed structures of the first three members of the homologous series alkanes, alkenes and alcohols.

Applying facts

15 By using suitable examples, differentiate between the terms 'molecular formula', 'fully displayed structural formula' and 'condensed structural formula'.

16 How does the structural formula show whether a compound is saturated or unsaturated?

17 **a** Discuss, using an example, how you can determine the homologous series a compound belongs to when given the compound name.

   b Using an example, describe how you would work out the formula of a compound given its name.

   c Using an example, describe how you would determine the name of a compound given the formula.

Analysing data

18 Pentane, pentene and pentanol can have many structural isomers. Which homologous series do each of these compounds belong to? Explain what is meant by the term 'structural isomers'. How many isomers of each exist? Draw and name the isomers of each of these compounds.

15 Sources of hydrocarbon compounds

Learning objectives

- Identify **natural gas** and **petroleum** as **natural sources** of hydrocarbons.
- Describe the separation of petroleum into useful fractions by **fractional distillation**.
- Name the **main fractions** obtained from the fractional distillation of petroleum and state their uses.
- Explain what is meant by the term **cracking** and state the importance of cracking.
- Describe **thermal** and **catalytic cracking of alkanes**.

Hydrocarbons are organic compounds composed of **carbon** and **hydrogen** atoms only. Alkanes and alkenes are both hydrocarbons. Naturally occurring hydrocarbons were formed deep under the Earth's crust and are extracted in their liquid form as petroleum or crude oil and in their gaseous form as natural gas. These are used as fuels. Without fossil fuels, most people could not drive their cars. They could not turn on their lights or heat or cool their homes. This is because most of the energy needed to do these things currently comes from fossil fuels.

The crude oil and natural gas that have been extracted over the past century were formed millions of years ago. Crude oil and natural gas were formed from the remains of tiny sea animals and plants which sank to the bottom of the seabed and were buried under layers of sand and silt. Due to anaerobic conditions at this depth, total decomposition of these dead plant and animals was not possible. The partially decomposed plant and animal remains continued to be buried under layers of sand and silt over the course of millions of years, placing them under immense pressure. This increased pressure, together with the natural heat from the Earth, resulted in these partially decomposed remains forming crude oil and natural gas deposits which are extracted today.

Natural sources of hydrocarbons

There are **two** natural sources of hydrocarbons: natural gas and crude oil (or petroleum).

- **Natural gas**

  Natural gas is a mixture of the first four **alkanes**, approximately 80–90% methane (CH_4) with small amounts of ethane (C_2H_6), propane (C_3H_8) and butane (C_4H_{10}). Before natural gas is sold commercially, the propane and butane are removed, leaving a mixture of **methane** and **ethane**. The **propane** and **butane** are then liquefied under pressure to produce liquefied petroleum gas, also known as LPG or 'bottled gas', which is used for cooking. The mixture of methane and ethane, known as commercial natural gas, is used to produce electricity, and for cooking and heating in homes. Commercial natural gas is also liquefied under pressure and is used as a cleaner-burning fuel to power vehicles worldwide.

- **Crude oil (or petroleum)**

  Crude oil is a yellow to black oily liquid found in the earth. It is a complex mixture consisting of a large number of different solid and gaseous hydrocarbons dissolved in liquid hydrocarbons, mainly alkanes and some ringed compounds. To make it useful, petroleum is separated into its different components (or 'fractions') by **fractional distillation** at an oil refinery.

Fractional distillation of crude oil

When extracted from the ground, crude oil contains many impurities which must be removed before any processing can occur. The impurities are first removed from the crude oil and then it is heated to about 400 °C and treated to remove sulfur to reduce pollution. This produces a mixture of liquid and vapour which is piped into the bottom part of a **fractionating tower**. The **vapours** rise up the tower and the viscous heavy liquid fraction, known as **bitumen** or **asphalt**, sinks to the bottom of the tower and is tapped off.

The vapours rising up the tower pass through a series of bubble caps and trays where they may **condense**. The **temperature decreases** going up the tower and the lower the boiling point of the hydrocarbon, the further the vapour will rise before condensing. The liquids produced when the vapours condense are tapped off at the different levels. Gases that do not condense are removed at the top of the tower as **refinery gas**. Each fraction tapped off is a mixture of hydrocarbons with similar sized molecules and boiling points. The different fractions have different **uses**. They are mainly used as fuels and lubricants, and to manufacture a variety of petrochemicals.

Table 15.1 and Figure 15.1 summarise the main fractions from crude oil and their uses.

At the top of the column the smaller molecules (which are more volatile, ignite easily and have a low boiling point) are obtained. The smallest molecules consist of one to four carbon atoms and this fraction, called **refinery gas**, is processed into **liquified petroleum gas (LPG)**. **LPG** is stored in steel cylinders and sold as gas used for cooking. **Petrol** or **gasoline** is the next fraction, which consists of molecules with five to ten carbon atoms. This fraction is used as fuel for internal combustion engines, in vehicles such as cars, light aircraft and boats. The next fraction obtained is **naphtha**, which is very important as chemical feedstock in the production of a wide range of petrochemicals, such as plastics and drugs.

Kerosene oil, the next fraction obtained, contains 10 to 14 carbon atoms and is used as fuel for jet engines, cooking, heating and lighting in homes. The **diesel fraction** consisting of 14 to 20 carbon atoms is used to power diesel engines in cars, trucks, buses, trains, tractors, boats and generators. While diesel is a cheaper fuel than petrol, when burnt it is not as clean as petrol. It produces higher levels of soot and particulate matter, which can lead to more smoky exhaust gases being produced.

Fuel oils are used to fuel factory boilers, power stations and ships. **Lubricating oils** and **waxes** are the next fraction to be obtained. Lubricating oils are used to lubricate mechanical parts in vehicles and machinery. Waxes are used in the manufacture of wax paper, polishes, petroleum jelly and candles.

Bitumen is the last fraction, and it is used in surfacing roads, car parks and airport runways. It is also used to manufacture roofing materials.

Table 15.1 *Fractions of crude oil, their boiling points and length of their carbon chains*

Name of fraction	Boiling point/°C	Number of carbon atoms	Uses
Refinery gas	below 25	1–4	Fuel for domestic use
Petrol	25–170	5–10	Fuel for internal combustion engine
Naphtha	127–217	8–12	To manufacture petrochemicals
Kerosene oil	170–250	10–14	Fuel for jet engines, cooking, heating, lighting
Diesel oil	250–350	14–20	Fuel for diesel engines
Fuel oil, lubricating oil and waxes	350–400	18–30	Fuel for power stations, factories and ships Lubricants in machinery and vehicle engines Used to make polishing waxes, petroleum jelly, candles
Bitumen (asphalt)	above 400	more than 30	Surfacing roads, car parks, airport runways Roofing

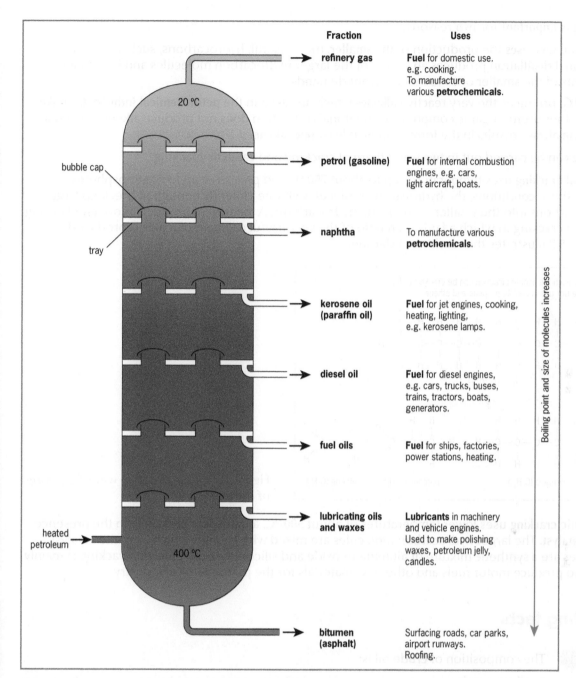

Fraction	Uses
refinery gas	**Fuel** for domestic use. e.g. cooking. To manufacture various **petrochemicals.**
petrol (gasoline)	**Fuel** for internal combustion engines, e.g. cars, light aircraft, boats.
naphtha	To manufacture various **petrochemicals.**
kerosene oil (paraffin oil)	**Fuel** for jet engines, cooking, heating, lighting, e.g. kerosene lamps.
diesel oil	**Fuel** for diesel engines, e.g. cars, trucks, buses, trains, tractors, boats, generators.
fuel oils	**Fuel** for ships, factories, power stations, heating.
lubricating oils and waxes	**Lubricants** in machinery and vehicle engines. Used to make polishing waxes, petroleum jelly, candles.
bitumen (asphalt)	Surfacing roads, car parks, airport runways. Roofing.

20 °C

bubble cap

tray

heated petroleum

400 °C

Boiling point and size of molecules increases

Figure 15.1 *Uses of the fractions produced by fractional distillation of crude oil*

Cracking hydrocarbons

When crude oil is fractionally distilled, more of the larger hydrocarbon molecules are produced than the smaller hydrocarbons. The larger hydrocarbons are less useful than the smaller ones, so the larger hydrocarbons can be converted to the more useful smaller hydrocarbons by the process of **cracking.**

Cracking is the process by which long chain hydrocarbon molecules are broken down into shorter chain hydrocarbon molecules by breaking carbon–carbon bonds.

Cracking is **important** for **two** reasons:

- Cracking **increases** the production of the **smaller**, more useful, hydrocarbons, such as petrol. Fractional distillation produces an excess of the larger hydrocarbon molecules and insufficient amounts of the smaller ones to meet current demands.

- Cracking produces the very reactive **alkenes** which are used in the **petrochemical industry** to make many other useful organic compounds. Fractional distillation does not produce alkenes, whereas cracking always results in the formation of at least **one alkene**.

Cracking can be carried out in **two** ways: thermal cracking and catalytic cracking.

- **Thermal cracking** uses temperatures up to about 750 °C and pressures up to 70 atmospheres. Under these conditions, the hydrocarbon molecules vibrate violently enough to break up large hydrocarbons into the smaller more useful hydrocarbons. A mixture of products is obtained during thermal cracking in which a fairly high ratio of the very useful alkene molecules is produced. Figure 15.2 illustrates the cracking of decane.

Decane from the naphtha fraction can be cracked to form pentane (for use in petrol), propene and ethene

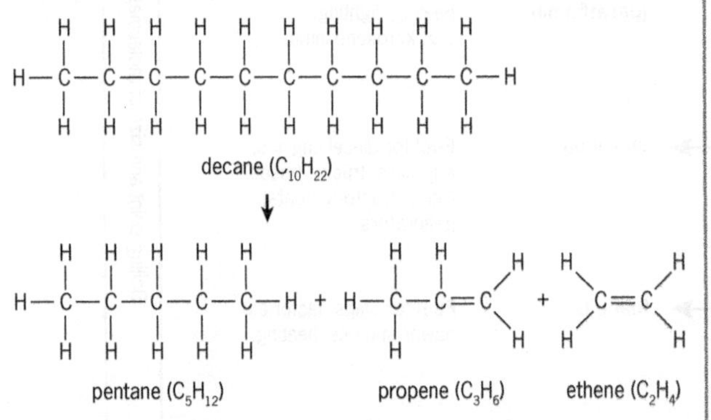

decane ($C_{10}H_{22}$)

pentane (C_5H_{12}) propene (C_3H_6) ethene (C_2H_4)

Figure 15.2 *One possible way of cracking of decane*

- **Catalytic cracking** uses lower temperatures of about 500 °C, at fairly low pressures in the presence of a **catalyst**. The larger hydrocarbon molecules are mixed with zeolites which form the catalyst. Zeolites are a synthetic mixture of aluminium oxide and silicon dioxide. Catalytic cracking is mainly used to produce motor fuels and other raw materials for the petrochemical industry.

Recalling facts

  The composition of crude oil is:

a alkanes only

b alkenes only

c only large hydrocarbons

d a mixture of different hydrocarbons

  What is the method used to separate the different fractions contained in crude oil:

a distillation

b fractional distillation

c cracking

d catenation

3 Refinery gas is used:

   a as fuel for motor vehicles

   b as fuel for domestic cooking

   c to manufacture solvents

   d as fuel for jet engines

4 Naphtha is a fraction that consists of _____ carbon atoms:

   a 18–30

   b 10–14

   c 8–12

   d 14–20

5 When crude oil enters the fractionating column and is heated it:

   a condenses

   b vaporises

   c melts

   d combusts

6 The boiling point of kerosene is:

   a 25–170 °C

   b 170–250 °C

   c 250–350 °C

   d 350–400 °C

7 Natural gas is made up of:

   a 80–90% butane

   b 80–90% propane

   c 80–90% methane

   d 80–90% ethane

8 Liquefied petroleum gas (LPG) is made up of:

   a propane and methane

   b propane and butane

   c methane and butane

   d methane and ethane

9 Bitumen is mainly used for:

   a fuel for motor vehicles

   b lubricating machinery

   c surfacing roofs and roads

   d making polishes and candles

10 The following statements are true about cracking except:
 a Only shorter chain alkane molecules are formed.
 b Shorter chain alkane and alkene molecules are formed.
 c Conditions for thermal cracking are 700 °C and 70 atmospheres pressure.
 d Conditions for catalytic cracking are 500 °C in the presence of zeolites.

11 Discuss how crude oil was formed.

12 Discuss the two methods used to crack alkanes.

13 Natural gas is another source of hydrocarbons. What are the main components of natural gas. State the uses of natural gas.

Analysing data

14 Briefly outline how the components of crude oil are obtained. What is the name of the separation process used and the principle involved in the separation technique used? Give the boiling points and the range of the number of carbon atoms in the hydrocarbon chain of a light fraction, a heavy fraction and a medium fraction.

15 Nonane (C_9H_{20}) belongs to the homologous series alkanes; these molecules can undergo cracking and the products of this process are very important. Discuss this statement. Your answer must include the meaning of cracking, the importance of cracking large alkanes, an equation showing the products formed when nonane undergoes cracking and the uses of the members of the homologous series these products belong to.

16 Reactions of carbon compounds

Learning objectives

- Describe the reactions of the homologous series **alkanes and alkenes**.
- Link the **reactivity** of the alkanes and alkenes to their **functional groups**.
- Describe a **chemical test** to distinguish between an alkane and an alkene.
- Explain how the **properties** of the alkanes and alkenes influence their uses.
- Describe the **production of biogas**.
- Use the functional groups to identify **alcohols**, **acids** and **esters**.
- Describe the reactions of **ethanol**.
- Describe the **fermentation process** which **converts carbohydrates to ethanol**.
- Describe the reactions of **ethanoic acids**.
- Explain the **hydrolysis of esters** including **saponification**.
- Compare **soapy** and **soapless detergents**.

The **chemical reactions** of carbon compounds are determined by the reactions of the **functional group** (or groups) present in the compounds.

The alkanes: C_nH_{2n+2}

Alkanes are **saturated** hydrocarbons, meaning they have only **single bonds** between adjacent carbon atoms. Alkanes with 1 to 4 carbon atoms in their molecules are **gases** at room temperature, those with 5 to 16 carbon atoms are **liquids** and those with 17 or more carbon atoms are **solids**. Alkanes are colourless compounds with a characteristic odour. They are molecular compounds; hence they are non-polar and therefore are immiscible with water but soluble in most organic solvents, such as tetrachloromethane. There is a general increase in the melting and boiling points of alkanes with increasing molecular mass. It should be noted that straight chain molecules have greater interaction than branched chain molecules; therefore, the greater the branching, the lower the boiling point of the alkane. The densities of the alkanes increase down the series; they are also less dense than water. As the molecules become larger, they evaporate less easily and become less flammable.

Alkanes are relatively **unreactive** because the carbon–carbon single bonds in their molecules are strong and not easily broken.

Reactions of alkanes

- **Alkanes burn easily in air or oxygen**

  Alkanes undergo **complete combustion** when burnt in excess air or oxygen to form **carbon dioxide** and **water** as steam. They burn with **clear, blue, non-smoky flames** because they have a **low** ratio of carbon to hydrogen atoms in their molecules. All the carbon is converted to carbon dioxide and no unreacted carbon remains in the flames to make them smoky. The reactions are **exothermic**, producing large amounts of heat energy.

  For example: $C_3H_8(g) + 5O_2(g) \longrightarrow 3CO_2(g) + 4H_2O(g)$ ΔH –ve

  Incomplete combustion of alkanes occurs when there is an insufficient supply of air or oxygen. The alkanes burn with a smoky or sooty red or yellow flame producing carbon dioxide, carbon monoxide and water in the form of steam.

  For example: $2C_3H_8(g) + 9O_2(g) \longrightarrow 4CO_2(g) + 2CO + 8H_2O(g)$ ΔH –ve

- **Alkanes undergo substitution reactions with halogens**

Under the correct conditions, alkanes undergo **substitution reactions** with **halogens**. In these reactions, the hydrogen atoms in the alkane molecules are replaced by halogen atoms such as chlorine or bromine. For the reaction to occur, energy in the form of **light** is required; ultraviolet light works best. This is a good example of a photochemical reaction – a reaction that needs light to occur. The products of the halogenation of alkanes are known as **haloalkanes** or **alkyl halides**.

Example 1

The reaction between methane and chlorine

In the dark, **no** reaction occurs. In bright light or ultraviolet light, a **rapid** reaction occurs. In dim light, a **slow substitution** reaction occurs in stages, where one hydrogen atom is replaced by one chlorine atom at a time:

$$CH_4(g) + Cl_2(g) \xrightarrow{light} \underset{\text{monochloromethane}}{CH_3Cl(g)} + \underset{\text{hydrogen chloride}}{HCl(g)}$$

$$CH_3Cl(g) + Cl_2(g) \xrightarrow{light} \underset{\text{dichloromethane}}{CH_2Cl_2(l)} + HCl(g)$$

$$CH_2Cl_2(l) + Cl_2(g) \xrightarrow{light} \underset{\text{trichloromethane}}{CHCl_3(l)} + HCl(g)$$

$$CHCl_3(l) + Cl_2(g) \xrightarrow{light} \underset{\text{tetrachloromethane}}{CCl_4(l)} + HCl(g)$$

The overall reaction:

$$CH_4(g) + 4Cl_2(g) \xrightarrow{light} CCl_4(l) + 4HCl(g)$$

Similar substitutions occur with **bromine vapour** or **bromine solution** and with other alkanes, though the reactions are slower. During the reaction between bromine and any alkane, the colour of the bromine **slowly** fades from **red brown** to **colourless** in the presence of **UV light**. This indicates that the bromine is being used up in the substitution reaction.

The organic product is bromomethane. One of the hydrogen atoms in the methane has been replaced by a bromine atom, so this is the first step in the substitution reaction. However, the reaction does not stop there, and all the hydrogens in the methane can in turn be replaced by bromine atoms. Write out all the steps for the replacement of all the hydrogens in methane by bromine!

The speed of the halogenation reaction depends on the reactivity of the halogen: the more reactive the halogen, the faster the reaction; therefore the reaction with fluorine is faster than with iodine. Light intensity also affects the speed of the reaction: the more intense the light, the faster the reaction. The size of the alkane determines the reactivity of the alkanes and hence the speed of the halogenation reaction. The smaller the alkane, the more reactive is the alkane and the faster the halogenation reaction; therefore the halogenation of methane is fastest.

The alkenes: C_nH_{2n}

Alkenes are unsaturated hydrocarbons because they each contain one carbon–carbon double bond. The presence of this double bond as their functional group makes alkenes more reactive than alkanes.

The physical properties of the alkenes are similar to those of the alkanes. A similar pattern exists to that of the alkanes in terms of the physical states of the alkenes. The boiling points of the alkenes increase with increasing molecular mass, while the flammability decreases.

Reactions of alkenes

- **Alkenes burn easily in air or oxygen**

  Alkenes burn in air or oxygen to form **carbon dioxide** and **water** as steam. They burn with **smoky yellow flames** because they have a higher ratio of carbon to hydrogen atoms in their molecules than alkanes. Not all the carbon is converted to carbon dioxide and the unreacted carbon remains, giving the flames a yellow, smoky appearance. This is one reason why alkenes are not used as fuels. The reactions are **exothermic**. The equations for propene and butene burning in air or oxygen respectively are given:

  for example: $2C_3H_6(g) + 9O_2(g) \longrightarrow 6CO_2(g) + 6H_2O(g)$ ΔH −ve

  $C_4H_8(g) + 6O_2(g) \longrightarrow 4CO_2(g) + 4H_2O(g)$ ΔH −ve

- **Alkenes undergo addition reactions**

  Alkenes undergo **addition reactions** with other small molecules in which the alkene and the other molecule react to form **one** molecule. One bond in the double bond is broken and the compound formed is **saturated** (it has no double bonds). As can be seen in Figure 16.1, X–Y symbolises a small molecule with a single covalent bond between two atoms or small groups of atoms within the molecule. When a reaction occurs between the alkene molecule and X–Y, one of the bonds in the carbon–carbon double bonds breaks together with the covalent bond between X–Y. A single bond now exists between two carbon atoms with the double bond and X bonds to the carbon atom on one side of the original double bond and Y bonds to the carbon atom on the other side.

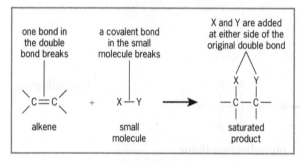

Figure 16.1 *Summary of addition reactions of alkenes*

Table 16.1 *Addition reactions of alkenes*

Reaction	Equation and conditions for reactions of ethene	Product
Hydrogenation Addition of **hydrogen** The hydrogen adds across the C=C bond of the alkenes.	 or propene + hydrogen $\xrightarrow[\text{5 atm, 150 °C}]{\text{Ni catalyst}}$ propane or $C_3H_6(g)$ + $H_2(g)$ $\xrightarrow[\text{5 atm, 150 °C}]{\text{Ni catalyst}}$ $C_3H_8(g)$	Alkanes
Halogenation Addition of **halogens** (chlorine gas, bromine vapour, or a solution of bromine in water or tetrachloromethane). If bromine is added, then the bromine vapour or bromine solution changes colour **rapidly** from **red-brown to colourless.** Chlorine reacts much faster than bromine, iodine reacts slowly. In this reaction the halogen adds across the C=C bond of the alkenes.	ethene + chlorine → **1,2-dichloroethane** or $C_2H_4(g) + Cl_2(g) \longrightarrow C_2H_4Cl_2(l)$	Haloalkanes
Addition of **hydrogen halides (HX)**, (hydrogen chloride, hydrogen bromide or hydrogen iodide). The H–X adds across the C=C bond of the alkenes.	ethene + hydrogen bromide → **monobromoethane** or $C_2H_4(g) + HBr(g) \longrightarrow C_2H_5Br(l)$	Haloalkanes
Hydration Addition of **water** in the form of steam. A mixture of steam and alkene is passed over a catalyst. The molecule of water adds across the C=C bond of the alkenes.	ethene + water → **ethanol**, using $\xrightarrow[\text{70 atm, 300 °C}]{\text{H}_3\text{PO}_4 \text{ in sand catalyst}}$ or $C_2H_4(g) + H_2O(g)$ $\xrightarrow[\text{70 atm, 300 °C}]{\text{H}_3\text{PO}_4 \text{ in sand catalyst}}$ $C_2H_5OH(l)$	Alcohols

Table 16.1 *Continued*

Reaction	Equation and conditions for reactions of ethene	Product
Oxidation Addition reaction with **acidified potassium manganate(VII) solution**. The acidified potassium manganate (VII) solution changes colour rapidly from **purple to colourless**. The alkene **reduces** the purple (MnO_4^-) ion to the colourless (Mn^{2+}) ion.	 ethene from oxidising agent ethane-1,2-diol or $C_2H_4(g) + H_2O(l) + [O] \longrightarrow C_2H_4(OH)_2(l)$	Dialcohols
Polymerisation	When exposed to high pressure, a catalyst and heat, alkene molecules open up their C=C bond and join with each other to undergo addition reactions to form large molecules called **polyalkenes**, e.g. ethene forms **polyethene** (see page 280).	Polyalkenes

Distinguishing between an alkane and an alkene

An alkane can be distinguished from an alkene by reacting both with **bromine** solution or **acidified potassium manganate(VII)** solution. Alkanes and alkenes have different functional groups, and the alkanes are saturated compounds, whereas the alkenes are unsaturated compounds. So the tests outlined in Table 16.2 are used to check whether the compound contains a carbon–carbon double bond, which means it is **unsaturated**.

Table 16.2 *Distinguishing between an alkane and an alkene*

Test	Observations and their explanations	
	Alkane	Alkene
Add **bromine solution**, i.e. bromine dissolved in water (bromine water) or in tetrachloromethane	The solution stays **red-brown**. **No reaction** occurs between the alkane and bromine under normal laboratory conditions.	The solution **rapidly** changes colour from red-brown to **colourless**. A **rapid addition reaction** occurs between the alkene and bromine solution forming a **colourless** haloalkane.
Add **acidified potassium manganate(VII) solution**	The solution stays **purple**. **No reaction** occurs between the alkane and acidified potassium manganate(VII) solution.	The solution **rapidly** changes colour from purple to **colourless**. A **rapid addition reaction** occurs during which the alkene reduces the purple MnO_4^- ion to the **colourless** Mn^{2+} ion.

Note In **UV light**, alkanes cause a solution of bromine to **slowly** change colour from red-brown to **colourless** due to the **slow substitution** reaction occurring.

Uses of alkanes and alkenes

Uses of alkanes

- Alkanes are used as **fuels** for the following reasons:
  - They **burn** very easily.
  - They release large amounts of **energy** when they burn because the reactions are exothermic.
  - They burn with **clean blue flames** which contain very little soot.
  - They are easy to **store**, **transport** and **distribute**.
- Alkanes are used as **solvents** because they are **non-polar** and are able to dissolve other non-polar solutes. For example, hexane and heptane are used as solvents for making fast-drying glues and extracting oils from seeds.
- The halogenated hydrocarbons, such as chlorofluorocarbons (or CFCs), are used as aerosols, refrigerants and propellants. The destruction of the ozone layer in the atmosphere has been attributed to CFCs. These compounds are being switched to more environmentally friendly products. They are also used as solvents for dry cleaning and as anaesthetics. They can also be used as pesticides.

Biogas production

Biogas is a **renewable energy source**. It is produced by naturally occurring anaerobic bacteria breaking down organic matter in the absence of oxygen in an **anaerobic digester**. The organic matter can be manure, sewage, organic waste generated in the kitchen or other food industry and garden waste. The biogas produced is a mixture of approximately **60% methane, 40% carbon dioxide** and traces of other gases, e.g., hydrogen sulfide. The composition of biogas varies, depending on the type of organic matter used in the process.

Biogas can be used directly as a **fuel** for cooking, heating and to generate electricity, or it can be upgraded to almost pure methane, known as **biomethane**, by removal of the other gases. Biomethane can also be used as fuel in vehicles designed to utilise liquified natural gas (LNG) as their fuel source. This alternative and renewable fuel source reduces the demands on fossil fuels.

The residual matter after the anaerobic digestion is complete can be used as fertilisers, so nutrients are added back to the soil. Biogas production is an environmentally friendly process because it reduces the quantity of waste which enters landfills and dumps.

Uses of alkenes

Alkenes are used as **starting materials** in the manufacture of a wide variety of important chemicals because they readily undergo **addition reactions**. They are used to manufacture ethanol and other **alcohols**, **antifreezes** such as ethane-1,2-diol, **synthetic rubbers** and a variety of **haloalkanes**. Because they can undergo polymerisation reactions, they are used to manufacture a wide range of polymers, also known as **plastics** (see page 280).

Margarines and solid cooking fats are produced from vegetable oils by a process known as hardening. Vegetable oils are soft and contain esters of long chain carboxylic acids with numerous double bonds. These are called polyunsaturated esters. These oils undergo the process of hydrogenation in which hydrogen atoms are added across the double bonds to make saturated hard fats with higher melting points. Polyunsaturated oils are thought to be healthier than saturated fats.

Ethene is produced by unripe fruits in minute quantities and this compound assists in the ripening of the fruits. Unripe fruits such as bananas and tomatoes, for example, are shipped green and this prevents them from spoiling before they reach the consumers. The fruits are then exposed to ethene gas which ripens the fruit.

Recalling facts

1 What are the products of complete combustion of an alkane?

  a carbon dioxide only

  b carbon monoxide and water

  c carbon dioxide and water

  d carbon dioxide, carbon monoxide and water

2 Which statement is NOT correct about the reaction of methane and chlorine?

  a Ultraviolet light is necessary for the reaction.

  b The reaction does not occur in the dark.

  c The hydrogen atoms are replaced by chlorine atoms.

  d The reaction occurs quickly in dim light.

3 Which statement is correct when distinguishing between an alkane and an alkene?

  a An alkane rapidly changes bromine water from red-brown to colourless.

  b When an alkene is added to bromine water, there is no colour change.

  c A colour change from purple to colourless occurs when an alkane is added to acidified potassium(VII) solution.

  d A colour change from purple to colourless occurs when an alkene is added to acidified potassium(VII) solution.

4 Which is NOT correct when an alkene is burnt?

  a Carbon dioxide and water are produced.

  b The reaction is exothermic.

  c A blue flame is produced.

  d A smoky yellow flame is produced.

5 Which of the following is NOT a necessary condition for the formation of ethanol from ethene?

  a H_3PO_4 in a sand catalyst

  b 70 atm, 300 °C

  c 5 atm, 150 °C

  d addition of water in the form of steam

6 Which of the following statements is NOT true?

  a Alkanes are used as solvents.

  b Alkanes release a large amount of energy when burnt.

  c Alkanes are clean-burning fuels.

  d Alkanes produce a smoky yellow flame when burnt in plenty of air.

7 Which is NOT correct about biogas?

a It is a renewable source of energy.

b It can be used directly as a fuel.

c It can be converted to pure methane.

d It is produced by breaking down organic matter in the presence of oxygen.

8 Alkenes are used to produce all of the following except:

a antifreeze

b synthetic rubbers

c polymers

d biomethane

9 Give five uses of alkanes and alkenes.

Applying facts

10 Alkanes are saturated and alkenes are unsaturated. Discuss this statement in terms of the types of bonds or functional groups these compounds possess and their chemical reactivity. Describe a test to distinguish between unsaturated and saturated compounds.

11 a Using a suitable example, discuss what is meant by the term 'substitution reaction'. In your explanation you must state the conditions necessary, the homologous series with which this type of reaction occurs, write equations and formulae for all the steps which can occur for complete substitution, and name the products formed in each step.

b What factors affect the rate of substitution reactions?

12 Discuss the five different types of reactions that occur with members of the homologous series alkenes. You should choose a member of the series and state the conditions necessary for the reactions, giving the products and the necessary balanced equations for each reaction. Also explain the importance of each of these reactions.

Analysing data

13 Are alkanes soluble in water? Explain your answer.

Alcohols: $C_nH_{2n+1}OH$ or R–OH

Alcohols (or **alkanols**) have the **hydroxyl group, –OH**, as their functional group. All alcohols undergo similar reactions because they all contain the **hydroxyl group**; however, the strength of the reactions **decreases** as the number of carbon atoms per molecule increases.

General physical properties of alcohols

Alcohols are colourless sweet-smelling liquids that have low boiling points. The boiling points of the alcohols increases as the number of carbon atoms increases. As the number of carbon atoms increases, the size of the molecules increases and so do the intermolecular forces, resulting in an increase in the energy required to break these bonds; hence the increasing boiling points. These covalent molecules are **polar** because they possess the polar **–OH group**. Because of this:

- Alcohols are **less volatile** than their corresponding alkanes. Because of the polar –OH groups, the forces of attraction between alcohol molecules are stronger than the forces between non-polar alkane molecules with the same number of carbon atoms. All alcohols are **liquids or solids** at room temperature. Their boiling points **increase** as the number of carbon atoms per molecule increases.

- Alcohols are **soluble** in water because water is a polar solvent. Their solubility **decreases** as the number of carbon atoms per molecule increases.

Alcohols undergo combustion, reactions with reactive metals, dehydration and oxidation. These reactions are demonstrated here using ethanol.

Reactions of ethanol

- **Ethanol burns easily in air or oxygen**

Ethanol burns in excess air or oxygen to produce **carbon dioxide** and **water** as steam. It burns with a **clear, blue, non-smoky flame** because of the **low** ratio of carbon to hydrogen atoms in the molecules. Incomplete burning occurs if the air or oxygen supply is insufficient, producing carbon (smoky flame), carbon monoxide, carbon dioxide and water just like the alkanes and alkenes. The reaction is **exothermic** The balanced equation for the combustion of ethanol in excess air or oxygen is:

$$C_2H_5OH(l) + 3O_2(g) \longrightarrow 2CO_2(g) + 3H_2O(g) \qquad \Delta H \text{ –ve}$$

- **Ethanol reacts with reactive metals**

Ethanol reacts with reactive metals (sodium and lithium, for example) to give the metal **ethoxide** (C_2H_5OX) where X is the reactive metal, and **hydrogen**. The metal displaces the hydrogen from the hydroxyl group (–OH) and forms hydrogen gas, so effervescence is observed. A colourless solution is produced. The reaction is like that of a metal and water except that it is less vigorous. The balanced equation for the reaction of ethanol with sodium is:

$$2C_2H_5OH(l) + 2Na(s) \longrightarrow 2C_2H_5ONa(\text{alc sol}) + H_2(g)$$
$$\text{sodium ethoxide}$$

Note 'alc sol' is 'alcohol solution'

Sodium ethoxide is an ionic compound which contains the ethoxide ion $C_2H_5O^-$.

- **Ethanol undergoes dehydration**

Ethene is produced when ethanol reacts with dehydrating agents, such as anhydrous aluminium oxide or concentrated sulfuric acid. A molecule of water is lost when ethanol is dehydrated. A double bond is formed between the two adjacent carbon atoms containing the hydroxyl group where a water molecule is lost.

For example: ethanol can be **dehydrated** to **ethene** in two ways:

- Heating ethanol at a temperature of about 170 °C with excess concentrated sulfuric acid. The acid acts as a catalyst:

$$C_2H_5OH(l) \xrightarrow[\text{170 °C}]{\text{conc. } H_2SO_4} C_2H_4(g) + H_2O(g)$$

- Passing ethanol vapour over heated aluminium oxide. The aluminium oxide acts as a catalyst.

- **Ethanol undergoes oxidation**

Ethanol is **oxidised** to **ethanoic acid** when heated with acidified potassium manganate(VII) solution or acidified potassium dichromate(VI) solution. Ethanol acts as a **reducing agent**.

$$C_2H_5OH(l) \quad + \quad 2[O] \longrightarrow CH_3COOH(aq) \quad + \quad H_2O(l)$$

| ethanol | from oxidising agent | ethanoic acid |

Orange acidified potassium dichromate(VI) crystals can be used in the **breathalyser test** to determine the alcohol content of a driver's breath. The driver blows over the crystals and if ethanol vapour is present, it **reduces** the **orange** dichromate(VI) ion ($Cr_2O_7^{2-}$) to the **green** chromium(III) ion (Cr^{3+}). This turns the crystals green.

- **Ethanol reacts with alkanoic acids**

Ethanol reacts with alkanoic acids to produce an **ester** and **water** (see page 270).

Production of ethanol by fermentation of carbohydrates

Ethanol can be produced by using **yeast** to **ferment** carbohydrates under **anaerobic** conditions (without oxygen, Figure 16.2). Yeasts are microorganisms which produce enzymes that break down complex carbohydrates into simple sugars, mainly glucose. They then produce the enzyme **zymase**, which changes the simple sugars into **ethanol** and **carbon dioxide**, as shown in the equation below:

$$C_6H_{12}O_6(aq) \xrightarrow{\text{zymase in yeast}} 2C_2H_5OH(aq) + 2CO_2(g) \qquad \Delta H\ -ve$$
$$\text{glucose} \hspace{5cm} \text{ethanol}$$

Fermentation stops when the concentration of ethanol in the fermentation mixture reaches about 14%. At this concentration, the ethanol starts to denature the zymase and this stops it from working. Ethanol which is about 96% pure is then obtained from the fermentation mixture using **fractional distillation** (see page 29), collecting the fraction that distils at 78 °C (Figure 16.3).

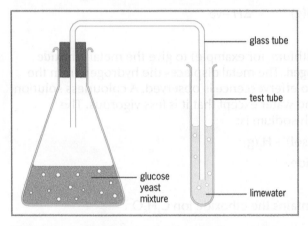

Figure 16.2 *Ethanol production by fermentation*

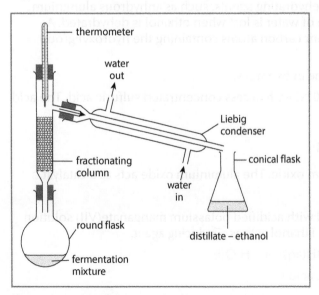

Figure 16.3 *Separation of ethanol produced by fermentation using fractional distillation*

Fermentation of carbohydrates is used to produce a variety of different **alcoholic beverages**, including wine and rum.

- **Wine** is mainly made from **grapes** in a winery. The yeast is added to the crushed grapes (known as must) and it ferments the sugars present under anaerobic conditions. During the fermentation process, ethanol and carbon dioxide are produced. When fermentation is complete, the wine is clarified and aged before bottling. Air should not come into contact with the wine because certain aerobic bacteria **oxidise** the ethanol to **ethanoic acid**, or vinegar, causing the wine to become sour:

$$C_2H_5OH(aq) + O_2(g) \xrightarrow{\text{anaerobic bacteria}} CH_3COOH(aq) + H_2O(l)$$
$$\text{ethanoic acid}$$

In the Caribbean, many different fruits, flowers and plant materials are fermented to produce wines. Fruits and other starchy materials (such as mangoes, pommecythere and pineapple), flowers (such as hibiscus flowers) and other plant materials (such as the petals from sorrel and extracts from the aloe vera plant) are used.

- **Rum** is made from **molasses** in a rum distillery. The yeast is added to the molasses and it ferments the sugars present, mainly sucrose, glucose and fructose. The yeast secretes two enzymes: invertase and zymase. The invertase catalyses the conversion of sucrose into glucose and fructose and the zymase catalyses the breakdown of glucose and fructose into ethanol and carbon dioxide. The mixture is then **fractionally distilled**. The distillate is diluted with water and transferred to oak barrels to be aged. After the aging process, more water is added to decrease the alcohol content and then various aged rums are blended to produce the different brands produced by the different manufacturers.

Alkanoic acids: $C_nH_{2n+1}COOH$ or R–COOH

Alkanoic acids (or **carboxylic acids**) have the **carboxyl** group, **–COOH**, as their functional group. The carboxyl group gives this group of compounds its acidic properties, relatively high boiling points and its solubility in water.

Alkanoic acids have higher boiling points than their corresponding alkanols and are less volatile than the corresponding alkanes with the same number of carbon atoms. The molecules are **polar** due to the **–OH** part of the functional group being polar. Like alcohols, alkanoic acids are **less volatile** than their corresponding alkanes and are **soluble** in water. As the molecular mass of the alkanoic acid increases, the solubility in water decreases because the attractive force of the –OH group decreases with increasing number of carbon atoms in the hydrocarbon chain. When they dissolve in water they **partially** ionise, and are therefore **weak acids**:

for example: $CH_3COOH(aq) \rightleftharpoons CH_3COO^-(aq) + H^+(aq)$
                   ethanoic acid   ethanoate ion

and

                   $C_2H_5COOH(aq) \rightleftharpoons C_2H_5COO^-(aq) + H^+(aq)$
                   propanoic acid   propanoate ion

Reactions of aqueous ethanoic acid

Aqueous solutions of alkanoic acids react in a similar way to inorganic acids, such as hydrochloric acid, though the reactions are **slower** because the acids are weak. The hydrogen in the functional group can be replaced directly or indirectly by a metal to form a salt. The salts formed by ethanoic acid are called **ethanoates**.

- **Aqueous ethanoic acid reacts with reactive metals**

  Ethanoic acid reacts with reactive metals, such as sodium, magnesium and calcium, to form a **salt** and **hydrogen** gas:

for example: $Mg(s) + 2CH_3COOH(aq) \longrightarrow (CH_3COO)_2Mg(aq) + H_2(g)$
magnesium ethanoate

- **Aqueous ethanoic acid reacts with metal oxides and metal hydroxides**

   Ethanoic acid reacts with metal oxides and hydroxides to form a **salt** and **water**:

   for example: $CuO(s) + 2CH_3COOH(aq) \longrightarrow (CH_3COO)_2Cu(aq) + H_2O(l)$
copper(II) ethanoate

   $LiOH(aq) + CH_3COOH(aq) \longrightarrow CH_3COOLi(aq) + H_2O(l)$
lithium ethanoate

- **Aqueous ethanoic acid reacts with metal carbonates**

   Ethanoic acid reacts with metal carbonates to form a **salt**, **carbon dioxide** and **water**:

   for example: $ZnCO_3(s) + 2CH_3COOH(aq) \longrightarrow (CH_3COO)_2Zn(aq) + CO_2(g) + H_2O(l)$
zinc ethanoate

Reactions of anhydrous ethanoic acid

Anhydrous (water-free) ethanoic acid reacts with **alcohols** to produce an **ester** and **water** (see below).

Esters: $C_nH_{2n+1}COOC_xH_{2x+1}$ or R–COO–R′

An **ester** is formed when an **alkanoic acid** reacts with an **alcohol**. The reaction is a type of **condensation reaction** where the two molecules join to form a larger molecule with the loss of a water molecule. This condensation reaction is known as **esterification**, and it requires concentrated sulfuric acid and heat. As can be seen in the equation below, there is a two-way arrow signifying that the reaction is an equilibrium reaction, so there will never be complete conversion of all the reactants, that is, the alkanoic acid and the alcohol to the ester and water. All four compounds (the two reactants and the two products) would be in the final mixture. The ester is separated by fractional distillation.

It should also be noted that the OH from the carboxyl group of the alkanoic acid and the H from the hydroxyl group of the alcohol form the water in the reaction:

$$\text{alkanoic acid} + \text{alcohol} \underset{\text{heat}}{\overset{\text{conc. } H_2SO_4}{\rightleftharpoons}} \text{ester} + \text{water}$$

Example 2

ethanoic acid	butanol	butyl ethanoate	water

or $CH_3COOH(l) + C_4H_9OH(l) \underset{\text{heat}}{\overset{\text{conc. } H_2SO_4}{\rightleftharpoons}} CH_3COOC_4H_9(l) + H_2O(l)$

The concentrated sulfuric acid is added for **two** reasons:

- To act as a **catalyst** to **speed up** the reaction.

- To **remove the water** produced during the reaction. This favours the forward reaction and **increases the yield** of ester.

Esters have the **ester group**, **–COO–**, as their functional group:

$$-\overset{\displaystyle O}{\underset{\displaystyle ||}{C}}-O-$$

Many esters are found naturally. Those with a low number of carbon atoms in their molecules are volatile liquids (short chain esters) which usually have very distinctive sweet, fruity smells. They are found especially in flowers and fruit. Animal fats and vegetable oils are esters formed from **fatty acids** (long chain alkanoic acids), and **glycerol** (an alcohol).

Writing the formulae and names of esters

When writing formula and name of an ester:

- **Formula:** the part from the **acid** comes first
  the part from the **alcohol** comes second.
- **Name:** the prefix from the **alcohol**, ending in '**-yl**', comes first
  the prefix from the **acid**, ending in '**-anoate**', comes second.

Example 3

$$C_3H_7COOH \quad + \quad CH_3OH \rightleftharpoons C_3H_7COOCH_3 \quad + \quad H_2O$$

butanoic aid   methanol   methyl butanoate

Table 16.3 *Formulae and names of some esters*

Alkanoic acid	Alcohol	Ester
CH_3COOH ethanoic acid	C_2H_5OH ethanol	$CH_3COOC_2H_5$ ethyl ethanoate
$HCOOH$ methanoic acid	C_2H_5OH ethanol	$HCOOC_2H_5$ ethyl methanoate
CH_3COOH ethanoic acid	CH_3OH methanol	CH_3COOCH_3 methyl ethanoate
C_2H_5COOH propanoic acid	CH_3OH methanol	$C_2H_5COOCH_3$ methyl propanoate
C_2H_5COOH propanoic acid	C_3H_7OH propanol	$C_2H_5COOC_3H_7$ propyl propanoate

Hydrolysis of esters

During **hydrolysis**, molecules of a compound are broken down into smaller molecules by reacting the compound with **water**. Hydrolysis of esters can be carried out by heating the ester with a dilute acid or an aqueous alkali.

- **Acid hydrolysis** involves heating the ester with dilute hydrochloric or sulfuric acid. The acid acts as a **catalyst**. The products are the **alkanoic acid** and the **alcohol** from which the ester was formed:

$$C_2H_5COOC_3H_7(aq) + H_2O(l) \overset{H^+ \text{ ions}}{\rightleftharpoons} C_2H_5COOH(aq) + C_3H_7OH(aq)$$
propyl propanoate   propanoic acid   propanol

- **Alkaline hydrolysis** involves heating the ester with potassium or sodium hydroxide solution. The products are the **potassium** or **sodium salt** of the **alkanoic acid** and the **alcohol** from which the ester was formed. This is a two-stage process. The propanoic acid and propanol are formed first, as in the process of acid hydrolysis. Then the propanoic acid is neutralised by potassium hydroxide to form potassium propanoate. The equations for stage I and II are:

Stage I

$$C_2H_5COOC_3H_7(aq) + H_2O(l) \underset{}{\overset{OH^- \text{ ions}}{\rightleftharpoons}} C_2H_5COOH(aq) + C_3H_7OH(aq)$$

propyl propanoate   propanoic acid   propanol

Stage II

$$C_2H_5COOH(l) \quad + \quad KOH(aq) \quad \rightleftharpoons \quad C_2H_5COOK(aq) \quad + \quad H_2O(l)$$

propanoic acid   potassium hydroxide   potassium propanoate   water

The overall reaction is illustrated in the equation:

$$C_2H_5COOC_3H_7(aq) + \quad KOH(aq) \quad \longrightarrow \quad C_2H_5COOK(aq) \quad + \quad C_3H_7OH(aq)$$

propyl propanoate   potassium hydroxide   potassium propanoate   propanol

Saponification of fats and oils – making soap

Saponification refers to the process that produces **soap**. During saponification, large ester molecules found in animal fats and vegetable oils undergo **alkaline hydrolysis** by being boiled with concentrated potassium or sodium hydroxide solution. The reaction produces **soap**, which is the potassium or sodium salt of a long chain alkanoic acid (**fatty acid**) and **glycerol** ($C_3H_5(OH)_3$). The soap made from the salt of sodium is hard soap and that from the salt of potassium is soft soap.

A simplified equation for this reaction is:

$$\text{fat or oil} + NaOH \xrightarrow{\text{heat}} \text{sodium salt of a long chain alkanoic acid} + \text{glycerol}$$

The fat **glyceryl octadecanoate** (($C_{17}H_{35}COO)_3C_3H_5$) is an ester of **octadecanoic acid** ($C_{17}H_{35}COOH$) and **glycerol** ($C_3H_5(OH)_3$). Saponification of glyceryl octadecanoate by boiling with sodium hydroxide solution, forms **sodium octadecanoate** ($C_{17}H_{35}COONa$) and **glycerol**. Sodium octadecanoate, also called sodium stearate, is the most common form of **soap** (Figure 16.4).

$$(C_{17}H_{35}COO)_3C_3H_5(l) + 3NaOH(aq) \xrightarrow{\text{heat}} 3C_{17}H_{35}COONa(aq) + C_3H_5(OH)_3(aq)$$

glyceryl octadecanoate   sodium octadecanoate   glycerol
(fat)   (soap)

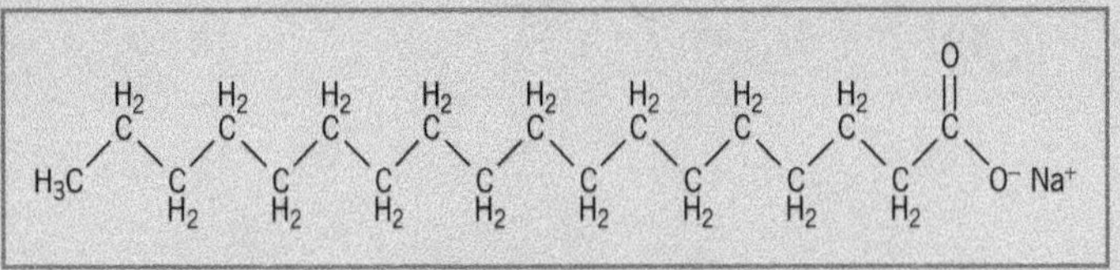

Figure 16.4 *A soap molecule*

Sodium palmitate is another example of soaps. Here palmitic acid is hexadecanoic acid.

Soapy and soapless detergents

Soapy and **soapless detergents** are organic substances which are added to water to remove dirt, for example, from the skin, clothes, household surfaces and floors.

- **Soapy detergents** are made by boiling animal fats or vegetable fats and oils with concentrated potassium or sodium hydroxide solution. They may be simply called **soaps**, for example, sodium octadecanoate, $C_{17}H_{35}COO^-Na^+$.
- **Soapless detergents** are formed from **petroleum**. They are also known as 'synthetic detergents' and may be simply called **detergents**, for example, sodium dodecyl sulfate, $C_{12}H_{25}OSO_3^-Na^+$.

The detergent molecule consists of a hydrophilic or polar water-loving head and a non-polar hydrophobic tail. The hydrophobic tail is grease-loving but water-hating. The tail comprises the fatty part of the molecule (see Figure 16.5). Grease and oils are non-polar molecules and are immiscible in water. In other words, they do not dissolve in water. To remove dirt which is attached to the grease and oils from surfaces, these surfaces must be in contact with a detergent and water mixture. The non-polar tail of the detergent molecules affixes itself to the grease and oil while the hydrophobic head stays dissolved in the water. When there is constant agitation of the mixture, the dirt is extricated from the surface and the hydrophobic tails of the detergent molecules attach themselves all around the grease molecules while the hydrophobic heads remain in the water (see Figure 16.6). This keeps the dirt dispersed in the water and when the surface is rinsed the detergent–grease complexes are removed.

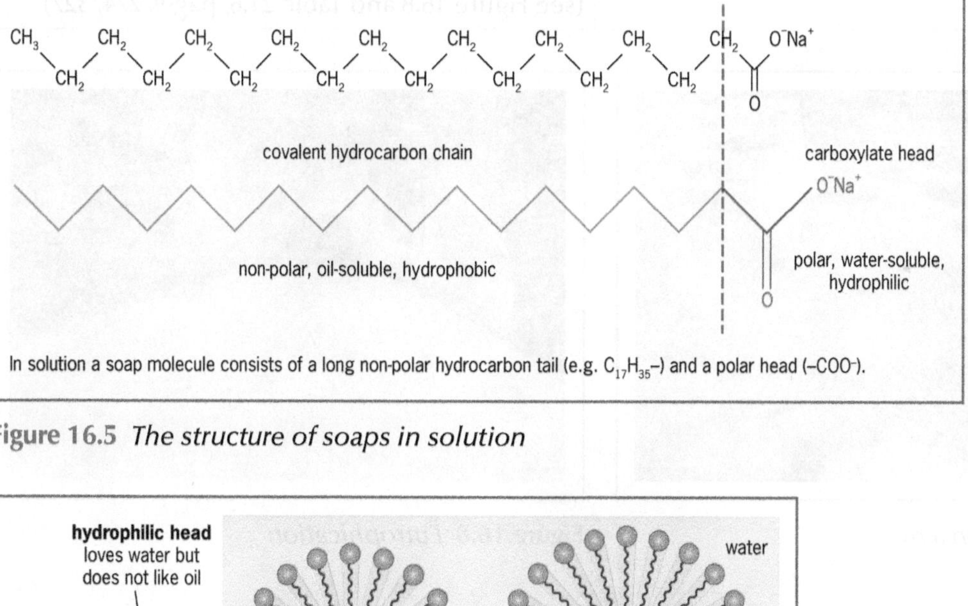

![Diagram showing the structure of a soap molecule: a covalent hydrocarbon chain labelled CH₃, CH₂ repeating units ending in a carboxylate head O⁻Na⁺. The chain is non-polar, oil-soluble, hydrophobic; the carboxylate head is polar, water-soluble, hydrophilic.]

In solution a soap molecule consists of a long non-polar hydrocarbon tail (e.g. $C_{17}H_{35}-$) and a polar head ($-COO^-$).

Figure 16.5 *The structure of soaps in solution*

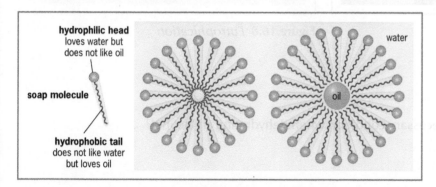

hydrophilic head
loves water but does not like oil

soap molecule

hydrophobic tail
does not like water but loves oil

water

oil

Figure 16.6 *Formation of a detergent–grease complex*

The differences between soaps and soapless detergents are given in Table 16.4.

Table 16.4 *The differences between soapy and soapless detergents*

Soapy detergents	Soapless detergents
Manufactured from fats and oils, a **renewable** resource which will not run out.	Manufactured from petroleum, a **non-renewable** resource which will eventually run out.
Do not lather easily in hard water containing Ca^{2+} and Mg^{2+} ions. Their calcium and magnesium salts are insoluble and form unpleasant **scum** (see page 336). This wastes soap, discolours clothes and forms an unpleasant grey, greasy layer around sinks, baths and showers.	Lather easily in hard water. Their calcium and magnesium salts are soluble, so they **do not** form scum.
Are **biodegradable**, meaning they are broken down by bacteria in the environment. They **do not** cause foam to form on waterways such as lakes and rivers, or in sewage systems.	Some are **non-biodegradable**. These can cause **foam** to form on waterways and in sewage systems (Figure 16.7). This causes aquatic organisms to die because oxygen can no longer dissolve in the water, and it makes sewage treatment difficult. Most modern soapless detergents are now biodegradable.
Do not contain phosphates, so they **do not** cause eutrophication of aquatic environments.	Some contain **phosphates**, added to improve their cleaning ability. Phosphates cause pollution of aquatic environments by causing the rapid growth of green algae known as **eutrophication** (see Figure 16.8 and Table 21.6, pages 274, 327).

Figure 16.7 *Foam on a river*

Figure 16.8 *Eutrophication*

Recalling facts

 14 Which is NOT a necessary condition when dehydrating an alcohol?

   a conc. H_2SO_4

   b 170 °C

   c Ni catalyst

   d aluminium oxide

15 When ethane is burnt in oxygen:

    a carbon dioxide is produced only.

    b carbon dioxide and water are produced.

    c the reaction is endothermic.

    d a sooty flame is produced.

16 When ethanol reacts with sodium:

    a covalent sodium ethoxide is produced.

    b sodium displaces hydrogen from ethanol.

    c carbon dioxide is produced.

    d a blue solution is formed.

17 In the following reaction:

$$C_2H_5OH(l) + 2[O] \longrightarrow CH_3COOH(aq) + H_2O(l)$$

the ethanol is:

    a behaving as an oxidising agent   **c** undergoes hydrogenation

    b behaving as a reducing agent   **d** reduced

18 In the production of ethanol by fermentation which statement is NOT correct:

    a ethanol and carbon dioxide are produced.

    b zymase in yeast breaks down complex carbohydrates.

    c the reaction is anaerobic.

    d ethanol destroys the zymase enzyme.

19 When a metal carbonate reacts with ethanoic acid:

    a a salt is produced only.

    b salt and water are produced only.

    c a salt, water and carbon dioxide are produced.

    d a salt, water and hydrogen gas are produced.

20 Name the following ester:

$C_2H_5COOCH_3$

    a methyl propanoate

    b ethyl propanoate

    c butyl methanoate

    d ethyl butanoate

21 When ethyl ethanoate undergoes alkaline hydrolysis using sodium hydroxide:

    a sodium ethanoate is produced only.

    b ethanoic acid and ethanol are produced only.

    c the reaction occurs in one step.

    d sodium ethanoate and ethanol are produced.

22 Soapless detergents are:

    a natural

    b synthetic

    c biodegradable

    d made from renewable resources

23 Saponification is:

    a acid hydrolysis of large esters

    b alkaline hydrolysis of large esters

    c when fats and oils are boiled with an alkali

    d when glycerol is one of the products of the reaction

24 List three general properties of alcohols.

25 Write the equations and observations for the reactions of ethanol with **a** excess air and **b** sodium.

26 Alkanoic acids are weak acids. Explain.

Applying facts

27 There are two different ways of making ethanol. One is via a natural process and the other is from using hydrocarbons. Name each of these methods and outline how ethanol is produced using each of these two methods. Your answer must include the starting materials, the conditions, procedure and equations for the reactions.

28 Alkanoic acids undergo reactions in a similar way to inorganic acids, except these reactions are slower. Give two such reactions. Include balanced equations in your answer.

29 **a** What is an ester?

    b State two uses of esters.

    c **i** Write an equation for the reaction between propanoic acid and propanol, showing the formation of the water molecules.

       ii Name the ester formed.

      iii Why is concentrated sulfuric acid used in this reaction?

30 Describe how soaps are used to remove dirt from clothing. Include in your discussion how the grease–detergent complex is formed.

17 Polymers

Learning objectives

- Describe the term **polymers**.
- Explain the formation of **addition** and **condensation polymerisation** and give examples.
- Deduce the structure of polymers given a **monomer**.
- Deduce the structure of a monomer given the polymer.
- State the uses of **addition** and **condensation polymers**.
- Discuss the positive and negative effects of **plastics**.

Polymers are large molecules (macromolecules) which are made from many repeating small molecules, known as **monomers**, bonded together. They are formed from hydrocarbons and hydrocarbon derivatives. There are different types of polymers. Some occur in nature, including wool, hair, rubber, proteins, starches and cellulose; while others are synthetic and are referred to as plastics, for example, polystyrene, synthetic rubber, polyester, Teflon, PVC and nylon. Polymers are everywhere and form a part of our daily lives. In fact, it can be said that synthetic polymers have revolutionised our society. While polymers have benefitted humankind, there are ill-effects of these plastics on society, and for this reason it is important to understand the chemistry of polymers, so that their manufacture, use and recycling can efficiently and effectively benefit society.

*A **polymer** is a macromolecule formed by linking together 50 or more monomers, usually in chains.*

Formation of polymers

A polymer may contain thousands of monomers. They are typically in the form of long chains, often with cross links. The reaction by which a polymer is formed from monomers is known as **polymerisation**. There are **unsaturated monomers**, which are unsaturated hydrocarbons, such as those which belong to the homologous series alkenes. Another type of monomers are **bifunctional monomers**. A **bifunctional monomer** contains two functional groups, which can be identical or different. The functional groups include the hydroxyl group (OH) and/or carboxyl group (COOH). Examples of these are ethane 1,2-diol and amino acids. These **bifunctional monomers** bind with other bifunctional monomers. There are **two** types of polymerisation reactions and the polymer formed depends on the type of monomer (unsaturated or bifunctional) used to make up the polymers (Table 17.1). The two types of polymerisation reactions are as follows:

- **Addition polymerisation** occurs when **unsaturated** monomers, such as **alkenes**, are linked together to form a **saturated** polymer known as an **addition polymer**. One bond in the double bond of each alkene molecule breaks and the molecules bond to one another in chains by single covalent bonds between adjacent carbon atoms. In the presence of heat, pressure, and a suitable catalyst these unsaturated monomers bond with each other, forming long chains containing between 50 and 50 000 monomers. The resulting structure is named the poly(unsaturated monomer) and is represented by the structure of the saturated monomer in brackets and an "*n*" representing the number of repeating units. For example, the polymer ethene is named poly(ethene) and its diagrammatic representation is shown in Table 17.3 (see page 279). There is no loss of atoms during addition polymerisation. Addition polymers are made from small alkenes, such as ethene and propene. These small alkenes are produced from the cracking of large alkanes, such as naphtha and other petroleum fractions. Some examples of addition polymers are polyethene and polypropene, which are made of repeating units of ethene and propene, respectively, forming long chains (see Table 17.2 for the classification of polymers and 17.3 for the formation of different polymers).

- **Condensation polymerisation** involves linking monomers together in chains by eliminating a **small molecule**, usually water, from between adjacent monomers. A hydrogen atom comes from one of the bifunctional monomer units and the OH comes from the other adjacent bifunctional monomer. When this small molecule is eliminated only then can the monomers link and bond to form the long chains. Other small molecules that can be lost during condensation polymerisation are hydrogen chloride HCl and ammonia (NH_3). For this to occur, the monomer molecules must be **bifunctional monomers**. The polymers formed are known as **condensation polymers**. Examples of condensation reactions are found in the manufacture of polyester, polyamide, proteins and polysaccharides. These condensation polymers have specific linkages: polyesters have an ester link, polyamides have an amide or peptide link, polysaccharides have an ether link. Table 17.2 gives examples of condensation polymers and Table 17.3 gives the formation of the characteristic links found in condensation polymers.

Table 17.1 *Addition and condensation polymerisation compared*

Addition polymerisation	Condensation polymerisation
The polymer is the **only product.**	**Two products** are formed, the polymer and small molecules, usually water.
The polymer is made from monomers which are all the **same.**	The polymer is often made from **more than one** type of monomer.
The **empirical formula** of the polymer is the **same** as the monomer from which it was formed; no atoms are lost during its formation.	The **empirical formula** of the polymer is **different** from the monomers; atoms are lost during its formation.

Table 17.2 *Classification of polymers*

Type of polymerisation	Type of polymer	Examples	
		Synthetic	Natural
Addition polymerisation	Polyalkene	Polyethene	None exist
		Polypropene	
		Polychloroethene (polyvinyl chloride or PVC)	
		Polystyrene (Styrofoam)	
Condensation polymerisation	Polyester	Polyethylene terephthalate (PET, Terylene or Dacron)	None exist
	Polyamide	Nylon	Proteins
	Polysaccharide	None exist	Starch
			Glycogen (animal starch)
			Cellulose

Table 17.3 *Formation of the different polymers*

Type of polymer	Type of linkage between monomers	Structure and name(s) of the monomer(s)	Structure and name of the polymer
Polyalkene	Alkane $-\overset{\mid}{\underset{\mid}{C}}-\overset{\mid}{\underset{\mid}{C}}-$	n ethene + n ethene	polyethene
		n chloroethene + n chloroethene	polychloroethene or polyvinyl chloride (PVC)
		n + n	If X = **CH$_3$**, the polymer is **polypropene**. If X = **C$_6$H$_5$**, the polymer is **polystyrene**
Polyester	Ester $-\overset{O}{\overset{\|}{C}}-O-$ or $-COO-$	n diacid + n dialcohol Y and Y represent variable hydrocarbon groups	a polyester
Polyamide	Amide (peptide) $-\overset{O}{\overset{\|}{C}}-\overset{H}{\underset{\mid}{N}}-$ or $-CONH-$	n diacid + n diamine Y and Y represent variable hydrocarbon groups	a polyamide
		n amino acid + n amino acid	a protein
Polysaccharide	Ether $-O-$	n monosaccharide (C$_6$H$_{12}$O$_6$) $\quad n$ monosaccharide (C$_6$H$_{12}$O$_6$) e.g. glucose, where X represents C$_6$H$_{10}$O$_4$	a polysaccharide

Note $-O-H \quad H-$ represents the loss of a water molecule (H$_2$O) from between adjacent monomers.

Uses of polymers

Synthetic polymers, commonly known as **plastics**, have a great many uses because their properties make them superior to many other materials. Table 17.4 and Figure 17.1 give examples of the uses of plastics based on the following properties:

- They are durable, that is, they are resistant to physical and chemical damage, and biological decay.
- They are easily moulded into many different shapes.
- They are light but strong.
- They are translucent and can be easily dyed resulting in different colours.
- They can be made to be rigid or flexible.
- They are good thermal and electrical insulators.
- They can be easily welded or joined.
- They can be spun into fibres because their molecules are extremely long.

Table 17.4 *Uses of polymers*

Polymer type	Name of polymer	Uses of polymer
Polyalkene	Polyethene	To make plastic bags, plastic bottles, plastic chairs, insulation around electrical wires, washing up bowls, buckets, tubing, packaging for food and cling wrap for wrapping fresh vegetables and food.
	Polychloroethene (PVC)	To make water and sewer pipes, guttering, window and door frames, water-proof plastic sheeting, surgical gloves and insulation for electrical wires and cables.
	Polypropene	To make ropes, carpets, plastic toys, plastic food containers and furniture.
	Polystyrene (Styrofoam)	To make containers for fast food and drinks, packaging materials and insulation materials.
Polyester	Polyethylene terephthalate (PET, Terylene or Dacron)	To make PET bottles for soft drinks. Fibres are used to make clothing, boat sails, carpets and fibre filling for winter clothing, sleeping bags and pillows.
Polyamide	Nylon	Fibres are used to make fishing lines and nets, ropes, carpets, parachutes, tents and clothing, especially if stretch is required, e.g. sports wear and nylon stockings.
	Protein	To build body cells, hair and nails. To make enzymes and antibodies.
Polysaccharide	Starch and glycogen	Stored as food reserves in living organisms. When needed, they can be broken down into glucose which is used in respiration to produce energy.
	Cellulose	To build plant cells walls.

Section B: Organic chemistry

Figure 17.1 *Uses of plastics*

Impact of synthetic polymers (plastics) on the environment

While **plastics** have many positive uses, **synthetic polymers** can have **harmful effects** on living organisms and the environment (pages 329):

- Most plastics are made from a **non-renewable resource** (petroleum). Their manufacture is contributing to the depletion of petroleum world wide.

- Most plastics are **non-biodegradable**. Microbes cannot decompose them naturally, nor are they decomposed by air. Waste plastics build up in the environment causing pollution of land and water.

- Most plastics are directly harmful to **aquatic organisms**, such as sea turtles and sea birds, due to ingestion, entanglement and suffocation.

- Various **toxic chemicals** are released into the environment during the manufacture of plastics, and some of these continue to be released from the plastic items during use and when discarded. For example, plastic foam uses chlorofluorocarbons (CFCs) in its manufacturing process and, as time passes, these gases escape from the plastic foam and are released into the atmosphere. CFCs are greenhouse gases; they react with ozone and deplete the ozone layer in the upper atmosphere and therefore contribute to global warming. Plastics include compounds called 'phthalates' and bisphenol-A (BPA) which, through scientific research, has been shown to affect genital development in boys and can cause breast cancer.
- Many plastics are **flammable**; they therefore pose fire risks.
- When burnt, plastics produce **dense smoke** and **poisonous gases**, such as carbon monoxide. PVC produces chlorine gas and nylon produces hydrogen cyanide, which can lead to air pollution.

Recalling facts

1 Which statement is TRUE about polymers?

  a They can be natural only.

  b They can be natural and synthetic.

  c They are made up of unsaturated monomers only.

  d They can be synthetic only.

2 All the polymers listed below are formed by condensation polymerisation except:

  a polyethene

  b nylon

  c dacron

  d glycogen

3 Which of the following is a natural polymer?

  a polyethene

  b nylon 6

  c cellulose

  d Styrofoam

4 The type of linkage in starch is:

  a amide

  b ester

  c ether

  d alkane

5 Which is NOT TRUE about condensation polymerisation?

  a Only one product is formed.

  b Two products are formed.

  c Water is a product.

  d The monomer molecule must have two functional groups.

6 The type of linkage in polystyrene is:

   a amide

   b alkane

   c ester

   d ether

7 The type of linkage in Terylene is:

   a amide

   b ester

   c ether

   d alkane

8 Which of the following is NOT a use of plastic?

   a water pipes

   b food packaging

   c ropes

   d antibodies

9 Which of the following is NOT a property of plastics?

   a durable

   b easily dyed

   c lightweight but strong

   d not easily moulded

10 Synthetic polymers are all of the following except:

   a plastics

   b made from renewable resources

   c most are non-biodegradable

   d releases toxic gases when burnt

11 Define the term polymer.

12 Condensation polymerisation involves the loss of a small molecule. Give three examples of such molecules.

Applying facts

13 Using a named monomer, explain what is meant by the term 'addition polymerisation'. Include in your explanation the conditions necessary, and a drawing of a partial structure showing at least three monomer units. Are any atoms lost during addition polymerisation?

14 Natural polymers are examples of condensation polymerisation. Using a named natural polymer, discuss how it is formed from its monomer units. In your explanation you must include the structure of the monomers involved, an equation showing the formation of the link, the name of the link and a diagram showing the link within the structure of the polymer.

15 List six properties of plastics and name examples in which they are used in everyday life.

Analysing data

16 Deduce from the structure the monomers present:

17 Plastics have both negative and positive impacts in society. Discuss this statement.

Section C
Inorganic chemistry

In this section

Characteristics of metals

- General properties of metals; bonding in the metal lattice; equations of metals with oxygen, water and dilute acids; equations of metal oxides, hydroxides, nitrates and carbonates with acids; action of heat on oxides, carbonates, nitrates and hydroxides of metals

The reactivity, extraction and uses of metals

- Reactivity series of metals; method of extraction of metals; extraction of aluminium; extraction of iron; uses of iron, aluminium and lead; definition of an alloy

Impact of metals on living systems and the environment

- Conditions essential for corrosion; detrimental and beneficial corrosion; importance of metals and their compounds in living organisms; harmful effects of metals and their compounds on living organisms and the environment

Non-metals

- Physical properties of non-metals; reactions of non-metals with oxygen and metals; reducing and oxidising properties of non-metals; laboratory preparation of carbon dioxide, oxygen and ammonia; collection of carbon dioxide, oxygen and ammonia; harmful effects of non-metals and their compounds on living systems and the environment

Water

- Properties of water; function of water in living systems; solvent properties of water; two types of water hardness; methods of large-scale treatment of water for domestic purposes; treatment of water in the home; softening water

Green Chemistry

- Principles of Green Chemistry; examples of Green Chemistry products used in industry

Qualitative analysis

- Tests used in the identification of cations and anions; tests to identify cations using aqueous sodium hydroxide, aqueous ammonia and aqueous potassium iodide; ionic equations for the reactions occurring in the tests; tests to identify common anions; ionic equations for the reactions occurring in the tests; tests to identify O_2, H_2, CO_2, HCl, NH_3, Cl_2, SO_2, NO_2 and water vapour

18 Characteristics of metals

Learning objectives

- Describe the **general properties of metals.**
- Explain these properties in terms of the **bonding** that exists in the **metal lattice.**
- Describe and write balanced equations of metals with oxygen, water and dilute acids.
- Describe and write balanced equations of **metal oxides, hydroxides, nitrates** and **carbonates with acids.**
- Describe the **action of heat** on **oxides, carbonates, nitrates** and **hydroxides of metals.**

Metals are elements that are found mainly in Groups I, II and III of the periodic table, and between Groups II and III as the transition metals. The atoms of most metals have 1, 2 or 3 valence electrons. Metals have been used for thousands of years and metals make up most of the elements found in the Earth's crust. Metals are very useful because of their properties, and life as we know it would not be possible without metals. Metals are found in our cars, aeroplanes, ships, pots, cutlery and jewellery.

Physical properties of metals

Metals have common **physical properties** as a result of the **metallic bonding** between metal atoms in the metallic lattice (see page 81).

- Metals have **high melting and boiling points.** There are strong forces of attraction between the delocalised negatively charged 'sea of electrons' and the positive metal ions. Therefore, high temperatures are necessary to break the metallic bonds and displace the ions from within the metal lattice.
- Metals are **solid at room temperature** (except mercury). Mercury has a melting point of −38.87 °C and a boiling point of 356.90 °C.
- Metals are **good conductors of electricity** (both in the solid and liquid state, Figure 18.1) and heat (Figure 18.2). For conduction of heat and electricity, there must be free charged particles, and metals have the delocalised electrons which carry heat and electrical energy. When metals are heated at one end, the positive metal ions vibrate more energetically, transferring energy to the delocalised electrons. These free electrons move to other parts of the metals and transfer heat energy to other positive ions.

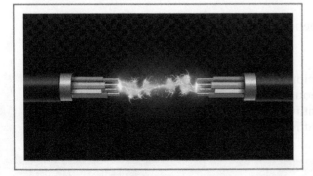

Figure 18.1 *Metal wires conducting electricity*

Figure 18.2 *Metals used as pots and pans because they are good conductors of heat*

- The strong attraction between the positive ions in the crystal lattice for the delocalised electrons (metallic bonding which occurs in metals, page 81) results in metals being hard and strong. In general, the more delocalised electrons there are, the harder the metal.
- Metals are **malleable** (can be hammered into thin sheets, Figure 18.3) and **ductile** (can be drawn into thin wires). Metals consists of layers of metal atoms (page 81) and these layers can slide over each other and not disturb the existing metallic bonds between the metal atoms. These bonds are therefore flexible but strong.

Figure 18.3 *Metals are ductile and malleable, gold can be pulled into wire and beaten into sheets to make jewellery*

- Metals are **shiny** or **lustrous** in appearance (Figure 18.4). The metals shine because the 'sea of electrons' absorb the energy from the light and generate a second wave of light which radiates from the surface. In other words, a metal's shine is really reflected light.

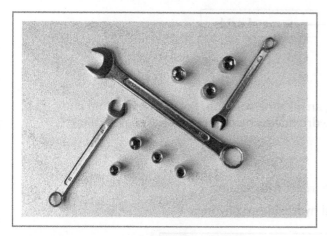

Figure 18.4 *Metals have a shiny lustre*

- Metals have **high densities** because the atoms of the metallic structure are tightly packed together, resulting in a large mass in a small volume.

Chemical properties of metals

When they react, metals ionise by **losing** electrons to form positive **cations**. The metal behaves as a **reducing agent** because it gives electrons to the other reactant (it causes the other reactant to **gain** electrons). This results in the formation of **ionic compounds**.

$$M \longrightarrow M^{n+} + ne^-$$

Some metals react vigorously, even violently, with acids, oxygen and water, whilst others are relatively unreactive. Potassium, sodium, calcium and magnesium are the most reactive, whilst aluminium, zinc and iron are less reactive, and copper and silver are relatively unreactive.

Reactions of metals with dilute acids

When a metal reacts with dilute hydrochloric or sulfuric acid, it forms a **salt** and **hydrogen**:

$$\text{metal + acid} \longrightarrow \text{salt + hydrogen}$$

It should be noted that dilute nitric acid has oxidising powers and so does not follow the trend of hydrochloric acid or sulfuric acid to produce a salt and hydrogen gas. Also, reactive metals, such as potassium, sodium, calcium and magnesium are very reactive with dilute acids. The acid and metal that are used determine the salt produced by the reaction. Chlorides are formed by hydrochloric acid; sulfates are formed by sulfuric acid:

for example: $2K(s) + 2HCl(aq) \longrightarrow 2KCl(aq) + H_2(g)$

                 $Zn(s) + H_2SO_4(aq) \longrightarrow ZnSO_4(aq) + H_2(g)$

Reactions of metals with oxygen

Different metals show varying reactions when exposed to air. The surface of reactive metals are immediately oxidised when exposed to oxygen, while the less reactive metals display little or no reaction on exposure to oxygen. Potassium and sodium react violently on exposure to oxygen and, because of this reaction, they are stored under paraffin oil. The paraffin oil acts as a shield, ensuring that the metal does not come into contact with oxygen. When a metal reacts with oxygen, it forms a **metal oxide,** which is an ionic compound. Aluminium, zinc and lead(II) oxide are **amphoteric.** The oxides of the other metals are **basic:**

$$\text{metal + oxygen} \longrightarrow \text{metal oxide}$$

for example: $2Ca(s) + O_2(g) \longrightarrow 2CaO(s)$

                 $2Zn(s) + O_2(g) \longrightarrow 2ZnO(s)$

Some metal oxides can dissolve in water, forming an alkaline solution. Potassium, sodium and calcium oxide dissolve in water to form soluble hydroxides. The other oxides are insoluble.

Reactions of metals with water

Some metals react with water whereas others only react with steam.

- When a metal reacts with **water**, it forms a **metal hydroxide** and **hydrogen**:

$$\text{metal + water} \longrightarrow \text{metal hydroxide + hydrogen}$$

for example: $Mg(s) + 2H_2O(l) \longrightarrow Mg(OH)_2(aq) + H_2(g)$

                 $2Na(s) + 2H_2O(l) \longrightarrow 2NaOH(aq) + H_2(g)$

- When a metal reacts with **steam**, it forms a **metal oxide** and **hydrogen**:

$$\text{metal + steam} \longrightarrow \text{metal oxide + hydrogen}$$

for example: $2Al(s) + 3H_2O(g) \longrightarrow Al_2O_3(s) + 3H_2(g)$

                 $Zn(s) + H_2O(g) \longrightarrow ZnO(s) + H_2(g)$

Table 18.1 *Summary of reactions of metals with dilute acids, oxygen and water*

Metal	Description of the reaction with dilute acids	Description and equation of the reaction when the metal is heated in air	Description and equation of the reaction with water
Potassium	Reacts extremely violently.	Burns vigorously with a lilac flame. White powdery solid formed. $4K(s) + O_2(g) \longrightarrow 2K_2O(s)$	Reacts very vigorously with cold water. Lilac flame observed. $2K(s) + 2H_2O(l) \longrightarrow 2KOH(aq) + H_2(g)$
Sodium	Reacts violently.	Burns vigorously with an orange flame (Figure 18.5a). White powdery solid formed. $4Na(s) + O_2(g) \longrightarrow 2Na_2O(s)$	Reacts vigorously with cold water. Orange flame observed. $2Na(s) + 2H_2O(l) \longrightarrow 2NaOH(aq) + H_2(g)$
Calcium	Reacts fairly violently.	Burns very easily with a brick red flame (Figure 18.5b). White powdery solid formed. $2Ca(s) + O_2(g) \longrightarrow 2CaO(s)$	Reacts moderately with cold water. $Ca(s) + 2H_2O(l) \longrightarrow Ca(OH)_2(aq) + H_2(g)$
Magnesium	Reacts very vigorously.	Burns easily with a bright white flame. White powdery solid formed. $2Mg(s) + O_2(g) \longrightarrow 2MgO(s)$	Reacts very slowly with cold water, slowly with hot water. Magnesium hydroxide is formed. $Mg(s) + 2H_2O(l) \longrightarrow Mg(OH)_2(aq) + H_2(g)$ Reacts vigorously with steam. Magnesium oxide is formed. $Mg(s) + H_2O(g) \longrightarrow MgO(s) + H_2(g)$
Aluminium	Reacts vigorously.	Burn when heated strongly, especially if powdered. Aluminium forms a white powdery oxide. Zinc oxide is yellow when hot but white when cold. Iron(II) and iron(III) oxide are black. $4Al(s) + 3O_2(g) \longrightarrow 2Al_2O_3(s)$ $2Zn(s) + O_2(g) \longrightarrow 2ZnO(s)$ $3Fe(s) + 2O_2(g) \longrightarrow Fe_3O_4(s)$	Do not react with cold water or hot water. React with steam. $2Al(s) + 3H_2O(g) \longrightarrow Al_2O_3(s) + 3H_2(g)$ $Zn(s) + H_2O(g) \longrightarrow ZnO(s) + H_2(g)$ $3Fe(s) + 4H_2O(g) \longrightarrow Fe_3O_4(s) + 4H_2(g)$
Zinc	Reacts fairly vigorously.		
Iron	Reacts very slowly.		
Copper	Do not react with dilute acids.	$2Cu(s) + O_2(g) \longrightarrow 2CuO(s)$	Do not react with water or steam.
Silver		Does not react, even when heated very strongly.	

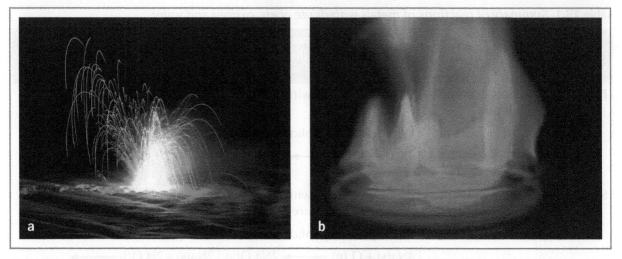

Figure 18.5 *Sodium explodes in water to produce an orange flame **a**, while calcium produces a brick red flame **b***

Reactions of metal compounds

All metal oxides, hydroxides and carbonates react with **dilute acids**, and many metal hydroxides, carbonates and nitrates decompose when heated.

Reactions of metal compounds with dilute acids

Metal oxides and hydroxides are all bases and are therefore neutralised by dilute hydrochloric acid and sulfuric acid to form a salt and water. These reactions are exothermic and feel warm to the touch. The reactions of the metal oxides and hydroxides are shown below:

- **Metal oxides** react with acids to form a **salt** and **water**:

$$\boxed{\text{metal oxide + acid} \longrightarrow \text{salt + water}}$$

for example: $Al_2O_3(s) + 6HCl(aq) \longrightarrow 2AlCl_3(aq) + 3H_2O(l)$

- **Metal hydroxides** react with acids to form a **salt** and **water**:

$$\boxed{\text{metal hydroxide + acid} \longrightarrow \text{salt + water}}$$

for example: $Ca(OH)_2(s) + H_2SO_4(aq) \longrightarrow CaSO_4(aq) + 2H_2O(l)$

- **Metal carbonates** react with acids to form a **salt, carbon dioxide** and **water**:

$$\boxed{\text{metal carbonate + acid} \longrightarrow \text{salt + carbon dioxide + water}}$$

for example: $MgCO_3(s) + 2HNO_3(aq) \longrightarrow Mg(NO_3)_2(aq) + CO_2(g) + H_2O(l)$

It should be noted that sulfuric acid is dibasic and, depending on the ratio of acid to carbonate used in the reaction, a normal or acidic salt can be formed:

$$Na_2CO_3(s) + H_2SO_4(aq) \longrightarrow Na_2SO_4(aq) + H_2O(l) + CO_2(g)$$

or

$$Na_2CO_3(s) + 2H_2SO_4(aq) \longrightarrow 2NaHSO_4(aq) + H_2O(l) + CO_2(g)$$

- Zinc, lead and aluminium oxide and hydroxide are amphoteric in nature and therefore react with **alkalis**:

for example: $Al_2O_3(s) + 2NaOH(aq) \longrightarrow 2NaAlO_2(aq) + H_2O(l)$
sodium aluminate

- **Metal nitrates** react with dilute acids to produce a salt and nitric acid.

The nitrates of metals such as Na, K, Mg, Al, Cu, Fe and Zn do not react with dilute sulfuric acid. The nitrates of lead and calcium readily react with dilute sulfuric acid to produce white precipitates of lead sulfate and calcium sulfate, respectively, and nitric acid, as shown in the chemical equations:

$$Pb(NO_3)_2(aq) + H_2SO_4(aq) \longrightarrow PbSO_4(s) + 2HNO_3(aq)$$
$$Ca(NO_3)_2(aq) + H_2SO_4(aq) \longrightarrow CaSO_4(s) + 2HNO_3(aq)$$

Silver and lead nitrates react with dilute hydrochloric acid to produce silver and lead chloride, respectively, as shown in the chemical equations below, while most other metal nitrates do not react with dilute hydrochloric acid.

$$Pb(NO_3)_2(aq) + 2HCl(aq) \longrightarrow PbCl_2(s) + 2HNO_3(aq)$$
$$AgNO_3(aq) + HCl(aq) \longrightarrow AgCl(s) + HNO_3(aq)$$

Decomposition of metal compounds when heated

Compounds of potassium and sodium are **stable** and do not decompose on heating or, in the case of the nitrates, decompose only slightly. Compounds of other metals decompose when heated and the ease of decomposition increases going **down** the reactivity series (see page 295). More stable compounds are formed by potassium and sodium because they either do not decompose (hydroxide and carbonate) or decompose slightly (nitrate), whereas other metals form unstable compounds that decompose easily, for example, carbonates, hydroxides and nitrates of lead and silver.

Metal oxides can be decomposed by heat to give the elemental metal and oxygen. The more reactive the metal, or the higher the metal is in the reactivity series, the higher the temperature required to allow the metal oxide to decompose into the metal and oxygen. For example, for metals like aluminium the temperature is many thousands of degrees Celsius. For this reason the metal oxides formed from metals high up in the reactivity series require the process of electrolysis to be reduced (see page 298). Metal oxides formed from metals low down in the reactivity series (for example, white silver oxide) undergo thermal decomposition at the temperature of a Bunsen flame.

$$2Ag_2O(s) \xrightarrow{\text{heat}} 4Ag(s) + O_2(g)$$

Gases produced during decomposition of metal compounds, such as oxygen, nitrogen dioxide, carbon dioxide or water vapour, can be confirmed by the tests given in Table 24.9 (see page 357).

Table 18.2 *The effect of heat on metal carbonates, hydroxides and nitrates*

Metal	Metal compounds		
	Hydroxides	Carbonates	Nitrates
Potassium Sodium	The hydroxides are stable; they **do not** decompose.	The carbonates are stable; they **do not** decompose.	Decompose slightly to form the **metal nitrite** and **oxygen**: e.g. $2NaNO_3(s) \longrightarrow 2NaNO_2(s) + O_2(g)$ $2KNO_3(s) \longrightarrow 2KNO_2(s) + O_2(g)$
Calcium Magnesium Aluminium Zinc Iron Lead Copper	Decompose to form the **metal oxide** and **water** (as steam): e.g. $Mg(OH)_2(s) \longrightarrow MgO(s) + H_2O(g)$	Decompose to form the **metal oxide** and **carbon dioxide**: e.g. $PbCO_3(s) \longrightarrow PbO(s) + CO_2(g)$	Decompose to form the **metal oxide**, **nitrogen dioxide** and **oxygen**: e.g. $2Mg(NO_3)_2(s) \longrightarrow 2MgO(s) + 4NO_2(g) + O_2(g)$
Silver	Silver hydroxide is too unstable to exist.	Silver carbonate is too unstable to exist.	Decomposes to form **silver**, **nitrogen dioxide** and **oxygen**: $2AgNO_3(s) \longrightarrow 2Ag(s) + 2NO_2(g) + O_2(g)$

Recalling facts

1 Which of the following is NOT a physical property of metals?

   a lustrous

   b strong

   c solid

   d non-conductor

2 Which of the following is true when metals react?

   I Metals ionise by losing electrons.

   II Metals behave as an oxidising agent.

   III An ionic compound is formed.

   a I only

   b II and III only

   c I and III only

   d I, II and III

3 Calcium and water produces:

   a calcium oxide and hydrogen gas

   b calcium oxide and water

   c calcium hydroxide and water

   d calcium hydroxide and hydrogen gas

4 Magnesium hydroxide reacts with sulfuric acid to give:

a magnesium sulfate only

b magnesium sulfate and water

c magnesium sulfate, carbon dioxide and water

d none of the above

5 Which of the following is NOT true about the reactions of zinc:

a reacts fairly vigorously with dilute acids

b powdered zinc burns when heated strongly

c reacts with cold water

d reacts with steam

6 When potassium carbonate is heated it produces:

a potassium oxide only

b carbon dioxide only

c potassium oxide and carbon dioxide

d none of the above

7 Sodium nitrate decomposes on heating to produce:

a $NaNO_2(g)$ only

b $NaNO_2(g)$ and $O_2(g)$

c $NaNO_2(s)$ and $O_2(g)$

d none of the above

8 Silver nitrate decomposes on heating to give:

a silver nitrite only

b silver nitrite and oxygen

c silver nitrite and nitrogen dioxide

d silver, nitrogen dioxide and oxygen

9 Metal oxides when heated give:

a the metal only

b the metal and water

c the metal and oxygen

d the metal, water and oxygen

10 Lead(II) nitrate reacts with sulfuric acid to produce:

a lead(II) sulfate, water and nitrogen dioxide

b lead(II) sulfate, water and nitrogen gas

c lead(II) sulfate and nitric acid

d lead(II) sulfate and nitrogen dioxide

11 State where on the periodic table metals can be found.

12 Which of the following metal nitrates, Mg, Na, Zn, Al, Pb, Ag and Cu, react with:

a dilute sulfuric acid

b dilute hydrochloric acid

Write equations to represent the reactions that occur.

Applying facts

13 Give three physical properties of metals and explain these properties, relating them to the type of bonding which exists in the metallic lattice structure.

14 Arrange the following carbonates in order of their increasing ease of decomposition:

copper carbonate, aluminium carbonate, zinc carbonate and magnesium carbonate

Write equations representing the decomposition of each carbonate.

15 Name the products formed and write balanced equations when potassium nitrate and magnesium nitrate are heated.

16 Do potassium hydroxide, sodium hydroxide and silver hydroxide decompose on heating? Explain your answer.

17 A metal carbonate can form two salts when reacting with sulfuric acid. Using a named example, write balanced equations for the production of both salts.

18 Write equations for the reaction of each of the following metals with oxygen: potassium, sodium, calcium and magnesium.

19 Sodium reacts with cold water to give a gas. Write a balanced equation with state symbols for the reaction.

20 Write equations for the reaction of calcium, zinc and magnesium with **a** hydrochloric acid and **b** sulfuric acid.

19 The reactivity, extraction and uses of metals

Learning objectives

- Explain the basis of the **reactivity series of metals**.
- Deduce information about metals when using the reactivity series.
- Explain how the position of a metal in the reactivity series determines its **method of extraction**.
- **Outline the extraction of aluminium** from the electrolysis of purified aluminium oxide.
- Outline the essential reactions in the **extraction of iron using haematite or magnetite, limestone and coke in a blast furnace.**
- Describe the **uses of aluminium, iron and lead**, relate these uses to the properties of the metals.
- Explain what is an **alloy** is.
- Discuss why metal alloys are used instead of the pure metal.
- Relate the uses of aluminium, iron and lead alloys to their properties.

The reactivity of metals varies greatly and this has an impact on whether the metals occur in their free or combined state in the Earth's crust, their method of extraction and their uses. When metals are arranged in order of how reactive they are, the **reactivity series of metals (Table 19.1)** is produced. Carbon and hydrogen are included in the series even though they are non-metals. This was done to show the ease with which they act as reducing agents when reacting with metal oxides (p. 298). The inclusion of hydrogen is further explained on page 298.

The reactivity series of metals

The **reactivity series of metals** (Table 19.1) arranges the metals in order from the most reactive (potassium) to the least reactive (gold). It tells us how easily the metal atom loses electrons (ionises) to form cations, its reducing ability (see page 296), its reactivity, and its behaviour in displacement reactions which determines a suitable method to extract metals form its ores.

Table 19.1 *The reactivity series of metals*

Metal	Symbol	Reactivity
Potassium	K	most reactive
Sodium	Na	
Calcium	Ca	
Magnesium	Mg	
Aluminium	Al	
(Carbon)	(C)	**Increasing:**
Zinc	Zn	• ease of ionisation
Iron	Fe	• reactivity
Lead	Pb	• strength as a reducing agent
(Hydrogen)	(H)	• stability of compounds
Copper	Cu	
Mercury	Hg	
Silver	Ag	
Gold	Au	least reactive

- Metals at the **top** of the series ionise the most easily, which makes them the **most reactive**. Potassium is the most reactive and gold the least reactive because potassium ionises easily and gold does not. The most reactive metals are the **strongest reducing agents** because they give away electrons the most easily. In other words, they are easily oxidised. Their ions are very **stable**, which makes their compounds very stable. These metals tarnish or corrode very easily.

- Metals at the **bottom** of the series ionise the least easily which makes them the **least reactive**. They are the **weakest reducing agents** because they give away electrons the least easily. Their ions are very **unstable**, which makes their compounds very unstable.

- The electropositivity of the metals decreases on moving down the reactivity series.

The reactivity series is based on the following:

- How vigorously the metals react with **dilute acids** (hydrochloric acid and sulfuric acid), **oxygen** and **water/steam** (see Table 18.1, page 289). Potassium, sodium, calcium and magnesium are the most reactive metals with dilute acids, oxygen and water/steam. Copper is the least reactive metal with oxygen and sliver does not react with dilute acids, oxygen and water/steam.

- How easily metal compounds are **decomposed** when they are heated (see Table 18.2, page 292 and page 291 for oxides). The stability of the compounds formed by very reactive metals is high. Therefore carbonates and hydroxides of potassium and sodium are stable and do not decompose when heated, but their nitrates slightly decompose on heating. Silver compounds are so highly unstable that only silver nitrate exists (the hydroxide and carbonate do not). Silver nitrate when heated decomposes very easily.

$$\text{Silver nitrate} \xrightarrow{\text{heat}} \text{silver + nitrogen dioxide + oxygen}$$

The ease of decomposition of the hydroxides, carbonates and nitrates of the other metals increases in the following order: calcium, magnesium, zinc, aluminium, iron, lead and copper.

$$\text{Calcium carbonate} \xrightarrow{\text{heat}} \text{calcium oxide + carbon dioxide}$$

Copper compounds decompose easily because copper is least reactive, forming very unstable compounds while calcium compounds decompose least because calcium is highly reactive and forms very stable compounds.

- Whether or not a metal will **displace** another metal from its compounds (see below). A more reactive metal displaces a less reactive metal from its compounds.

Displacement reactions

A **displacement reaction** occurs when a metal in its free state takes the place of another metal in a compound. A **more reactive metal** always displaces a **less reactive metal** from its compounds. Atoms of the more reactive metal **ionise** to form ions and the ions of the less reactive metal are **discharged** to form atoms.

$$C \quad + \quad DX \quad \longrightarrow \quad CX \quad + \quad D$$

⋮	⋮	
higher	lower	
in the series	in the series	
than D	than C	

- C is higher in the reactivity series, therefore it is **more** reactive than D. C **ionises** to form C^{n+} ions:

$$C \longrightarrow C^{n+} + ne^-$$

- D is lower in the reactivity series, therefore it is **less** reactive than C. The D^{n+} ions are **discharged** to form D atoms:

$$D^{n+} + ne^- \longrightarrow D$$

A more reactive metal can displace a less reactive metal from its oxide. Therefore, magnesium being higher in the reactivity series can reduce aluminium oxide to aluminium as seen in the equation:

$$3Mg(s) + Al_2O_3(s) \longrightarrow 3MgO(s) + 2Al(s)$$

Potassium, sodium and calcium can also reduce aluminium oxide to aluminium, being higher up in the reactivity series.

These are also **redox reactions** (see page 163). The metal in its free state is a **stronger** reducing agent than the metal in the compound.

For example: $Fe(s) + PbSO_4(aq) \longrightarrow FeSO_4(aq) + Pb(s)$

Ionically: $Fe^0(s) + Pb^{2+}(aq) \longrightarrow Fe^{2+}(aq) + Pb^0(s)$

Iron is higher up in the series, making it more reactive than lead, and therefore displaces the lead from its aqueous solution.

Zinc can displace copper from copper sulfate and iron from iron sulfate because zinc is higher up in the reactivity series than iron or copper.

For example: $Zn(s) + CuSO_4(aq) \longrightarrow ZnSO_4(aq) + Cu(s)$

Ionically: $Zn^0(s) + Cu^{2+}(aq) \longrightarrow Zn^{2+}(aq) + Cu^0(s)$

For example: $Zn(s) + FeSO_4(aq) \longrightarrow ZnSO_4(aq) + Fe(s)$

Ionically: $Zn^0(s) + Fe^{2+}(aq) \longrightarrow Zn^{2+}(aq) + Fe^0(s)$

Let us explain what happens when a piece of zinc metal is placed in about 5 cm³ of copper(II) sulfate solution contained in a test tube.

The reaction is as stated above

$$Zn(s) + CuSO_4(aq) \longrightarrow ZnSO_4(aq) + Cu(s)$$

Zinc being more reactive than copper (see Table 19.1) would ionise and the Zn^{2+} ions would enter the solution.

$$Zn(s) \longrightarrow Zn^{2+}(aq) + 2e^-$$

The Cu^{2+} ions in the copper(II) sulfate solution are discharged and copper atoms are produced.

$$Cu^{2+}(aq) + 2e^- \longrightarrow Cu(s)$$

A copper precipitate, pink in colour, develops on the zinc which falls off when disturbed into the solution. The blue colour of the copper (II) sulfate solution gradually fades as the blue Cu^{2+} ions are discharged. The size of the zinc strip decreases as the Zn^{2+} ions go into solution.

The overall ionic equation for the reaction is:

$$Zn(s) + Cu^{2+}(aq) \longrightarrow Zn^{2+}(aq) + Cu(s)$$

If a piece of copper was placed into zinc(II) sulfate solution in a test tube there would be no reaction. Copper is below zinc in the reactivity series (Table 19.1), therefore copper cannot displace zinc from the zinc(II) sulfate and hence no reaction occurs.

The reactivity series of metals can be used to predict:

- The products of displacement reaction – the metal higher up in the series will displace the metal in a compound which is lower down in the series. Magnesium will displace iron. One can use displacement reactions to determine the positions of metals in the reactivity series if their reactions are similar. The higher metal will always displace the lower metal.

- The reactivity of metals towards each other – how far apart metals are from each other in the series gives an indication of how vigorously one metal reacts with water, for example, than another. The further away they are from each other in the series, the more vigorously the one higher in the series will react than the one lower down in the series. Sodium will form sodium hydroxide and hydrogen gas with cold water; aluminium will only react with steam.

Even though **hydrogen** is a non-metal, it is included in the reactivity series of metals because it can be used in comparing the reactivities of the metals. If the metals are above hydrogen in the reactivity series, they can react with the acid and displace the hydrogen in the acid. If the metals are lower than hydrogen in the reactivity series, they will not react with the acid and will not displace the hydrogen in the acid. The further away the metal is from hydrogen as the series is ascended – that is, the higher up the metal is from hydrogen – the more vigorous is the reaction between the metal and the acid.

The extraction of metals from their ores

Silver, gold and other unreactive metals can be mined directly from the Earth's crust, where they occur in their **free elemental state**. Most metals are found combined with other elements in impure ionic compounds, known as **ores**. The metals must be **extracted** from these ores. Metal oxides, sulfides and carbonates are some of the most important ores.

During extraction from its ore, the metal cations are discharged to form atoms by **gaining** electrons. The extraction of metals is therefore a **reduction process**:

$$M^{n+} + ne^- \longrightarrow M$$

Choosing an extraction method

The extraction method used depends on the **position** of the metal in the reactivity series:

- Metals **high** in the reactivity series (**aluminium and above**) are extracted by **electrolysis of their molten ores**. They require a **powerful method** of reduction because they form very stable ions which are difficult to reduce. Electrolysis is a powerful method, but it uses a lot of energy and is very expensive.
- Metals **lower down** in the series (**zinc and below**) are extracted by **heating their ores with a reducing agent** such as carbon, carbon monoxide or hydrogen. They require a **less powerful method** of reduction than electrolysis because their ions are less stable and are easier to reduce. Heating their ores with a reducing agent is a less powerful method, uses less energy and is less expensive than electrolysis.

Extraction of aluminium

Aluminium is always found in the Earth's crust combined with other elements. In other words, it exists as ores of the element. Bauxite is the main ore of aluminium and aluminium is extracted using the process of **electrolysis**. The formula and the main reactant in the extraction of aluminium is given below:

Ores: **bauxite** – impure, hydrated aluminium oxide, $Al_2O_3 \cdot xH_2O$.

         cryolite – sodium aluminium fluoride, Na_3AlF_6

The electrolysis process occurs in a large carbon (graphite) lined steel tank, as shown in Figure 19.1. The steel tank forms the electrolytic cell and the carbon lining acts as the negative cathode in the electrolysis process. Huge blocks of carbon, suspended in the middle of the tank, act as the positive anode, as shown in Figure 19.1.

- The bauxite is **purified**. This forms pure, anhydrous aluminium oxide, also known as **alumina**, Al_2O_3.
- The **alumina** is dissolved in **molten cryolite** at about 950 °C to separate the ions. The melting point of alumina is 2050 °C and molten alumina is a poor conductor. Dissolving it in molten cryolite reduces its melting temperature, which reduces the energy required. The solution produced is also a better conductor than molten alumina because its ions are now mobile.

- The molten solution of alumina in cryolite is **electrolysed** in an electrolytic cell.
  - The **aluminium ions** move towards the **cathode** and are **reduced** to form aluminium atoms:

    $$Al^{3+}(l) + 3e^- \longrightarrow Al(l)$$

    Three moles of electrons are needed to discharge one mole of aluminium.

    Molten aluminium collects at the bottom of the cell. It is tapped off and made into blocks or sheets.
  - The **oxide ions** move towards the **anode** and are **oxidised** to form oxygen gas:

    $$2O^{2-}(l) \longrightarrow O_2(g) + 4e^-$$

    Oxygen gas is evolved at the anode. The oxygen gas oxidises the carbon anodes forming carbon dioxide. The anodes must be replaced periodically as they disintegrate because of the reaction with the oxygen gas.

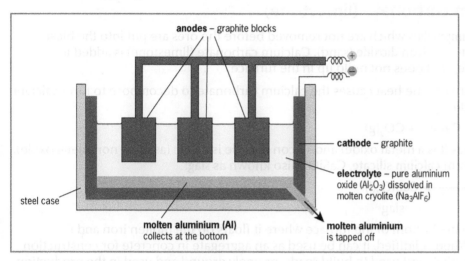

anodes – graphite blocks

cathode – graphite

electrolyte – pure aluminium oxide (Al_2O_3) dissolved in molten cryolite (Na_3AlF_6)

steel case

molten aluminium (Al) collects at the bottom

molten aluminium is tapped off

Figure 19.1 *Electrolytic cell for the extraction of aluminium*

Extraction of iron

The most widely used metal in the world is **iron**. It is used in the construction, vehicle and equipment manufacturing industries. It is abundantly found as ores in the Earth's crust. Haematite, magnetite and iron pyrites are the main ores in which iron is found. The most important ores from which iron is extracted are haematite and magnetite; their chemical formulae are given below:

Ores: **haematite** – impure iron(III) oxide, Fe_2O_3

magnetite – impure iron(II, III) oxide, Fe_3O_4

Extraction of iron from haematite and magnetite is carried out by reducing the ores using the reducing agent, **carbon monoxide (CO)**, in a **blast furnace** (see Figure 19.2). The furnace is a chimney-like structure 30 metres high made of steel and has an inner lining of fireproof bricks.

- A mixture of the **iron ores**, **coke** (carbon) and **limestone** (calcium carbonate) is added through the top of the furnace by means of a hopper.
- **Hot air** is blown in through the bottom of the furnace.
- In the **bottom** part of the furnace, coke reacts with the oxygen in the air to produce **carbon dioxide**:

    $$C(s) + O_2(g) \longrightarrow CO_2(g) \quad \Delta H \text{ –ve}$$

The reaction is **exothermic**. The heat produced keeps the bottom of the furnace at a temperature of about 1900 °C. The carbon dioxide moves up the furnace.

- As it reaches the **middle** part of the furnace, the carbon dioxide reacts with more of the hot coke, and is reduced to **carbon monoxide:**

$$CO_2(g) + C(s) \longrightarrow 2CO(g)$$

The carbon monoxide moves up the furnace.

- In the **top** part of the furnace, the carbon monoxide **reduces** the iron ores to **iron:**

$$Fe_2O_3(s) + 3CO(g) \longrightarrow 2Fe(l) + 3CO_2(g)$$

and $Fe_3O_4(s) + 4CO(g) \longrightarrow 3Fe(l) + 4CO_2(g)$

The **molten iron** runs to the bottom of the furnace and is tapped off. The iron, known as '**pig iron**', is impure. It contains about 4% carbon, and other impurities such as silicon and phosphorus. Most of the pig iron is purified and converted into an alloy of iron known as **steel.**

The role of calcium carbonate (limestone)

Iron ores contain a lot of **impurities** which are not removed before the ores are put into the blast furnace. The main impurity is **silicon dioxide** (sand). Calcium carbonate (limestone) is added to remove the silicon dioxide, so it does not build up in the furnace.

- In the **top** part of the furnace, the heat causes the calcium carbonate to decompose to form **calcium oxide** and carbon dioxide:

$$CaCO_3(s) \longrightarrow CaO(s) + CO_2(g)$$

- Calcium oxide is basic (as it is a metal oxide) and silicon dioxide is acidic (as it is a non-metal oxide). The two then react to form **calcium silicate**, $CaSiO_3$, also known as **slag:**

$$CaO(s) + SiO_2(s) \longrightarrow CaSiO_3(l)$$
$$\text{slag}$$

The molten slag runs to the bottom of the furnace where it floats on the molten iron and is tapped off separately. When solidified, it can be used as an aggregate in concrete for construction purposes, mixed with asphalt and used to build roads, or finely ground and used in the production of cement.

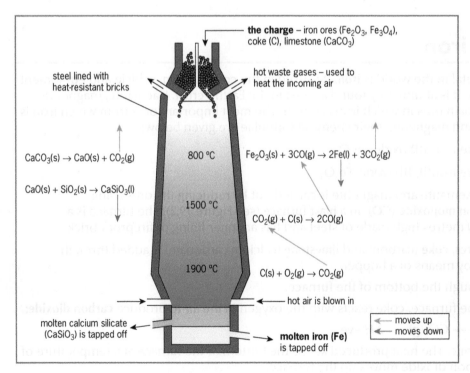

Figure 19.2 *A blast furnace used for extracting iron*

Uses of metals

Metals are used in the manufacture of items which are used in our daily lives. The physical and chemical **properties** of metals, such as strength, density, melting point, conductivity, resistance to corrosion and chemicals, and cost, determine their uses.

Table 19.2 *Properties and uses of the metals aluminium, iron and lead*

Metal	Used to make	Properties of the metal
Aluminium	Cans to store drinks	Resistant to corrosion; malleable so is easily shaped; non-toxic; low density so is light in weight.
	Overhead electrical cables	Good conductor of electricity; resistant to corrosion; light in weight; ductile so easily drawn out into wires.
	Window frames	Resistant to corrosion; light in weight.
	Cooking utensils, e.g. saucepans and baking trays	Good conductor of heat; resistant to corrosion; light in weight; non-toxic; can be polished to have a shiny, attractive appearance.
	Foil used in cooking and pouches used for food cooking, storage and re-heating	Does not react with the food due to its unreactive aluminium oxide coating; non-toxic; highly reflective so keeps in heat.

(*Continued*)

Table 19.2 *Continued*

Metal	Used to make	Properties of the metal
Wrought iron (rarely used)	Ornamental iron work	Malleable and ductile so is easily shaped; strong, which makes it resistant to stress; easily welded.
Lead	Lead-acid batteries, e.g. car batteries	Good conductor of electricity; very resistant to corrosion.
	Radiation shields, e.g. against X-rays	High density so prevents radiation from passing through.
	Keels for sailboats; lead weights, e.g. fishing and diving weights	High density so is heavy; very malleable so is easily shaped.

Alloys and uses of alloys

Alloys are **mixtures** of two or more metals, though a few also contain non-metals. Alloys are produced to improve or to modify the properties of metals. Aluminium, iron and lead are used extensively to manufacture **alloys** because they are easily alloyed with other metals (Table 19.3). The atoms of the metals in an alloy are usually of different sizes. This changes the regular packing of the atoms, which makes it more difficult for them to slide over each other when force is applied. This usually makes alloys **harder** and **stronger** than the pure metals. They are also usually more **resistant to corrosion** and are often used in place of pure metals.

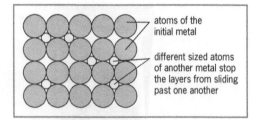

atoms of the initial metal

different sized atoms of another metal stop the layers from sliding past one another

Figure 19.3 *Arrangement of atoms in an alloy*

Table 19.3 *Composition, uses and properties of some common alloys*

Name of alloy	Composition	Uses	Properties of the alloy
Duralumin	Approximately **94% aluminium** alloyed with 4% copper and small amounts of magnesium and manganese.	To construct aircraft and the bodies of motor vehicles.	• Stronger, harder and more workable than aluminium. • Light in weight and resistant to corrosion.
Magnalium	Approximately **95% aluminium** alloyed with 5% magnesium.	To manufacture aircraft and motor vehicle parts.	• Stronger, more workable and lighter in weight than aluminium. • More resistant to corrosion than aluminium.
Mild steel	**Iron** alloyed with less than 0.25% carbon.	To construct buildings, bridges, oil rigs, ships, trains and motor vehicles. To make 'tin cans' to store food; 'tin cans' are made of steel coated in a thin layer of tin which prevents corrosion. To make wire and nails.	• Harder and stronger than iron. • Malleable and ductile so is easily shaped. • Easy to weld.
High carbon steel	**Iron** alloyed with 0.25% to 1.5% carbon.	To make cutting tools, chisels, knives, drill bits and masonry nails.	• Harder than mild steel, but more brittle.
Stainless steel	About **70% iron** alloyed with 20% chromium and 10% nickel.	To make cutlery, kitchen equipment, sinks, catering equipment, surgical equipment and surgical implants. In the construction of modern buildings.	• Harder, stronger and much more resistant to rusting (corrosion) than carbon steels. • Malleable, ductile and easy to work with. • Has a very shiny, attractive appearance.
Cast iron	About **96% iron** and 4% carbon.	To make small castings, e.g. cylinder blocks in engines, railings, gates, manhole covers, hinges and cast iron cookware.	• Easy to cast into exact shapes. • Hard, but more brittle than steel; it shatters rather than bends when hit.
Lead solder	About **60% lead** alloyed with 40% tin.	To join metal items together, e.g. wires and pipes.	• Has a low melting point (lower than lead), so melts easily when joining the metals. • As resistant to corrosion as lead, but harder and stronger.

Recalling facts

1 Which is NOT true as you descend the reactivity series of metals?

   a The metal's ease of ionisation decreases.

   b The metal's reactivity increases.

   c The strength of the metal as a reducing agent decreases.

   d The stability of the compounds of the metals decreases.

2 In the extraction process of iron, which chemical equation represents the reaction occurring in the middle of the furnace?

   a $CO_2(g) + C(s) \longrightarrow 2CO(g)$

   b $C(s) + O_2(g) \longrightarrow CO_2(g)$

   c $Fe_2O_3(s) + 3CO(g) \longrightarrow 2Fe(l) + 3CO_2(g)$

   d $Fe_3O_4(s) + 4CO(g) \longrightarrow 3Fe(l) + 4CO_2(g)$

3 What is the function of the limestone in the extraction process of iron?

   a to remove coke

   b to remove silicon dioxide

   c to form carbon monoxide

   d to form pig iron

4 An alternative reducing agent in the extraction of iron is:

   a H_2 **b** $CaCO_3$ **c** CaO **d** $CaSiO_3$

5 The cathode in the electrolytic cell used to extract aluminium from its ore is:

   a platinum

   b graphite

   c steel

   d copper

6 One of the main ores of iron is:

   a bauxite

   b cryolite

   c haematite

   d silicate

7 Alumina is dissolved in molten sodium aluminium fluoride, Na_3AlF_6, to:

   a increase the melting point

   b decrease the melting point

   c form carbon dioxide

   d form oxide ions

8 Which of the following is used in the manufacture of aircraft bodies?

a stainless steel

b magnalium

c mild steel

d solder

9 Which of the following does NOT occur at the anode during electrolysis to produce aluminium?

a aluminium is formed

b the oxide ions move towards it

c the anode degenerates

d carbon dioxide is formed

10 One of the major impurities found in the ores of iron is:

a cryolite

b silicon dioxide

c sulfur

d coke

11 a What is meant by the term the 'reactivity series of metals'?

b Explain how the metals are placed in order in the reactivity series.

c What information about metals can be predicted from the reactivity series of metals?

12 Why is hydrogen included in the reactivity series of metals?

Applying facts

13 Explain the following in terms of the reducing power of metals and/or their position in the reactivity series.

a Why do potassium and sodium carbonates and hydroxides not decompose on heating?

b Silver hydroxide and silver carbonate do not exist.

c Iron carbonate is more easily decomposed than calcium carbonate.

d Why are displacement reactions described as redox reactions?

e During the excavation of ancient cities, iron objects are not found but gold objects are.

14 Explain how the reactivity series is used to choose a method of extraction of a metal from its ore.

15 **a** Briefly describe the electrolytic extraction of aluminium from bauxite. Include balanced chemical equations to support your answer. You should include in your answer the following:

  i the reason for adding cryolite

  ii the materials the electrodes are made of

  iii an explanation of why the anodes must be periodically replaced.

  b Give three uses of aluminium and relate these uses to the properties of aluminium.

16 **a** Explain, in terms of the arrangement of atoms in the metallic lattice, why an alloy is stronger than a pure metal.

  b Name one alloy of aluminium and one alloy of iron and give the composition and use of each. Also relate the property of the alloy to the uses mentioned.

  c Give one use of the metal lead and relate this use to the properties of lead.

  d Give the composition of an alloy of lead and state its use.

Analysing data

17 In the extraction of iron from its ores explain:

  a the use of coke

  b why hot air is blown in through the bottom of the furnace

  c the function of limestone

  Include balanced equations to support your answers

20 Impact of metals on living systems and the environment

Learning objectives

- Describe the conditions essential for **corrosion** and state how corrosion can be prevented.
- Explain how corrosion can be **detrimental** and **beneficial**.
- Discuss the **importance of metals and their compounds in living organisms**.
- Discuss the **harmful effects of metals and their compounds on living organisms and the environment**.

Certain **metal ions** play vital roles in living organisms while others can be extremely harmful. Metal ions have substantial roles in biological systems. Structurally, they are fundamental to the bones and teeth. They are also important in intra- and inter-cellular biological processes. For example, they are necessary in the maintenance of electrical charges and osmotic pressure, in photosynthesis and in electron transfer processes. They are also key to the proper functioning of nerve cells, muscle cells, the brain and the heart and for the transportation of oxygen. The **environment** can have a significant effect on metals used in everyday activities.

Corrosion of metals

Corrosion takes place when the surface of a metal is gradually worn away by reacting with chemicals in the environment, mainly **oxygen** and **water vapour**. Certain chemicals, such as sodium chloride and some pollutants, speed up the process. When a metal corrodes, it is oxidised to form the **metal oxide**. Salts may also form, for example, the reaction of metals with carbon dioxide forms carbonates. In general, the **higher** a metal is in the reactivity series, the **faster** it corrodes. Also, metals that are closer to the sea corrode faster than the same metals further inland because of the increased amount of sodium chloride in the atmosphere (Figure 20.1).

Figure 20.1 *Seawater corrosion*

Iron and aluminium corrode in different ways and the corrosion can be **detrimental** or **beneficial**.

The corrosion of aluminium

The corrosion of aluminium is generally **beneficial**. When a fresh piece of aluminium is exposed to air, it immediately forms a layer of **aluminium oxide** (Al_2O_3). This layer **adheres** to the metal surface, does not flake off and is relatively unreactive. It therefore protects the aluminium from further corrosion. The thickness of this layer can be increased by **anodising** (see page 200). The oxide layer on the aluminium makes the surface harder and allows the absorption of dyes. Anodised aluminium can therefore be used to make pots and pans, car rims (Figure 20.2) and be used in satellites.

Figure 20.2 *Car rims made of anodised aluminium*

The corrosion of iron – rusting

The corrosion of iron is **detrimental**. When iron and steel objects are exposed to oxygen and moisture, they immediately begin to corrode forming mainly **hydrated iron(III) oxide**, $Fe_2O_3 \cdot xH_2O$, commonly known as **rust**. The corrosion of iron and steel is called **rusting** (Figure 20.3). Rust does not adhere to the iron below; it **flakes off** instead. This exposes fresh iron to oxygen and moisture, which then rusts, and the rust flakes off. The process continues and the iron is gradually worn away. As iron and steel are used extensively in the iron and steel industry – in buildings, roofs, bridges, and to manufacture vehicles and other equipment – this corrosion is detrimental.

Chemically, hydrated iron(III) oxide and its formation are represented by the following chemical equation:

$$4Fe(s) + 3O_2(g) + xH_2O(l) \longrightarrow 2Fe_2O_3 \cdot xH_2O_{(s)}$$

Rusting is a redox reaction. Iron is oxidised to iron(III) ions by losing electrons, as represented by the following ionic equation:

$$Fe(s) \longrightarrow Fe^{3+}(s) + 3e^- \qquad \text{(oxidation)}$$

The oxygen then gains the electrons produced in the oxidation of iron and forms oxide ions. This is reduction and is represented as follows:

$$O(g) + 2e^- \longrightarrow O^{2-}(s) \qquad \text{(reduction)}$$

Figure 20.3 *Rusting of iron*

Investigating the conditions necessary for rusting

For rusting to occur, three things need to be present:

- iron
- water (moisture)
- oxygen.

To investigate the conditions necessary for rusting, we can design an experiment to observe the effects of removing oxygen and moisture (see Figure 20.1). The experiment is carried out in this way:

1 Put a clean steel nail into a test tube; add enough water to cover **half** the nail; and cork the tube. Label this test tube "A".

2 Place a second clean steel nail into another test tube that contains boiled water which was allowed to cool quickly. Boiling the water removes any dissolved oxygen that may be present in the water. Rapid cooling of the boiled water is essential to ensure that no oxygen dissolves in the boiled water again. Cover the nail completely with the boiled water, so that it is not exposed to any oxygen. Pour a small amount of oil down the side of the test tube so that a thin layer forms on top of the water. This prevents any oxygen from dissolving in the boiled water. Cork the tube and label it "B".

3 Place a third clean steel nail into a dry test tube with some calcium chloride; cork the tube and label it "C". The calcium chloride absorbs any moisture from the air in the test tube.

4 Leave the three test tubes for five days.

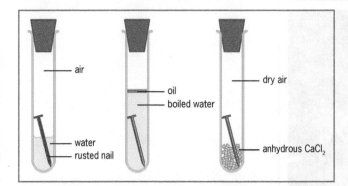

Figure 20.4 *Investigating the conditions necessary for rusting*

- Tube A contains a steel nail exposed to both oxygen and moisture.
- Tube B contains a steel nail exposed to moisture only.
- Tube C contains a steel nail exposed to oxygen only.

Results

Only tube "A", which contained water that covered half the nail, would have rusted. Only this tube had both conditions of moisture and oxygen necessary for rusting. Tubes "B" and "C" only had one of the conditions necessary for rusting and, as such, rusting of the steel nail did not occur in these tubes.

Rust prevention

There are several treatments that can prevent or slow the rusting of iron. These include painting (Figure 20.5) or coating the surface with a thin layer of protective metal or plastic, or a thin film of grease or oil. Sacrificial protection is another method of preventing rusting from occurring (Figure 20.6). Iron and steel can be protected from rust by electrically attaching a more reactive metal, such as zinc, to its surface (see Table 19.1). The more reactive metal oxidises more readily than iron and so 'sacrifices' itself while the iron does not rust. Another example is the use of blocks of aluminium at the foot of the steel pillars that support oil rigs to prevent corrosion of the iron metal. Aluminium is more reactive than iron (see Table 19.1) and therefore oxidises more readily than iron and so 'sacrifices' itself.

Figure 20.5 Painting to prevent rusting of iron and steel

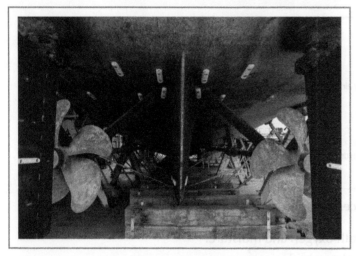

Figure 20.6 Yacht hull with zinc blocks for corrosion protection against the effects of seawater

The importance of metals and their compounds in living organisms

The human body requires certain **metal ions** in relatively large quantities (more than 100 mg per day). These are called **macrominerals** and include calcium, potassium, sodium and magnesium. Others, known as **microminerals** or **trace minerals**, are needed in much smaller quantities, for example, iron, zinc, manganese, cobalt, copper, molybdenum, selenium and chromium. Plants also require minerals for healthy growth and development.

Table 20.1 *The importance of metals and their compounds in living organisms*

Metal ion	Importance in living organisms
Magnesium	Essential for green plants to produce the green pigment, **chlorophyll**, found in chloroplasts. Chlorophyll absorbs sunlight energy so that plants can manufacture their own food by **photosynthesis**: $$6CO_2(g) + 6H_2O(l) \xrightarrow[\text{(absorbed by chlorophyll)}]{\text{sunlight energy}} C_6H_{12}O_6(aq) + 6O_2(g)$$ glucose A shortage of magnesium causes **chlorosis** where the leaves of plants become yellow. Over 300 biochemical reactions in the human body require magnesium ions because they help many enzymes to function. *Leaves showing chlorosis*
Iron	Essential for animals to produce the red protein, **haemoglobin**, found in red blood cells. Haemoglobin carries oxygen around the body for cells to use in **respiration** to produce energy: $$C_6H_{12}O_6(aq) + 6O_2(g) \longrightarrow 6CO_2(g) + 6H_2O(l) + energy$$ A shortage of iron leads to **anaemia** where the number of red blood cells is reduced causing tiredness and a lack of energy. ANAEMIA NORMAL *Lack of iron causes anaemia*
Calcium	Essential to produce **calcium hydroxyapatite** $(Ca_{10}(PO_4)_6(OH)_2)$ in the bones and teeth of animals. A shortage of calcium leads to **rickets** in children where the legs become bowed, and **osteoporosis** in adults where the bones become weak and brittle. *Rickets in children*
Zinc	Important for the functioning of the immune system, for wounds to heal, and for the growth and repair of cells and tissues.
Sodium and **potassium**	Important for impulses to be transmitted along nerves and for muscles to contract.

Note Chlorophyll and haemoglobin are known as **organometallic compounds** because they are organic compounds whose molecules contain metal ions.

Harmful effects of metals and their compounds

The ions of certain transition metals and metalloids, known as **heavy metal ions**, are **toxic** to living organisms, especially when they combine with organic compounds to form **organometallic compounds**. These metal ions occur naturally; however, **pollution** caused by human activities is causing their concentrations within the environment to increase.

Pollution is the contamination of the natural environment by the release of unpleasant and harmful substances into the environment.

Heavy metal ions are **persistent**, meaning they remain in the environment for a long time. These non-degradable heavy metals can increase in concentration from the environment to the first organism in a food chain (**bioaccumulation**) and then increase in concentration as they traverse one trophic level to the next higher level (**biomagnification**) in a food chain. These two processes enable small concentrations of these pollutants to find their way into organisms through the food chain, eventually reaching harmful levels in top consumers such as birds of prey and large fish. Eating **large fish**, such as sharks, marlin and tuna, is the major source of ingested **mercury** in humans.

Table 20.2 *Harmful effects of metal ions on living organisms*

Metal ion	Sources in the environment	Harmful effects
Lead	Discarded lead-acid batteries; manufacture and recycling of lead-acid batteries; mining of lead ores; extraction and refining of lead from its ores; lead-based paints; car exhaust fumes when using leaded petrol in some countries, lead shots from ammunition, lead pipes in old buildings.	• Damages various body tissues and organs, e.g. the kidneys, liver, bones, muscle and nervous system, particularly the brain. • Interferes with the normal formation of red blood cells, which leads to **anaemia**. • Particularly harmful to young children as it can cause behavioural problems and learning disorders.
Arsenic	Mining of certain metals, mainly gold; extraction and refining of metals; burning fossil fuels, especially coal. Volcanic eruptions.	• Causes changes in pigmentation and thickening of the skin, and can cause **cancer**. • Damages the nervous system, heart, lungs and blood vessels.
Cadmium	Discarded nickel–cadmium batteries; cigarette smoke; burning fossil fuels; incinerating waste; extraction and refining of metals. *Nickel–cadmium batteries*	• Damages the kidneys, liver and respiratory system if inhaled. • Can cause bones to become weakened and fragile, leading to **osteoporosis**.

Metal ion	Sources in the environment	Harmful effects
Mercury	Discarded fluorescent light bulbs; discarded mercury thermometers from laboratories and hospitals; burning coal in coal-fired power plants; extraction and refining of metals and emissions from volcanoes.  *A compact fluorescent light bulb containing mercury vapour*	• Damages the central nervous system, resulting in loss of muscular co-ordination, numbness in the hands and feet, and impaired hearing, sight and speech – a condition known as **Minamata disease**.

Disposal of solid waste containing heavy metals

Disposal of solid waste containing **heavy metals** is a serious problem. This waste includes:

- lead-acid batteries from cars, trucks, other vehicles and boats
- nickel-cadmium batteries
- fluorescent light bulbs which contain mercury vapour
- hospital and laboratory thermometers which contain mercury.

These items should not be disposed of in **landfills** since groundwater and nearby soil could be contaminated, and they should not be **incinerated** because harmful gases containing the metal ions could be released into the air. The more items containing heavy metals that are **recycled**, the more the problem of their disposal will be solved. Iron, aluminium, copper and zinc can be easily separated and recycled from waste. Waste from electronic technology is rapidly increasing in our landfills; while some of these wastes can be recycled some electronic wastes are difficult to recycle. Recycling electronic waste can expose workers to potentially harmful heavy metals such as cadmium.

Recalling facts

  Which of the following metals is a micromineral?

    a calcium   **c** potassium

    b manganese   **d** sodium

  Which of the following metals is essential to form haemoglobin?

    a calcium   **c** sodium

    b zinc   **d** iron

3 The importance of zinc in living organisms is:

a to prevent rickets

b essential to heal wounds

c to prevent Minamata disease

d transmission of impulses along nerves

4 The metal arsenic causes:

a anaemia

b cancer

c osteoporosis

d Minamata disease

5 Which of the following is NOT a heavy metal?

a lead

b zinc

c mercury

d cadmium

6 Which statements are true about heavy metals?

I Heavy metals are non-toxic to living organisms.

II Heavy metals persist in the environment.

III Heavy metals are used to make light bulbs and batteries.

a I and II only

b I and III only

c II and III only

d I, II and III

7 The rate at which most metals corrode depends on all of the following except:

a their reactivity

b their colour

c the presence of sodium chloride

d the presence of water and oxygen

8 Which of the following statements are true about anodised aluminium?

I The oxide layer on the aluminium becomes thinner.

II The anodised aluminium is more corrosion resistant.

III The anodised surface can easily absorb dyes.

a I and II only

b II and III only

c I and III only

d I, II and III

9 Which of the following does NOT occur when metals corrode?

    a form metal oxides

    b are oxidised

    c are reduced

    d can form salts, e.g. carbonates

10 The corrosion of aluminium:

    a is beneficial

    b is detrimental

    c forms rust

    d forms iron oxide

11 Explain what is meant by the term 'corrosion'. What are the conditions necessary for corrosion to occur?

Applying facts

12 Metals in trace amounts are essential to both plants and animals. Give three examples of such metals and explain their role in living systems. Also, state the effects of their absence to living systems.

13 Discuss the sources and possible toxic effects of three named heavy metals.

14 State some sources of heavy metals that can enter as solid waste in our landfills. What are the ill effects of these heavy metals if they are allowed to enter our landfills? What is a possible solution to reducing these heavy metals entering our landfills?

Analysing data

15 'Rusting of iron is said to be a redox reaction.'

    a Explain this statement, giving a definition of the term 'redox' and equations for each stage of the reaction.

    b Does the base of an iron window frame rust faster than the top of the window frame? Explain.

    c An iron window frame rusts faster next to the sea. Explain.

    d Aluminium window frames last longer than iron window frames. Explain why.

    e Name three methods that can be used to slow or prevent rusting.

16 'There is a concentration of heavy metals in the tissues of animals at the top of the food chains.' Would smaller fishes have lower concentrations of heavy metals than larger fishes? Explain this using the occurrence of Minamata disease in a person eating large species of fish, rather than small species of fish.

21 Non-metals

Learning objectives

- Describe the **physical properties of non-metals**.
- Describe the **reactions of non-metals with oxygen** and **metals**.
- Explain the **reducing and oxidising properties of non-metals**.
- Describe the **laboratory preparation of carbon dioxide, oxygen and ammonia**.
- Discuss the method of **collection of carbon dioxide, oxygen** and **ammonia** based on their properties.
- Relate the properties of oxygen and carbon dioxide to their uses.
- State the uses of various non-metals and their compounds.
- Discuss the **harmful effects of non-metals and their compounds on living systems and the environment**.

Non-metals are elements that are found mainly in the upper right-hand portion of the periodic table in Groups V, VI, VII and 0. The atoms of most non-metals have 5, 6, 7 or 8 valence electrons (electrons in the outermost 'shell' of the atom). Non-metals behave differently to and display properties different from those of metals. Most of the non-metals are gases (hydrogen, oxygen, nitrogen), one is a liquid (bromine) and the others are solids (iodine, carbon, silicon, sulfur). The most reactive (fluorine) and least reactive (noble gases) elements are non-metals.

Non-metals undergo different types of bonding. A non-metal bonds with a metal to form an ionic bond. The metal forms the cation and the non-metal forms the anion. The resulting compounds are solids. Non-metal atoms bond with other non-metal atoms to form covalent bonds, which form diatomic molecules. These diatomic molecules have weak intermolecular forces of attraction between them. Under normal conditions these diatomic molecules are gases, liquids or volatile solids. Examples of these include the diatomic molecules hydrogen, nitrogen, fluorine, chlorine, bromine and iodine. The outer shells of the non-metals in Group 0 of the noble gases are full (or contain a full octet) and for this reason they exist as individual atoms and are not reactive. Diamond and graphite are allotropes of carbon, and it was seen in Chapter 5 (page 84) how the bonding within these allotropes influences their properties.

Physical properties of non-metals

The physical properties of non-metals vary because of the different ways in which non-metal atoms are bonded in their elements. However, non-metals have the following **general physical properties**:

- Most non-metals have **low** melting and boiling points.
- Non-metals can be **solid**, **liquid** or **gas** at room temperature.
- Non-metals are **poor** conductors of electricity and heat (except graphite).
- Non-metals in the solid state are **weak** and **brittle**. They are not malleable or ductile except carbon, which can be pulled into carbon fibres.
- Non-metals in the solid state are **dull** in appearance and are not sonorous.
- Non-metals usually have **low** densities.

Table 21.1 *Specific properties and occurrences of certain non-metals*

Non-metal	Properties and occurrence
Hydrogen (H_2)	A neutral gas at room temperature. Colourless, odourless and tasteless.
	Virtually insoluble in water.
	Less dense than air; hydrogen is the lightest known element.
	Mainly exists combined in compounds such as water, acids and most organic matter.
Chlorine (Cl_2)	An acidic, yellow-green, poisonous gas with a strong odour.
	Moderately soluble in water.
	Denser than air.
	It is highly reactive and so occurs combined in metal chlorides, e.g. sodium chloride or rock salt.
Oxygen (O_2)	A gas at room temperature. Neutral, colourless, odourless and tasteless.
	Slightly soluble in water.
	Slightly denser than air.
	Exists uncombined in the air, also combined in water, silicates, oxides and salts.
Carbon (C)	Has two main allotropes, diamond and graphite (see page 84):
	• **Diamond:**
	○ An extremely hard, transparent, colourless, sparkling solid.
	○ Has a very high melting point.
	○ Does not conduct electricity.
	• **Graphite:**
	○ A soft, flaky, opaque, dark grey solid.
	○ Has a very high melting point.
	○ Conducts electricity.
	Exists as diamond and graphite, coal, mineral oils, carbonates, hydrogen carbonates, organic matter and carbon dioxide gas.
Sulfur (S)	A solid at room temperature. Yellow powdery solid. Allotropes include: rhombic and monoclinic sulfur.
	Exists in the uncombined or elemental state as natural deposits near hot springs and volcanic regions. Also combined in metal sulfides and sulfates.
Nitrogen (N_2)	A gas at room temperature. Neutral, colourless, odourless and tasteless.
	Virtually insoluble in water.
	Slightly less dense than air.
	Exists uncombined in the atmosphere, also combined as metal nitrates, ammonium compounds and proteins.

Chemical properties of non-metals

- When they react with **metals**, non-metals ionise by **gaining** electrons to form negative **anions**. The non-metal behaves as an **oxidising agent** since it removes electrons from the metal (it causes the metal to **lose** electrons). This results in the formation of **ionic compounds**:

$$N + ne^- \longrightarrow N^{n-}$$

- When non-metals react with other **non-metals**, they **share** valence electrons. This results in the formation of **covalent compounds**. The non-metals may behave as **oxidising** or **reducing agents**.

Reactions of non-metals with metals and oxygen

- Reactions between non-metals and **metals** are **redox reactions** in which the non-metal acts as the oxidising agent and the metal acts as the reducing agent.
- Reactions between non-metals and **oxygen** are **redox reactions** in which oxygen acts as the oxidising agent and the other non-metal acts as the reducing agent. The product of the reaction is a **non-metal oxide**. Most non-metal oxides are **acidic**, for example, carbon dioxide (CO_2), sulfur dioxide (SO_2), sulfur trioxide (SO_3) and nitrogen dioxide (NO_2). A few are **neutral**, for example, water (H_2O), carbon monoxide (CO) and nitrogen monoxide (NO).

Table 21.2 *Reactions of some non-metals with metals and with oxygen*

Non-metal	Reaction with metals (using calcium as an example)	Reaction with oxygen
Hydrogen	Produces **metal hydrides**: $Ca(s) + H_2(g) \longrightarrow CaH_2(s)$ calcium hydride	Burns with a very pale blue flame to produce **water** as steam: $2H_2(g) + O_2(g) \longrightarrow 2H_2O(g)$
Chlorine	Produces **metal chlorides**: $Ca(s) + Cl_2(g) \longrightarrow CaCl_2(s)$ calcium chloride	———
Oxygen	Produces **metal oxides**: $2Ca(s) + O_2(g) \longrightarrow 2CaO(s)$ calcium oxide	———
Carbon	———	Burns to produce either carbon monoxide or carbon dioxide: • In a limited supply of oxygen, **carbon monoxide** is formed: $2C(s) + O_2(g) \longrightarrow 2CO(g)$ • In a plentiful supply of oxygen, **carbon dioxide** is formed: $C(s) + O_2(g) \longrightarrow CO_2(g)$
Sulfur	Produces **metal sulfides**: $Ca(s) + S(s) \longrightarrow CaS(s)$ calcium sulfide	Burns with a blue flame to form **sulfur dioxide**: $S(s) + O_2(g) \longrightarrow SO_2(g)$
Nitrogen	Produces **metal nitrides**: $3Ca(s) + N_2(g) \longrightarrow Ca_3N_2(s)$ calcium nitride	Reacts with oxygen, if the temperature is high enough, to form **nitrogen monoxide**: $N_2(g) + O_2(g) \longrightarrow 2NO(g)$

Behaviour of non-metals as oxidising and reducing agents

Unless reacting with oxygen, non-metals usually act as **oxidising agents**. However, hydrogen, carbon and sulfur can also act as reducing agents.

Non-metals acting as oxidising agents

- **All** non-metals act as oxidising agents when reacting with **metals** (see Table 21.2).
- **Oxygen** and **chlorine** act as oxidising agents in **all** reactions.

For example:

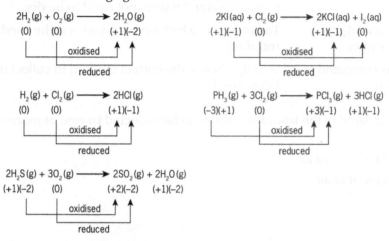

Let us examine the reaction of hydrogen sulfide and oxygen. Oxygen causes the oxidation number of sulfur to increase from −2 to +2. In the reaction with potassium iodide, chlorine removes electrons from the I⁻ ions causing their oxidation number to increase from −1 to 0. In the reaction with phosphorus trihydride (PH₃), chlorine causes the oxidation number of phosphorus to increase from −3 to +3.

Non-metals acting as reducing agents

- **Hydrogen, carbon, sulfur** and **nitrogen** act as reducing agents when reacting with **oxygen** (see Table 21.2).
- **Hydrogen** and **carbon** act as reducing agents when reacting with **metal oxides**. They reduce the metal ions to produce metal atoms.

For example:

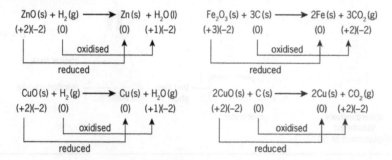

In the reaction between zinc oxide and hydrogen, the oxidation number of zinc decreases from +2 to 0, caused by the hydrogen. In the reaction of copper oxide and hydrogen, the oxidation number of copper decreases from +2 to 0, caused by the hydrogen. In the reaction of iron(III) oxide and carbon, the oxidation number of iron changes from +3 to 0, caused by the carbon. In the reaction of copper oxide and carbon, the oxidation number of copper decreases from +2 to 0, caused by the carbon.

Laboratory preparation of gases

When choosing a **method** for the laboratory preparation of a gas, the following must be taken into consideration: the reactants and the conditions, the properties of the gas, the method of collection of the gas, safety considerations, choice of apparatus and finally testing to ensure that the gas that is prepared is the correct gas. It is therefore very important to consider the properties of the gas when deciding on the method of preparation. The properties to be considered are given in Table 21.3.

Table 21.3 *Properties to be considered when choosing a method to prepare a gas*

Property to consider	Reason
Solubility of the gas in water.	To determine whether the gas can be collected by bubbling it through water if it does not need to be dry.
Reactivity of the gas with different drying agents.	To determine which drying agents can be used if a dry gas is required.
Density of the gas compared to the density of air.	To help choose the correct method to collect the gas if it has been dried.

When gases are prepared in the laboratory, they can be collected by one or more of the following techniques:

- downward displacement of air
- upward displacement of air
- over water
- in a syringe.

If a gas is less dense than air, it can be collected by **the downward displacement of air technique** or upward delivery (Figure 21.1). Gases such as hydrogen and ammonia can be collected by the downward displacement of air method. Conversely, gases which are denser than air can be collected by **the upward displacement of air technique** or downward delivery (Figure 21.1). Sulfur dioxide, carbon dioxide and chlorine can be collected by this technique.

Gases which are insoluble or slightly soluble in water and do not react with water can be collected **over water** (Figure 21.1). This method cannot be used if the gas is required to be dry. Gases such as oxygen, carbon dioxide, nitrogen and hydrogen can be collected using this method. An advantage of this technique is that we can visually tell when the gas jar or container is filled with the gas.

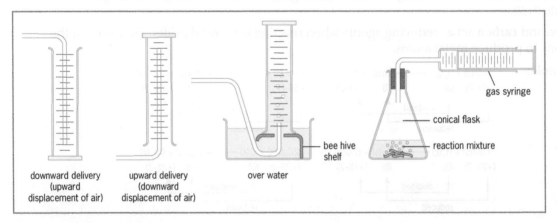

downward delivery
(upward
displacement of air)

upward delivery
(downward
displacement of air)

over water

bee hive
shelf

gas syringe

conical flask

reaction mixture

Figure 21.1 *Four different methods for collecting gas*

Another method that can be used to collect **any** gas is collecting it **in a syringe** as shown in Figure 21.1. This method has advantages, such as the gas can be transported without difficulty, a known volume of gas can be delivered to another container by simply securely attaching the syringe to the other container and pushing the plunger to the appropriate graduation mark, the residual gas remains uncontaminated, and we can visually determine when the syringe is full. A disadvantage of this method is that, if the gas evolves quickly, the syringe will fill quickly and the collection of the gas may be challenging to control.

Gases which are produced must be collected dry or dried because water is an impurity. The drying agent normally used is concentrated sulfuric acid. However, some gases cannot be dried using concentrated sulfuric acid because they react with the acid: ammonia and hydrogen sulfide are examples. Calcium oxide is another drying agent and can be used to dry ammonia.

Laboratory preparation of carbon dioxide and oxygen

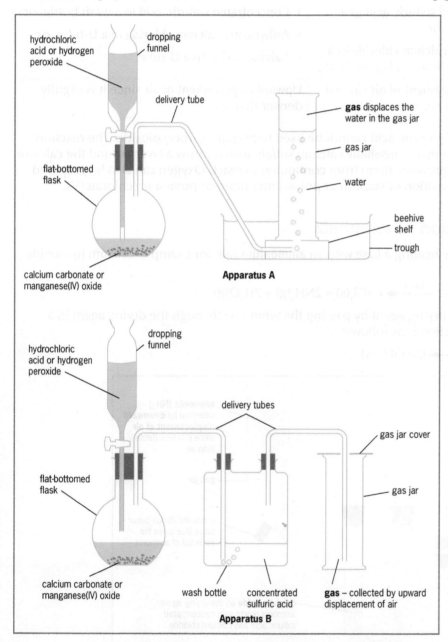

Figure 21.2 *Apparatus used for the laboratory preparation of oxygen and carbon dioxide*

Table 21.4 *Laboratory preparation of carbon dioxide and oxygen*

	Carbon dioxide (CO_2)	Oxygen (O_2)
Method	Reacting a **carbonate** with an **acid**, usually calcium carbonate and hydrochloric acid: $CaCO_3(s) + 2HCl(aq) \longrightarrow$ $\quad CaCl_2(aq) + CO_2(g) + H_2O(l)$	Decomposition of **hydrogen peroxide** using a **catalyst** of manganese(IV) oxide: $2H_2O_2(l) \xrightarrow{MnO_2} 2H_2O(l) + O_2(g)$
Apparatus	For **wet** carbon dioxide: apparatus **A** For **dry** carbon dioxide: apparatus **B**	For **wet** oxygen: apparatus **A** (Figure 21.2) For **dry** oxygen: apparatus **B** (Figure 21.2)
Drying agent	• **Concentrated sulfuric acid** in a wash bottle, or • Anhydrous **calcium chloride** in a U-tube (as shown in Figure 21.3)	• **Concentrated sulfuric acid** in a wash bottle, or • Anhydrous **calcium chloride** in a U-tube, or • **Calcium oxide** in a U-tube
Collection of the dry gas	**Upward displacement of air** since it is denser than air.	**Upward displacement of air** since it is slightly denser than air.

Note Calcium carbonate and sulfuric acid cannot be used to prepare carbon dioxide. The reaction quickly stops because it makes **insoluble** calcium sulfate which forms a layer around the calcium carbonate crystals and prevents them from continuing to react. Oxygen can also be prepared by the thermal decomposition of sodium or potassium nitrate or potassium chlorate(V).

Laboratory preparation of ammonia

Ammonia can be prepared by heating a **base** with an **ammonium salt**, for example, calcium hydroxide and ammonium chloride:

$$Ca(OH)_2(s) + 2NH_4Cl(s) \xrightarrow{heat} CaCl_2(s) + 2NH_3(g) + 2H_2O(g)$$

Calcium oxide is used as the drying agent by passing the ammonia through the drying agent in a U-tube (Figure 21.3). The reaction is as follows:

$$CaO(s) + H_2O(l) \longrightarrow Ca(OH)_2(s)$$

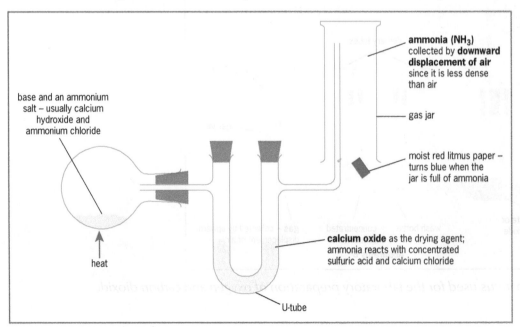

Figure 21.3 *The laboratory preparation of dry ammonia*

Note Ammonia reacts with water to form ammonium hydroxide solution, therefore **cannot** be collected by bubbling it through water. Ammonium nitrate is not used in the laboratory preparation of ammonia because it is highly explosive and can decompose to produce nitrous oxide and water vapour. Another ammonium salt that can be used in the reaction is ammonium sulfate.

Uses of carbon dioxide and oxygen

Because of their **properties**, carbon dioxide and oxygen have many uses.

Uses of carbon dioxide

Table 21.5 *Uses and properties of carbon dioxide*

Uses	Properties
In **fire extinguishers** when liquefied under pressure	Non-flammable Denser than air so it smothers the flames and keeps oxygen out. Used in fires where water cannot be used, for example, in fires caused by electrical short circuits.
To make **carbonated soft drinks**	Dissolves in the drink under pressure and bubbles out when pressure is released. Adds a pleasant tingle and taste.
As a **refrigerant** in the solid state ('dry ice')	Sublimes at -78.5 °C so keeps frozen foods at a very low temperature and does not leave a liquid residue when it sublimes to a gas.
As an **aerosol propellant** for certain foods, e.g. whipped cream	Relatively inert
Used to **fill containers** (silos) for storing grains	This inhibits fungal and bacterial growth on the grains.
Used as a **flooding gas** to pressurise oil wells	To increase output when extracting oil.
Used as an **alternative chemical** in the treatment of alkaline wastewater	Is a safer alternative than mineral acid and is effective in lowering the pH of the alkaline wastewater.

Uses of oxygen

Oxygen is essential for living organisms to carry out **aerobic respiration** and produce **energy**. It is therefore used:

- In **hospitals** to help patients with breathing difficulties and to ease certain medical disorders, including emphysema, asthma, chronic bronchitis, Covid-19, treating persons suffering from carbon monoxide poisoning and heart disease.
- On **aeroplanes** and **submarines** for people onboard to breathe in emergencies.
- In **spacesuits** for astronauts to breathe.
- In **breathing apparatus** for mountaineers and scuba and deep-sea divers.
- To **destroy** bacteria.

Oxygen is essential for **combustion** to occur. It is therefore used:

- In **welding torches** to burn the acetylene or hydrogen and produce extremely high-temperature flames.
- In the liquid state it is used to burn the fuel to produce the thrust in **rocket engines**.
- In the **production of energy** in industrial processes, generators, cars, aeroplanes and ships.

Uses of non-metals and their compounds

Non-metals and their compounds have a great many uses in industry and everyday life. Figures 21.4 through 21.9 give some uses of some non-metals and their compounds.

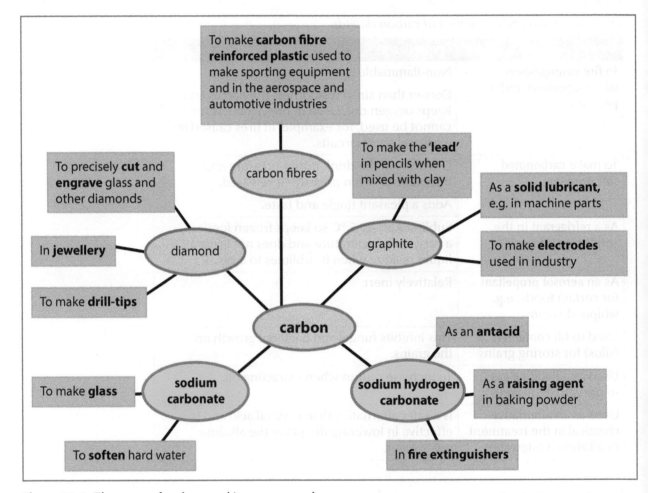

To make **carbon fibre reinforced plastic** used to make sporting equipment and in the aerospace and automotive industries

carbon fibres

To make the **'lead'** in pencils when mixed with clay

To precisely **cut** and **engrave** glass and other diamonds

As a **solid lubricant,** e.g. in machine parts

In **jewellery**

diamond

graphite

To make **electrodes** used in industry

To make **drill-tips**

carbon

As an **antacid**

To make **glass**

sodium carbonate

sodium hydrogen carbonate

As a **raising agent** in baking powder

To **soften** hard water

In **fire extinguishers**

Figure 21.4 *The uses of carbon and its compounds*

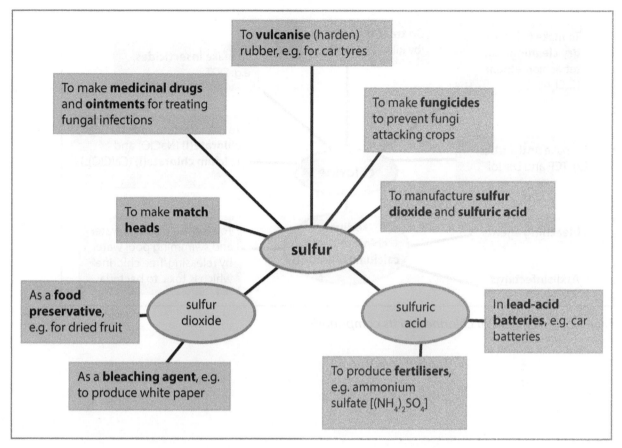

Figure 21.5 *The uses of sulfur and its compounds*

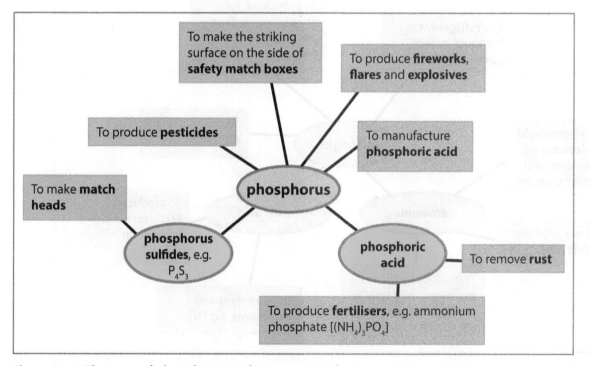

Figure 21.6 *The uses of phosphorus and its compounds*

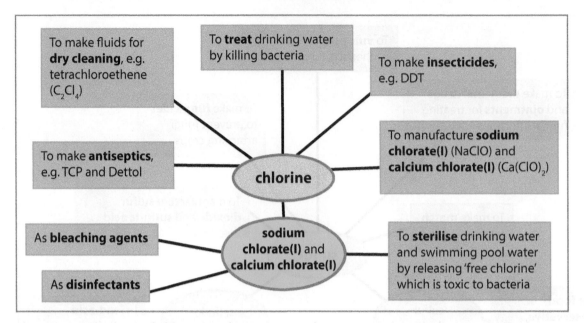

Figure 21.7 *The uses of chlorine and its compounds*

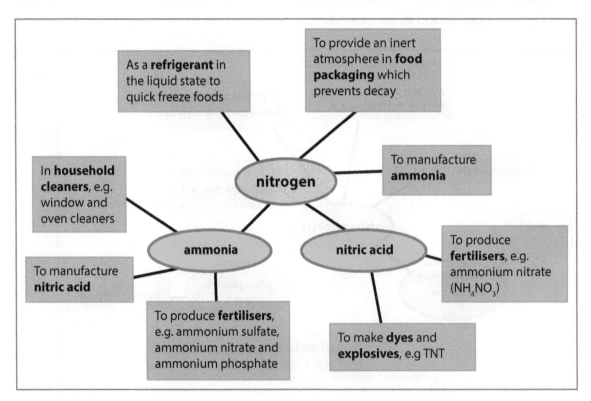

Figure 21.8 *The uses of nitrogen and its compounds*

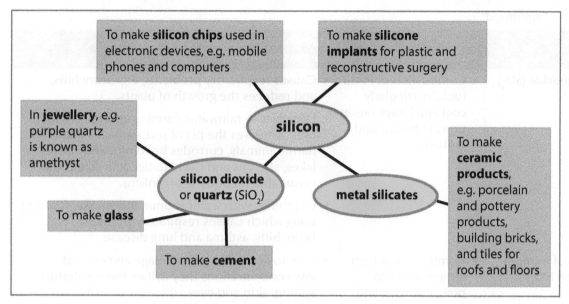

Figure 21.9 *The uses of silicon and its compounds*

Harmful effects of non-metals and their compounds

Some compounds of non-metals can be harmful to living organisms and the environment. Human activities are causing an increase in their concentrations within the environment. These result in pollution of natural resources, such as air and water. Release of waste gases and particulates in the atmosphere lead to air pollution. Nitrates, phosphates, untreated sewage, detergents and fertilisers being leached or released into our waterways lead to water pollution. Table 21.6 summarises the harmful effects of some compounds of non-metals.

Table 21.6 *Harmful effects of some compounds of non-metals*

Pollutant	Sources in the environment	Harmful effects on living organisms and the environment
Carbon dioxide (CO_2)	• Complete combustion of fossil fuels, particularly in power stations, industry, motor vehicles and aeroplanes.	• Builds up in the upper atmosphere enhancing the **greenhouse effect** and **global warming**, which is causing polar ice caps and glaciers to melt, sea levels to rise, low-lying coastal areas to flood, changes in global climate and more severe weather patterns. • Some is absorbed by oceans causing **ocean acidification**, which is expected to affect the ability of shellfish to produce their shells, and of reef-building corals to produce their skeletons.
Carbon monoxide (CO)	• Incomplete combustion of fossil fuels which occurs mainly in motor vehicles.	• Combines with haemoglobin more easily than oxygen. This reduces the amount of oxygen that gets to body cells which reduces respiration and mental awareness. It causes dizziness, headaches and visual impairment, and can lead to unconsciousness and death.

(Continued)

Table 21.6 *Continued*

Pollutant	Sources in the environment	Harmful effects on living organisms and the environment
Sulfur dioxide (SO_2)	• Combustion of fossil fuels, particularly coal and heavy oils in power stations and industry.	• Causes respiratory problems, e.g. bronchitis, and reduces the growth of plants. • Dissolves in rainwater, forming **acid rain**. Acid rain decreases the pH of soil, damages plants, harms animals, corrodes buildings, and causes lakes, streams and rivers to become acidic and unsuitable for aquatic organisms. • Combines with water vapour and smoke, forming **smog** which causes respiratory problems, e.g. bronchitis, asthma and lung disease.
Oxides of nitrogen (NO and NO_2)	• Combustion at high temperatures in power stations and engines of motor vehicles which causes nitrogen and oxygen in the air to react.	• Very toxic. Cause lung damage and even at low concentrations they irritate the respiratory system, skin and eyes. • Cause leaves to die and reduce plant growth. • Dissolve in rainwater producing **acid rain** (see above).
Hydrogen sulfide (H_2S)	• Decomposing organic waste in farmyards, landfills and garbage dumps. • A waste product from petroleum refineries.	• Extremely toxic. Even low concentrations irritate the eyes and respiratory system. • Combines readily with haemoglobin in the same way as carbon monoxide (see above).
Carbon particles (C)	• Combustion of fossil fuels. • Bush fires and cigarette smoke.	• Coat leaves which reduces photosynthesis, and blacken buildings. • Combine with water vapour and sulfur dioxide to form **smog** (see above).
Chlorofluorocarbons (CFCs)	• Used in refrigerators and air conditioners as a refrigerant, and in some aerosol sprays as a propellant.	• Break down the **ozone layer** in the upper atmosphere. This allows more ultraviolet light to reach the Earth's surface which is leading to more people developing skin cancer, cataracts and depressed immune systems.
Pesticides, e.g. insecticides, fungicides and herbicides	• Used in agriculture to control pests, diseases and weeds. • Used to control vectors of disease, e.g. mosquitoes.	• Become **higher in concentration** up food chains and can harm top consumers. • Can harm **useful** organisms as well as harmful ones, e.g. bees which are crucial for pollination in plants.
Nitrate ions (NO_3^-) and phosphate ions (PO_4^{3-})	• Chemical fertilisers used in agriculture. • Synthetic detergents.	• Cause **eutrophication**, i.e. the rapid growth of green plants and algae in lakes, ponds and rivers, which causes the water to turn green. The plants and algae begin to die and are decomposed by aerobic bacteria which multiply and use up the dissolved oxygen. This causes other aquatic organisms to die, e.g. fish.

Figures 21.10 to 21.12 show some of the harmful effects of compounds of non-metals.

Figure 21.10 *Damage to plants and building from acid rain*

Figure 21.11 *Smog formation*

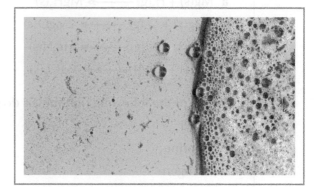

Figure 21.12 *Eutrophication*

Disposal of solid waste containing plastics

Plastics are organic compounds composed of non-metallic elements. They are made mainly from hydrocarbons obtained from natural gas, crude oil and coal. Most plastics are **non-biodegradable**, so they remain in the environment for a very long time. Because of this, getting rid of solid waste containing plastics is a major problem:

- **Toxic gases** are produced when plastics burn. Disposal of plastics in incinerators can cause air pollution and health problems.

- **Toxic chemicals** are continually released from some plastics. These chemicals can contaminate soil and groundwater when plastics are disposed of in landfills.

- About 25% of all solid waste going to **landfills** is composed of plastics. More and more land is being used up to dispose of these plastics.

- Plastics often end up in **lakes, rivers** and **oceans** when not disposed of correctly and can harm aquatic organisms (see page 280–281).

The more plastic items that are **recycled**, the more the problem of their disposal will be solved.

Figure 21.13 *Solid waste containing plastics*

Recalling facts

1 Which of the following is true when a non-metal reacts with oxygen?

   I   Oxygen acts as a reducing agent.

   II It is a redox reaction.

   III The product of the reaction is a non-metal oxide.

   a I only

   b I and II only

   c II and III only

   d I, II and III

2 Which of the following equations does NOT represent the reaction between magnesium and a non-metal?

   a $Mg(s) + H_2(g) \longrightarrow MgH_2(s)$

   b $2Mg(s) + O_2(g) \longrightarrow 2MgO(s)$

   c $3Mg(s) + N_2(g) \longrightarrow Mg_2N(s)$

   d $Mg(s) + Cl_2(g) \longrightarrow MgCl_2(s)$

3 Which of the following non-metals does NOT react with oxygen?

   a sulfur

   b chlorine

   c nitrogen

   d hydrogen

4 Which of the following properties is NOT considered when preparing a gas?

   a colour

   b density

   c reactivity

   d solubility

5 Oxygen is used in _____

   a refrigerants

   b aerosol propellants

   c spacesuits

   d fire extinguishers

6 Sodium hydrogencarbonate ($NaHCO_3$) has the following uses except:

   a as a raising agent

   b as an antacid

   c as a water softener

   d in fire extinguishers

7 Which is NOT a greenhouse gas?

a H_2O

b CO_2

c CH_4

d N_2

8 Nitrogen is used to make all the following except:

a fertilisers

b household cleaners

c explosives

d pesticides

9 Which of the following is TRUE about plastics?

I Most are non-biodegradable.

II When burnt they produce toxic gases.

III Plastics cannot be recycled

a I and II only

b I and III only

c II and III only

d I, II and III

10 Which of the following gases breaks down the ozone layer?

a CH_4

b CO_2

c CO

d CFCs

11 List the physical properties of non-metals.

12 What are the properties of gases that need to be taken into consideration when preparing a gas in the laboratory? Explain why each of these properties is important in the method chosen.

13 Several drying agents can be used when preparing oxygen and carbon dioxide gases in the laboratory. Name them.

14 List four uses each of carbon dioxide and oxygen.

15 Give five uses each of the following non-metals and their compounds:

a nitrogen

b phosphorus

c sulfur

Applying facts

16 'Reactions between non-metals and oxygen are redox reactions.' Using your knowledge of oxidation and reduction, and a suitable equation, explain this statement.

17 Both carbon and hydrogen can act as reducing agents when reacting with metal oxides. Explain this statement using equations and oxidation numbers.

18 Describe the laboratory production of ammonia. Your answer must include a labelled diagram of the apparatus used, the reactants and the drying agent. Explain why ammonia cannot be collected by bubbling through water.

19 Discuss the sources and the harmful effects of the following on the environment:

a hydrogen sulfide

b carbon dioxide

c pesticides

20 Most plastics are non-biodegradable. Discuss the major negative effects of non-biodegradable plastics on the environment. How may the problem of plastics filling up our landfills be reduced?

22 Water

Learning objectives

- Describe the unique properties of **water**.
- Relate the unique properties of water to its functions in **living systems**.
- Discuss the consequences of the **solvent properties of water**.
- Distinguish between the two types of **water hardness**.
- Describe the methods of **large-scale treatment of water for domestic purposes**.
- Discuss methods in which water can be **treated at home**.
- Describe how hard water can be **softened**.

Water is essential for all life forms and is the most common substance found on Earth; it covers three quarters of the Earth's surface and can exist in three states: as a solid (ice), liquid (water) and gas (water vapour). The state in which water exists depends on the temperature and pressure. All organisms are made up of water, which is a simple molecule containing two atoms of hydrogen and one atom of oxygen. The structure of water gives it its unique properties. Water molecules are **polar** (see page 79). The partial positively charged hydrogen atoms and partial negatively charged oxygen atoms of water molecules are attracted to each other forming **hydrogen bonds**. Hydrogen bonds are generally **stronger** than the intermolecular forces between other molecules and they have a significant effect on the **physical properties** of water. These properties are important to **living organisms**.

The unique properties of water

- **Water has a maximum density at 4 °C**

    Density is a measure of the closeness with which molecules are packed together. It is defined as:

    $$\text{density} = \frac{\text{mass}}{\text{volume}}$$

    The density of a substance with a fixed mass decreases when its volume decreases and increases when its volume increases.

    When most substances solidify from the liquid state they contract. Water is unique in that when it solidifies into ice it expands and becomes less dense. When water is cooled to 4 °C it **contracts** and becomes denser. If it is cooled below 4 °C, it starts to **expand** and become less dense. It continues to expand until it freezes at 0 °C. As a result, ice at 0 °C **floats** on water as it forms. This can be explained by the hydrogen bonding which exists in water. There are more spaces in the ice because the hydrogen bonds do not allow the water molecules to line up efficiently as they do in the liquid state. Therefore the water molecules are more compact in the liquid state than in solid ice.

    When a pond, lake or river freezes in winter, ice forms on the surface and this layer forms a barrier between the water below the ice and the cold air, offering insulation and stopping the rest of the water from getting cold as quickly. The warmer, denser water remains below the ice. **Aquatic organisms** are able to survive the winter by staying in the water beneath the ice.

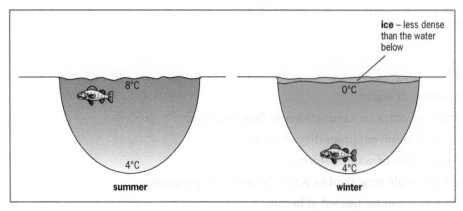

Figure 22.1 *Water temperatures in a pond or lake in the summer and winter*

- **Water has a high heat of vaporisation**

  Volatility refers to how readily/easily a substance vaporises, and **the heat of vaporisation** is the amount of heat energy required to change a liquid to a gas. A lot of heat energy is required to change liquid water to water vapour, due to the hydrogen bonds which exist between the water molecules. Therefore, water has a **high heat of vaporisation** and hence the **volatility** of water is low.

  When water evaporates from the surface of an organism, it removes a lot of heat energy from the organism, making sweating and transpiration efficient **cooling** mechanisms.

- **Water has relatively high melting and boiling points**

  Compared with other molecules of a similar size, water has relatively high melting and boiling points (0 °C and 100 °C, respectively). Therefore water is **not very volatile**. More energy must be supplied to break the hydrogen bonds that hold the water molecules together, so it has a higher boiling point. This means that liquid water turns into a vapour at a much higher temperature, so it has low volatility. At the temperatures experienced on Earth, most water is in the liquid state. This means that seas, rivers, lakes and ponds exist and provide an environment for aquatic organisms.

- **Water has a high specific heat capacity**

  It requires a **lot of heat energy** to increase the temperature of water by 1 °C. As a result, water can absorb a lot of heat energy without its temperature changing very much.

  - Since the bodies of living organisms contain between 60% and 70% water, they can absorb a lot of heat energy without their body temperatures changing very much. So they can survive in extremes of temperature.
  - As atmospheric temperatures change, the temperatures of large bodies of water, such as lakes and seas, do not change very much. Therefore, aquatic organisms do not experience extreme fluctuations in the temperature of their environment.
  - In coastal areas, temperatures remain cooler because the water absorbs large amounts of heat during the day and slowly releases the heat energy during the night.

- **Water dissolves a large number of substances**

  Water is commonly referred to as the universal solvent because it can dissolve many substances. Being **polar**, water can dissolve both ionic and polar covalent compounds making it an excellent solvent. As can be seen in Figure 22.2, the water molecules and ionic compounds are separate. The ionic bonds between the sodium and chloride ions are weakened by the polar attraction of the water molecules, dissociating the sodium and chloride ions. The slightly charged areas (dipoles) of the water molecules are attracted to the opposing charge on the sodium and chloride ions, forming hydrated shells, thus dissolving the ionic sodium chloride compound. Figure 22.3 shows how ethanol mixes with water. The ethanol molecule contains a polar O–H bond just like the water molecule. The polar water molecules interact strongly with the polar bond in the ethanol, forming a mutual attraction between the dipoles.

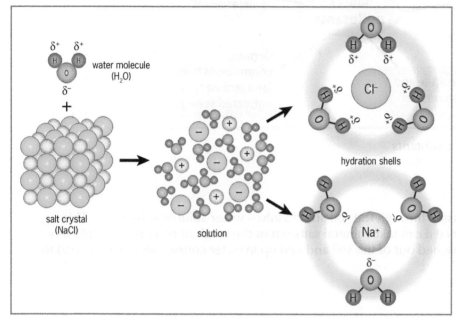

Figure 22.2 *Water dissolving an ionic compound*

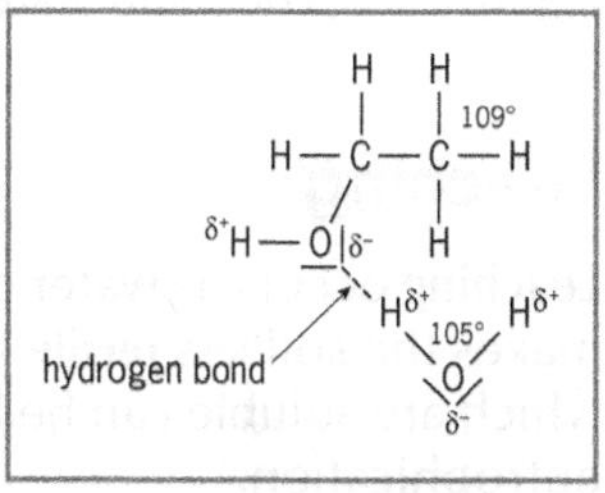

Figure 22.3 *Water mixes completely with polar covalent substances like ethanol*

This is **important** to living organisms because:

○ Water dissolves chemicals in the cells of organisms so that **chemical reactions** such as respiration can occur.

○ Water dissolves useful substances, such as food and mineral salts, so they can be **absorbed** into the bodies of organisms and **transported** around their bodies.

○ Water dissolves waste and harmful substances so they can be **excreted** from living organisms, for example, urea dissolves in water forming urine.

The solvent properties of water can also be **detrimental** because they can cause water to become **hard** or **polluted** and mineral salts to be **leached** out of the soil.

Consequences of water's solvent properties

Water pollution

Water pollution is the contamination of water bodies, usually because of human activities reducing the ability of the body of water to provide essential substances to ecosystems and making it toxic to humans and the environment. Figure 22.4 shows how water becomes **polluted** when it dissolves harmful substances in the environment.

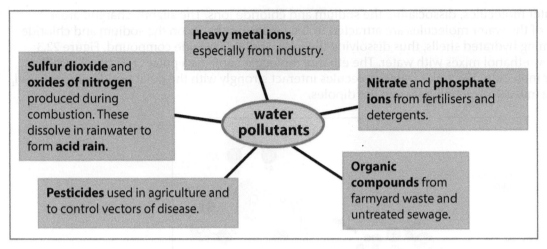

Figure 22.4 *The main water pollutants*

Leaching

Leaching occurs as water passes through the soil and dissolves water-soluble substances. This makes the soil **less fertile** since it can take mineral salts out of the reach of plant roots. Fertilisers which are soluble can be leached out of the soil and end up in water courses and this can lead to eutrophication.

Water hardness

Dissolved **calcium** and **magnesium salts** cause water to become hard. Hard water leaves limescale in kettles, for example. **Hard water** does not lather easily with soap, whereas **soft water** lathers easily with soap. When soap, sodium octadecanoate ($C_{17}H_{35}COONa$), is added to water containing dissolved Ca^{2+} or Mg^{2+} ions (hard water), insoluble calcium and magnesium octadecanoate form. This is commonly called **scum**:

for example: $2C_{17}H_{35}COONa(aq) + Ca^{2+}(aq) \longrightarrow (C_{17}H_{35}COO)_2Ca(s) + 2Na^+(aq)$
                            soap   scum

Hard water is **inconvenient** because:

- It causes unpleasant scum to form (Figure 22.5). Scum discolours clothes and forms a grey, greasy layer around sinks, baths and showers.

- It **wastes** soap. Soap only lathers when all the Ca^{2+} or Mg^{2+} ions have been precipitated out as scum.

- It causes **limescale** (see page 339) to be deposited in kettles, boilers and hot water pipes (Figure 22.6). This wastes electricity and can block pipes.

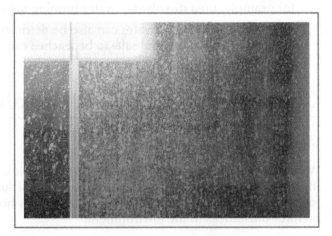

Figure 22.5 *Soap scum forms on shower screens*

Figure 22.6 *Limescale on a sink, a tap and a kettle element*

There are **two** types of water hardness:

- **Temporary hardness**

  Dissolved **calcium hydrogen carbonate** ($Ca(HCO_3)_2$) and **magnesium hydrogen carbonate** ($Mg(HCO_3)_2$) cause temporary hardness. It is found in limestone-rich areas. When rainwater containing dissolved carbon dioxide passes through limestone (calcium carbonate, $CaCO_3$), soluble calcium hydrogen carbonate forms which dissolves in the rainwater:

  $$CaCO_3(s) + H_2O(l) + CO_2(g) \longrightarrow Ca(HCO_3)_2(aq)$$

  Temporary hardness **can** be removed by **boiling** the water (see page 339).

- **Permanent hardness**

  Dissolved **calcium sulfate** ($CaSO_4$) and **magnesium sulfate** ($MgSO_4$) cause permanent hardness. Permanent hardness **cannot** be removed by **boiling**.

Treatment of water for domestic use

Water from natural sources is usually contaminated and is not safe for human consumption. To make water safe for domestic use, it is **treated** using various different methods.

Large-scale treatment of water

The following steps can be used to treat water before it is piped to homes:

- **Screening.** Large suspended debris such as plastic bottles, branches and leaves are removed using wire meshes.

- **Flocculation.** Certain chemicals, such as alum (aluminium sulfate) and lime are added so that fine suspended solid particles clump together to form larger particles called **floc.**

- **Sedimentation.** The water is then allowed to flow into a reservoir where the floc is allowed to settle.

- **Filtration.** The clear water above the floc is passed through **filters** to remove any remaining particles. This filtration system is made of a bed of gravel and sand. Activated carbon filters can also be used to deodorise the water. Filtration also removes some microorganisms, for example, bacteria and viruses.

- **Chlorination. Chlorine gas** or **monochloroamine** (NH_2Cl) are added to kill any remaining bacteria and viruses. The amount of chlorine used to sterilise the water is safe for human consumption. The water is now sterile and can be released into the water pipeline system where a person can turn the tap, fill a glass and directly consume water that is safe for drinking.

Methods to treat water in the home

- **Boiling**

  This is a very simple and easy technique of purifying water at home. Most microorganisms can be killed by **boiling** water for 15 minutes.

- **Filtering**

  Fibre filters can be used to remove suspended particles. **Carbon filters** containing activated charcoal can be used to remove dissolved organic compounds, odours and unpleasant tastes. These filters can be attached to the tap or the pipelines and must be replaced often; otherwise the filters could support microbial growth and contaminate the water supply to your home. Another type of filter system which can be used at home is a filter pitcher (Figure 22.7), where water is filled into a pitcher and the water passes through an activated charcoal cartridge which acts like the filter mentioned above. These filters must also be replaced often to prevent microorganisms growing in them and contaminating the water.

Figure 22.7 *A home water filter pitcher and replaceable cartridge*

- **Chlorinating**

  Microorganisms can be destroyed by adding **sodium chlorate(I)** solution (NaClO) which is found in chlorine-based bleaches. To kill microorganisms without leaving any bad taste, 10 drops of chlorine-based bleach is added to 5 litres of water and left to stand for 30 minutes. **Calcium chlorate(I)** tablets ($Ca(ClO)_2$) can also be added to water to destroy microorganisms, making the water safe for consumption.

Methods to soften hard water

Hard water can be converted to **soft** water by removing the dissolved Ca^{2+} or Mg^{2+} ions. All methods remove both temporary and permanent hardness, except boiling.

- **Boiling**

  Boiling removes **temporary hardness** by causing dissolved calcium hydrogencarbonate and magnesium hydrogencarbonate to decompose:

  for example: $$Ca(HCO_3)_2(aq) \xrightarrow{\text{heat}} CaCO_3(s) + H_2O(l) + CO_2(g)$$

  The insoluble carbonates precipitate out, thereby removing the Ca^{2+} and Mg^{2+} ions. The calcium carbonate produced is also known as **limescale** or **kettle fur**. Permanent hardness is not removed using this method.

- **Adding washing soda, sodium carbonate**

  Sodium carbonate, added to hard water, causes dissolved Ca^{2+} or Mg^{2+} ions to precipitate out as **insoluble** calcium carbonate and magnesium carbonate. These can then be filtered off.

  Removing **temporary hardness**:

  for example: $$Ca(HCO_3)_2(aq) + Na_2CO_3(aq) \longrightarrow CaCO_3(s) + 2NaHCO_3(aq)$$

  Removing **permanent hardness**:

  for example: $$CaSO_4(aq) + Na_2CO_3(aq) \longrightarrow CaCO_3(s) + Na_2SO_4(aq)$$
  Ionically: $$Ca^{2+}(aq) + CO_3^{2-}(aq) \longrightarrow CaCO_3(s)$$
  $$MgCl_2(aq) + Na_2CO_3(aq) \longrightarrow MgCO_3(s) + 2NaCl(aq)$$

- **Ion-exchange**

  Water is slowly passed through an ion-exchange column in a water-softening device (Figure 22.8). The column contains an **ion-exchange resin** called **zeolite, Na_2Z**. Any Ca^{2+} and Mg^{2+} ions in the water **displace** the Na^+ ions and are absorbed into the zeolite. The Na^+ ions enter the water but do not cause it to be hard:

  for example: $$Ca^{2+}(aq) + \underset{\substack{\text{ion-exchange} \\ \text{resin}}}{Na_2Z(s)} \longrightarrow CaZ(s) + 2Na^+(aq)$$

Figure 22.8 *An ion-exchange water softening device*

- ## Distillation

Water is boiled and the steam is condensed to form pure **distilled water** which is collected in a separate container. Any dissolved salts and microorganisms are left behind. This method is not an economical method to produce potable water as it utilises a large amount of energy to heat the water. Solar stills (Figure 22.9) can be used to produce distilled water on a small scale. The sun's energy is used to evaporate impure water (e.g. salt water), which then cools, condenses and is collected as potable water.

Figure 22.9 *A solar still*

- ## Reverse osmosis

Water is forced through a **differentially permeable** membrane under pressure and dissolved substances remain behind on the pressurised side. This removes Ca^{2+} and Mg^{2+} ions in the water as well as other ions, contaminants and most microorganisms. Desalination plants use this technology to produce fresh water from seawater (Figure 22.10).

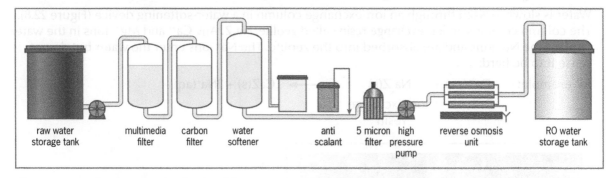

Figure 22.10 *Fresh water is obtained from seawater by reverse osmosis*

Recalling facts

1 The unique properties of water can be attributed to:

   a covalent bonding

   b ionic bonding

   c hydrogen bonding

   d metallic bonding

2 Water molecules are _____ because each molecule has a side that has a partial positive charge and a side that has a partial negative charge.

a non-polar

b polar

c volatile

d cohesive

3 All of the following are classified as special properties of water except:

a relatively high melting point

b high specific heat capacity

c relatively high viscosity

d density abnormality

4 One detrimental effect of water being able to dissolve many substances is:

a dissolving waste products so that they can be excreted

b mineral salts can be leached out of soil

c dissolving substances facilitating absorption in organisms

d dissolving chemicals in cells facilitating chemical reactions to occur

5 Which of the following is NOT a water pollutant?

a nitrate ions

b pesticides

c heavy metals

d carbon ions

6 Permanent hardness is caused by:

a $CaCO_3$

b $CaSO_4$

c $MgSO_3$

d $Ca(HCO_3)_2$

7 Which of the following is NOT a method used to soften water?

a boiling

b chlorination

c ion-exchange

d reverse osmosis

8 Which is NOT a method used to treat water at home to make it safe to consume?

a boiling

b chlorination

c filtration

d flocculation

9 Which of the following is TRUE about scum?

   I It forms around sinks and showers.

   II It is a precipitate of Ca^{2+} and Mg^{2+} ions.

   III It is a precipitate when soap is mixed with soft water.

   a I only

   b II only

   c I and II only

   d I, II and III

10 Water attains maximum density at _____ °C

   a 100   **b** 0   **c** 4   **d** −4

11 What is meant by the following terms?

   a polar molecule

   b specific heat capacity

   c heat of evaporation

   d hardness of water

   e soft water

   f scum

12 Water is described as a 'universal solvent' and when it dissolves harmful substances it becomes polluted. List the main pollutants of water.

Applying facts

13 **a** Distinguish between temporary and permanent hardness of water.

   b Explain the effect of heating on the temporary and permanent hardness of water. Explain with the aid of an equation the cause of limescale build-up in a kettle.

   c Describe one way in which water can be treated to remove both the temporary and permanent hardness of water. Support your answer with an equation.

14 **a** Explain each stage of the process of producing drinking water from natural fresh water sources.

   b Describe the industrial process of obtaining drinking water from seawater.

   c Distillation is another method of producing drinking water. Is this method economically feasible? Explain your answer.

15 Describe two methods of treating water at home to ensure that it is safe for drinking.

Analysing data

16 List the unique properties of water. Explain how water being a polar molecule accounts for these unique properties.

23 Green Chemistry

Learning objectives

- Define the term **Green Chemistry**.
- Outline the principles of **Green Chemistry**.
- Cite some examples of Green Products produced in industry.

The concept of **Green Chemistry**, also known as **sustainable chemistry**, was established by Paul Anastas and John Warner in 1990 and provides a framework for chemists to use when designing new materials, chemical products and processes. Its primary aim is to reduce the flow of **chemical pollutants** into the environment.

Green Chemistry is the utilisation of a set of principles in the design, manufacture and application of chemical products that reduces or eliminates the use and generation of hazardous substances.

Green Chemistry, as stated in the definition, strives to reduce or eliminate the use and generation of hazardous waste substances. In decreasing or eradicating dangerous waste usage or creation, many positive advantages to human health, the environment, the economy and business result.

Figure 23.1 summarises some of the benefits of Green Chemistry. Using the principles of Green Chemistry can lead to cleaner air and water supply, and the production of safer chemical and food products for use and consumption by humans and animals. Hazardous waste substances can disrupt ecosystems, and plants and animals can suffer the ill effects of exposure to these substances. These effects can be averted when hazardous waste production is minimised or eliminated. Global warming, ozone depletion and smog formation would be greatly reduced, positively benefitting our environment. There would also be a great reduction in sending hazardous waste to landfill. The benefit to business is tremendous as there are fewer synthetic steps in the manufacturing process, and less energy and water consumption, producing greater yields of products. Waste reduction and elimination lead to less money being spent on hazard waste remediation (removal of pollution or contaminants) and disposal. These contribute to businesses making more profit. There is also reduced use of non-renewable petroleum products.

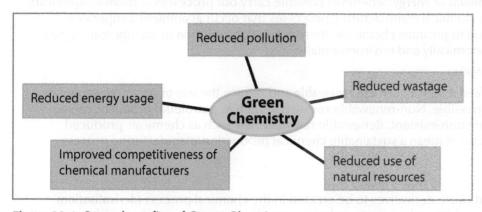

Figure 23.1 *Some benefits of Green Chemistry*

The twelve principles of Green Chemistry

Green Chemistry has **twelve** principles:

1 Prevent waste

Design processes that **prevent waste** from being produced rather than having to treat waste or clean it up afterwards. Manufacturing procedures must be designed to enhance the amount of product obtained while minimising the amount of waste produced.

2 Maximise atom economy

Design processes which incorporate most or all of the starting materials into the final products so that **few atoms are wasted**. Any products from the reaction that are not useful lead to more waste generation and a decrease in atom economy.

3 Design less hazardous chemical syntheses

Design processes that use and generate substances which are as **non-toxic** as possible to humans and the environment. When less toxic starting material is used less toxic waste is formed, reducing the risk to humans and the environment and also reducing expenditure in disposing of the hazardous waste substances.

4 Design safer chemicals and products

Design chemical products, whether medical or industrial, that are as effective as possible functionally whilst being as **non-toxic** as possible. We need to study the functionality of chemicals in living things and the environment and apply our findings in the design of intended products so that a safer and more effective product is obtained.

5 Use safer solvents and auxiliaries

Avoid using solvents, separating agents and other additional (auxiliary) chemicals, or replace them with **safer alternatives.** Solvents and other auxiliary chemicals increase risks such as flammability and instability, so these materials must be recyclable and have low toxicity, and must use a minimum amount of energy for the reaction to occur. Steps in the manufacturing process that use auxiliary chemicals must be eliminated or minimised or safer alternatives used, to avoid risks to the environment and employees and the production of hazardous waste materials.

6 Increase energy efficiency

Use the **minimum amount of energy**: whenever possible carry out processes at room temperature and pressure. When chemical manufacturing processes that occur at ambient temperature and pressure are used to produce chemicals, there is less consumption of energy, leading to a reduced impact economically and environmentally.

7 Use renewable feedstocks

Use raw materials (feedstocks) which are **renewable** and reduce the use of non-renewable raw materials wherever possible. Non-renewable resources, such as petroleum products, can be depleted and become non-existent. Renewable raw materials such as chemicals produced from biological processes mean a sustainable chemical production/manufacturing process can be used.

8 Reduce derivatives

Avoid processes that cause derivatives to be created in the chemical process (**derivatisation**) because they require additional reagents and can generate waste, for example, avoid temporarily modifying physical and chemical processes to prevent unwanted reactions. During a chemical reaction, chemicals are added to protect a certain part of a molecule from change while other parts of the molecule undergo change. The addition of these chemicals increases the amount of waste generated, increasing risks to the environment and humans. Enzymes can be used in chemical processes to effect changes to the part of the molecules which need to be changed since enzymes are specific in their actions and this will eliminate the use of chemicals to protect the part of the molecule which does not have to undergo change.

9 Use catalysts rather than stoichiometric reagents

Use **catalysts** whenever possible because they are effective in small amounts, can carry out a single reaction many times, cause reactions to occur faster and at lower temperatures, and reduce the production of unwanted and hazardous by-products. The use of catalysts leads to higher atom economies in reactions.

10 Design for degradation

Design chemical products so that, when their functional life ends, they **break down** into harmless products by UV light, water or naturally occurring microorganisms, so that they do not persist in the environment (Figure 23.2, 23.3, 23.4). If products are not biodegradable, such as plastics made from petroleum, they will accumulate and remain in the environment and will continue to harm plants and animals and the environment.

Figure 23.2 *Biofuels are made from renewable raw materials such as maize and oil palm*

Figure 23.3 *Biodegradable plastic bags*

Figure 23.4 *Environmentally friendly disposable tableware*

11 Analyse in real-time to prevent pollution

Monitor the progress of any chemical process to prevent accidents or unexpected reactions which could lead to the formation of any unwanted or hazardous by-products. These unwanted or hazardous substances can be expelled into the environment and cause harm or pollute the environment.

12 Minimise the potential for accidents

Choose reagents to be used in chemical processes which keep the possibility of **chemical accidents** to a minimum, for example, explosions, fires and the release of toxic substances. Procedures should also be designed to minimise risk.

Innovations in Green Chemistry

The benefits of practising the principles of Green Chemistry in the production of products are recognised worldwide with positive benefits economically and environmentally and will lead to a cleaner and more sustainable planet. To encourage and promote research and education in the field of Green Chemistry, the US Environmental Protection Agency (EPA) and the **ACS Green Chemistry Institute®** sponsors awards in this field. The Presidential Green Chemistry Challenge Award is one such award.

Some examples of Green Chemistry accomplishments in the fields of pharmaceuticals, paints, detergents and housewares are discussed below.

- Elevance Renewable Sciences uses the catalytic chemical process called *metathesis* to break down natural oils and recombine the fragments into high-performance chemicals to produce specialty chemicals for many uses, such as highly concentrated cold-water detergents that provide better cleaning with reduced energy costs.

- Merck and Codexis developed a second-generation green synthesis of sitagliptin (an anti-diabetic medication to treat type 2 diabetes). An enzymatic-catalysed manufacturing process was developed which not only eliminates the use of a metal catalyst but also increases the yield and safety and reduces waste production.

- Codexis uses an engineered enzyme and a low-cost feedstock which optimise both the enzyme and the chemical process to manufacture the drug Simvastatin, a prescription drug for treating high cholesterol. The drug is produced more cost effectively, decreasing the hazard and waste produced. This drug had been manufactured by a multistep process which used large amounts of hazardous reagents and produced a large amount of toxic waste in the manufacturing process.

- Innovations in the plastics world include NatureWorks using a method where microorganisms convert cornstarch into a resin that is just as strong as the rigid petroleum-based plastic currently used for containers such as water bottles and yogurt pots. Also, biodegradable bags can be manufactured using starch and calcium carbonate, which completely break down into carbon dioxide, water and biomass that can be composted.

- The paint industry has successful innovations in producing green paints. Procter & Gamble and Cook Composites and Polymers made a green alternative to fossil-fuel-derived paint resins and solvents, cutting hazardous volatiles by 50 percent, using soya oil and sugar. Sherwin-Williams developed water-based acrylic alkyd paints with low amounts of volatile organic compounds (VOCs) that can be made from recycled soda bottle plastic (PET), acrylics and soybean oil (Figure 23.6).

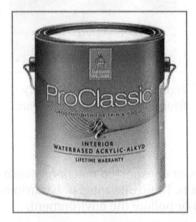

Figure 23.5 *Sherwin-Williams water-based acrylic alkyd paints with low VOCs*

- Biodegradable and phosphate-free and chlorine-free raw materials are used by Seventh Generation in the manufacture of green cleaning products such as laundry and dishwashing detergents; paper products such as paper towels and diapers; and personal care products such as body washes and lotions. The packaging for these products is manufactured from recycled materials.

Recalling facts

1 Which of the following statements is/are true about the term Green Chemistry?

I   It is also known as 'sustainable chemistry'.

II It reduces or eliminates the creation of dangerous waste products.

III It has positive advantages for the environment.

a I only

b II and III only

c I and III only

d I, II and III

2 Which of these is NOT a benefit of using the principles of Green Chemistry in designing new chemical products and processes?

a cleaner air and water

b reduction of hazardous waste production

c reduction in smog formation

d increased use of non-renewable petroleum products

3 Which of these is NOT a principle of Green Chemistry?

a prevent waste production

b minimise atom economy

c use safer solvents

d use renewable feedstocks

4 Which of the following is NOT an example of a product being produced using the principles of Green Chemistry?

a Simvastatin drug for treating high cholesterol

b compostable film

c Sherwin-Williams acrylic alkyd paints

d ammonia produced by the Haber process

5 Which of the following statement(s) is/are true when designing for biodegradation?

I The product must decompose into harmless products in water.

II UV light could decompose the product into harmless substances.

III The products persist and accumulate in the environment and take a long time to decompose.

a I only

b I and II only

c I and III only

d I, II and III

6 Which statement is correct when using a catalyst rather than stoichiometric reagents in Green Chemistry?

I A catalyst leads to a lower atom economy in reactions.

II A catalyst causes reactions to occur faster at lower temperatures.

III A catalyst reduces the production of unwanted and hazardous by-products.

a I and II only

b I and III only

c II and III only

d I, II and III

7 Define the term 'Green Chemistry'.

Applying facts

8   Identify and discuss FIVE principles of Green Chemistry.

Analysing data

9   Discuss how Green Chemistry leads to a cleaner and more sustainable earth, citing benefits in the fields of human health, the environment, and economy and business.

10   A tourist resort is close to both the ocean and a river. Every so often there are soap suds in the river water. Also, the river water sometimes has a high algal bloom and the odour emanated is foul. Use your knowledge gained from Green Chemistry to solve this problem.

11   A manufacturer producing chemicals has been getting complaints about pollution occurring from his factory in the air and waterways. His accountant has also indicated that the cost of raw material is increasing, and product production has decreased, which is leading to increases in product cost. Also, there is a product equivalent to the manufacturer's product being sold at the same cost and is marketed as being 'Green'. The CEO approaches you as the person in charge of product development to assist in making the firm more competitive. Using your knowledge of Green Chemistry, discuss how you would solve the stated problems.

24 Qualitative analysis

Learning objectives

- Describe **physical tests** that can be used in the **identification of cations and anions.**
- Describe **tests to identify cations using aqueous sodium hydroxide, aqueous ammonia and aqueous potassium iodide.**
- Give the results and write **ionic equations for the reactions occurring in the tests.**
- Describe **tests to identify common anions.**
- Give the results and write **ionic equations for the reactions occurring in the tests.**
- Describe **tests to identify O_2, H_2, CO_2, HCl, NH_3, Cl_2, SO_2, NO_2 and water vapour.**

Qualitative analysis involves **identifying** the components of a single substance or a mixture, for example, identifying the cation and anion present in an ionic compound. When identifying the cations and anions in an inorganic salt, reactions which produce a precipitate, a colour change and/or the evolution of a gas are used, so that we can easily use our senses of sight and smell in the identification process. The following steps are involved when qualitatively analysing an inorganic salt:

Step a Preliminary examination of the solid salt. The general appearance and physical properties of the salt are noted. These give important information and can be used to narrow the identity of the cations and anions present. It should be noted that the information gathered from the preliminary examination is not confirmatory.

Step b Determination of the cation present by carrying out reactions on the salt in solution and confirmatory tests.

Step c Determination of the anion present by carrying out reactions on the salt in solution and confirmatory tests.

Table 24.1 gives the possibilities for a particular colour and appearance of an unknown salt on preliminary examination.

Table 24.1 *Possible colours and appearance of an unknown salt*

Observation	Inference
Black	CuO, CuS, FeO, FeS, PbS, I_2 crystals
Blue	Copper salt
Brown	PbO_2, I_2 solution
Reddish-brown	Fe^{3+}, copper
Green/light green	Cu^{2+}, Fe^{2+}, Ni^{2+}
Orange	$K_2Cr_2O_7$, PbO
Yellow	PbO, PbI_2, AgBr, AgI
Purple	$KMnO_4$
White	Na^+, K^+, Ca^{2+}, Zn^{2+}, Pb^{2+}, Al^{3+}
Deliquescent	Chloride or nitrate

The possible identity of cations and anions based on solubility of the inorganic salt in water can be determined using Tables 6.1 and 6.2 (pages 94 and 95).

Identifying cations

Reaction with aqueous sodium hydroxide (sodium hydroxide solution)

Metal cations form insoluble metal hydroxides when they react with aqueous sodium hydroxide:

$$M^{n+}(aq) + nOH^-(aq) \longrightarrow M(OH)_n(s)$$

To identify the metal or ammonium ion in an unknown ionic compound, make a **solution** of the solid in distilled water. Then add aqueous sodium hydroxide **dropwise** and note the **colour** of any **precipitate** that forms. Add **excess** aqueous sodium hydroxide and look to see whether the precipitate **dissolves**. If **no** precipitate is seen, warm gently and test for **ammonia** gas (see Table 24.9, page 357). Table 24.2 and Figure 24.2 give observations made when aqueous sodium hydroxide is added and the identity of the cation present.

Table 24.2 *Reactions of cations with aqueous sodium hydroxide (NaOH(aq))*

Cation	Colour of precipitate on adding aqueous sodium hydroxide dropwise	Identity of precipitate	Reaction equation	Effect of adding excess aqueous sodium hydroxide to the precipitate
Ca^{2+}	White	Calcium hydroxide	$Ca^{2+}(aq) + 2OH^-(aq) \longrightarrow Ca(OH)_2(s)$ white	Precipitate remains, i.e. it is **insoluble** in excess NaOH(aq).
Al^{3+}	White	Aluminium hydroxide	$Al^{3+}(aq) + 3OH^-(aq) \longrightarrow Al(OH)_3(s)$ white	Precipitate dissolves forming a colourless solution, i.e. it is **soluble** in excess NaOH(aq).
Pb^{2+}	White	Lead(II) hydroxide	$Pb^{2+}(aq) + 2OH^-(aq) \longrightarrow Pb(OH)_2(s)$ white (see Figure 24.1)	Precipitate dissolves forming a colourless solution, i.e. it is **soluble** in excess NaOH(aq).
Zn^{2+}	White	Zinc hydroxide	$Zn^{2+}(aq) + 2OH^-(aq) \longrightarrow Zn(OH)_2(s)$ white	Precipitate dissolves forming a colourless solution, i.e. it is **soluble** in excess NaOH(aq).
Cu^{2+}	Blue	Copper(II) hydroxide	$Cu^{2+}(aq) + 2OH^-(aq) \longrightarrow Cu(OH)_2(s)$ blue (see Figure 24.1)	Precipitate remains, i.e. it is **insoluble** in excess NaOH(aq).

Cation	Colour of precipitate on adding aqueous sodium hydroxide dropwise	Identity of precipitate	Reaction equation	Effect of adding excess aqueous sodium hydroxide to the precipitate
Fe^{2+}	Green	Iron(II) hydroxide	$Fe^{2+}(aq) + 2OH^-(aq) \longrightarrow Fe(OH)_2(s)$ green (see Figure 24.1)	Precipitate remains, i.e. it is **insoluble** in excess NaOH(aq).
Fe^{3+}	Red-brown	Iron(III) hydroxide	$Fe^{3+}(aq) + 3OH^-(aq) \longrightarrow Fe(OH)_3(s)$ red-brown (see Figure 24.1)	Precipitate remains, i.e. it is **insoluble** in excess NaOH(aq).
NH_4^+	**No** precipitate. **Ammonia** is evolved on warming which changes moist red litmus paper blue.	–	$NH_4^+(aq) + OH^-(aq) \longrightarrow$ $NH_3(g) + H_2O(l)$	–

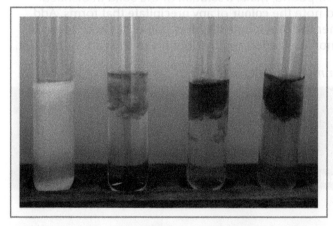

Figure 24.1 *From left to right, precipitates of lead(II) hydroxide, copper(II) hydroxide, iron(II) hydroxide and iron(III) hydroxide*

Calcium hydroxide, copper(II) hydroxide, iron(II) hydroxide and **iron(III) hydroxide** are **basic hydroxides** so they do not react with sodium hydroxide. When excess aqueous sodium hydroxide is added to these precipitates they **remain.**

Aluminium hydroxide, lead(II) hydroxide and **zinc hydroxide** are **amphoteric hydroxides**. They react with the excess sodium hydroxide forming soluble salts, hence the precipitates **dissolve.**

Ammonium hydroxide is soluble, therefore, no precipitate forms. When the mixture is warmed, ammonia gas is produced because the ammonium ion and the hydroxide ion react, as shown in the following equation:

$$NH_4^+(aq) + OH^-(aq) \longrightarrow NH_3(g) + H_2O(l)$$

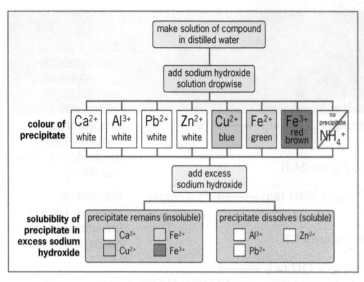

Figure 24.2 *Identification of cations using aqueous sodium hydroxide*

Reaction with aqueous ammonia (ammonium hydroxide solution)

The metal cations, except the Ca^{2+} ion, form insoluble metal hydroxides with ammonium hydroxide solution:

$$M^{n+}(aq) + nOH^-(aq) \longrightarrow M(OH)_n(s)$$

To identify the metal ion in an unknown ionic compound, make a **solution** of the solid in distilled water. Then add aqueous ammonia **dropwise** and note the **colour** of any **precipitate** that forms. Add **excess** aqueous ammonia and look to see whether the precipitate **dissolves**. Table 24.3 and Figure 24.3 give the observations made when aqueous ammonia is added and the identity of the cations present.

Table 24.3 *Reactions of cations with aqueous ammonia ($NH_4OH(aq)$)*

Cation	Colour of precipitate on adding aqueous ammonia dropwise	Identity of precipitate	Reaction equation	Effect of adding excess aqueous ammonia to the precipitate
Ca^{2+}	No precipitate	–	–	–
Al^{3+}	White	Aluminium hydroxide	$Al^{3+}(aq) + 3OH^-(aq) \longrightarrow Al(OH)_3(s)$ white	Precipitate remains, i.e. it is **insoluble** in excess $NH_4OH(aq)$.
Pb^{2+}	White	Lead(II) hydroxide	$Pb^{2+}(aq) + 2OH^-(aq) \longrightarrow Pb(OH)_2(s)$ white	Precipitate remains, i.e. it is **insoluble** in excess $NH_4OH(aq)$.
Zn^{2+}	White	Zinc hydroxide	$Zn^{2+}(aq) + 2OH^-(aq) \longrightarrow Zn(OH)_2(s)$ white	Precipitate dissolves forming a colourless solution, i.e. it is **soluble** in excess $NH_4OH(aq)$.
Cu^{2+}	Blue	Copper(II) hydroxide	$Cu^{2+}(aq) + 2OH^-(aq) \longrightarrow Cu(OH)_2(s)$ blue	Precipitate dissolves forming a deep blue solution, i.e. it is **soluble** in excess $NH_4OH(aq)$.

Cation	Colour of precipitate on adding aqueous ammonia dropwise	Identity of precipitate	Reaction equation	Effect of adding excess aqueous ammonia to the precipitate
Fe^{2+}	Green	Iron(II) hydroxide	$Fe^{2+}(aq) + 2OH^-(aq) \longrightarrow Fe(OH)_2(s)$ green	Precipitate remains, i.e. it is **insoluble** in excess $NH_4OH(aq)$.
Fe^{3+}	Red-brown	Iron(III) hydroxide	$Fe^{3+}(aq) + 3OH^-(aq) \longrightarrow Fe(OH)_3(s)$ red-brown	Precipitate remains, i.e. it is **insoluble** in excess $NH_4OH(aq)$.

Aluminium hydroxide, lead(II) hydroxide, iron(II) hydroxide and **iron(III) hydroxide** do not react with ammonium hydroxide. When excess aqueous ammonia is added, these precipitates **remain**.

Zinc hydroxide and **copper(II) hydroxide** do react with ammonium hydroxide. They react with the excess aqueous ammonia forming complex soluble salts, hence the precipitates **dissolve**.

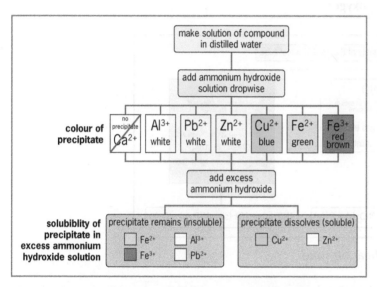

Figure 24.3 *Identification of cations using aqueous ammonia*

To distinguish between the Al^{3+} ion and the Pb^{2+} ion

Putting the results of the previous two tests together, the Al^{3+} **ion** and the Pb^{2+} **ion** are the only cations which cannot be distinguished. To distinguish between these, make a solution of the solid, add a few drops of **potassium iodide solution** and look for the appearance of a **precipitate** (Figures 24.4 and 24.5):

- Al^{3+} **ion: no** precipitate forms.
- Pb^{2+} **ion: a bright yellow** precipitate of **lead(II) iodide** forms:

$$Pb^{2+}(aq) + 2I^-(aq) \longrightarrow PbI_2(s)$$
yellow

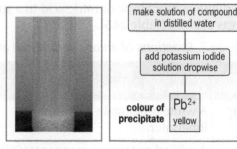

Figure 24.4
Precipitate of lead(II) iodide

Figure 24.5 *Test to distinguish between Al^{3+} ions and Pb^{2+} ions*

Identifying anions

Effect of heat on the solid

Heat a small quantity of the **solid** in a **dry** test tube and test the **gas** evolved (see Table 24.9, page 357 for the tests to identify gases). Table 24.4 and Figure 24.6 give the observation after heating the solid sample and the possible anion present.

Table 24.4 *Effect of heat on the solid*

Anion	Observations/ results of gas tests	Identity of gas(es) evolved	Reaction equation
CO_3^{2-}	A white precipitate forms in limewater.	**Carbon dioxide**	$CO_3^{2-}(s) \xrightarrow{\text{heat}} O^{2-}(s) + CO_2(g)$
NO_3^- of potassium or sodium	A glowing splint relights.	**Oxygen**	$2NO_3^-(s) \xrightarrow{\text{heat}} 2NO_2^-(s) + O_2(g)$
NO_3^- of calcium and below	A brown gas is seen and a glowing splint relights.	**Nitrogen dioxide and oxygen**	$4NO_3^-(s) \xrightarrow{\text{heat}} 2O^{2-}(s) + 4NO_2(g) + O_2(g)$

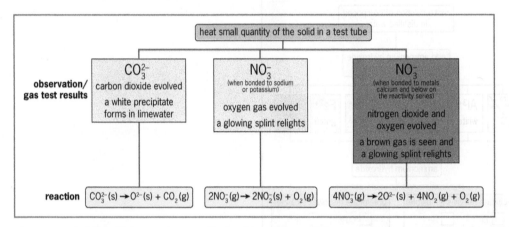

Figure 24.6 *Identifying anions: effect of heat on solid*

Further test to identify the nitrate ion

Add concentrated sulfuric acid and a few copper turnings to a sample of the **solid** in a **dry** test tube and heat. A **blue** solution forms and brown **nitrogen dioxide** gas is evolved.

Reaction with dilute acid

Add dilute hydrochloric or nitric acid to a spatula of the **solid** in a test tube, heat if necessary, and test the **gas** evolved (Table 24.5).

Table 24.5 *Reactions of anions with dilute acid*

Anion	Results of gas tests	Identity of gas evolved	Reaction equation
CO_3^{2-}	A white precipitate forms in limewater.	**Carbon dioxide**	$CO_3^{2-}(s) + 2H^+(aq) \longrightarrow CO_2(g) + H_2O(l)$
SO_3^{2-}	Acidified potassium manganate(VII) solution changes from purple to colourless.	**Sulfur dioxide**	$SO_3^{2-}(s) + 2H^+(aq) \longrightarrow SO_2(g) + H_2O(l)$

Reaction with concentrated sulfuric acid

Add a few drops of concentrated sulfuric acid to a small amount of the **solid** in a dry test tube and test the **gas** evolved. The carbonate, sulfite, chloride (Cl⁻), bromide (Br⁻) and iodide (I⁻) ions can be identified using this test (Table 24.6 and Figure 24.7)

Table 24.6 *Reactions of anions with concentrated sulfuric acid*

Anion	Observations/results of gas tests	Identity of gas evolved/product
CO_3^{2-}	A white precipitate forms in limewater.	**Carbon dioxide**
SO_3^{2-}	Acidified potassium manganate(VII) solution changes from purple to colourless.	**Sulfur dioxide**
Cl^-	White fumes form with ammonia gas.	**Hydrogen chloride**
Br^-	A red-brown gas is seen.	**Bromine**
I^-	A grey-black solid forms which sublimes to form a purple vapour if heated.	**Iodine**

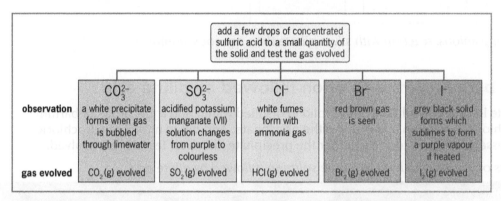

Figure 24.7 *Identifying anions: reactions with concentrated sulfuric acid*

Reaction with silver nitrate solution followed by aqueous ammonia

Make a **solution** of the solid in dilute nitric acid. Add a few drops of silver nitrate solution and observe the **colour** of the precipitate. Add aqueous ammonia and look to see whether the precipitate **dissolves**. The chloride (Cl⁻), bromide (Br⁻) and iodide (I⁻) ions can be identified by this test (Table 24.7 and Figure 24.8).

Table 24.7 *Reactions of anions with silver nitrate solution followed by aqueous ammonia*

Anion	Observations when silver nitrate solution is added	Identity of precipitate	Reaction equation	Observation when aqueous ammonia is added
Cl^-	A **white** precipitate forms which becomes slightly purple-grey in sunlight.	**Silver chloride**	$Ag^+(aq) + Cl^-(aq) \longrightarrow AgCl(s)$ white	Precipitate dissolves forming a colourless solution, i.e. it is **soluble** in aqueous ammonia.
Br^-	A **cream** precipitate forms which becomes slightly green in sunlight.	**Silver bromide**	$Ag^+(aq) + Br^-(aq) \longrightarrow AgBr(s)$ cream	Precipitate partially dissolves, i.e. it is **slightly soluble**.
I^-	A **pale yellow** precipitate forms.	**Silver iodide**	$Ag^+(aq) + I^-(aq) \longrightarrow AgI(s)$ pale yellow	Precipitate remains, i.e. it is **insoluble**.

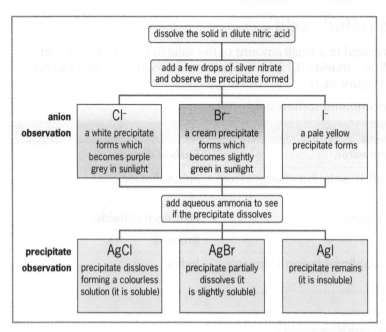

Figure 24.8 *Identifying anions: reaction with silver nitrate then aqueous ammonia*

Reaction with barium nitrate solution followed by dilute acid

To identify the **sulfate ion**, make a **solution** of the solid in distilled water. Add a few drops of barium nitrate (or barium chloride) solution and observe the precipitate. Add dilute nitric or hydrochloric acid, heating if necessary, and look to see whether the precipitate **dissolves.** Test any **gas** evolved.

Table 24.8 *Reactions of anions with barium nitrate solution followed by dilute acid*

Anion	Observations when barium nitrate solution is added	Identity of precipitate	Reaction equation	Observations when dilute acid is added
CO_3^{2-}	A white precipitate forms.	**Barium carbonate**	$Ba^{2+}(aq) + CO_3^{2-}(aq) \longrightarrow BaCO_3(s)$ white	Precipitate **dissolves**; it reacts releasing **carbon dioxide**: $CO_3^{2-}(s) + 2H^+(aq) \longrightarrow CO_2(g) + H_2O(l)$
SO_3^{2-}	A white precipitate forms.	**Barium sulfite**	$Ba^{2+}(aq) + SO_3^{2-}(aq) \longrightarrow BaSO_3(s)$ white	Precipitate **dissolves**; it reacts releasing **sulfur dioxide** on heating: $SO_3^{2-}(s) + 2H^+(aq) \longrightarrow SO_2(g) + H_2O(l)$
SO_4^{2-}	A white precipitate forms.	**Barium sulfate**	$Ba^{2+}(aq) + SO_4^{2-}(aq) \longrightarrow BaSO_4(s)$ white	Precipitate **remains**; it does not react with dilute acid.

Identifying gases

Gases are often liberated when inorganic salts are heated or when reacted with reagents. A variety of tests, including noting the colour and smell of the gas, reaction to a burning splint and colour change to moist litmus paper can be performed in the laboratory to identify different **gases.**

Table 24.9 *Identifying gases*

Gas	Properties	Test	Explanation of test
Oxygen (O_2)	Colourless and odourless	• Causes a **glowing splint** to glow brighter or **relight**.	• Oxygen supports combustion.
Hydrogen (H_2)	Colourless and odourless	• Causes a **lighted splint** to make a **'squeaky pop'** and be extinguished.	• Hydrogen reacts explosively with oxygen in the air to form steam: $2H_2(g) + O_2(g) \longrightarrow 2H_2O(g)$
Carbon dioxide (CO_2)	Colourless and odourless	• Forms a **white precipitate** in **limewater** (calcium hydroxide solution).	• Insoluble, white calcium carbonate forms: $Ca(OH)_2(aq) + CO_2(g) \longrightarrow CaCO_3(s) + H_2O(l)$ white
		• The precipitate **redissolves** on continued bubbling.	• Soluble calcium hydrogencarbonate forms: $CaCO_3(s) + H_2O(l) + CO_2(g) \longrightarrow Ca(HCO_3)_2(aq)$
		• Turns moist blue litmus paper **faint red.**	• CO_2 gas slightly acidic
		• **Extinguishes** a glowing splint.	• CO_2 does not burn or support combustion
Hydrogen chloride (HCl)	Colourless, with sharp, acid odour	• Forms **white fumes** when brought near a drop of **concentrated ammonia solution** on a glass rod.	• White fumes of ammonium chloride form: $NH_3(g) + HCl(g) \longrightarrow NH_4Cl(s)$
Ammonia (NH_3)	Colourless, with pungent odour	• Turns **moist red litmus paper blue.**	• Ammonia reacts with water on the paper forming alkaline ammonium hydroxide: $NH_3(g) + H_2O(l) \rightleftharpoons NH_4OH(aq)$
		• Forms **white fumes** when brought near a drop of **concentrated hydrochloric acid** on a glass rod.	• White fumes of ammonium chloride form: $NH_3(g) + HCl(g) \longrightarrow NH_4Cl(s)$
Chlorine (Cl_2)	Yellow-green, with sharp, choking odour	• Causes **moist blue litmus paper** to turn **red** and then bleaches it **white.**	• Chlorine reacts with water on the paper forming two acids, hydrochloric acid (HCl) and chloric(I) acid (HClO): $Cl_2(g) + H_2O(l) \longrightarrow HCl(aq) + HClO(aq)$ Chloric(I) acid oxidises coloured litmus to colourless.

(*Continued*)

Table 24.9 *Continued*

Gas	Properties	Test	Explanation of test
Sulfur dioxide (SO$_2$)	Colourless, with pungent odour	• Turns **acidified potassium manganate(VII) solution** from **purple** to **colourless**.	• Sulfur dioxide reduces the purple MnO_4^- ion to the colourless Mn^{2+} ion.
		• Turns **acidified potassium dichromate(VI) solution** from **orange** to **green**.	• Sulfur dioxide reduces the orange $Cr_2O_7^{2-}$ ion to the green Cr^{3+} ion.
Nitrogen dioxide (NO$_2$)	Brown, with sharp, irritating odour	• A **brown gas** • Causes **moist blue litmus paper** to turn **red**.	• Nitrogen dioxide reacts with water on the paper forming two acids, nitrous acid (HNO$_2$) and nitric acid (HNO$_3$): $2NO_2(g) + H_2O(l) \longrightarrow HNO_2(aq) + HNO_3(aq)$
Water vapour (H$_2$O)	Colourless and odourless	• Causes **dry cobalt(II) chloride paper** to change from **blue to pink**.	• Water vapour changes blue, anhydrous cobalt(II) chloride (CoCl$_2$) to pink, hydrated cobalt(II) chloride (CoCl$_2$·6H$_2$O).
		• Causes **anhydrous copper(II) sulfate** to change from **white to blue**.	• Water vapour changes white, anhydrous copper(II) sulfate (CuSO$_4$) to blue, hydrated copper(II) sulfate (CuSO$_4$·5H$_2$O).

Recalling facts

1 On preliminary examination the colour of a solid salt sample is described as reddish-brown. This indicates that the salt may be:

   a I$_2$

   b PbO

   c Fe^{3+} salt

   d Fe^{2+} salt

2 When aqueous sodium hydroxide is added to a salt solution in a test tube, a white precipitate is formed which is insoluble in excess aqueous sodium hydroxide solution. When aqueous ammonia is added to the salt solution, no precipitate is formed, even when excess aqueous ammonia solution is added. The cation present is:

   a Al^{3+}

   b Ca^{2+}

   c Pb^{2+}

   d Zn^{2+}

3 When aqueous sodium hydroxide is added to a salt solution, no precipitate is formed, but a pungent gas which turns moist red litmus paper blue evolves. The cation present is:

a Ca^{2+}

b Fe^{3+}

c NH_4^+

d Zn^{2+}

4 What is the colour of the precipitate formed in the following equation?

$$Fe^{2+}(aq) + 2OH^-(aq) \longrightarrow Fe(OH)_2(s)$$

a blue

b green

c red-brown

d white

5 To distinguish between Al^{3+} ions and Pb^{2+} ions which of the following is added to a solution of the salt?

a aqueous sodium hydroxide

b aqueous ammonium

c potassium iodide solution

d potassium dichromate solution

6 When silver nitrate is added to a salt solution, a pale-yellow precipitate is formed, which is insoluble in aqueous ammonia. The possible identity of the anion is:

a chloride

b bromide

c fluoride

d iodide

7 When a small quantity of solid is heated in a dry test tube, oxygen gas evolves. The identity of the salt could be:

a sodium carbonate

b sodium nitrate

c calcium nitrate

d sodium sulfate

8 When barium nitrate solution is added to a salt solution, followed by dilute hydrochloric acid, a white precipitate which is insoluble in dilute hydrochloric acid is formed. The possible identity of the anion is:

a CO_3^-

b CO_3^{2-}

c SO_3^{2-}

d SO_4^{2-}

9 Water vapour causes anhydrous copper(II) sulfate to change from:

    a blue to pink

    b blue to white

    c white to blue

    d pink to blue

10 A colourless, odourless gas which extinguishes a lighted splint making a squeaky popping sound is:

    a oxygen

    b hydrogen

    c carbon dioxide

    d hydrogen chloride

11 What are the steps involved in determining the identity of an inorganic salt?

Applying facts

12 Describe a chemical test for the following gases:

    a chlorine

    b carbon dioxide

    c ammonia

    d water vapour

    e nitrogen dioxide

In your answer describe the colour of the gas, its reaction with litmus paper and its reaction to a lighted splint.

Analysing data

13 Name a salt that, when heated, produces a brown gas which rekindles a glowing splint. What is the name of the gas?

14 When concentrated sulfuric acid is added to a solid in a test tube, a gas that gives a white precipitate with aqueous silver nitrate is formed. What is the anion present in the solid?

15 Describe tests that could be used to distinguish between calcium, aluminium, zinc and lead cations.

16 When sodium hydroxide was added to a solution of substance F, a white precipitate was formed. Another sample of solution F was acidified and lead(II) nitrate solution was added to it. A yellow precipitate was formed. Deduce the identity of substance F.

17 A student dissolved Substance C in water and performed the tests shown in the table.

Test	Observation	Inference
Colour and appearance of solid salt.	Greenish white crystalline solids.	
To the solution in the first test tube sodium hydroxide was added dropwise and then added in excess.	A green precipitate insoluble in excess was obtained.	
To the solution in the second test tube aqueous ammonia was added dropwise then in excess.	A green precipitate insoluble in excess was obtained.	
To the solution in the third test tube silver nitrate solution was added, then aqueous ammonia was added.	A white precipitate was formed which dissolved on addition of aqueous ammonia.	

State the inference after analysing the observations for each test, giving ionic equations and deduce the possible ions and the identity of the salt.

Index

Page numbers along with 't' an 'f' refers to table and figure respectively